# The Subject(s) of Human Rights

In the series *Asian American History and Culture*, edited by Cathy J. Schlund-Vials, Shelley Sang-Hee Lee, and Rick Bonus. Founding editor, Sucheng Chan; editors emeriti, David Palumbo-Liu, Michael Omi, K. Scott Wong, and Linda Trinh Võ.

Also in this series:

Malini Johar Schueller, *Campaigns of Knowledge: U.S. Pedagogies of Colonialism and Occupation in the Philippines and Japan*
Crystal Mun-hye Baik, *Reencounters: On the Korean War and Diasporic Memory Critique*
Michael Omi, Dana Y. Nakano, and Jeffrey Yamashita, eds., *Japanese American Millennials: Rethinking Generation, Community, and Diversity*
Masumi Izumi, *The Rise and Fall of America's Concentration Camp Law: Civil Liberties Debates from the Internment to McCarthyism and the Radical 1960s*
Shirley Jennifer Lim, *Anna May Wong: Performing the Modern*
Edward Tang, *From Confinement to Containment: Japanese/American Arts during the Early Cold War*
Patricia P. Chu, *Where I Have Never Been: Migration, Melancholia, and Memory in Asian American Narratives of Return*
Cynthia Wu, *Sticky Rice: A Politics of Intraracial Desire*
Marguerite Nguyen, *America's Vietnam: The* Longue Durée *of U.S. Literature and Empire*
Vanita Reddy, *Fashioning Diaspora: Beauty, Femininity, and South Asian American Culture*
Audrey Wu Clark, *The Asian American Avant-Garde: Universalist Aspirations in Modernist Literature and Art*
Eric Tang, *Unsettled: Cambodian Refugees in the New York City Hyperghetto*
Jeffrey Santa Ana, *Racial Feelings: Asian America in a Capitalist Culture of Emotion*
Jiemin Bao, *Creating a Buddhist Community: A Thai Temple in Silicon Valley*
Elda E. Tsou, *Unquiet Tropes: Form, Race, and Asian American Literature*
Tarry Hum, *Making a Global Immigrant Neighborhood: Brooklyn's Sunset Park*
Ruth Mayer, *Serial Fu Manchu: The Chinese Supervillain and the Spread of Yellow Peril Ideology*
Karen Kuo, *East Is West and West Is East: Gender, Culture, and Interwar Encounters between Asia and America*
Kieu-Linh Caroline Valverde, *Transnationalizing Viet Nam: Community, Culture, and Politics in the Diaspora*
Lan P. Duong, *Treacherous Subjects: Gender, Culture, and Trans-Vietnamese Feminism*
Kristi Brian, *Reframing Transracial Adoption: Adopted Koreans, White Parents, and the Politics of Kinship*
Belinda Kong, *Tiananmen Fictions outside the Square: The Chinese Literary Diaspora and the Politics of Global Culture*
Bindi V. Shah, *Laotian Daughters: Working toward Community, Belonging, and Environmental Justice*

*A list of additional titles in this series appears at the back of this book*

Edited by
Cathy J. Schlund-Vials,
Guy Beauregard, and
Hsiu-chuan Lee

# THE SUBJECT(S) OF HUMAN RIGHTS

## Crises, Violations, and Asian/American Critique

With an Afterword by Madeleine Thien

TEMPLE UNIVERSITY PRESS
*Philadelphia • Rome • Tokyo*

TEMPLE UNIVERSITY PRESS
Philadelphia, Pennsylvania 19122
*tupress.temple.edu*


Published 2020

Library of Congress Cataloging-in-Publication Data

Names: Schlund-Vials, Cathy J., 1974- editor. | Beauregard, Guy Pierre, editor. | Lee, Hsiu-chuan, editor. | Thien, Madeleine, 1974- writer of afterword.
Title: The subject(s) of human rights : crises, violations, and Asian/American critique / edited by Cathy J. Schlund-Vials, Guy Beauregard, and Hsiu-chuan Lee ; with an afterword by Madeleine Thien.
Description: Philadelphia : Temple University Press, 2020. | Series: Asian American history and culture | Includes bibliographical references and index. | Summary: "This work takes seriously the ways in which Asian American studies has from its founding engaged with humanitarian crises and large-scale violations. Committed to extending this critical work across local/global, domestic/international, and immigrant/refugee frames, this collection relocates Asian America from the periphery to the center of human rights critique"—Provided by publisher.
Identifiers: LCCN 2019010532 (print) | LCCN 2019981205 (ebook) | ISBN 9781439915721 (cloth) | ISBN 9781439915738 (paperback) | ISBN 9781439915745 (ebook)
Subjects: LCSH: Human rights—Asia. | Human rights—North America. | Asians—Social conditions. | Asian Americans—Social conditions. | Human rights in literature. | Asian Americans—Study and teaching. | Asia—Relations—North America. | North America—Relations—Asia.
Classification: LCC JC599.A78 S93 2020 (print) | LCC JC599.A78 (ebook) | DDC 323.1195/07—dc23
LC record available at https://lccn.loc.gov/2019010532
LC ebook record available at https://lccn.loc.gov/2019981205

9 8 7 6 5 4 3 2 1

# Contents

# Acknowledgments

From the beginning, Sara Cohen and Aaron Javsicas at Temple University Press were amazingly supportive of *The Subject(s) of Human Rights*. Such support, predicated on a truly capacious vision of how this collection functioned as both conversation starter and field interrogator, was unwavering from proposal to final submission. This aspirational engagement with collection topic and project focus was likewise reflected in all our interactions with Ashley Petrucci, Gary Kramer, and other members of the Temple University Press team, including most recently Sarah Munroe, who has maintained momentum and commitment. Admittedly, *The Subject(s) of Human Rights* reflects the provocative suggestions put forth by the anonymous readers, who pushed us (as editors) and our contributors to clarify the intellectual, academic, and activist stakes of such human rights inquiry and critique. To that end, the contributors to this collection have very much been part of this larger publishing journey; the originality of their ideas coupled with the willingness to revise made this a joyous editing endeavor. Jamie Armstrong, editorial project manager at Amnet Systems, deserves considerable praise for guiding the manuscript at a critical production stage. We are also indebted to the unparalleled generosity of Dinh Q. Lê, whose "Burma," from the evocative *Fragile Spring* series, serves as the cover for this collection.

This collection is very much the culmination of a conversation that began in Taiwan at the 2015 Summer Institute in Asian American Studies (SIAAS), which was in major part funded by The Ministry of Science and Technology in Taiwan (MOST 102-2420-H-009-004-MY3), National Taiwan Normal University and the College of Liberal Arts at National Taiwan University.

Accordingly, *The Subject(s) of Human Rights* is wonderfully beholden to those who comprise the SIAAS collective: Guy Beauregard, Pin-chia Feng, Shyh-jen Fuh, Hsiu-chuan Lee, and Andy Chih-ming Wang. As Guy Beauregard eloquently characterizes, this critical conversation would not have happened without them; it would also not have occurred without the work of SIAAS participants who, in substantive and substantial ways, helped reframe, rethink, and re-engage with many of the pressing issues addressed in this collection. The Ministry of Science and Technology in Taiwan (MOST 104-2410-H-003-034-MY3 and MOST 107-2410-H-002-048-MY3), along with the College of Liberal Arts at National Taiwan University, provided key support to conceptualize, edit, and contribute to this collection and is gratefully acknowledged. The Ministry of Science and Technology in Taiwan funded the three Summer Institutes in Asian American Studies (2013, 2014, 2015) that brought this collection "into being" and provided significant research support. And, the Department of English at National Taiwan Normal University provided integral organizing support for what served as the genesis conference event for this collection.

Last, but certainly not least, the editors would like to acknowledge the advice, support, and friendship of those who make doing this work worthwhile and such labor rewarding: Joan Chiung-Heui Chang, Iping Liang, Ioana Luca, and Christopher Vials.

# The Subject(s) of Human Rights

# Introduction

## *The Subject(s) of Human Rights: Recalibrating Asian/American Critique*

Guy Beauregard,
Cathy J. Schlund-Vials, and
Hsiu-chuan Lee

On February 2, 1948, U.S. president Harry S. Truman issued a "Special Message to Congress on Civil Rights." In this dispatch, the thirty-third commander-in-chief succinctly outlined ten recommendations, which included antidiscrimination laws at home, a permanent Commission on Civil Rights, a federal protection against lynching, statehood for Hawaii and Alaska, antiracist naturalization laws, and the "settling [of] the evacuation claims of Japanese Americans." On this final point, Truman explained,

> During the last war more than one hundred thousand Japanese Americans were evacuated from their homes in the Pacific states solely because of their racial origin. Many of these people suffered property and business losses as a result of this forced evacuation and through no fault of their own. The Congress has before it a procedure by which claims based upon these losses can be promptly considered and settled. . . . We in the United States are working in company with other nations who share our desire for enduring world peace and who believe with us that, above all else, men must be free. We are striving to build a world of amity of nations—a world where men may live under governments of their own choosing and under laws of their own making. (*Public Papers* 125)

Five months later, on July 2, President Truman signed the "Japanese-American Claims Act," which authorized the settlement of property loss claims. Congress appropriated $38 million to settle a total of 23,000 claims for damages totaling $131 million; the final claim was adjudicated in 1965, the same year that the Hart-Celler Act, known as the Nationality and Immigration Act, was passed.[1]

Such state-directed reparative acts, which occurred forty years before U.S. president Ronald Reagan signed into law the Civil Liberties Act of 1988 (known more colloquially as the Japanese American Redress Act), have largely been disremembered within Asian American studies, a multivalent interdiscipline born out of mid-twentieth-century civil rights struggles, antiwar protests, and third-world liberation movements. Indeed, while the Japanese American incarceration/internment occupies a prominent civil rights position as an apex of anti-Asian nativism and as an index of anti-Asian racism, less recollected is the degree to which it was, in its immediate aftermath, comprehended as a human rights flashpoint. As striking is Truman's own connection vis-à-vis human rights given that it was under his administration that the United States would become the first—and, at the time of writing, still the only—nation to use atomic weapons in a war; it was his executive-level sponsorship that presaged the codification and implementation of the Marshall Plan; it was during his administration that the United States occupied Okinawa and mainland Japan and entered the Korean War; and last, but certainly not least, it was during his presidency (with considerable U.S. support) that the United Nations would pass—on December 10, 1948—the Universal Declaration of Human Rights (UDHR), which has become the standard on which to evaluate international rights violations.[2]

Situated adjacent attempts to settle reparations at home, rights declarations abroad, militarism in Asia and the Pacific, and a past/present Cold War/War on Terror imaginary, the multivalent domestic and international politics outlined above accentuate the ways in which Asian American studies as an interdiscipline has, in ways that have not always been adequately recognized, been oriented within and around human rights. Accordingly, if, as Lisa Lowe evocatively observes in "The International within the National," a "tireless reckoning" with the past is integral to the field (30), then foundational to Asian American studies' diverse critical engagements is an indefatigable attention to the ways in which the United States has historically been an exclusionary, antirights nation. From Chinese immigration restrictions to the denial of naturalized citizenship for Asian migrants, from the aforementioned incarceration of Japanese Americans to the present-day deportation of Southeast Asian Americans, and from yellow peril characterizations to more recent acts of Islamophobia, Asian Americans have consistently been subjected to human rights violations. Shifting from domestic imaginaries to U.S. foreign policy, Asian subjects—particularly over the course of the twentieth century and into the twenty-first—have been in various ways firsthand witnesses to American war-making, settler colonialism, military occupation, collateral damage, and displacement.

*The Subject(s) of Human Rights: Crises, Violations, and Asian/American Critique* takes seriously the ways in which Asian American studies has from its founding "tirelessly reckon[ed]" with humanitarian crises and large-scale violations. Committed to extending this critical work across local/global, domestic/international, and immigrant/refugee frames, this collection relocates the imagined geographies of Asian America from the periphery to the center of human rights critique. In doing so, we wish to underline both the aspirations of the discourses of human rights encoded in documents such as the UDHR and the widely acknowledged failures of such discourses to prevent ongoing forms of imperialism, militarism, genocidal violence, and other wide-scale human rights violations. This duality is by now widely recognized in contemporary scholarship, even as the implications and possible outcomes of this duality remain hotly contested. Randall Williams, for example, juxtaposes the "impressive array of human rights" set forth in the UDHR with the need to confront "a grim postwar reality" marked by subjugation, starvation, and extermination (xvi)—and, in doing so, forcefully calls for an anti-imperialist internationalism. Christine Hong, drawing on the work of Williams and others to focus on "the dominant human rights framing of North Korea" (511), takes aim at the discourse of human rights as "a ruling idea of the present that obscures the brutality of the imperial past and disavows the violence of the imperial present" (515). Such powerful anti-imperialist critiques have in contemporary scholarship been supplemented by the work of other scholars who have insisted in different ways on other forms of interventionary work. Rajini Srikanth, for example, has investigated how readers and viewers accustomed to responding to traumatic and sensational stories and images may learn to "acquire the skills to engage 'quiet' (i.e., devoid of rhetoric and diction that is laden with images of obvious cruelty and abuse) narratives of human rights abuse"—how, in short, we may learn "to discern the monumental apparatus of oppression that regulates all aspects of an individual's or group's life" (80). Engagement with what Srikanth calls "cognitive and interpretive responsibility" (80) has been extended by Crystal Parikh, who in *Writing Human Rights* sets out to read "the political theory of human rights through the ethical deliberations staged in narratives authored by contemporary American writers of color" (2). Our collection shares Parikh's commitment to neither "uniformly and summarily celebrate *nor* dismiss human rights" (2).[3] But in this collection we also extend our analytic scope more widely than the United States in the ways proposed by Parikh, even as we admire her commitment to developing "a human rights method" (22).

Specifically, Parikh's study sets out to investigate "the ethico-politics that minor American literatures engage," a process through which "*the subject of human rights has largely been imagined as a latently American one—always already, that is, American in character and desires*" (3; emphasis added). In a sophisticated argumentative move, Parikh also underlines how "human rights are imagined to be that which *others*—other people in other places—need, while Americans always already enjoy an exceptional 'good life,' not only in terms of material comforts and political freedoms, but in the sense of the good moral life of *bios*, by which Greek philosophy designated the 'proper' form of living" (3). Parikh argues that "the social and historical location of these particular minor subjects proves an indispensable fulcrum for reading the possibilities of human rights against the mandates of possessive individualism, multicultural neoliberalism, and modern state sovereignty" (3). But we contend that this framing of subjects of human rights as "*always already . . . American in character*" gives too much away, even as it may arguably be the case in the context of the textual archive that Parikh assembles and discusses. By contrast, our collection works with a broader archive, a critical project that has been enabled by the form of a multiauthored collection with contributions and critiques coming from a wider range of locations—both in North America and in Asia—than a single-authored study could reasonably be expected to provide. The diversity of geographical imaginings at work in the essays that follow is not a simple matter of plurality; as discussed below, it has implications for how we configure and attempt to recalibrate our understanding of Asian/American critique.

In our collection, this critique focuses on what we call "subject(s) of human rights," through which we attempt to bring together three interrelated critical projects: a sharper understanding of how Asian/Americans have been subjected to human rights violations, a refocused concern with how Asian/Americans have also acted as subjects of history and social agents attempting to effect forms of change (progressive or otherwise), and a collective intervention into academic subjects organizing and regulating the sorts of knowledge produced around such subjects. Across various sites, the contributors to this collection engage with the possibilities and the limits of the histories and stories that have circulated and the forms of knowledge that have been produced around discourses of "human rights" as they have intersected—at times spectacularly and at times more quietly—with uneven relations of power and movements of people in and around Asia, the Pacific, and North America.

In this collection, we propose that critically engaging with "subject(s) of human rights" in the ways noted above requires a fundamental rethinking of Asian America's imagined geographies. In doing so, we take inspiration from critical initiatives including events organized through the SIAAS project—a multicampus initiative discussed in more detail below—that have, as Chih-ming Wang puts it, "attempted to hold onto the pluralities of Asia and America" ("Asian American Critical Work" 66). We will return to the topic of what Wang calls "at-times unexpected reconfigurations of Asia" ("Asian

American Critical Work" 67) that characterize both the SIAAS project and the critical work performed by many of the essays in this collection. At this point, however, we wish to turn to some of the stakes involved in conceptualizing "America" as plural, notably through forms of Asian/Canadian critical work that we argue, following Wang, can open new possibilities for "tracking other trajectories of transpacific contacts" ("Asian American Critical Work" 67). The entanglement of various "American" sites in Asian American studies has long been recognized, from the groundbreaking historical studies on permeable U.S.-Canadian borderlands in the Pacific Northwest (Chang), to innovative scholarship on "hemispheric Orientalism" (E. Lee) and its relevance to understanding settler colonialism in the Americas (Day), to examinations of the politics of the "Asian Canadian questions" that have informed Asian American knowledge production (Beauregard). The generative nature of these conversations has taken a significant step forward in recent years following attempts by scholars to think through the stakes involved in developing forms of "Asian Canadian critique beyond the nation" (C. Lee and Kim). It is amid such developments that we wish to foreground Lisa Yoneyama's brief yet resonant observations on what she calls "possibilities of Asian/Canadian transnationality." Accessing Iyko Day's work, Yoneyama acknowledges Canada's distinct racial formation before observing how "Canada's political reality—in which state-sanctioned multicultural and humanitarian nationalism are supplemented by the ethnonationalisms of different diasporic and migrant populations—has made it especially difficult for many of [her] students to articulate a sustained critique from the position of 'Asian Canadians'" ("Possibilities" 197). Indeed, the pedagogical challenges described here, marked by state-directed attempts to co-opt and contain dissonant histories, remain prominent in Canada—even as newly articulated subject positions are not (as some of the contributions to this collection make clear) reducible to the terms set by such forms of multicultural or humanitarian governmentality. Despite—or perhaps precisely due to—this particular sociopolitical situation, Yoneyama proposes the development of critically intersecting work linking "Asian/Canadian critique" with "transpacific Asian/American critique," through which we may "relearn how Canada as a subimperial nation has been deeply implicated in the transpacific Cold War order" ("Possibilities" 197). Yoneyama's call for us to address "the often disavowed, yet shared and deeply interconnected genealogies of violence" that constitute the contemporary world ("Possibilities" 198) names precisely the critical work to which we as editors of this collection aspire.

Such aspirations have led us to revisit the notion of "Asian/American critique" as it was memorably elaborated in David Palumbo-Liu's monumental study *Asian/American: Historical Crossings of a Racial Frontier*. In a well-known formulation, Palumbo-Liu theorizes the term *Asian/American* as one marking "*both* the distinction installed between 'Asian' and 'American' *and* a dynamic, unsettled, and inclusive movement" (1)—with such distinctions and movements having profoundly uneven effects on subjects in Asia, the Pacific, and North America. We remain inspired by Palumbo-Liu's observation that "the very shape and character of the United States in the twentieth century—specifically, in the imaginings of modern American development in the global system—is inseparable from historical occasions of real contact between and interpenetrations of Asia and America, in and across the Pacific Ocean" (2). But we also insist that Asian/American critique as it is conceptualized and mobilized in this collection must at the same time reckon with distinct and uneven forms of "contact" in specific sites in Asia and the Pacific. In this respect, our work also takes inspiration from more recent studies by scholars such as Keith Camacho, Erin Suzuki, Yên Lê Espiritu, and (again) Lisa Yoneyama as their works address historical and ongoing forms of imperial, settler-colonial, and militarized violence in Asia, the Pacific, and North America.

The relevance of this recent work to envisioning a recalibrated Asian/American critique has been powerfully expressed in Yoneyama's work on what she calls "cold war ruins," glossed as "traces of geohistorical violence" (*Cold War Ruins* 210). Yoneyama writes, "When critically illuminated, ruins are repositories of debris that in the present offer wisdom associated with failed strategies, unrealized possibilities, and paths that could have but were never taken. They remind us, too, of the excisions and exclusions in what appears complete and victorious, as in the Cold War's triumphant, forward-looking ideologies—of liberation, the new international order, postcolonial nation-building, economic take-off, and so forth" (*Cold War Ruins* 210). To Yoneyama's list, we might also add the promises of discourses of human rights to somehow finally and adequately "right wrongs"—promises that appear increasingly dubious, as recently underlined by Samuel Moyn in *Not Enough*, in these neoliberal times.[4] Acknowledging such challenges, Yoneyama observes that "ruins are vestiges bequeathed to us that are at once liabilities endured from the past and assets for the future, both repressive and emancipatory" (*Cold War Ruins* 210). In working across the varied and shifting imagined geographies of Asian America to articulate new forms of Asian/American critique, the contributors to this collection address what we might call "the ruins of human rights" as they have promised and foreclosed new subject positions, critical stances, and possibilities for envisioning a more just world.

As noted above, an important catalyst for this collection has been the SIAAS project, notably the 2015 Summer Institute in Asian American Studies held in Taipei, Taiwan.[5] This summer institute, along with other SIAAS events, was organized with a view to furthering Asian American studies from transpacific—and, in particular, Asian—perspectives. Gathering scholars and students from Asia, the Pacific, North America, and beyond, the SIAAS project not only extended Asia's engagement with Asian American studies but also attempted to "reactivate" Asian American critical discourse in the geohistorical contexts of Asian/American intersections.[6] Indeed, if recent developments in and recalibrations of Asian Canadian studies have effectively complicated some of the geographical imaginaries and established paradigms of Asian American studies, Asian American studies in Asia has in our view further unsettled—productively—the boundaries and epistemologies of North America–centered Asian American studies. Be it a release of "Asian America" from ethno-minoritized identity categories; a mobilization of inter-Asian geohistorical genealogies; a challenge to disciplinary distinctions between Asian, American, and Asian American studies; or an evocation of the intersecting trajectories of immigration, migration, wars, colonialism, imperialism, and capitalism across the Pacific—in each of these ways, Asian American studies in Asia has extended Asian/American time-space and helped bring additional sociohistorical materiality into Asian American studies.[7]

Among the many topics about which Asian American studies in Asia has been concerned, human rights stands out as one of the most crucial. This may be because the issue of "rights" is inevitably contested for those moving between, living beyond, and in many cases struggling with dual or multiple affiliations with nation-states. While the emergence and solidification of nation-states along the development of Western modernity has consolidated the idea of civil rights, the "rights" for immigrants, migrants, refugees, diasporic subjects, alien residents, war prisoners, indigenous peoples, migrant workers, the racialized, and the colonized remain unsettled and contested. One case in point, as foregrounded earlier in this introduction, is that the discourse of civil rights as promulgated by Truman in 1948 has proved to be inadequate to address the rights violations imposed on Asian subjects. The mass incarceration of Japanese Americans, for example, is irreducible to a civil rights discourse that attempts to focus on supposedly "domestic" issues alone. As Kandice Chuh acutely points out, the internment/incarceration of Japanese Americans underscores the entanglement of U.S. nationalism with the "'transnationalization' of Japaneseness"—"the conversion of the threat of Japanese empire into Japanese (American) racial difference by governmental and legal apparatuses of U.S. nationalism" (59). The "transnational," according to Chuh, must be taken as an essential "cognitive analytic" in order to trace "the incapacity of the nation-state to contain and represent fully the subjectivities and ways of life that circulate within the nation-space" (62).

If Chuh reminds us of the importance of "the transnational within the national" (69), Brian Masaru Hayashi in *Democratizing the Enemy* attends to the different factions of Japanese Americans, who are divided along the lines of generations, immigration status, class, and prefectural origins in Japan, to demonstrate the inadequacy of the discourse of civil rights to account for contentious national and ethno-familial identifications. Unconstrained by the dominant interpretation of Japanese Americans as a racialized minority in U.S. domestic politics, Hayashi suggests to look "beyond the national borders" (8) to recognize the residents of Japanese origin as first and foremost *humans in motion*, seeking individual and familial well-being between nations before being subjected to U.S. nationalist and assimilationist policies. Appositely titling the prologue to his book as "Beyond Civil Rights" and the epilogue as "Toward Human Rights," Hayashi pushes us to consider human rights as a core subject in discussing Asian/American immigration, migration, diasporas, and wars.

Building on this existing scholarship, this collection brings to the fore Asian/American national and transnational "lifeworlds" (a term used in Christopher Lee's essay in this collection) as contested sites of human rights practices and violations, (de)formations and transformations. One objective of this volume is to attempt to restore to presence "the subjects of human rights," including subjects impacted by militarism, refugees, repatriated persons, trafficked migrant workers, and so on—subjects who have been rendered invisible or relegated to the position of the inhuman. In "The Intimacies of Four Continents," Lisa Lowe concludes her study of Chinese indentured laborers in the Caribbean in the nineteenth century by advocating a project of "visualizing, mourning, and thinking 'other humanities' within the received genealogy of 'the human'" (208).[8] Likewise, by intervening into the intersections of state ideologies, imperialism, cold war militarism, and neoliberal capitalism across Asia/America, this collection provides renewed meditations on contested meanings of "the human" and "human rights." It seeks to ask: Who are entitled to be viewed as human subjects? Who are positioned as inhuman? Which subjects serve as the practitioners of human rights?

By drawing critical force from Asian American studies in and about Asia, this collection seeks to "reengage" Asia as it has been entwined with Asian/American and transpacific trajectories and discourses.[9] In addition to conceiving of Asia as offering a contextual enlargement of Asian American studies, this collection attempts to probe into cases of human rights violations and critiques by connecting Asian politics to forces taking place in and beyond the imagined geographies of "Asia." Rika Nakamura has contended that one benefit of "the intellectual encounter between Asia and Asian America" is that "Asian American studies as [a] racial minority discourse forces ethno-racial majority Asians . . . to reflect upon the racial, ethnic, and (neo)colonial relations in our own lands while critiquing the inequalities that are taking place in and across Asia" (251). Extending Nakamura's ethically grounded injunction, this collection investigates how Asian/American histories and stories can invigorate our understanding of Asian cultural politics in the ongoing struggles over power and representation in Asia and across the Pacific.

The first section of this collection investigates the stakes involved in "recollecting human rights" across Asian/American sites. It opens with Min-Jung Kim's powerful essay on the nexus of "militarism, neocolonialism, state building, and securitization" in South Korea. In this essay, Kim examines how U.S. military presence on the Korean peninsula has been justified through discourses of humanitarianism and reproduced through modes of South Korean governmentality that foreground what Kim calls "the logics of militarization and securitization." Through an investigation of the impacts of the U.S.–South Korea SOFA (Status of Forces Agreement) first signed in 1966, Kim draws attention to the environmental damage caused by the U.S. military; the deaths of two young South Korean girls crushed by U.S. military vehicles in 2002; and the lives of *kijichon*, or "camptown," prostitutes working near U.S. military bases, with a focus on the brutal murder of Yun Geum Yi in 1992. Through a careful consideration of these cases, Kim underlines the daunting challenges involved in rethinking human rights not as a universal discourse but as one that cannot, in the case of South Korea, be disentangled from the intersections of imperialism, state ideologies, and gender.

Christopher Lee's essay follows Kim's call for a "context-specific analysis" by focusing on the particularities of "how Chinese migrants became intertwined in the emerging international refugee regime" in the early Cold War period. Drawing attention to a profound reorganization of transpacific migrant lifeworlds linking Guangdong, Hong Kong, and Canada after 1947, Lee focuses on subjects of human rights who are in motion but also regulated through the categories of "the (immediate) relative" and "the refugee." While such categories were used by states and colonial authorities to attempt to manage the movements of Chinese migrants, they also, as Lee points out, offered opportunities for activists to challenge the Canadian federal government's exclusionary immigration policies. Lee's essay turns from this shifting and contested legal terrain to the immigrant family narrative, focusing on the work of Chinese Canadian author Judy Fong Bates to argue that her work conveys not simply what happened through a history of transpacific migration "but also what could have happened." Through a bold turn to Hannah Arendt's 1943 essay "We Refugees," Lee shows that Fong Bates's writing reveals "how the transnational lifeworld of Chinese migration came under tremendous strain" in the 1950s, revealing as well what Lee identifies as "the inability of post-1947 political frameworks to attend to the complexities of displacement."

Lee's focus on displaced subjects gains further historical depth in Masumi Izumi's essay on what she calls "a formerly unknown group of subjects": Japanese/Canadians who played on the legendary Vancouver Asahi baseball team before returning to Japan or being forcibly "repatriated" to Japan by the Canadian federal government after World War II. Subjected to incarceration, dispossession, and either forced relocation east of the Rocky Mountains or "repatriation" to Japan (a country many nisei in Canada had never visited), Japanese Canadians have long been recognized as subjects of human rights violations. Izumi's essay adds to our understanding of the history of Japanese Canadians by observing how the 2014 release of a film named *The Vancouver Asahi* set in motion possibilities to reconnect, through social media and other means, with the families and the descendants of members of this baseball team living in Japan after the forced dismantling of the Asahi in 1942. In Izumi's analysis, the contemporary popularization of the Asahi baseball team has enabled new historical subjects to emerge through access to previously inaccessible archives in Japan and through the telling of previously unknown stories across national boundaries.

Vinh Nguyen's essay concludes the opening section by discussing how Vietnamese diasporic subjects have through the discourse of human rights remembered histories of forced migration. Nguyen takes as his starting point the 2015 commemoration of the fortieth anniversary of the end of the Vietnam War, with a particular focus on the proposed state-sponsored construction in Ottawa of the Memorial to the Victims of Communism. Nguyen's nuanced analysis emphasizes how former Vietnamese refugees cannot be adequately understood as "passive, helpless, or empty of history and politics, even when they are victims"; instead, as Nguyen underlines, former refugees have actively adopted and mobilized human rights discourse to reshape what he calls "the conditions of refuge(es), past and present." In putting forth this position, Nguyen's essay shows how the struggles over the contentious memorial and the 2015 passing of Bill S-219 (known as the Journey to Freedom Day Act) not only reveal attempts to further consolidate notions of Canada as a presumed "land of refuge" and attempts to obscure Canadian complicity in supporting military violence in Asia; such struggles also open space, in Nguyen's account, to recognize new speaking positions at a moment in which the notion of "rights" remains unresolved.

The second part of this collection takes its cue from Nguyen's interventionary work to attempt to track "impossible subjects" that emerge at the intersections of race, gender, sexuality, and labor. This section opens with Yin Wang's examination of African American writer James Baldwin's remarkable engagement with the Vietnam War. Building on a renewed contemporary interest in Baldwin's critiques of antiblack racism in the United States and his varied contributions to black liberation struggles, Wang's essay shifts our focus to his unflinching denunciations of American military activity in Asia, foregrounding his analyses of colonialism inside and outside the United States. In doing so, Wang examines a number of key moments and sites: Baldwin's participation in—and his theorization of—the International War Crimes Tribunal, a 1966 nonstate initiative calling for U.S. war criminals to be brought to justice; his 1970 Turkish interviews, in which he critiqued white-centered middlebrow media depictions of U.S. militarism in Asia as an attempt to assist "the lesser races of the world"; and his post-1965 novels as robust depictions of how African American characters were deeply entangled in American wars in and against Japan, Korea, and Vietnam.

The complex forms of cross-identification identified by Wang in Baldwin's varied oeuvre find a different form of expression in Christopher B. Patterson's investigation of what he calls "migrant domestic workers in the plural." Moving across scattered sites in Asia and the Pacific—including the Philippines, Bahrain, Micronesia, and Hawaii—Patterson develops a multifaceted critique of discourses that position Filipinas working abroad as "national heroes" and discourses of neoliberalism used to depict familiar "'self-making' trajectories [of migrant workers] that have characterized the Asian American model minority." To extend this analysis, Patterson discusses literary texts by Kristiana Kahakauwila and Mia Alvar and the ways these texts depict migrant workers, foregrounding (in Patterson's account) discourses of "matronlyness," the policing of sexualities, and "willfullness" in Asian and Pacific spaces. Through his analysis, Patterson not only foregrounds the diversity of experiences in the Filipino/a migrant labor diaspora; he also focuses on Hawaii and Micronesian Islands as spaces indelibly marked by colonialism and U.S. militarism, not excluding the lasting damage caused by U.S. atomic testing in the Marshall Islands from 1946 to 1958.

Grace Hui-chuan Wu extends Patterson's focus on migrant labor diasporas by examining narrative representations of Southeast Asian migrant workers in Taiwan. In doing so, Wu's essay helps complicate received notions of migration that assume a unidirectional movement of subjects from Asia to America. What happens to accounts of the subjects of human rights when we take seriously the trajectories of inter-Asian migration, in this case linking the Philippines, Vietnam, and Taiwan? Building on the groundbreaking work of scholars such as Amie Parry, who proposed in 2012 to read Ku Yuling's creative nonfiction text *Our Stories* in relation to Asian American critique, Wu presents a comparative reading of texts by Southeast Asian migrant workers in Taiwan and by Taiwanese activist Ku Yu-ling. In doing so, Wu's essay uncovers some fascinating points of connection, including the pivotal role of Lucie Cheng, a former director of the UCLA Asian American Studies Center who helped found *4-Way Voice*, a newspaper for Southeast Asian migrant workers and immigrants in Taiwan. Wu is not, however, content to simply identify points of contact with what is already widely considered to be "Asian American" critical work. She instead asks: How might texts by and about Southeast Asian migrant workers in Taiwan help make "the inhumanity of global capitalism visible"? And how might such texts enable new social relations to push beyond "the racial hierarchies of the world economic order"? Analyzing the limits and possibilities of tropes of slavery, community building, and identity politics, Wu argues that we cannot be content with "humanitarian" reading practices that reaffirm the agency of reading subjects, instead calling for us to envision "new social relations and collectively historicize incongruities between labor migration, globalization, and human rights."

Annie Isabel Fukushima concludes this section with an ambitious critical account of "tethered subjectivities" spanning Asia, the Pacific Islands, and the continental United States. Her essay begins with the Korean-operated Daewoosa factory in American Samoa, a site where trafficked migrant workers from Vietnam and China worked alongside Samoan workers. While the owner of this factory was eventually convicted and sentenced to forty years in prison, Fukushima nevertheless reads this case as a failure to facilitate human rights in the Asia-Pacific region insofar as it affirmed, rather than contested, U.S. colonial presence in the region. Extending her discussion to address what she calls "factories, farms, and fisheries"—encompassing, among other subjects, Thai farm workers in Hawaii and the story of Sonny, a fisher from Indonesia whose journey took him to Australia, Fiji, American Samoa, and eventually California—Fukushima foregrounds key moments in the history of U.S. imperialism and colonial rule, including California's 1850 "Act for the Government and Protection of Indians," the annexation of Hawaii in 1898, and the partitioning of the Samoan archipelago in 1899. In doing so, her essay tracks how rights-based forms of subjectivity are inextricably tied to settler-colonial logics. Drawing on the work of Gayatri Chakravorty Spivak, Fukushima proposes the notion of "hacking" as a way of undoing discourses of human trafficking and human rights, urging us to envision new ways to challenge rights violations that do not, at the same time, affirm U.S. settler-colonial presence.

The third and final section of this collection asks what it would mean to envision the limits of human rights as they become visible through varied aftermaths, afterlives, and aesthetics. In her essay, Cathy J. Schlund-Vials revisits the topic of atrocity tourism in Cambodia. Drawing on recent controversies involving the widely popular downloadable game *Pokémon Go*, wherein museums dedicated to recollecting large-scale human loss and mass violence were listed as viable play sites, Schlund-Vials considers the exploitative registers and problematic dynamics of "atrocity tourism," a voyeuristic practice that privileges consumption over commemoration. Focusing her attention on Cambodia's Tuol Sleng Genocide Museum, Schlund-Vials explores the possibilities and, more significant, the limitations of such spaces, which troublingly eschew victimhood in favor of spectacularized perpetratorhood. Through tactical juxtaposition and comparative reframing, Schlund-Vials argues that the critique of consumptive practices vis-à-vis

*Pokémon Go* strategically disremembers the commercial dimensions of contemporary atrocity tourism. Such critiques lay bare the extent to which Tuol Sleng Genocide Museum—along with its companion site, Choeung Ek Killing Field and Genocide Center—as vexed memorials to a genocide that, due to a paucity of Khmer Rouge defendants and in the absence of victim reparation, has yet to be juridically reconciled.

Dinidu Karunanayake extends this turn to the aftermaths of human rights violations by focusing on internally displaced persons (IDPs) after the official conclusion of the Sri Lankan civil war in 2009. Discussing the last phase of the war, named "Humanitarian Operation" by the Sri Lankan government, Karunanayake draws attention to the disjunction between its destructive outcomes (including an estimated 21,200–28,200 deaths and over 275,000 IDPs) and the state's discursive framing of these events as a just war fought in the interests of civilians' rights and freedom. In doing so, this essay underlines ongoing crises of citizenship and human rights in Sri Lanka after the presumed end of the civil war. Karunanayake supplements this critique of state actions and state discourses by turning to two texts: *Handmade: Stories of Strength Shared through Recipes from the Women of Sri Lanka*, a text that "probes postwar legacies and human rights through the concept of food"; and an art project named *The Incomplete Thombu*, which presents oral testimonies and hand-sketched plans through which internally displaced subjects could present remembered notions of "home." The notion of "incompletion" foregrounded in Karunanayake's essay speaks powerfully to violent pasts that are in Sri Lanka not yet past. Emphasizing the "participant-centric methodology" at work in the texts he discusses, Karunanayake calls for the forging of a "mnemonic citizenship" not bound to categories and discourses produced by the state.

An analogous if not identical critique of relations between the nation-state and its citizens informs Mayumo Inoue's investigation of how the Okinawan archipelago has been, in his account, "constituted as a racialized space of disciplinary and regulatory extraction within the imperial world through a series of interstate diplomatic treaties, wars, and events" involving (among other actors) the United States, the Ryukyu Kingdom, and Japan. Inoue's essay takes on this topic via Michel Foucault's 1976 lecture addressing what he calls "a new right" distinct from "the old right of sovereignty." Inoue argues that working toward such "a new right" in the context of Okinawa requires a two-sided critique of, one the one hand, U.S. imperialism and the production of nation-state forms in East Asia and, on the other, nationalist desires to claim specific "populations" as putative targets of discipline. Inoue extends this critique through an analysis of two texts: Sai Yoichi's 1985 feature-length film *Let Him Rest in Peace* and Shinjo Takekazu's 2010 poem "Rupture—Henoko." Through his readings of these texts, Inoue directs our attention to ways in which "antiwar and anticolonial imaginations can critically exit what Foucault calls 'the subject-to-subject cycle'" dependent on the sovereign power of the state, thereby calling for "an aesthetic and erotic disarticulation of the biopolitical terms of life and death enforced by the state."

Christine Kim extends this section's focus on the aesthetic through an examination of texts produced by North Korean defectors including Shin Dong-hyuk, Jang Jin-sung, and others. Kim locates her reading of these texts by carefully investigating how a "political archive of post-WWII thought" produces "human rights as a racialized project." Her essay then situates the genre of life writing by North Korean defectors within this discourse to consider how such writing illustrates "the conceptual limitations of the human." By focusing on the limits of what it means to be "human," Kim calls for a rethinking of "the guiding logics of human rights"—and the bases of dominant reading practices. As Kim concludes, "In unpacking the human/inhuman binary logic that shapes human rights discourse and operates along national and racialized lines, we can begin to interrogate not just the cultural fantasies of North Korean inhumanity but also those that imagine the Western subject as universal and the fears and anxieties that underpin both."

This collection ends with an afterword by writer Madeleine Thien on "the act of listening." Thien's narrative account takes as a starting point a set of sixty-five bronze bells buried in the tomb of the Marquis Yi of Zeng after his death in 433 B.C., bells that lay silent underground until their rediscovery some twenty-five hundred years later. How might we understand the nature of this silence? For Thien, "unofficial history, encoded in multiple and interlocking silences, is etched on the air; *we could even say it is the air itself.*" Tracking complex interwoven routes through Russia, China, Vienna, Shanghai, Cambodia, and the uncovering of the sixty-five bronze bells in Hubei Province in China in 1977, Thien affirms the writer's task as a lifelong attempt "to practice the art of listening." For Thien, "to deny the personhood of others is to believe that the boundaries of their bodies do not exist and require neither reciprocity nor dignity. We, the fortunate, occupy the land they once inhabited, use the resources they once controlled, and take ownership of the labor we now demand from them. Thus diminished, it is only a matter of time before political and geopolitical forces seek to erase their bodies from the landscape and their voices from the field of sound." Thien's insistence that acts of listening are necessary for any sound to exist stands as succinct summation of the limits and possibilities of this collection and its varied attempts to address "the subject(s) of human rights"—subjects for whom, as Thien shows us, silence continues to repeat, with structures that might nevertheless still be heard.

## NOTES

1. Before 1965, U.S. immigration policy contained nation-based quotas that privileged non-Asian, non-African, and non–Latin American countries. The 1965 Hart-

Celler Act removed these quotas in favor of a hemispheric delineation. To wit, 120,000 immigrants were granted legal entry from the Western hemisphere; 170,000 were afforded entry from the Eastern hemisphere. The act also contained seven preferences; these preferences largely focused on family reunification and employment (specifically for those in the hard sciences). This piece of legislation is responsible for the first en masse immigration of individuals from Asian nation-states since the passage of the 1882 Chinese Exclusion Act. While the act was very much consistent with the liberal logics of the U.S. Civil Rights movement (via the elimination of racially inflected quotas), it was also linked to the foreign policy fact of militarized engagements abroad, notably in Southeast Asia.

2. Here is it important to acknowledge that human rights should not simply be understood as a post-1945 discourse (as discussed above) concurrent with military occupation, attempted forms of state-directed reparations, and the 1948 adoption of the UDHR. Instead, as Samuel Moyn's revisionary history *The Last Utopia* persuasively argues, we also need to understand human rights as a discourse that leapt into vastly wider use in the English language—including, for example, in the Anglo-American press (231)—in the 1970s, a period that directly overlapped and intersected with the rise of Asian American studies as an interdiscipline.

3. Parikh observes, "As any even cursory review of the twentieth century makes evident, human rights principles and instruments have been severely limited in terms of legal implementation and enforceability. And yet . . . human rights remain deeply meaningful methods of political and moral imagining, especially for subjects whose recognition by the state is tenuous, if not altogether foreclosed" (86).

4. In addressing the limits of his foundational work *The Last Utopia*, Moyn flatly acknowledges that "human rights became our highest ideals only as material hierarchy remained endemic or worsened" (*Not Enough* 220). Crucial to Moyn's assessment is a "missed connection": "Precisely because the human rights revolution has focused so intently on state abuses and has, at its most ambitious, dedicated itself to establishing a guarantee of sufficient provision, it has failed to respond to—or even recognize—neoliberalism's obliteration of any constraints on inequality" (*Not Enough* 216–217).

5. This summer institute, organized around the theme of "The Subject(s) of Human Rights," was held in Taipei from July 16 to 19, 2015.

6. A detailed introduction to and reflections on the SIAAS project can be found in "The SIAAS Project: Reactivating Asian American Critical Work," a special forum published in *Amerasia Journal* 42.3 (2016): 43–68.

7. The history and development of Asian American studies in Asia has been dealt with in numerous publications in Asia and the United States. Some key English-language sources include Wong; Wang, *Asian American Studies*; Aimin; Feng.

8. This idea has been further elaborated by Lowe in the revised (and substantially expanded) version of this essay in the introductory chapter (also titled "The Intimacies of Four Continents") of *The Intimacies of Four Continents* (Durham, NC: Duke University Press, 2015).

9. For a discussion of the potential of Asian American studies to "re-engage" Asia, see H. Lee.

## WORKS CITED

Aimin, Chen. "Asian American Literary Studies in China." *Amerasia Journal* 38.2 (2012): 155–161.

Beauregard, Guy. "Asian American Studies, Asian Canadian Questions." *Amerasia Journal* 33.2 (2007): xxi–xxviii.

Camacho, Keith L. *Cultures of Commemoration: The Politics of War, Memory, and History in the Mariana Islands.* Honolulu: University of Hawaii Press, 2011.

Chang, Kornel. *Pacific Connections: The Making of the U.S.-Canadian Borderlands.* Berkeley: University of California Press, 2012.

Chuh, Kandice. "Nikkei Internment: Determined Identities/Undecidable Meanings." *Imagine Otherwise: On Asian Americanist Critique.* Durham, NC: Duke University Press, 2003. 58–84.

Day, Iyko. "Transnationalism Within." *Canadian Literature* 227 (2015): 198–199.

Espiritu, Yên Lê. *Body Counts: The Vietnam War and Militarized Refuge(es).* Oakland: University of California Press, 2014.

Feng, Pin-chia. "East Asian Approaches to Asian American Literature Studies: The Case of Japan, Taiwan, and South Korea." *The Routledge Companion to Asian American and Pacific Islander Literature.* London: Routledge, 2014. 257–267.

Hayashi, Brian Masaru. *Democratizing the Enemy: The Japanese American Internment.* Princeton: Princeton University Press, 2004.

Hong, Christine. "Reframing North Korean Human Rights: Introduction." *Critical Asian Studies* 45.4 (2013): 511–532.

Lee, Christopher, and Christine Kim. "Asian Canadian Critique beyond the Nation." *Canadian Literature* 227 (2015): 6–14.

Lee, Erika. "Hemispheric Orientalism and the 1907 Pacific Coast Race Riots." *Amerasia Journal* 33.2 (2007): 19–47.

Lee, Hsiu-chuan. "Re-engaging 'Asia.'" *Amerasia Journal* 42.3 (2016): 47–51.

Lowe, Lisa. "The International within the National: American Studies and Asian American Critique." *Cultural Critique* 40 (1998): 29–37.

———. "The Intimacies of Four Continents." *Haunted by Empire: Geographies of Intimacy in North American History.* Ed. Ann Laura Stoler. Durham, NC: Duke University Press, 2006. 191–212.

Moyn, Samuel. *The Last Utopia: Human Rights in History.* 2010. Cambridge, MA: Belknap, 2012.

———. *Not Enough: Human Rights in an Unequal World.* Cambridge, MA: Belknap, 2018.

Nakamura, Rika. "What Asian American Studies Can Learn from Asia: Towards a Project of Comparative Minority Studies." *Inter-Asia Cultural Studies* 13.2 (2012): 251–266.

Palumbo-Liu, David. *Asian/American: Historical Crossings of a Racial Frontier.* Stanford: Stanford University Press, 1999.

Parikh, Crystal. *Writing Human Rights: The Political Imaginaries of Writers of Color.* Minneapolis: University of Minnesota Press, 2017.

*Public Papers of the Presidents of the United States, Harry S. Truman, 1945–1953.* Washington, DC: United States Government Printing Office, 1966.

Srikanth, Rajini. "Quiet Prose and Bare Life: Why We Should Eschew the Sensational in Human Rights Language." *Frame* 27.1 (2014): 79–99.

Suzuki, Erin. "Transpacific." *The Routledge Companion to Asian American and Pacific Islander Literature.* Ed. Rachel C. Lee. London: Routledge, 2014. 352–364.

Wang, Chih-ming. "Asian American Critical Work in a Transpacific and Inter-Asia Nexus." *Amerasia Journal* 42.3 (2016): 63–68.

———, ed. *Asian American Studies in Asia*. Special issue of *Inter-Asia Cultural Studies* 13.2 (2012).

Williams, Randall. *The Divided World: Human Rights and Its Violence*. Minneapolis: University of Minnesota Press, 2010.

Wong, Sau-ling C. "When Asian American Literature Leaves 'Home': On Internationalizing Asian American Literary Studies." *Crossing Oceans: Reconfiguring American Literary Studies in the Pacific Rim*. Hong Kong: Hong Kong University Press, 2004. 29–40.

Yoneyama, Lisa. *Cold War Ruins: Transpacific Critique of American Justice and Japanese War Crimes*. Durham, NC: Duke University Press, 2016.

———. "Possibilities of Asian/Canadian Transnationality." *Canadian Literature* 227 (2015): 196–198.

# PART I

## Recollecting Human Rights

# 1

# Human Rights and South Korea

## *U.S. Imperialism, State Ideologies, and Camptown Prostitution*

MIN-JUNG KIM

Violations are often committed in the Orwellian name of human rights themselves, cloaked in the palliative rhetoric of humanitarian intervention, [and] the chivalric defense of women and children. . . . [The] discursive victory of human rights means that ours is at once the Age of Human Rights and the Age of Human Rights Abuse.

—JOSEPH R. SLAUGHTER, *Human Rights, Inc.*

If human beings have universal and inalienable rights, why do human beings need to be protected from the state, and more pointedly, why must they be protected by the very state they are being protected from?

—GREG A. MULLINS, "Paradoxes of Neoliberalism and Human Rights"

Drafted by the delegations of fifty-eight states and revised over the course of three years in the aftermath of World War II, and with egalitarian aspirations to alleviate the suffering of humankind, the 1948 United Nations' Universal Declaration of Human Rights (UDHR) was a significant international response to human rights violations and wartime atrocities. However, an industry of scholars skeptical about the formulation of human rights have pointed out the problems with the claims in the UDHR, with how to adjudicate them, and with human rights discourse at large. One of the most stringent critics of the UDHR, Joseph R. Slaughter argues that "international human rights is a notoriously feeble legal regime" with only "optional protocols" whereby individual states may "ratify legal conventions without extending to their citizens the right to lay claim to those rights" ("Enabling Fictions" 56). Belinda Walzer states that while important for the value on human dignity and respect for the rights of individuals, the UDHR promotes "notions of individuality and a subject of rights who is predicated upon an Enlightenment notion of liberal subjectivity" (436). Elizabeth Anker also asserts that the language of human rights "marshal[s] a highly abstract, disembodied, and anemic vision of human selfhood" (16) "that yield[s] a highly truncated, decorporealized vision of the subject—one that paradoxically negates core dimensions of embodied experience" (2). Relatedly, Luce Irigaray has contended that the UDHR "may be a moving document, but from the very first article, I, as a woman, no longer feel 'human,' for I am not 'born free and equal in dignity and rights' [to other 'men']" (ix).

In addition to the problem inherent in the UDHR of evocations of abstract and decontextualized human condition, human rights discourse has been and continues to be used by states as a ploy to depoliticize or mask violent political operations, such as colonialism and imperialism. There is a long history of Western states casting their militaristic interventions as civilizational crusades, presenting themselves as charitable benefactors who are solely guided by the egalitarian principles of human rights. Human rights discourse is, of course, not equivalent to humanitarianism. In theory, humanitarianism is a doctrine that finds benevolence, sympathy, and compassion as natural to humankind and that these qualities can enable individuals to develop a moral obligation to relieve the suffering of others. And while humanitarianism and human rights share common origins "in natural law and the notion of inherent human dignity," human rights is primarily a juridical discourse, and humanitarianism remains a moral one (Wilson and Brown, qtd. in Goldberg and Moore 14). Yet because humanitarianism and human rights share common ground, including their focus on what it means to be a human—to have rights to dignity and to help secure those rights for others through one's humane qualities—humanitarianism has been a critical component in human rights, with productive as well as dangerous ramifications. Julie Stone Peters argues sharply that "the grounding of humanitarian principles in rights, and of rights in humanitarian principles, fused the sentimental with a political program" (23). As Leticia Sabsay further contends, the creation of "'the suffering other' as mute and helplessly un-nurtured, violated, or deprived body demands affective responses willing to commit to humanitarian enterprises, thereby moralizing otherwise potentially political claims" (280).

Moreover, the limitation of human rights both in theory and in practice becomes starkly evident when turning to geopolitical contexts with overlapping sociopolitical trajectories such as militarism, neocolonialism, state building, and securitization, such as South Korea. The first part of this essay will concentrate on the nation space of South Korea of the Park Chung Hee (1962–1979) regime to consider its fraught relationship to human rights because of the interlocking histories of U.S. imperialism, anti-Communism, capitalism, military dictatorship, and national sovereignty. It will then turn to contemporary instances of human rights violations in light of the ongoing reality of U.S. hegemony and the unequal terms of the U.S.–Republic of Korea Status of Forces Agreement (SOFA). The last part of the essay will focus in particular on camptown (*kijichon*) prostitution of roughly the 1960s–1980s to contend that, embedded in multiple ideologies and oppressive structures such as patriarchy and gender ideologies, debt-peonage of the club system, racism and violence from clients, U.S. extraterritorial hegemony in Asia, and the South Korean state's complicity and tacit support of camptown prostitution, the lives of camptown women call into question the viability of universal and normative discourse of human rights.

## U.S. Imperialism and the South Korean State

A documentary produced in 1950 by the U.S. Armed Forces, "Crime of Korea," serves as an apt example of how the U.S. government has relied on the moral high ground of humanitarianism to justify its military presence in Korea and future involvement in world affairs. This black-and-white film does offer an unrelenting portrayal of the reality of the Korean War (1950–1953) by repeatedly showing images and clips of the destruction of homes and buildings, orphaned children crying on the streets, mothers and wives hunched over next to their dead husbands and sons, lamenting and mourning, and the endless lines of dead bodies. Yet, as Lilie Chouliaraki points out, it is precisely the media's showcasing of the suffering of distant others that is the key to humanitarian practices.[1] As Didier Fassin keenly articulates, "the portrayal of the recipients of humanitarian action as vulnerable—which is key to the whole humanitarian machine—depicts these subjects almost exclusively as the carriers of bodies subjected to naked violence."[2] In this light, what is striking about the documentary *Crime of Korea* is the rhetoric in the narration voice-over by Humphrey Bogart, the promotion of the United States to its self-proclaimed status as a humanitarian champion of the world. In the voice of Bogart as a war correspondent, the film begins with the narrative that after the surrender of Japan in 1945, "every GI was a symbol of liberation to the natives." Five years later, in 1950, the war correspondent returns to Korea, to the war zone with "American and other United Nations troops bringing liberation," "the brilliant leadership of the United States working with other United Nations forces."

Worth noting here is that there is a glaring distortion of facts in the film. At one point, Bogart mentions the area of Taejon in South Korea, along with images of piles and lines of dead bodies—"these were prisoners of the Communists," "shot with their hands tied behind their backs. . . . These men and women were not killed accidentally in the heat of battle. They were murdered cold-bloodedly, deliberately, butchered to spread terror" by "communist monsters." Contrary to the film's presentation, the "Taejon Massacre" was not committed by North Korean forces but was a massacre by the South Korean state of between four thousand and seven thousand local political prisoners—men, boys, and some women who had been jailed, many of those accused as pro-Communists. Transported in trucks, some attended by U.S. military personnel, they were slaughtered, shot, buried alive, and thrown into pits and dumped with earth. This atrocity blatantly took place under U.S. supervision, for American officers stood idly by, watching as the slaughter continued, photographing for their records but doing nothing to stop it (Cumings 1).

In addition, the film constructs the narrative of U.S. occupation in Korea after Japanese surrender as governed by purely humanitarian principles to assist a backward nation to development. The film attempts to redefine and reaffirm the United States' status as a harbinger of world security by turning to images of U.S. defense plants with weaponry in the factory lines and Americans industriously moving about in workplaces. It proceeds to state emphatically that there will not be any more wars "as long as we remain vigilant and strong." "The cost will not be small. Liberty is never cheap." Then, returning to the scenes of dead bodies in in Korea, it states, "Let us not forget this. For our sake as well as for the rest of the world. Remember this. If we value our lives, our home, and our freedom, let us remember the crime of Korea."[3] This single film is just one example of the ways that a particular brand of moral humanitarianism has been in the service of the consolidation of U.S. imperial hegemony in the twentieth century and in the present, as in the destruction of the Afghan state under the claims to save the women and children. Elizabeth Swanson Goldberg goes as far as to assert that human rights and humanitarianism are in fact "extensions of political power within imperial frameworks that claim to critique imperialism" but that may ultimately end up "reinforcing" it (111).

U.S. presence in Korea cannot be reduced summarily as American violence and aggression disguised as humanitarianism and aid. The specifics of U.S. foreign policy notwithstanding, quite a few South Koreans who lived through the Korean War as children have benevolent associations with individual American soldiers. The traumatic experiences of war—death, families torn apart, scarcity of food, destruction of homes—have also engendered among South Koreans a strong collectivist nationalist sentiment of hard work and individual sacrifice for national strength and unity. Issues on which South Koreans are divided today, such as national security, politics, and foreign policy, are polarized by age more than anything else. Divisive positions on the Republic of Korea's National Security Act, which has been enforced since 1948, is a case in point: many among those who are in favor of keeping it were born before or shortly after the Korean War. The purpose of the National Security Act, "to secure the security of the State and the subsistence of the freedom of nationals, by regulating any anticipated activities compounding the safety of the State" ("National Security Act"), has also been used in dictatorships and military regimes to suppress activities against "the safety of the State," such as political protests and voicing of pro-Communist or anti-South Korean state sentiments, or even sentiments against the ruling state. Though some of the clauses have been amended over the years, the National Security Act stipulates that "any person who praises, incites, or propagates the activities of an anti-government organization, a member thereof of the person who has received an order from it, or who acts in concert with it, or propagates or instigates a rebellion against the State, with the knowledge of the fact that it may endanger the existence and security of the State of democratic fundamental order, shall be punished by imprisonment for not more than seven years" ("National Security Act"). This National Security Act can be and has been employed as a justification for human rights violations, using police and state force against citizens.

Without doubt, throughout the dictatorship of Park Chung Hee (1962–1979) and the military regimes of Chun Do Hwan (1979–1988) and Roh Tae Woo (1988–1993), South Koreans have not blindly upheld or endorsed the state's views and human rights violations as a necessary condition for national security and economic development. The student democracy movement, labor protests, and the work of individual journalists, scholars, artists, and ordinary citizens have been a critical part in the long, painful history of struggles against state's use of military police and suppression of dissent. However, the urgency of nation building after the war, the continuing threat from North Korea, and the state's dependence on the United States for its military defense have made a special place for anti-Communism and capitalist development as official state ideologies that many citizens, especially those who were born during the Korean War, have come to accept. Even South Koreans who were born after 1950, who did not experience the war firsthand, have been raised in a political and social climate where anti-Communism has been the state ideology, including monthly nationwide defense training drills and mandatory anti-Communism ethics classes and speech, essay, and art contests in schools.

State intervention in the everyday life of its citizenry during the Park Chung Hee regime is best illustrated in the amendment, on March 10, 1973, of the "Punishment of Minor Offenses Act," which basically made individual expression illegal by enforcing regulations on men's hair length and style and women's skirt lengths. For about ten years that followed, men with hair covering their ears on the sides and shirt lapel in the back, or with a perm, could be seized by the police, who carried hair clippers. And since women were prohibited from wearing miniskirts that rose more than seventeen centimeters from the knees, the police could be seen carrying rulers to measure skirt lengths on the streets. The government's claim that not "decadence" and "promiscuity" but only industry and hard work are the prescriptions for fortifying the nation against the threat of Communism and other foreign invasions further contributed—as in the anxiety over women's skirt lengths—to the limited construction of women's roles as supportive spouses, homemakers, and mothers.

In sum, for several decades after the Korean War, the South Korean state posited national security, economic prosperity, and political stability as preconditions for, or equivalent to, rights as citizens. Thus, human rights, in the normative sense of dignity, right to free expression of opinion and speech, and choice of life and individual development, were forcefully compromised and curtailed by the official state ideologies of anti-Communism, capitalism, and the neocolonial discourse of the United States as an ally and benefactor. At the same time, it seems that the case of South Korea is an apt illustration of what John Lechte and Saul Newman articulate in their provocative study on Giorgio Agamben and the politics of human rights, that there is "a fundamental and perhaps irreconcilable tension between the principle of national sovereignty and that of human rights," insofar as human rights "necessarily imply *a limitation* on state power" (vii; emphasis added). Lechte and Newman point out that "sovereignty embodies a desire for autonomy . . . a self-enclosed solipsistic identity that refuses to recognize or answer to anything other than itself" and that human rights in theory "seek to call sovereignty into account, make it answer to universal principles of justice, therefore invoking an alternative ontology of the human, which exceeds the order of the state, [and] are thus an anathema to it" (vii). As Lechte and Newman go on to note, if, at its heart, "state sovereignty is about security," even where human rights may be "at least formally a part of the constitutional order, it must always give way to the exigencies of security" (vii).

The condition of national partition in Korea, which remains as a "ceasefire," and thus the ongoing possibility of the eruption of war, has made the logics of militarization and securitization the dominant modes of South Korean state governmentality.[4] The condition of "a state of emergency" has also been used by the South Korean government to operationalize its power as absolutely sovereign, not necessarily including the "right" to take the life of its citizens but, as during the Park Chung Hee regime, including the passage of orders that limit and monitor the everyday activities of its citizens. In this sense, Agamben's formulations of the paradox of sovereignty and the state of exception are fearfully relevant to the sociopolitical situation in South Korea. In his seminal work *Homo Sacer: Sovereign Power and Bare Life*, Agamben notes that "the paradox of sovereignty" lies in the fact that the sovereign "having the legal power to suspend the validity of the law, legally places himself outside the law" (15) and that, following Carl Schmitt, "the sovereign exception is the very possibility of juridical rule and, along with it the very meaning of State authority" (17). Thus, for Agamben, what is excluded is "not without relation to the rule," but on the contrary, "what is excluded in the exception maintains itself in relation to the rule in the form of the rule's suspension. The rule applies to the exception in no longer applying, in withdrawing from it. The state of exception is thus not the chaos that precedes order but rather the situation that results from its suspension" (18). As Agamben notes, "what is at issue in the sovereign exception is not so much the control or neutralization of an excess as the creation and definition of the very space in which the juridico-political order can have validity" (19). That the Park Chung Hee government in South Korea drew on the logic of a state of exception as a way to normalize its dictatorial and military regime is evidenced in its promotion of national security and nation building as defenses against Communist threat. More specifically, as I turn to in the last part of this paper on camptown prostitution, the Park Chung Hee regime exercised sovereign power by creating laws that could be suspended around U.S. military bases, producing women in camptowns as "bare life," whose "inclusive exclusion" in the state was defined by their abandonment from law.

## U.S. Militarism and SOFA

The formation of U.S. military bases in South Korea is part of the much longer history of its global empire building, with the establishment of its bases around the world that can be traced as early as 1898 in Guantanamo, Cuba, after defeating Spain (Hohn and Moon 7). The history of U.S. military bases in South Korea, Japan and Okinawa, and West Germany in particular reveal that during and after World War II these locations became intimately connected in the larger strategic planning of the United States as a way to ensure the nation's political and economic ambitions and as critical sites for U.S. Cold War battles against the Communist bloc. Some seventy thousand troops were stationed in South Korea in 1953; the country was additionally of value because of its proximity to Japan, since the United States along with countries in the North Atlantic Treaty Organization (NATO) feared that the Soviet Union could regard South Korea as "a dagger or a launching pad for an invasion of Japan" (Hohn and Moon 10). At the time of writing, 28,500 U.S. soldiers are stationed in South Korea.

U.S. military presence overseas was far from evenly distributed, not just in the size and number of its troops but in their composition. Unlike in Japan, Okinawa, and West Germany, where military duty would normally last two to three years and families often accompanied soldiers, service in South Korea, considered far too dangerous a post for families, was and remains a one-year rotation term. This difference has important implications for the nature of interaction between the military, which is composed mostly of men and very few women, and the host communities. Another crucial difference is the specific natures of the SOFAs that the United States has with host countries.

A SOFA was first signed between the United States and twelve NATO countries in 1951 after World War II. During the 1950s, the United States had SOFAs with forty-nine countries, and by 2008, with more than one hundred nations (Hohn and Moon 14). As diplomatic agreements facilitating the military alliance between the United States and the host governments, SOFAs touch on several areas, though the content and the specifics may differ, often a reflection of the nature of the host country's relation to the United States. The U.S.–Republic of Korea (ROK) SOFA, first signed in 1966, includes articles on various issues concerning the legal status of U.S. military personnel and their dependents, as well as of Koreans employed on the military bases—specifications regarding criminal jurisdiction over U.S. military personnel, the U.S. military's use of land for compounds or maneuver areas, environmental damage resulting from military exercises, passport and visa law exemptions of U.S. military personnel and their dependents from regulation by the Republic of Korea, and the restricted labor rights of Koreans employed on bases. Unlike the U.S.-Germany SOFA, the U.S.-ROK SOFA is far more flexible about the U.S. military's use of land and the environment. In 2000, the U.S. military admitted to dumping formaldehyde in the Hangang River in South Korea and apologized, though they were not held accountable in any legal way (Power). In 2011, it was reported that U.S. military had buried drums of Agent Orange at Camp Carroll in Waegwan, North Gyeonsang Province, and though the joint environmental probe by United States Forces Korea (USFK) and the Environment Ministry found no evidence of Agent Orange or its risk to human health, the U.S. military admitted to burying chemicals at the site (Power). In addition to the serious damage to the environment, the occurrence of some high-profile crimes has prompted calls for revision of the SOFA through protests from civic groups such as Solidary for Peace and Reunification of Korea, especially as the disparities between the U.S.-ROK SOFA and the U.S.-Germany SOFA became more evident. As Hohn and Moon point out, although in principle SOFAs were designed to facilitate the military alliance between the United States and the "host" county, insofar as they work to protect the rights and the privileges of the U.S. military personnel, "despite the absence of formal colonies, [they] have undermined national sovereignty and contain the contradiction of American liberal imperialism" (15).

While most Koreans may not encounter U.S. military personnel, those who live near the bases or even in areas not immediately adjacent but in the many regions and provinces outside the city of Seoul can be affected, and with some of the most tragic outcomes, as in the deaths of two fourteen-year-old girls, Mi Sun Shim and Hyo Soon Shin. On June 13, 2002, in a narrow two-lane road about ten miles north of Seoul in Yangju, Uijeongbu, Mi Sun Shim and Hyo Soon Shin were run over and crushed to death by a U.S. military armored vehicle ("Two S Korean Teenagers"). The twelve-foot-wide sixty-ton vehicle, used to clear mines, was part of a convoy moving to a training exercise (Ayling). The two girls were walking along the edge of a 4.2-meter-wide road, the main pathway for pedestrians in the area, when they were run over from behind by the vehicle, as another convoy of U.S. military vehicles was coming from the opposite direction (Ayling). Sergeant Mark Walker, who was at the wheel of the vehicle, has been quoted as saying that he was on the radio and could not hear a warning about the girls from the vehicle commander Sergeant Fernando Nino ("Bush Effigy Burned"). Sergeant Nino argued that he had alerted Sergeant Walker to the presence of the girls, while Walker claimed that he never heard the warning because, apparently, of a defective communications system ("Korean Anger").

This tragic incident provoked national outrage in South Korea. The Second Infantry Division of the U.S. Army had not informed the villagers of the off-base training mission beforehand. And even after the accident, declaring Highway 56 a critical link for the troops, U.S. military officials did not pull the mine-clearing vehicles off the roads (Ayling). Additionally, whereas the local police investigator in Uijeongbu initially saw the deaths of the girls as resulting from the driver's negligence, under the U.S.-ROK SOFA, U.S. soldiers are under U.S. jurisdiction and beyond the reach of South Korean law.[5]

The girls' deaths led to large-scale protests outside U.S. military bases and across cities in South Korea (with candlelight vigils in the center of Seoul gathering some twenty thousand people) to call for the amendment of the SOFA and for the two soldiers who were driving the vehicle to be turned over for trial in the South Korean court system. The South Korean Ministry requested that the USFK commander transfer jurisdiction to the Korean legal system, but the request was denied, with the judge advocate of USFK stating that the soldiers were performing assigned duties in official capacity and were thus subject to the SOFA. In November that year, under U.S. military court, the vehicle's commander and driver, Fernando Nino and Sergeant Mark Walker, were found not guilty of "negligent homicide" and were cleared of charges ("Korean Anger"). In the months before and after the verdict, posters of the two girls' crushed and mutilated bodies could be found in subway stations across Seoul, and the images still remain. The deaths of Shim and Shin were tragedies that fueled broad-scale anti-American sentiments for a number of reasons: the horrific nature of their deaths at a young, defenseless age; the U.S. military court ruling that cleared the two men in the vehicle; the unequal "agreement" of the U.S.-ROK SOFA that tapped into the public's own sense of powerlessness and subordination to the U.S. state; the frustration and anger at the South Korean government for its ineffectiveness in protecting the rights of its citizens; and the frustration with the plight of the nation at large.

Pointed out by various civic groups in South Korea as they continue to call for revisions to the SOFA, the category and nature of "official duty" of

U.S. military personnel can be open to interpretation, and since "criminal jurisdiction" involving military personnel on duty belongs to the U.S. military court, the South Korean government in effect has no legal jurisdiction involving American military personnel. With the United States exercising extraterritorial national sovereignty, the South Korean state can offer little legal protection to its citizens, especially to civilians living near or working in the bases. Though the situation may differ somewhat based on the ruling political party in South Korea at the time, far from the government taking more active measures, it is usually civic activists and groups who try to mobilize communities and people into action or pressure the government with regard to the specifics of U.S.-ROK relations and U.S. military presence.

The fate of two innocent young girls who died on their way to a friend's birthday party is a stark reminder of the dysfunctionality of any discourse on human rights in the context of U.S. imperialism and the South Korean state's subordinate status. But even in their deaths, the girls were stripped of their basic human rights to dignity and respect, denied their right to fair representation in court, and defenseless and powerless against U.S. hegemony. The South Korean state was impotent in protecting and securing basic human rights for its citizens in circumstances that involve its relationship to the U.S. state, although not necessarily complicit in the violent deaths of citizens.

## Camptown Prostitution

U.S. military intervention in South Korea coincided with the formation of camptowns or kijichons near the bases. Catering to the consumer needs of the American GIs, such camptowns consist of clothing stores, barber shops, and bars or clubs with English names, which the soldiers frequent off duty to drink beer, relax, and pick up women, the center of kijichon life (K. Moon 17). As Katherine Moon notes in her extensive and provocative study, *Sex Among Allies: Military Prostitution in U.S.-Korea Relations*, as manifestations of the U.S. military empire as a global and transnational phenomenon, camptowns are "hybrid and ambiguous spaces that blur national boundaries and sovereignty" (19), and kijichon prostitution is thus "a part of the U.S. military's chain of overseas camptowns which have thrived on prostitution in Asia (Vietnam, Thailand, Okinawa, and the Philippines, in addition to South Korea)" (15).

As Cynthia Enloe has argued, the ideology and lifestyle of the military establishment depend on highly gendered notions of femininity and masculinity, and the connection between military power and male heterosexual power often dictates the soldiers' relationships to the local community. Enloe asserts that "soldier-clients learn to view their masculinity—and the prowess of the nation they represent—as dependent on their sexual domination of the women who live near the base" ("Feminist Perspective" 101), and thus, the military base "is a package of presumptions about the male soldier's needs, the local society's sexual needs, and about the local society's resources for satisfying those needs" (*Bananas* 200). Camptown prostitution is therefore a highly particular kind of exploitative military, political, and sexual relationship, where the militarization of men takes place at the expense of the domination of poor, socially ostracized women, almost all of whom either have sought life in a camptown as a last resort for survival or have been sold into prostitution. Studies have documented that extreme poverty; being homeless, abandoned, or orphaned from the Korean War; abusive relationships; and physical beatings or rape from a male family member or from other men in the village were the most common reasons that women entered camptowns in the 1950s to 1970s. Sadly and ironically, societal labels that criminalize rape victims as "fallen," "ruined," and "whores" led women to regard camptowns as their only option, yet they continued to feel obligated to their duties as daughters and sisters by supporting aging parents and by providing schooling fees for male siblings. In 1966, among the 22,670 surveyed women in prostitution, 76 percent were either without a parent or without a place to stay, and among the 105 surveyed who were working in the Yongsan area in 1965, all were supporting from one to eight members of their family (*Sex Allies*). The few who were able to voluntarily leave camptowns as they reached middle age ended up resorting again to sex work, because factory work was the only other option for women without an education, but even this was available only to young women with agile hands and didn't provide enough money to support their own children (Sturdevant and Stoltzfus 239).

The lives of camptown prostitutes reveal that their victimization is compounded by a number of factors: South Korean national politics, U.S. hegemony, racism, sexism, patriarchy, poverty, and gender ideologies. The debt-peonage system of the clubs made incurring debts inevitable, since women who first entered a camptown needed to borrow money from the club owner to be supplied with clothes, makeup, bedding, and other necessities, and the clubs set impossible quotas for the number of drinks to sell and the number of men a night. Beatings and rape from club managers were common as well.

That prostitution entails multiple forms of violence, abuse, harassment, physical beatings, and emotional injury from pimps and clients has been widely documented. In an essay that powerfully argues against prostitution as a human rights violation that contradicts the UDHR's claims for the inalienable rights and dignity of the human person, Kathleen Barry contends that not just the prostitution of children or in cases without consent but all prostitution is a human rights violation: "Objectifying a human being, reducing her to a commodity to purchase, is an abusive act of power. It violates a person's human dignity and obliterates her human rights". Barry goes on to state that objectification provides the context for "other seemingly nonviolent behaviors that include humiliation, demeaning and degradation." Jessica Neuwith notes that prostitution is a violation of human rights because it is never unrelated to human trafficking: the "demand for prostitution fuels sex trafficking to supply it; not all prostituted women are sex trafficking victims, but all sex trafficking victims are sold into prostitution". In addition, Neuwith states that while women engaging in "survival sex" out of dire economic needs may "technically be consensual," prostitution cannot be viewed as an instance of "free will," since "there is no choice in the absence of the freedom to choose otherwise." There is a different view on this issue, one that advocates for prostitution as a human right—not as a way to protect pimps, but as a way to better protect sex workers for whom prostitution may be their only way to earn a living from being arrested, persecuted, and criminalized (Murphy).

What both sides seem to agree on, however, is that prostitutes suffer violence and danger on a daily basis. But women in kijichon prostitution are in an especially vulnerable and defenseless position because of the dynamics of U.S. imperialist relations to South Korea that further set the context for the vast power differences of race, gender, sexuality, nationality, and language. While one former prostitute was not afraid to admit that the GI clients treated her better than Korean men, most noted that they had to deal with the abusive behavior of clients—racism, insults to the women's lack of English language skills, and physical violence (Sturdevant and Stoltzfus). Some of the terms that the GIs used to refer to the women—"yellow monkey" and "little brown fucking machine"—were clear reenactments of racist and sexist stereotypes in the United States that determined camptown relations. Additionally, many of the camptown clubs and bars had "Korean citizens forbidden from entry" signs, which meant that the interaction between U.S. military personnel and Koreans took the form of American GI male customer/dominant nation and Korean female hostess/subordinate nation, a form that echoes and encapsulates the reality of U.S. military hegemony.

Kijichon women are stigmatized and ostracized from South Korean society, especially for their prostitution to *Yangnom*, a derogatory term for Western men. *Yangalbo* (Western whore), *Yangsaikshi* (Western bride), *Yanggongju* (Western princes), and UN Madam are common epithets in a society that, even today, would view taking one's own life as more honorable than prostitution for survival. Although camptown women have formed associations and societies among themselves (S. Moon 58), they have had little support from the larger community. Even until the late 1990s, South Korean feminist groups neglected camptown prostitution, with activists admitting that they had never placed kijichon prostitutes in any purview of exploitation or oppression, perceiving the women as "'too different' from themselves" (K. Moon 9).

Camptown prostitution came to public attention in 1992 with the horrifying death of Yun Geum Yi (age twenty-eight) by U.S. Second Division Private Kenneth Lee Mackle (age twenty) on October 28 in Dongducheon ("Report on US Crimes in Korea"). At the time that Yun's body was found in her room, the trunk of an umbrella had been penetrated twenty-seven inches into her rectum, and a coke bottle had been half inserted inside her vagina.[6] An autopsy that followed confirmed that two beer bottles had also been inserted inside Yun's uterus. Broken matches were found inside Yun's mouth, and her body, covered in severe contusions and bruises, had been sprayed with laundry detergent powder. Fingerprints on the beer bottles found inside Yun's uterus enabled the police to trace the killer.

Under the SOFA, crimes committed off duty are subject to South Korean court of law.[7] However, the clause on "Criminal Jurisdiction" in the SOFA (Article XXII 5 [d]) that states that the authorities of the Republic of Korea "shall give special consideration to a request from the military authorities of the United States for assistance in maintaining custody of an accused member of the United States armed forces, the civilian component, or a dependent" makes it difficult to say that the Korean court of law has full independence and autonomy of cases involving the U.S. military. At the first trial, Mackle received a life sentence without parole, but he later received a reduced sentence of fifteen years. Although imprisoned in Cheonan prison on May 17, 1994, Mackle returned to the United States in 2006 after being released on parole. Yun's murder is not exceptional by any case. There have been a number of murders of camptown prostitutes by U.S. military personnel, women strangled and beaten to death, bodies found with hangers inserted in the uterus ("Report on US Crimes in Korea").[8]

Yet what is truly appalling, as detailed extensively by Katherine Moon, Seungsook Moon, and Ji-Yeon Yuh, is that during the Park Chung Hee regime, the South Korean government promoted camptown prostitution as a way both to keep the American forces in South Korea happy and to bring in foreign currency. In 1961, Park Chung Hee had declared prostitution illegal with the Prostitution Prevention Law, but he revised his stance a year later, designating 104 special districts as exempt from the law, 60 percent in camptowns.[9] Far from intervening in the abuse and violence, by encouraging and legitimizing prostitution, the South Korean government, in effect, facilitated the human rights violations of the women. In addition, as part of the camptown cleanup campaign of the 1970s, the women were subjected to intrusive vaginal inspections and mandatory VD exams, which were initially enforced by U.S. authorities but eventually were actively supported by the South Korean government and medics. Some camptown women felt that having their bodies examined by U.S. medics, or being required by the U.S. military police to show valid VD ID cards, was a violation of their human rights as well as their rights as Korean citizens (K. Moon 131), but they were powerless to escape the practice.

As South Korea became more aware of camptown prostitution with the 1992 death of Yun Geum Yi, in 2004, Seoul Broadcasting Station aired a documentary, *Sex Allies: Kijichon Clean-Up Campaign*, which featured testimonies of former prostitutes and government authorities who had been in office during the 1960–1980s. Among the shocking details that emerged from the interviews was again that camptown prostitution was collaboratively promoted by the United States and the South Korean governments. A former U.S. military sergeant noted that gates outside the bases were referred to as "condom land," since the guards checked to make sure the men were carrying condoms and distributed them freely. One Korean civil official related that the camptown of Kunsan, "America Town," was a town planned and built specifically to cater to the needs of the GIs. Clubs, bars, and five-hundred-room units for prostitution were established, and shuttle service from the base was provided, with one thousand GIs arriving in the camptown on some nights. Moreover, former camptown women reiterated that low-tier government officials would visit them regularly to give classes in etiquette, good conduct, and the English language; applauded the women for being "civilian diplomats" and "true patriots" for contributing to the South Korean economy by earning U.S. dollars; and said that the women should be proud.

Women who tested positive in the routine biweekly VD checkup were quarantined in detention centers, referred to among the women as "monkey houses" for the bars and high walls and fences. Women were highly fearful of being detained because of the side effects of the penicillin injections, leaving some even paralyzed. Severe injuries also resulted from attempts to escape the center by jumping from the upper floors or walls. As a former medical worker who had administered the shots confirmed, the penicillin dosage was the amount designated by the U.S. government, which he acknowledged may have been too potent for South Korean women.

In 2014, 122 former camptown prostitutes, now aging and poor, sued the South Korean government, demanding compensation of $10,000 each, for encouraging them to work as prostitutes, violating their human rights by forcing them to undergo degrading checkups, and locking them up in quarantine centers till they were judged fit to go back to work (Park; Evans). Though the requested compensation may have been minimal, the women sought an apology and admission from the South Korean government of its responsibility for prostitution that served the U.S. military (Cain). In the ninth hearing of July 2016, Park Young Ja, the only one among the 122 women to testify publicly, stated that despite the shame of making her identity public, there was something she had to say (Jin). Opening her statement with "we have been abandoned by a country in which we were born," Park continued that the South Korean government created kijichon prostitution and profited from the exploitation and abuse of poor young women, many in their midteens who had nowhere to go or were sold into prostitution, who had to serve five men a night at minimum. Park added that the government furthered the oppression of the women by condoning the violence of the pimps and the club managers.

While some former camptown women choose to refer to themselves as comfort women, the term may not be the most appropriate since they were not forcibly taken to become sex slaves for the Japanese military during World War II. However, the South Korean government was responsible for the system in which the women would remain trapped in kijichon until old age, when they would no longer be useful as dollar-earning commodities. Park Young Ja's comment that she had been abandoned by her country is a poignant remark that human rights are not a natural right owned by all but a right determined by the state or available only to those who are positively incorporated and positioned to claim them within the nation.

Two and a half years after the women brought their case to court, in January 2017, the Seoul Central District Court came to a ruling: the South Korean government should provide $5,000 each to 57 of the 122 women who initially sued the government in 2014. The court stated that since the legal regulation that stipulates quarantine of carriers of contagious disease, which includes sexually transmittable conditions, was passed on August 19, 1977, it recognizes the South Korean government's forceful quarantine of women before the law as a violation in legal terms, and as such, only 57 women could be considered for compensation. The court, however, did not accept claims made by the camptown women that the South Korean government actively created camptowns to facilitate prostitution, or the claim that the camptown women had scarce autonomy in entering lives in prostitution or could not leave them freely. The court thus did not order that the South Korean government provide any form of additional compensation to the 57 women or to the remaining 63 women (since the case was brought to court in 2014, two women have died) whose histories in quarantine centers could not be considered "illegal" confinement or who had not been placed in such facilities. According to a statement released by Camptown Women Human Rights League in South Korea (established in 2012) after the January 2017 court ruling, although former camptown prostitutes are "not satisfied with the ruling," they believe that they have made partial progress insofar as the court ruling is a sign that the Korean government admits to some sense of responsibility. At the time of writing, the women have appealed against the January 2017 ruling, and the case is still on trial, being reviewed in the Seoul High Court.

## Conclusion

Although without any legal enforceability, the UDHR has served an important function. It has been used as a platform for local, international, diasporic, and nongovernment organizations to promote dignity, respect, and free choice as one's natural rights as a human being. There have been various movements to intervene in the violence inflicted and condoned by state regimes, such as torture, genocide, rape, human trafficking, child labor, social and economic disenfranchisement, extreme poverty, and environmental hazards, and political and civil rights as well as economic and cultural rights that include rights to food, housing, health, and education have become central to public discourses on human rights.

There is, however, a contradiction between the goals of the UDHR, for human rights to have universal reach and application, and the particularities of the world it seeks to address, which is conflict ridden, divided, and not without but with distinctions of "race, colour, sex, language, religion, political or other opinion, national or social origin, property, birth, or other status" (Article 2 UDHR). But the vague and naive universalist rhetoric of the UDHR can in fact work as a reminder of the daunting challenges ahead in making the doctrine into a reality: to transform the particularities of individuals and states to a universalized status.

The case of South Korea makes evident that multiple intersections—U.S. extraterritorial sovereignty, racism, South Korean state nationalism and anti-Communism, capitalism and nation building, patriarchy, and gender ideologies—trouble the status of human rights as a privileged and universal discourse. This is not to say that human rights are virtually nonexistent or ineffective in South Korea but to argue for the importance of engaging in the discourse and practice of human rights from the particularities of nationality, ethnicity, class, and gender, to name a few, and the ongoing imperative for context-specific analysis as a way to launch further critical conversations with and about other sites.

## Acknowledgments

I would like to thank the organizers of "The 2015 Summer Institute in Asian American Studies: The Subject(s) of Human Rights" (July 16–18, Taipei, Taiwan): Guy Beauregard, Pin-chia Feng, Shyh-jen Fuh, Hsiu-chuan Lee, and Chih-ming Wang. Special thanks to Guy Beauregard, Hsiu-chuan Lee, and Cathy Schlund-Vials for their detailed comments on an early version of this paper, and to Cathy for all the work in bringing this collection into form.

**NOTES**

1. Chouliaraki, qtd. in Sabsay 280.

2. Fassin, qtd. in Sabsay 280.

3. In the epilogue, a man in a suit urges viewers to buy defense bonds as a way to "share the responsibility to keep the country strong": "I have seen the crime of Korea. . . . When we Americans see something we don't like, something that we believe is wrong, something we consider a crime against mankind, we want to act. We want to put a stop

to what's wrong. *That's the kind of people we are*" (emphasis added). He also urges "all Americans to meet aggression wherever it strikes." See "Crime of Korea."

4. See also Lee, Jan, and Wainwright.

5. Under Article XXII 3 Criminal Jurisdiction, U.S. military authorities have "the primary right to exercise jurisdiction over members of the United States armed forces or civilian component, and their dependents, in relation to . . . (a-ii) offenses arising out of any act or omission done in the performance of official duty."

6. See also K. Moon 21 for the account of Yun's murder.

7. Article XXII 3 (b) states that "in the case of any other offense, the authorities of the Republic of Korea shall have the primary right to exercise jurisdiction."

8. See also *Sex Allies.*

9. See Park 76–78 for a more extensive description of the Prevention Law (the Yullak Prevention Law).

## WORKS CITED

Agamben, Giorgio. *Homo Sacer: Sovereign Power and Bare Life*. Trans. Daniel Heller-Roazen. Stanford: Stanford University Press, 1998.

Anker, Elizabeth. *Fictions of Dignity: Embodying Human Rights in World Literature.* Ithaca, NY: Cornell University Press, 2012.

Ayling, Sharon. "Killings of Young Girls by U.S. Troops Ignites Rage." *Workers World.* 1 August 2002. Web. 5 May 2015.

Barry, Kathleen. "Why Is Prostitution a Violation of Human Rights?" *Wordpress.* December 2013. Web. 6 July 2016.

"Bush Effigy Burned as US Troops Stand Trial for Girls' Death." *AFP.* 18 November 2002. Web. 5 May 2015.

Cain, Geoffrey. "'Comfort Women' Who Serviced US Soldiers Demand Justice." *Mintpressnews.* 12 September 2014. Web. 25 July 2016.

"Crime of Korea (1950)." *Armed Forces Screen Report* 125. Online video clip. YouTube, n.d. Web. 5 May 2015.

Cumings, Bruce. "The South Korean Massacre at Taejon: New Evidence on US Responsibility and Coverup." *Asia-Pacific Journal Japan Focus* 6.7 (2008): 1–4.

Enloe, Cynthia. *Bananas, Beaches, Bases: Making Feminist Sense of International Politics.* Berkeley: University of California Press, 1990.

———. "A Feminist Perspective on Foreign Military Bases." *The Sun Never Sets: Confronting the Network of Foreign U.S. Military Bases.* Ed. Joseph Gerson and Bruce Birchard. Boston: South End, 1991. 95–106.

Evans, Stephen. "Did Korea Encourage Sex Work at US Bases?" *BBC News Magazine.* 28 November 2014. Web. 24 July 2016.

Goldberg, Elizabeth. "Intimations of What Was to Come: Edwidge Danticat's *Farming of Bones* and the Indivisibility of Human Rights." Goldberg and Moore 103–119.

Goldberg, Elizabeth Swanson, and Alexandra Schultheis Moore, eds. *Theoretical Perspectives on Human Rights and Literature.* New York: Routledge, 2012.

Hohn, Maria, and Seungsook Moon. Introduction. *Over There: Living with U.S. Military Empire from World War Two to the Present.* Ed. Hohn and Moon. Durham, NC: Duke University Press, 2010. 1–36.

Irigaray, Luce. *Thinking the Difference: For a Peaceful Revolution.* Trans. Karin Montin. New York: Routledge, 1994.

Jin Ju Won. "Public Testimony of Kijichon Comfort Women." *Women's Newspaper.* 13 July 2016. Web. 28 July 2016.

"Korean Anger as US Soldiers Cleared." *BBC*. 22 November 2002. Web. 5 May 2015.

Lechte, John, and Saul Newman. *Agamben and the Politics of Human Rights: Statelessness, Images, Violence*. Edinburgh: Edinburgh University Press, 2013.

Lee, Seung-Ook, Najeeb Jan, and Joel Wainwright. "Agamben, Postcoloniality, and Sovereignty in South Korea." *Antipode* 46.3 (2014): 650–668.

Moon, Katherine H. S. *Sex among Allies: Military Prostitution and U.S.-Korea Relations*. New York: Columbia University Press, 1997.

Moon, Seungsook. *Militarized Modernity and Gendered Citizenship in South Korea*. Durham, NC: Duke University Press, 2005.

Mullins, Greg A. "Paradoxes of Neoliberalism and Human Rights." Goldberg and Moore 120–34.

Murphy, Catherine. "Sex Workers' Rights Are Human Rights." *Amnesty International*. 14 August 2015. Web. 20 July 2016.

"National Security Act (of South Korea)." *Wikipedia*. 1948. Web. 10 May 2015.

Neuwith, Jessica. "Amnesty International Says Prostitution Is a Human Right—but It's Wrong." *The Guardian*. 28 July 2015. Web. 8 June 2016.

Park, Jeong-Mi. "Paradoxes of Gendering Strategy in Prostitution Policies: South Korea's 'Toleration-Regulation Regime,' 1961–1979." *Women's Studies International Forum* 37 (2013): 73–84.

Peters, Julie Stone. "'Literature,' the 'Rights of Man,' and Narratives of Authority: Historical Backgrounds to the Culture of Testimony." Goldberg and Moore 19–40.

Power, John. "[Voices] Should SOFA Be Revised?" *Korea Herald*. 18 March 2003. Web. 5 June 2016.

"Report on US Crimes in Korea 1945–2001: 17. Crimes Committed by U.S. Soldiers after the Korean War." *Korea International War Crimes Tribunal*. 23 June 2001. Web. 8 May 2016.

Sabsay, Leticia. "Permeable Bodies: Vulnerability, Affective Powers, Hegemony." *Vulnerability in Resistance*. Ed. Judith Butler, Zeynep Gambetti, and Sabsay. Durham, NC: Duke University Press, 2016. 278–302.

*Sex Allies: Kijichon Clean-Up Campaign*. *Seoul Broadcasting System*. 2013. Online video clip. YouTube. Web. 25 July 2016.

Slaughter, Joseph R. "Enabling Fictions and Novel Subjects: The *Bildungsroman* and International Human Rights Law." Goldberg and Moore 41–64.

———. *Human Rights, Inc.: The World Novel, Narrative Form, and International Law*. New York: Fordham University Press, 2007.

Sturdevant, Saundra Pollock, and Brenda Stoltzfus, eds. *Let the Good Times Roll: Prostitution and the U.S. Military in Asia*. New York: New Press, 1992.

"Two S Korean Teenagers Run Over [by] US Military Vehicle." *AFP*. 14 June 2002. Web. 5 May 2015.

"The Universal Declaration of Human Rights." *The United Nations*. 10 December 1948. Web. 4 May 2015.

Walzer, Belinda. "The Right Time for Rhetoric: Normativity, *Kairos*, and Human Rights." *The Routledge Companion to Literature and Human Rights*. Ed. Sophia A. McClennen and Alexandra Schultheis Moore. London: Routledge, 2016. 433–440.

Yuh, Ji-Yeon. *Beyond the Shadow of Camptown: Korean Military Brides in America*. New York: New York University Press, 2004.

# 2

# After 1947

## *The Relative, the Refugee, and the Immigrant in the Chinese Canadian Family Narrative*

Christopher Lee

Well into the 1960s, most Chinese in Canada could trace their lineage to several hundred villages in southern China's Guangdong Province. Once in Canada, their lives were subject to multiple forms of racism and exclusion. Until 1947, Canadians were legally categorized as British subjects while all Chinese, regardless of their place of birth, were considered Chinese nationals. This policy mirrored legal definitions of citizenship in China since 1909, when the Qing state formally declared Chinese nationality a matter of paternal bloodline regardless of place of birth; this policy was retained by the Republic of China (ROC) after the 1911 Revolution and not revised until the early years of the People's Republic of China (PRC).[1] In 1947, the Canadian government repealed the 1923 Chinese Exclusion Act, which had practically halted immigration from China for twenty-five years. In the same year, Canadian citizenship was finally extended to Chinese and other minorities.[2]

While these changes were undoubtedly significant, Chinese immigration to Canada continued to be heavily restricted for the next two decades even while European immigration was actively encouraged. As Prime Minister William Lyon Mackenzie King declared in 1947, "The people of Canada do not wish as a result of mass immigration to make a fundamental alteration in the character of our population. Large-scale immigration from the Orient would change that fundamental composition of the Canadian population" (qtd. in Yee 118). While the promotion of white domesticity has long been a central trait of settler colonialism,[3] the ability to sponsor family members was limited when it came to those of non-European descent. After 1947, wives and unmarried children under the age of eighteen of Chinese holding

Canadian citizenship were deemed eligible for sponsorship.[4] But for many families that had endured decades of separation due to war and exclusion, these age and marital status restrictions, along with the application process itself, proved impossible to overcome as many adult children found themselves unable to join their parents in Canada. These restrictions would be gradually relaxed, but it was not until 1967 that remaining racial barriers in Canada's immigration policy were finally removed and replaced with an ostensibly universal point system.

Critics disagree about whether the postwar period was a slow but sure march toward national inclusion or a time when immigrants and minorities were being co-opted through promises of citizenship and assimilation.[5] What gets obscured in these debates is how this period marked a deep shift in the transnational migrant lifeworld that had evolved and persisted for more than a century. Up through the postwar period, the lives of most Chinese in Canada were intricately tied to social structures that had developed to accommodate extended familial separation across large geographic distances. This was a world in which symbolic and material ties to clan, locality, and dialect formed the backbone of migration and settlement networks.[6] These ties were so strong that, after the defeat of Japan in 1945, many overseas Chinese returned to China hoping to finally live out the "Gold Mountain dream" of using their earnings to establish a comfortable life back home. From this perspective, Canadian citizenship was more of an insurance policy in an uncertain world than a sudden change of identity or national loyalty.

This chapter focuses on the interplay between two categories that functioned as heuristic and regulating vehicles for Chinese migration to Canada between 1947 and 1967: the (immediate) relative and the refugee. Despite their apparently clear meanings, both categories were highly contested, and neither fit seamlessly into the complex lived realities of migration. Drawing on scholarship on how Chinese migrants became intertwined in the emerging international refugee regime, my goal is to track how the uncertainty generated by these two categories illuminates critical questions about agency and futurity. These questions, in turn, reflect the world order of the early Cold War period, a time in which the adversarial relationship between the PRC and Canada made it impossible to sustain the transnational lifeworld that had been inhabited by Chinese migrants since the mid-nineteenth century in the face of nationally bound categories of citizenship. Nevertheless, this process could not erase all traces of earlier forms of transnationalism. It is in this vein that I analyze how the immigrant family narrative that has dominated contemporary Chinese Canadian writing displays the repression of experiences of statelessness that fall outside its national framework. In order to elaborate this claim, I will turn to the work of Judy Fong Bates and consider how her deployment of filial sentimentality registers the lingering effects and affects of transnational subject-formation.

Before proceeding, a brief note about literary methodology. As many critics have pointed out, no genre in Asian Canadian and Asian American writing has been as prominent as the immigrant family narrative, what Min Hyoung Song defines as the "perpetual retelling of ethnic stories of arrival, struggle, adjustment, accommodation, and resistance that can span generations" (4). Although the immigrant family narrative has been widely criticized for perpetuating ideologies of upward mobility through assimilation and the accumulation of economic and social capital, its intergenerational form has proved to be indispensable for asserting the historical presence of Asians in Canada and the United States, thereby directly counteracting their stereotypical characterization as perpetual foreigners and newcomers. My argument in this chapter draws on Crystal Parikh's insight that immigrant family narratives are deeply intertwined with the entrenchment of human rights in the West after World War II. As Parikh notes, "Citizenship, and legal status more generally, is assumed to be a 'one-way descending flow of familial transmission,' whereby not only are children always 'naturally' attached to their parents' physical presence, but they inherit their parents' legal personhood as well" (230). In Canada, this process extended into immigration and citizenship laws that have come to be recognized as fundamental aspects of its liberal democracy. What interests me is how the privileging of the Western nuclear family led to conflicts with understandings and practices of kinship that stem from the clan and lineage formations that dominated southern China until the twentieth century. As much as the immigrant family narrative is marked by the hegemony of the former, it also registers the sometimes violent mistranslations that took place in order for Chinese (families) to be recognized as Canadian citizens. I will suggest below that the trope of filiality is a particularly revealing site in which to track these conflicts. As such, it provides a window into a narrative temporality that regards the Citizenship Act of 1947 not as a watershed event but rather as one moment in an extended process through which Chinese migrants and their descendants encountered and negotiated with the demands of the nation-state.

## Chinese Refugees, Canadian Relatives

If 1947 was a watershed year in Canadian history, 1949 was a cataclysmic one for many Chinese migrants and their families. After the establishment of the People's Republic of China (PRC), it was estimated that one-fifth of the 6.4 million people of Guangdong Province belonged to transnational households with ties to Southeast Asia, the Americas, and elsewhere.[7] These families were often categorized as landlords and capitalists and were subjected to intense scrutiny, surveillance, and even violence.[8] The uncertainties of life under Communist rule led to the departures of many returnees as well as family members who sought to join relatives already abroad.

From 1949 until the early 1970s, practically the only way for Chinese from Guangdong to come to Canada was through Hong Kong. The British colony had long been the main port of departure in the region, but since Canada still recognized the ROC and had no diplomatic offices in the mainland until it formally recognized the PRC in 1970, would-be migrants had to get to Hong Kong to apply for the requisite visas. In doing so, they became part of a mass movement of people across the border. Before 1949, the border between Hong Kong and the mainland was more or less an open one, and people frequently crossed back and forth. The population of Hong Kong swelled from 1.8 million in 1948 to 2.36 million by 1950, a number that would continue to grow in ensuing years as conditions across the border worsened for many (Mark 1146). By 1951, what had been an open border was closed by both sides, although illegal crossings continued across land, river, and sea. With a humanitarian crisis on its hands, the British colonial government established border controls that limited the number of new arrivals. However, the colonial authorities made a crucial exception for those from neighboring Guangdong Province (the ability to understand and speak local dialects became a key way for border guards to separate "local" migrants from those from other provinces). As a result, large-scale migration would continue, in "legal" as well as "illegal" forms, even after such allowances were revoked.[9]

In the early 1950s, this influx turned Hong Kong into a pivotal test case for the newly established international refugee regime. It soon became clear that the very meaning of this category, which had been devised with Europe in mind, was uncertain. While Britain had signed the 1951 Convention Relating to the Status of Refugees, its provisions did not apply to its overseas territories. With regard to Hong Kong, Britain's primary concern was to maintain colonial rule, which meant preserving a working relationship with the PRC (Peterson, "To Be or Not to Be" 174). While the colonial government initially referred to new arrivals as refugees, it soon stopped using the word altogether. By claiming that migrants were motivated by economic not political concerns, the British colonial government absolved itself of any responsibility as outlined in international law and reserved the right to deport arrivals. In this context, the very notion of a "Chinese refugee" indicated the uneasy intersection between migrant practices and postwar forms of state and colonial power.

In 1954, the United Nations High Commission of Refugees commissioned a report that sought to determine whether arrivals in Hong Kong were indeed refugees according to the criteria set out by General Assembly Resolution 428; the commission was also tasked with ascertaining their numbers and living conditions. The resulting Hambro Report, named after Edvard Hambro, the commission's Norwegian chair, estimated there were 285,000 refugees, another 100,000 refugees "sur place," and another 282,000 Hong Kong–born dependents of refugees (par. 114). As the Hambro Report reveals, the Hong Kong refugee crisis lay at the crosshairs of the intense rivalry between the PRC and the ROC. Then as now, formal recognition of one automatically precluded recognition of the other, which resulted in an unexpected problem: only states that recognized the existence of the PRC could technically recognize the refugees in Hong Kong as such on the grounds that they had left the territories of the PRC and were afraid of returning. However, countries that recognized the ROC, including Canada, could not make the same admission because arrivals in Hong Kong were technically able to seek protection from the ROC although this was practically impossible (Peterson, "To Be or Not to Be" 174; Hambro par. 127). In the end, the Hambro Report concluded that Chinese refugees did not fit the strict definitions set out by the UN, but "from a broader and humanitarian point of view" they were "*de facto* refugees" (par. 156). The report ultimately failed to convince other states to agree to large-scale resettlement (an exception was the United States, but even there, the Refugee Relief Act of 1953 only set aside five thousand visas for Asian refugees, of which two thousand were reserved for those who had passports issued by the ROC, a comparatively small amount in comparison with the number of displaced people).[10] In the end, the majority of migrants remained in Hong Kong and eventually were able to normalize their status.

Canada's subdued response to the refugee crisis was therefore unexceptional. In fact, it had no clear policy toward refugees during this period. Even though its officials were involved in drafting the 1951 UN Convention Relating to the Status of Refugees, Canada would not actually sign the convention until 1969. Until the 1970s, refugee policies tended to be ad hoc and subject to geopolitical as well as humanitarian concerns. In the 1950s, Chinese refugees were largely ignored even while refugees from Eastern European countries such as Hungary and Czechoslovakia were embraced. Nevertheless, the refugee crisis impacted Chinese activists and their allies in Canada who sought to liberalize immigration laws and often framed their demands in the emergent terms of global human rights. As Laura Madokoro argues, activists insisted that "full membership in Canadian society involved more than legal formalities: it required that Chinese Canadians be able to enjoy the same rights as others, including family reunification" ("Slotting" 34). The legal strategies adopted by these antiracist movements reflected what Stephanie Bangarth has identified as the postwar "evolution" from an earlier focus on "'British liberties' to [a] human rights approach" based on the "growing recognition . . . of the right not to suffer state discrimination." Activists appealed to the UN charter to argue that immigration restrictions violated the inherent rights of Chinese to establish a normal family life in Canada. For example, in a widely covered Supreme Court case, Leong Hung Hing, an elderly Canadian citizen of Chinese descent, fought to have his son by his second wife admitted even though Canadian law did not recognize polygamous arrangements; by the time the court ruled in his favor in 1952,

Leong had already died, prompting the immigration department to refuse admittance to his son on the basis that he had no sponsor in Canada.[11]

As the plight of those in Hong Kong began to draw worldwide attention, activists in Canada used the crisis to further their political objectives. As Madokoro succinctly puts it, "While states relied on official categories to delineate the legitimate means of movement and therefore restrict migration, migrants and their families saw these same designations as channels of mobility" ("Unwanted Refugees" 49). Wong Foon Sien, a prominent community leader in Vancouver who made a well-publicized trip to Ottawa every year to lobby for changes to immigration policy, pointed out in 1958 that relatives of Chinese in Canada were among those who had fled to Hong Kong. Wong and his allies demanded that Canada follow the lead of the United States in admitting refugees, with the key stipulation that all refugees admitted should be relatives of those already in Canada. However, immigration officials objected to the "blurring" of these categories and cited concerns about Communist infiltration as well as the honesty of applicants as reasons to reject his suggestions (Madokoro, *Elusive Refuge* 143–144). In response, Wong wrote, "Families of Chinese Canadians who are refugees in Hong Kong may have to return to China where an alien political philosophy and possibly severe punishment or death awaits them" (qtd. in Madokoro, *Elusive Refuge* 144). These appeals eventually failed: when the Canadian federal government finally approved the resettlement of a small number of refugees in 1962, it explicitly ruled out taking in relatives and actually failed to fulfill its quota based on this restrictive criterion (Madokoro, *Elusive Refuge* 145).

Labels such as "refugee" and "relative" were thus deployed by different states and colonial authorities to manage, facilitate, and often obstruct migration practices. As we have seen, these labels were incongruent with the complex realities of Chinese migration; more importantly, they demonstrate how migration itself was shaped by the geopolitical pressures of the Cold War. The congealing of these categories occurred at a time when this migrant lifeworld was increasingly unsustainable on both sides of the Pacific. In Canada, the transnational migrant family eventually gave way to another unit, the nuclear immigrant family, which was rare before 1947 due to anti-Asian exclusion and sex-segregated migration patterns. The Chinese population in Canada would reach gender parity by the 1970s. By then, immigration policies had changed to explicitly attract skilled and educated migrants, developments that further favored the consolidation of the immigrant family.

## Filiality and the Immigrant Narrative

The demographic changes of postwar Chinese migration would eventually shape the parameters of Chinese Canadian literature in English, which emerged in the 1970s as part of larger Asian Canadian cultural movements.[12]

As I have already mentioned, the most recognizable genre in Chinese Canadian writing is the immigrant family narrative, which usually foregrounds intergenerational conflict as a screen on which to explore issues such as race, identity, and assimilation, particularly among second-generation characters who tend to be the protagonists. Such texts have tended to focus on the nuclear family unit while portraying common practices associated with transnational migration, such as multiple households and cross-racial marriages, as outdated or even deviant.

In short, immigrant family narratives not only are marked by the collision of very different structures of kinship but also register how Western notions of domesticity came to be applied to all immigrant groups in no small part through state policies. In order to bridge these differences, the immigrant family narrative frequently invokes notions of filiality as the ethical and material basis of family relations. Whether as a core component of Confucian thought or as an everyday practice, filiality—and filial piety in particular—prescribes the attitudes, emotions, desires, and duties of children to their parents and forms the basis of larger social groupings based on clan and kinship. As Adam McKeown writes with regard to migrant sending areas in the late Qing period, "Lineages promoted the material interests of local farmers and elites within the trappings of ancestor worship and patriline that were both long-standing aspects of Chinese daily life and activities sanctioned and supported by Qing ideology" (104). These ties formed the material basis for transnational networks of movement and settlement that enabled Chinese to navigate the risks and perils of migration while shaping how migrants understood their life choices and trajectories.

Extending these relations to the present day, erin Khuê Ninh argues that under global capitalism, the (nuclear) immigrant family is marked by a discourse of filiality wherein "sacrifice, obedience, hierarchy, gratitude" (*Ingratitude* 11) frame "the parent-child relation as a debtor-creditor relation" that is "structural, a matter of position rather than payment, and places the child ever in violation" (16). For the Asian immigrant family, filiality is a biopolitical discourse that regulates the feelings, desires, and actions of younger generations, rendering them amendable to the economic demands of the family unit. It is therefore a system of "affective management" that conditions orientations, feelings, tendencies, and behaviors in order that a "growing child's polymorphous desires and aspirations . . . become affixed to constructs of economic pragmatism and social prestige" (Ninh, "Affect" 49). Transplanted into the realm of private domesticity, filiality not only prescribes the "right" kinds of feelings but also disciplines and represses what it considers to be deviant:

> Suppose a context where the merest outward display is forbidden—where any shift of facial expression, any heaviness of hand or step,

> the barest modulation of volume or tone in voice is liable to provoke further affliction—and in that context, anger may *learn* to become intransitive. It surrenders expression, direction, and object: it becomes a humming under the skin—a sensory experience. Such conditions are the production floor for the filial child: a subject in whom anger and resistance are best dissipated before they rise into word or action or conscious knowing, in whom obedience must become autonomic. Rather than wait for that which is potential to become a punishable actuality, filiality trains the model minority child to lose arguments affectively, long before words can be sharpened to a point. (Ninh, "Affect" 52)

The subdued emotional tenor engendered by filiality has been widely depicted in immigrant family narratives as something that needs to be overcome in order for the second-generation protagonist to free himself or herself through discourses of liberal individualism.[13]

Insofar as immigrant family narratives tend to privilege the rebellious second-generation subject, the opposition between "outward" forms of resistance and "inner" forms of repression can obscure articulations of filiality that do not follow a liberatory trajectory. In order to account for these alternatives, we might turn to the broader problematic of sentiment in the maintenance of family life. In her work on contemporary Chinese cinema, Rey Chow theorizes sentimentalism as an affective mode marked by "*an inclination or a disposition toward making compromises and toward making-do with even—and especially—that which is oppressive and unbearable*" (18; emphasis in original). Unlike the dialectic between repression and expression, sentimentalism is a "mode of endurance" that is "about what keeps and preserves, what holds things together" (18). It is closely tied to domesticity because it encompasses the double meaning of "being accommodating and being accommodated," the interpersonal dynamics necessary to maintain the home as the site of kinship even when the "homely" is "revealed to be oppressive and unbearable—indeed, uninhabitable" (19). From an ideological perspective, the "idealization of filiality" cannot but seem conservative, but it is also a highly portable and adaptable form of relationality: filial sentiment is the affective and material glue that holds families together, whether they are spread across continents or have come back together again.

## Alternative Lives and the Immigrant Memoir

For Chinese in Canada during the 1950s and 1960s, the gradual relaxation of immigration restrictions resulted in the reactivation of long-repressed filial ties. Contemporary Chinese Canadian writer Judy Fong Bates has frequently depicted recently reunited Chinese families living and working in small Ontario towns during this period, a setting that stems from her own story as a young girl who arrived in Canada in 1955. For this chapter, I will focus on her 2010 memoir, *The Year of Finding Memory*, which contains some of her most extensive reflections on these experiences. *The Year of Finding Memory* revolves around two trips that Fong Bates made as an adult to her home village in Kaiping, China, after a lifetime of absence. From the start, she presents herself as a well-integrated, independent, and for the most part content Chinese Canadian woman, someone who benefited tremendously from the sacrifices of her parents. Her journeys prompt her to search for more information about her parents, a quest that unwittingly uncovers residual traces of a transnational migrant lifeworld.

In *The Year of Finding Memory*, everything goes back to 1947 but not because of historical milestones—rather, 1947 is the year when Fong Bates's parents got married. For both her father, Fong Wah Yent, and her mother, Fong Yet Lan, it was their second marriage, and both had surviving children from previous unions. Her father first came to Canada in 1914 and worked for many years in small-town laundries. These years were spent separated from his first wife, who died suddenly around 1940 in the midst of the war with Japan. He would not see their four children again until 1947, when he moved back to China in the hope of enjoying a comfortable life. He had met Yet Lan years earlier when she was the village schoolteacher, but they had lost touch until she took the initiative to contact him to propose marriage. As Fong Bates writes, "In 1947, when he believed he was returning to China to stay, his feelings of joy and hope must have been euphoric. The war was over and he would finally be reunited with his children. He would marry a woman whom he respected. Together, they would put the anguish of those war years behind and build a new life" (218). These expectations would be shattered as her father returned to Canada in August 1949 in order to escape the impending Communist victory. The author, his youngest daughter, was born four months later. His family fractured again as his oldest children, who were ineligible for sponsorship, remained in China never to see their father again, while his wife and younger children made it to Hong Kong and eventually to Canada.

Fong Bates recounts her life within the framework of the immigrant family narrative, with its emphasis on displacement, resettlement, and assimilation, and her stay in Hong Kong comes across merely as a brief transition. She mentions that in 1953, she "fled" to Hong Kong with her mother, but she does not tell us how they got there (24). In a book about finding memories, the Hong Kong years are notably vague:

> We languished in Hong Kong for only two years, but in my hazy remembrance the time feels longer, another lifetime belonging to someone else. I have no memory of [half-brother] Doon living with

> us, and yet I know he did. He was in his late teens and spent his days exploring the city on his own and with other young relatives who were waiting to emigrate. That period of my life has left me with a vague but persistent impression of that city's excitement, a memory of constantly turning my head and looking, my mother holding me by the wrist while we walked along contested sidewalks, and through outdoor markets swarming with people. (27)

These descriptions support the author's claim that it was only in Canada that her sense of self became fully established, but seemingly minor details scattered throughout the text hint at what lies outside this framework. She mentions that her mother had once sought refuge in Hong Kong during the war with Japan and originally did not want to go to Canada, preferring instead to stay in Hong Kong and live on remittances from her husband. Fong Bates also learns later on that her mother's sponsorship application had been rejected twice by Canadian authorities before finally being approved for reasons that remain unclear (234).

These details begin to acquire different meanings when we read them as belonging to a transnational lifeworld. The fact that Fong Bates's mother had already spent time in Hong Kong places her in a mobile population of Guangdong residents who were familiar with border crossings before the early 1950s. Her knowledge of the city and her family ties there made her decision to leave her village much more manageable, while her reluctance to leave Hong Kong suggests that it was still possible to imagine (and indeed to prefer) being part of a transnational family supported by remittances, arrangements that would have been well known to overseas Chinese families. We are reminded that the immigration process contains uncontrollable contingencies such as whims of bureaucrats, belying the common assumption that it is largely the result of choices and agency (I will return to this point shortly).

Moreover, these details indicate the text's interest in alternative life trajectories, ways in which the author's family history could have taken markedly different paths. Catherine Gallagher suggests that even though historical fiction contains invented elements, its defining constraint is that "it cannot contradict the historical record" (320), which functions as the "horizon of possibility" for judging whether events and other details are possible or probable.[14] Fiction and history constitute a "*modal* arc" (321; emphasis in original) in which space is created for speculation and judgment without fundamentally questioning the facticity of history. Even though a memoir such as *The Year of Finding Memory* necessarily emphasizes historicity (that is, it retells what has already happened), a similar arc between history and fiction operates as Fong Bates seeks to render judgment on herself and her family. In this context, alternative trajectories acquire their peculiar force through the awareness that they did not in fact take place. They are speculative, but, crucially, they function within the same discursive space that Gallagher identifies in the historical novel: they must be plausible within the historical world of the text. Put differently, the possibilities entertained by Fong Bates would have been applicable to many other would-be migrants who were converging in Hong Kong at the same time, facing similar conditions. In this sense, alternative trajectories provide a sense of the larger sociohistorical context in which Fong Bates's family story emerged by conveying not only what happened but also what could have happened. By excavating these possibilities, the text raises deeper questions about how its temporal and spatial parameters narrow a transnational lifeworld into a national narrative. It also asks: What kinds of relationships are possible if we look beyond restrictive itineraries of immigration and settlement? What psychic mechanisms are embedded in the very categories used to denote (im)migration? At stake in all this is nothing less than what makes *The Year of Finding Memory* legible as a Chinese Canadian narrative and the kinds of subjectivities that can be articulated through the exploration of intimate migrant family histories.

## "This Insane Optimism Which Is Next Door to Despair"

Hannah Arendt's challenging 1943 essay "We Refugees" explores the relationship between migration and character by turning a critical lens on Jewish émigrés such as herself. The essay begins with a striking gesture of disavowal as the speaker insists, "In the first place, we don't like to be called 'refugees.' We ourselves call each other 'newcomers' or 'immigrants'" (110). Much is at stake in these distinctions. Immigration, usually understood to be motivated by "purely economic reasons" (110), implies the exercise of rational choice, autonomy, and agency. By contrast, the refugee, completely divested of social status and forced to flee, is the quintessential figure of powerlessness. Describing the psychology of the immigrant as a refusal to engage with the horrific truth of statelessness, Arendt describes a pathological optimism that is manifested in the enthusiastic embrace of assimilation. In her view, the immigrant adopts an identity that masks the trauma of displacement through a kind of intentional forgetting: "The less we are free to decide who we are or to live as we like, the more we try to put up a front, to hide the facts, and to play roles" (115).

While Arendt recognizes that this "front" is a response to the fact that those who are "nothing but Jews" are "unprotected by any specific law or political convention" and therefore "nothing but human beings" (118), in a controversial move she also attributes a sense of ethical failure to the immigrant: "Lacking the courage to fight for a change of our social and legal status we have decided instead, so many of us, to try a change of identity" (116).[15]

What makes "We Refugees" particularly insightful is its focus on the mechanisms of repression and reinvention that distinguish the immigrant from the refugee. In Arendt's view, these processes are incomplete and ultimately ineffective. She writes hauntingly about how repressed memories erupt during the night, how those who "having made a lot of optimistic speeches, go home and turn on the gas or make use of a skyscraper in an unexpected way" (112). The "insane optimism" of the immigrant, she concludes, is "next door to despair" (113).

For the purposes of this discussion, I want to reframe Arendt's provocative claims to highlight how the immigrant is defined by an investment in futurity, however fraught. In texts such as *The Year of Finding Memory*, this pathological optimism is not so much a matter of feeling hopeful about the future but rather a dogged perseverance that both belongs to and disrupts the filial sentiment of accommodation, the affective strategies that orient the subject toward a future defined by kinship. Nevertheless, this sense of temporality is destroyed in the most traumatic event in the memoir: the suicide of the author's father in 1972. Fong Bates describes his death as "a sudden explosion of glass, hurling shards so small and fine they embedded themselves deep in our flesh, never to be removed" (5). For much of the text, this event lurks under the surface, rarely addressed until the second-to-last chapter. There, Fong Bates recounts how she visited her parents on the day he died. During lunch, her father accidentally spilled a bowl of soup, which drew a sharp scolding from her mother, but the conflict quickly dissipated. After Fong Bates left, her father quietly went to the basement and hanged himself out of his family's sight.

For Arendt, the act of suicide reveals the collapse of immigrant optimism as a dogged belief in the future suddenly gives way to a "quiet and modest way of vanishing" (114). In this context, suicide is an "apolog[etic]" kind of violence that reveals how the immigrant's "optimism is the vain attempt to keep head above water"; Arendt ruthlessly concludes, "Finally, they die of a kind of selfishness" (114). Ironically, this selfishness involves the extinction of the self; translated into the terms of filial sentimentality, it is the very opposite of accommodation, a refusal to repress the self in the name of accommodation. It is not surprising, then, that Fong Wah Yent's death unleashes other forms of "selfish" affect, feelings that exceed and undermine the maintenance of domesticity. Fong Bates repeatedly comes back to her mother's public displays of grief. As her husband's body was taken away from their house, she "let out a long painful moan. Her body crumpled and I could barely hold her up. At the same time her fingers dug into my shoulders. Everyone was watching us" (281). While much of the funeral "remains a blur," what stood out is "how inconsolable [her mother] was" (283). For Fong Bates, what is most disturbing about these memories is the *intensity* of her mother's grief in contrast to the "lack of affection" in their marriage. She writes, "Even now, when I think about the lack of affection in their marriage, the depth of her sorrow seems out of proportion. It didn't seem to matter whether she was standing or sitting; her body was crippled with grief. Every time I glanced at her, she was bent over, unable to straighten herself" (283). Why would her mother so deeply mourn a man with whom she shared an unhappy and often adversarial marriage—and what should we make of the stark mismatch between their relationship and her response to his death?

The impropriety of this scene stands in stark contrast with what might be described as the self-conscious propriety that characterizes the author/narrator's voice throughout *The Year of Finding Memory*: Fong Bates is reflective, wise, sometimes humorous, but never seems to indulge in sentimental excess. In other words, the tone of the memoir is decidedly in proportion, a state that connotes appropriateness, balance, and harmony. Her father's death, however, unleashes disproportionate affects of unusual intensity. In the prologue, Fong Bates writes, "In the months after my father's death, it seemed that whatever *equanimity* I was able to achieve could shatter in an instant. Without warning I would be seething with rage, then overcome by grief. But why was I angry again? with myself, for never learning how to read and write Chinese? for having parents so unlike me and so difficult to understand? at my father and what he had done to himself, what he had done to us?" (4; emphasis added). By placing uncontrollable feelings at the heart of the family unit, this passage recalls Ninh's point that filiality involves the repression of deviant feelings as well as Chow's observation that the mechanisms of accommodation function most acutely when the home proves to be unbearable. While excessive displays of grief are certainly not unknown in Chinese mourning practices, within the memoir's affective economy, the feelings described here stand in stark contrast with the routine repression of strong or negative affects in the Fong household, a deeply ingrained habit that infused their family life with bitterness, resentment, and melancholy, pierced only by occasional outbursts of rage that were quickly brought under control.

Fong Wah Yent's suicide upends the accommodationist tendencies of filial sentiment, with its emphasis on raising future generations at any cost. His death symbolically (if not in actual practice) deprives his family of the most important ingredient of filiality, a future in which to enact, inhabit, and reproduce kinship through the passing of generations. It also reveals him as a figure shorn of all dignity, finally defeated by a lifetime of hardship. As Fong Bates contemplates the meaning of his death, her thoughts resonate unexpectedly with Arendt's discussion of the immigrant: "The word *why* rings in my head. I can still see him, the way he looked at that last lunch, a man eaten away by despair and humiliation. . . . Was his final act a moment of selfish impulsiveness?" (286; emphasis in original). While filial relations do not stop with death (Fong Bates and her siblings observe the veneration of ancestors, for example), the text suggests that her family story somehow defies the closure offered by filial narratives. She writes that "his death haunts us like a dark shadow" and tells us, "Hardly a day goes by without my thinking of my father and his suicide," thoughts that "refuse to be pushed aside" (285–286). What is crucial here is not so much the accuracy of these descriptions but rather how the text's affective economy interrupts its formal coherence, a point that becomes evident when Fong Bates writes, "My father was an old man when he fitted that rope around his neck. Why could he not give us the gift of a peaceful ending? Was this his only way of making sure he would be remembered? Were we, his wife, his children, in some way culpable?" (286). Her father's death engenders a proliferation of guilt that infects everyone in the family including her father himself, whose death is now recast as a failure to persevere in the name of family. Fong Bates conveys this failure in formal terms, for what her father, who otherwise gave so much of his life to his family, finally withholds is "the gift of a peaceful ending."

In lieu of such a resolution, the text turns to another alternative life that once could have been but never came to be. In China, Fong Bates learns, to her surprise, that her parents were deeply attracted to each other when they first met. In fact, her father had wanted to take her as a second wife, much to the ire of his first wife, who then was still alive. Their romantic feelings had dissipated by the time they got married, and the stress of immigration and displacement further exacerbated their conflicts, creating an emotional atmosphere of bitterness and sadness that would permeate the author's childhood. Looking back on her mother's grief, Fong Bates asks whether it was directed less to her father's death than to the lingering memory of a "moment when the future held promise, when they might have been in love" before "love, transformed into contempt, had poisoned and wasted their lives" (287). Fong Bates suggests that her mother's disproportionate grief was released by the collapse of fantasies about what life could have been—which is to say that what her mother was actually mourning was the reality of what her life had actually come to be.

*The Year of Finding Memory* reveals, through its treatment of kinship and affect, how the transnational lifeworld of Chinese migration came under tremendous strain after 1947, invalidating life trajectories that it had sustained for centuries. The moment of promise now lost forever belonged to a world in which migration facilitated a different circuit of fantasies in which her father could still be recognized as an honored "Gold Mountain guest." In Canada, her parents' perseverance meant acting as if such a world could still be had as long as one held out for a better future by sheer determination. But as the genre of the immigrant family narrative shows, the futures that eventually became dominant would be shaped by the elusive promises of citizenship that was key to Canada's embrace of liberal democracy against the backdrop of an emerging international human rights regime. But while these changes offered new opportunities for Chinese migrants, their experiences continued to reveal the inability of post-1947 political frameworks to attend to the complexities of displacement. Caught between categories such as refugee and relative, the lives Chinese in Canada bore the memory of being what Arendt evocatively calls "nothing but human beings," traces of which persist in contemporary Chinese Canadian family narratives.

## NOTES

1. In the mid-1950s, largely in response to anti-Chinese unrest in Southeast Asia, the PRC started to revoke dual citizen status in order to encourage diasporic Chinese communities to localize their citizenship status. This policy marked the end, at least on mainland China, of the jus sanguinis approach taken by the Qing and ROC.

2. Even with these changes, Japanese Canadians were still denied citizenship rights and subject to deportation until 1949, and some Indigenous peoples did not receive citizenship rights until 1956, part of a colonial relationship that continues to this day. For more information about these changes, see Roy.

3. For an account of this history, see Perry.

4. The Chinese population in Canada before 1947 overwhelmingly consisted of men who lived apart from extended families in China. For this reason, Chinese during this period were often seen as part of a "bachelor community," although this label is not strictly accurate.

5. For contrasting accounts of the liberalization of immigration policy after World War II, see Roy; Thobani.

6. For historical background on Chinese migration, see Hsu, *Dreaming of Gold*; McKeown.

7. See Chan for more details.

8. For an account of overseas Chinese policy in the PRC, see Peterson, *Overseas Chinese*.

9. For a popular account of this history, see Chen.

10. For a detailed discussion of the Refugee Relief Act and its wide-ranging effects, see Hsu, *The Good Immigrants*.

11. For discussion of this case, see Roy 268.

12. For background on Asian Canadian cultural and activist movements, see Li; Lai.

13. Examples of Chinese Canadian authors who have explored this theme include SKY Lee, Wayson Choy, Jen Sookfong Lee, and, as I will discuss in more detail below, Judy Fong Bates.

14. My thanks to Colleen Lye for directing me to this source.

15. "We Refugees" has often been read as a rehearsal of arguments that would be developed in later works such as *The Origins of Totalitarianism*. There, Arendt famously argues that supposedly inherent human rights are "unenforceable—even in countries whose constitutions were based upon them—whenever people appeared who were no longer citizens of any sovereign state" (293). This diagnosis would in turn inspire later theorists such as Achille Mbembe and Giorgio Agamben.

## WORKS CITED

Arendt, Hannah. *The Origins of Totalitarianism*. New York: Harvest, 1968.

———. "We Refugees." *Altogether Elsewhere: Writers on Exile*. Ed. Marc Robinson. Boston: Faber and Faber, 1994. 110–119.

Bangarth, Stephanie. "'We Are Not Asking You to Open Wide the Gates for Chinese Immigration': The Committee for the Repeal of the Chinese Immigration Act and Early Human Rights Activism in Canada." *Canadian Historical Review* 84.3 (2003).

Chan, Shelly. "Rethinking the 'Left-Behind' in Chinese Migrations: A Case of Liberating Wives in Emigrant South China in the 1950s." *Proletarian and Gendered Mass Migrations: A Global Perspective on Continuities and Discontinuities from the Nineteenth to the Twenty-First Centuries*. Ed. Dirk Hoerder and Amarjit Kaur. Leiden: Brill, 2013. 451–466.

Chen, Bing'an. *Da tao Gang* [Escaping to Hong Kong]. Hong Kong: Xianggang zhong he chu ban, 2011.

Chow, Rey. *Sentimental Confabulations, Contemporary Chinese Films*. New York: Columbia University Press, 2007.

Fong Bates, Judy. *The Year of Finding Memory*. 2010. Toronto: Vintage, 2011.

Gallagher, Catherine. "What Would Napoleon Do? Historical, Fictional, and Counterfactual Characters." *New Literary History* 42.2 (2011): 315–336.

Hambro, Edvard (Hong Kong Refugees Survey Mission). *The Problem of Chinese Refugees in Hong Kong: Report Submitted to the United Nations High Commissioner for Refugees*. Leyden: A. W. Sijthoff, 1955.

Hsu, Madeline Y. *Dreaming of Gold, Dreaming of Home: Transnationalism and Migration between the United States and South China, 1882–1943*. Stanford: Stanford University Press, 2000.

———. *The Good Immigrants: How the Yellow Peril Became the Model Minority*. Princeton: Princeton University Press, 2015.

Lai, Larissa. *Slanting I, Imagining We: Asian Canadian Literary Production in the 1980s and 1990s*. Waterloo, ON: Wilfrid Laurier University Press, 2014.

Li, Xiaoping. *Voices Rising: Asian Canadian Cultural Activism*. Vancouver: University of British Columbia Press, 2007.

Madokoro, Laura. *Elusive Refuge: Chinese Migrants in the Cold War*. Cambridge, MA: Harvard University Press, 2016.

———. "'Slotting' Chinese Families and Refugees, 1947–1967." *Canadian Historical Review* 93.1 (2012): 25–56.

———. "Unwanted Refugees: Chinese Migration and the Making of a Global Humanitarian Agenda, 1949–1989." Diss. University of British Columbia, 2012.

Mark, Chi-Kwan. "The 'Problem of People': British Colonials, Cold War Powers, and the Chinese Refugees in Hong Kong, 1949–62." *Modern Asian Studies* 41.6 (2007): 1145–1181.

McKeown, Adam. *Chinese Migrant Networks and Cultural Change: Peru, Chicago, and Hawaii, 1900–1936*. Chicago: University of Chicago Press, 2001.

Ninh, erin Khuê. "Affect/Family/Filialty." *The Routledge Companion to Asian American and Pacific Islander Literature*. Ed. Rachel C. Lee. London: Routledge, 2014. 46–55.

———. *Ingratitude: The Debt-Bound Daughter in Asian American Literature*. New York: New York University Press, 2011.

Parikh, Crystal. *Writing Human Rights: The Political Imaginaries of Writers of Color*. Minneapolis: University of Minnesota Press, 2017.

Perry, Adele. *On the Edge of Empire: Gender, Race, and the Making of British Columbia, 1849–1871*. Toronto: University of Toronto Press, 2001.

Peterson, Glen. *Overseas Chinese in the People's Republic of China*. New York: Routledge, 2012.

———. "To Be or Not to Be a Refugee: The International Politics of the Hong Kong Refugee Crisis, 1949–55." *Journal of Imperial and Commonwealth History* 36.2 (2008): 171–195.

Roy, Patricia E. *The Triumph of Citizenship: The Japanese and Chinese in Canada, 1941–67.* Vancouver: University of British Columbia Press, 2007.

Song, Min Hyoung. "Asian American Literature within and beyond the Immigrant Narrative." *The Cambridge Companion to Asian American Literature.* Ed. Crystal Parikh and Daniel Y. Kim. New York: Cambridge University Press, 2015. 3–15.

Thobani, Sunera. *Exalted Subjects: Studies in the Making of Race and Nation in Canada.* Toronto: University of Toronto Press, 2007.

Yee, Paul. *Saltwater City: An Illustrated History of the Chinese in Vancouver.* Rev. ed. Vancouver: Douglas and McIntyre, 2006.

# 3

# The Vancouver Asahi Connection

## *(Re-)engagement of the Families of Returnees/Deportees in Japanese Canadian History*

Masumi Izumi

On a drizzling late afternoon on September 29, 2014, in downtown Vancouver, over a hundred Japanese young women anxiously lined up in front of the Centre for Performing Arts. The Red Carpet ceremony celebrated the world premiere of the film *The Vancouver Asahi* at the Vancouver International Film Festival (Ishii, *Bankuubaa no Asahi*). The film's director, Yuya Ishii, along with two lead actors, Kazuya Kamenashi and Satoshi Tsumabuki, were greeted with loud shrieks and waving hands. When the theater opened, it was filled with a larger crowd of English-speaking Asians of diverse genders and ages. They were Japanese Canadians, descendants of Japanese immigrants who came to Canada mostly before World War II. The film was a fictional representation of the true story of nisei (second-generation Japanese Canadian) baseball players and their issei (first-generation) and nisei fans in pre–World War II Vancouver. Before the show started, one elderly man walked onto the stage and stood next to the director and the actors. It was Kaye Koichi Kaminishi, the last known survivor of the former Asahi ballplayers. He played in the team's last years between 1939 and 1942 before it was disbanded due to the mass removal of Japanese Canadians from the west coast. Kaminishi greeted the audience in Japanese and thanked the director and everyone involved in the film production for trying to make the Asahi story known in Japan. Kaminishi received big cheers and heartfelt admiration from those in the theater.

During the making of *The Vancouver Asahi*, its producer consulted scholars of Japanese Canadian history and elders in the community. The director and actors, however, had no contact with the actual subjects of the story—members of the Japanese Canadian community who nurtured and cherished the baseball team. Perhaps because of this limitation, the movie lacked an urgent sense of storytelling or a compelling universal appeal to humanity. Despite its star-studded casting and abundant budget, the movie failed to achieve box office success after its release in Japan in December 2014. Director Ishii, a 2013 Japan Academy Award winner for his film *Fune o Amu* (English title *The Great Passage*), was more successful in depicting the psyche of youths in present-day Japanese society (Ishii, *Fune o Amu*). The opportunity to popularize the story of Asahi and historical experiences of Japanese Canadians among the general public in Japan was unfortunately missed.

Yet the release of *The Vancouver Asahi* produced an unintended result. It connected Japanese Canadians and scholars who study them to a formerly unknown group of subjects in the story, namely the families and descendants of the former Asahi members who had returned to Japan before World War II or those who were deported shortly after the war and did not return to Canada. Following World War II, after excluding all persons of Japanese racial origin from the west coast, the Canadian government forced Japanese Canadians to choose between "repatriation" after the war and immediate relocation east of the Rockies (Sunahara 113–124). Those who could not immediately move east signed up for repatriation. At the end of the war, the majority of the approximately ten thousand people who signed up for repatriation wished to stay in Canada, but the Canadian government refused to consider revocation of repatriation requests. After significant public criticism, the government eventually allowed revocation so those who wished to stay in Canada were allowed to do so (Bangarth). Those who chose to leave, which ended up to be about four thousand, were shipped to Japan in 1946. Their Canadian citizenship was stripped away when they embarked the ship, even though for many nisei, it was the first time they were to set foot in Japan. Thus, this policy is considered more of a "deportation" rather than "repatriation" (Sunahara 101–113). In this paper, I use the term *returnee* for those who had left Canada and remigrated to Japan before World War II and *deportee* for those who left Canada through the "repatriation" program in 1946. The returnees and deportees were severed from the Japanese Canadian community for almost seven decades, and their existence had been unknown since the Asahi was suddenly erased from the history of Canadian popular sports, along with the memory of a vibrant ethnic Japanese community in prewar British Columbia.

This chapter first documents the Asahi story from the team's birth to its dismantlement in 1942 and the community's recovery of the team's history since the 1990s. This story is important as it shows Japanese Canadians' adaptation to anti-Asian racial hostility in British Columbia, and because baseball not only united the Japanese community in Canada composed of people with diverse class, religious, and ideological affiliations but also provided a common ground where the Japanese and Caucasian players and fans could share enjoyment of the game. The later sections of this chapter elucidate how families and descendants of the former Asahi players in Japan connected with each other after the film's release and how such fortuitous reconnections led to the inclusion of the returnee/deportee stories into Japanese Canadian historiography.

The detention, dispossession, dispersal, and deportation of Japanese Canadians during and after World War II are among the most systematic state violence inflicted on a racial minority in Canadian history (Izumi, "Japanese Canadian Exclusion"). Twenty-two thousand people of Japanese descent living on the west coast were displaced from their homes, were banned from free movement, had their property confiscated, and were dispersed across the country. During the war, they were forced to live in horse stalls, wooden shacks and barracks in ghost towns, or barns with low-quality water on the sugar beet fields in the prairies. The government of British Columbia abandoned their responsibility for Japanese Canadian children's education. It was on top of this that four thousand were deported from their country of birth or of long-term residence. Although between one thousand and two thousand of the deportees eventually returned to Canada, an unknown number of them permanently settled in Japan in the postwar period (Kobayashi, *Demographic Profile* 51). Through the reinterpretation of Canadian history, which was an incremental process that developed as Canadian diversity increased since the 1960s, and through the Japanese Canadian Redress movement in the 1980s, those who stayed in or returned to Canada had a chance to speak of their wartime experiences and the longer history of anti-Asian movement in British Columbia. However, those who never returned to Canada did not have a chance to break their silence, as they were literally removed from the history of the nation.

Inclusion of the deportees' stories expands the subjects of human rights in Japanese Canadian history beyond familiar themes of anti-Asian discrimination and exclusion within North America. The reconnection of returnees and deportees among each other as well as to the Japanese Canadian community adds important new pieces of information to Japanese Canadian historiography and about the Asahi experience, which contains stories of migration, resilience under discrimination, cross-racial interactions, and erasure and recovery of a vernacular community history. The returnees' experiences that have been uncovered in Japan involved military service in the Japanese imperial army, the atomic bomb, survival in a war-torn country, and the reintegration of transnational subjects into an ethnic-based imaginary of the Japanese nation after World War II. These stories need to be recovered now because the descendants of transnational subjects who are searching their family histories are the last generation of people who had direct contact with the migrant generation, and the memories and records of these migration experiences will be lost forever if not preserved at this time.

## The Vancouver Asahi Baseball Club

From the beginning of the twentieth century, Japanese Canadians in Vancouver started living in the area adjacent to the Hastings Sawmill, a major employer of Japanese migrant laborers (Ayukawa 25). Soon the area around Powell Street came to be known as an ethnic Japanese community with houses and rooming houses owned by the Japanese as well as shops and offices catering to Japanese migrant laborers and immigrant families. There was a park at the physical center of the community, officially named Oppenheimer Park, but the residents called it "*Paueru Gurando*" (Powell Grounds)—the practice grounds as well as home field for the Asahi Baseball Club.

The Asahi was not the first baseball team that Japanese Canadians formed. The Vancouver Nippon Baseball Club was established as early as 1910 (Adachi, *Asahi: A Legend* 13). Baseball, in fact, was an extremely popular sport in Japan, and some young migrants might have played it in their home country. In the early 1910s, the size of the nisei population was increasing, and the community started to expand its programs for children. Unlike in the United States, where the immigration of new labor from Japan was halted after 1908, Japanese in Canada could continue to sponsor immigrants, and usually they invited male relatives or acquaintances from their home and neighboring villages. Through this channel, quite a number of issei were brought to Canada at young ages, and, with the increase of birth as female migration through marriage grew, the community leaders around Powell Street became concerned about disciplining the youths and preventing delinquency as well as promoting good health and strong spirit among children. Japanese Canadian youths faced special challenges as the community faced severe racial antagonism as well as structural discrimination in British Columbia. The 1907 racial riot in which white mobs shattered most of the store windows on Powell Street was still fresh in their memories. In 1912, the Vancouver Asahi Club was organized as a juvenile boy's club that provided athletic and martial arts programs "under *issei* supervision" (Hotchkiss 30). Baseball, of all the activities offered, was the most popular. In 1914, after a visit by the Keio University baseball team from Japan, a youth baseball team was established, with Ihachi Miyazaki (also known as Matsujiro Miyasaki) as a manager and coach.

Miyasaki, nicknamed "Bashamatsu" (*basha* means horse-drawn carriage), was from Kaideima village in Shiga Prefecture in Japan. He loved baseball (Miyazaki). The transnational familial and local connections ensured financial as well as material support for the Asahi team. Immigrants from prefectures that produced a large migrant population, such as Shiga and Wakayama, formed organizations based on their home village ties and favored their fellow villagers in hiring and granting other opportunities (Ayukawa 26). Kaideima villagers were particularly influential in businesses on Powell Street. Many of the players, mostly teenaged boys, were recruited from the graduates of the Vancouver Japanese Language School, whose major supporters were business owners on Powell Street. A majority of the original members of the Asahi were from Shiga, and the boys from families connected to the Kaideima village formed the core of the team for many years to come (Goto, *Bankuubaa Asahi Monogatari* 34–35).

Interestingly, the English-language sources and Japanese-language sources offer slightly different explanations for why the Vancouver Japanese Canadian community established the Asahi club. Canadian sources, such as Roy Hotchkiss's *Diamond Gods in the Morning Sun*, claim that the merchants and educators of the Powell Street community considered that baseball would alleviate racial hostility against the Japanese in Vancouver if Japanese Canadian children and Caucasian children played a common sport (Hotchkiss 30). On the other hand, sources by Japan-based writers, such as Ted Y. Furumoto's novel and comics by Hidenori Hara, underline the aspect of Japanese Canadians' competition against discriminatory Caucasians. Furumoto argues that the adults who nurtured the Asahi wished that the nisei youths could develop physical and mental strength from practicing baseball so that they would not be mentally or physically beaten down by racial discrimination (Furumoto, *Bankuubaa Asahi Gun* 32–33).

The Asahi team grew strong enough to compete in the International League, founded in 1918, which consisted of three Caucasian teams and the Asahi (Hotchkiss 32). As the Asahi became more competitive, the team attracted top players among Japanese Canadian ballplayers from different clubs. In 1919, the Asahi won the pennant of the Vancouver International League.

To compete against larger and more powerful Caucasian players, the Asahi had to excel in speed, technique, and synchronized movements that enabled unexpected strategies for scoring. The development of this kind of playing style, "brain ball," as some called it, was perfected by Harry Shigeichi Miyasaki, a Hawaii-born nisei (Hotchkiss 33). Miyasaki was on the 1919 International League Championship team and toured in Japan in 1921 with the team. In 1922, he became the coach and manager of the Asahi. Miyasaki endeavored to make the Asahi competitive by recruiting talented boys at a young age and developing tactical skills that would lead to scoring without power hitting. The batters used bunts, and the runners pushed into scoring positions through base stealing, hit and run, squeezes, and double steals. Miyasaki also emphasized the spirit of "team play," demanding the players to devote all efforts to winning, a style of baseball generally adopted in Japan (Jette 4). Superb ballplayers grew out of Miyasaki's coaching, the most famous being Roy Yamamura. Yamamura played shortstop, and his running speed made him a superb defender as well as leading base stealer in the Terminal League. He even signed with Vancouver's top-division team, Arrows, in 1931 and 1932. Yamamura coached the Asahi team as the player-manager between 1938 and 1941. The team moved on to the stronger Terminal League and won championships in 1926 and 1930. By that time, the Asahi was the most popular senior amateur baseball team in British Columbia, and its fans extended well into Caucasian population (Osborne).

Given prevailing anti-Asian sentiments, the Asahi players were initially met with unfair judgment or rough play. Harry Miyasaki adamantly prohibited any kind of challenge or even showing of discontent at those incidents and disciplined the players to stick to the spirit of "fair play" (Hotchkiss 43). Eventually as the team's reputation emerged, Caucasian fans started to protest the umpires' unfair calls. Grace Eiko Thomson, a nisei curator of the first museum exhibit of the Asahi Baseball Club, held in 2005 at the Japanese Canadian National Museum in Burnaby, British Columbia, emphasized the fact that baseball provided a rare space where Japanese Canadians and other Canadians could interact in equal status (Thomson). Thomson named the exhibit "Levelling the Playing Field: The Vancouver Asahi Baseball Team," which told how invigorating the Asahi was for Japanese Canadians, because they could play as well as or even better than Caucasian players as they overcame their physical disadvantage through hard practice and superb playing as well as tactical skills (Osborne; Thomson).

The Asahi team played in various leagues during the 1930s, but its popularity within and outside the Japanese Canadian community remained strong. By the late 1930s, when Kaye Kaminishi joined the team, the Asahi had five levels, from the Clovers or *gogun* (fifth team) for youngsters to *ichigun* (first team) at the top (Adachi, *Asahi 100th Anniversary* 103).

Kaminishi missed the last season of the Asahi because he visited his family in Hiroshima for six months in 1941. He and his mother caught the last ship departing Japan for North America, arriving in Vancouver on November 1 (Hotchkiss 88–89). In December after the Pearl Harbor attack, the whirlwind of events scattered the Asahi players. The team never reassembled after the war, and the Asahi became a legend.

Baseball nevertheless remained the most popular sport in the Japanese Canadian community for another decade including wartime. Kaminishi organized a softball team in Lillooet, a town with a self-supporting camp for the uprooted Japanese Canadians. He negotiated with a Royal Canadian Mounted Police officer to hold an exhibition match between the Japanese Canadian team and the Caucasian team in the town. The Japanese Canadian camp was separated by a river from the township of Lillooet, and the camp residents were not allowed to cross the bridge over the river without permission from the British Columbia Security Commission. Through the softball match, interactions between Japanese Canadians and the Caucasian population in the town started, which revitalized the economically degraded town (Shimokura).

In the postwar period, many former Asahi players kept in touch with each other and contributed to forming baseball clubs for second- and third-generation Japanese Canadians (Hotchkiss 208–224). As the years turned into decades, however, they retired from the sport. By the late 1960s, nisei baseball had "disappeared from the Canadian scene altogether" (Hotchkiss 233).

For the following two decades, the Japanese Canadian community went through the tumultuous period of historical reflections. The third generation, or sansei, started to get involved in the movement for social justice and ethnic cultural revival, influenced by the Asian American activists south of the border (Izumi, "Japanese Canadian Movement" 58–59). In 1977, the Japanese Canadian community celebrated the centennial of the first settlement of Japanese immigrant Manzo Nagano. As a part of the centennial events, the first Powell Street Festival was organized in Vancouver. It was the first postwar public celebration of Japanese culture and Japanese Canadian heritage for the uprooted community (Izumi, "Reclaiming and Reinventing" 321–322). As the Powell Street Festival turned into an annual event in Vancouver, and as the movement to demand reparation and redress for the Japanese American wartime internment progressed in the United States, Japanese Canadian activists organized themselves to demand racial justice in general and the governmental acknowledgment of the wartime injustice inflicted on Japanese Canadians (Omatsu). Publication of Joy Kogawa's acclaimed novel *Obasan* in 1981 added momentum to the redress movement in Canada, as the novel popularized the knowledge about the Japanese Canadian uprooting. A redress agreement was eventually settled by the National Association for Japanese Canadians through its negotiations with the Canadian government (Miki). In September 1988, Prime Minister Brian Mulroney announced the government's official apology and delivered individual monetary compensation to surviving Japanese Canadians whose human rights were infringed. During this time, however, the story of the Asahi was not brought to the forefront in the community's historical memory, except when the team's name appeared in the newspaper in the obituaries of former players and managers.

## Resurrection of the Asahi Story

The legend of the Asahi nevertheless survived in the community, owing to the connections between and occasional reunions of the former Asahi members. In 1990, after the passing of the aforementioned star player, Roy Yamamura, Pat Adachi, an adamant Asahi fan since the prewar period, decided to collect information about the team and compile a book to preserve its history

(Hotchkiss 265–270). After extensive research in Canada with many former Asahi players and families, who provided materials such as photographs, newspaper clippings, and oral history, Adachi completed *Asahi: A Legend in Baseball* in 1992. The story of the Asahi became accessible for late twentieth-century readers to learn about the pioneer ballplayers.

In the twenty-first century, the Asahi's fame was further restored in Canadian sports history. In 2003, a documentary film, *Sleeping Tigers: The Asahi Baseball Story*, was produced by Jari Osborne. That same year, the Asahi was inducted into the Canadian Baseball Hall of Fame. Five surviving Asahi players, Mike Maruno, Kaye Kaminishi, Mickey Maikawa, Ken Kutsukake, and Kiyoshi Suga, represented the team at the induction ceremony (Hotchkiss 276). For them, the applause they received was not only an acknowledgment of the team's erased history but also the vindication of the past persecution experienced by the Japanese Canadian community and their subsequent acceptance as full citizens of Canada (Hotchkiss 276–277). In 2005, the team was also inducted into the BC Sports Hall of Fame after sixty years of being buried in the sports history of their home province.

Norio Goto, a Japan-based retired sportscaster of the Chubu-Nippon Broadcasting Company (CBC), started to collect records of the Asahi after he met Kaminishi in Vancouver in the early 1990s. Goto, who had deep interest in both baseball and the history of Japanese emigration, produced a documentary about the Asahi, which was broadcast nationwide in 1994 on the Tokyo Broadcasting System (Goto, *Shirarezaru Kanada Asahi Gun*). Goto's 2010 book, *Bankuubaa Asahi Monogatari* (The Vancouver Asahi story), was based on an extensive study of articles related to baseball in the prewar Vancouver Japanese-language newspaper *Tairiku Nippo* (*The Continental Daily News*) and other historical materials on the team both in English and in Japanese. Goto had also conducted extensive interviews with surviving former players and other people related to the team. Goto's book has been translated into English and is now available to English-speaking readers (Goto, *Story of Vancouver Asahi*).

The media coverage about the vindication of the Asahi team's fame and the stories of surviving former members has uplifted the Japanese Canadian community, but it also had a side effect on the other side of the Pacific. Celebration of the legend of the Asahi prompted some Japanese nationals, children and relatives of the former ballplayers who returned to Japan, to look into their family history. At the same time, the renewed interest in the Asahi's story connected Japanese scholars of Japanese Canadian history to the Asahi families in Japan. These new relationships resulted in gathering and exchanging information about the Asahi across the Pacific, filling many gaps and correcting inaccuracies in the existing literature about the legendary baseball team.

These developments are significant for the field of ethnic studies, which has conventionally focused—and, in many instances, continues to focus—

on the experiences of immigrants who stayed and formed communities in North America. Since the end of the twentieth century, Donna Gabaccia and other scholars have pointed out the necessity to include return migration in the scope of immigration studies. Madeline Hsu has analogously elucidated how Chinese migrants maintained ties with their home villages after migrating to the United States and how migrants strategically chose between staying in the countries of destination and returning to the countries of origin. After the "transnational turn" of the field in the 1990s, more scholars have included return or circuit migration between Asia and North America in their scope of research. Historian John Price, for example, has analyzed how international relations between Asian nations and Canada have affected the transpacific migrants between the two regions. Meanwhile, some literary works connect Japanese, Japanese Americans, and Japanese and other Canadians in their plots, of which Ruth Ozeki's Booker Prize–shortlisted novel *A Tale for the Time Being* is one example. Still, few historical studies on Japanese Canadians written in English have included return migration as a subject of study (Izumi, "Japanese Canadian Movement").

Geographer Norifumi Kawahara has searched for return migrants from Canada in Wakayama, Nagano, Fukui, and other localities in Japan in order to collect alternative sources on Japanese Canadian history, but his work on this topic is so far available only in Japanese. Since return migrants are not organized like ethnic communities outside Japan, it is difficult for scholars to study return migrants' experiences or their sociological trends as a whole. In order to have interviews with the return migrants, scholars either have to focus on specific communities that have produced many emigrants, such as Shiga and Wakayama prefectures, or need to track others down through personal relationships (Kage). Encounters generated through the Asahi connection turned out to be invaluable assets, however accidental, for the development of the field.

## Connecting the Asahi History across the Pacific

Yoshiyasu Furumoto grew up listening to his father when he spoke about the baseball team he played for in Vancouver before he migrated to Japan. His father, Teddy Furumoto, told him how his team "used to play against the stronger *hakujin* [Caucasian] players and beat them" (*Bankuubaa Asahi Gun* 196–197). Teddy was one of the original members of the Asahi team and played as a pitcher, shortstop, or right fielder until 1925 (Adachi, *Asahi: A Legend* 21). He traveled to Japan shortly before the attack on Pearl Harbor and stayed there for the rest of his life. Yoshiyasu, born in Tokyo in 1948, never met his grandparents, who ran a rooming house in the Powell Street area and passed away in two separate camps in British Columbia during World War II.

After his father passed away, Furumoto saw the 1994 TBS documentary on the Asahi produced by Norio Goto. He learned that some Asahi players were still alive in Canada and decided to visit Canada to meet them. Learning that the elderly Asahi members wished their stories to be known in Japan, he published a novel based on the experience of his father under the pseudonym Ted Y. Furumoto. His novel, *Bankuubaa Asahi Gun*, was first published in 2008. Five years later, Hidenori Hara published a comic version of the story in a Big Comics series, targeting young male readers. In the following year, film director Yuya Ishii, deeply moved by the novel, turned the untold story of the prewar Japanese Canadian youths into the film *Bankuubaa no Asahi* (The Vancouver Asahi).

During the summer of 2014, as the Japanese mass media broadcast the release of Ishii's film, coverage of the Asahi story increased, and this induced other relatives of the Asahi players to come out and reconnect. Several individuals related to the Asahi players suddenly became "friends" through the social media platform Facebook. This group included Takashi Matsumiya in Kobe, Teruo Nakanishi in Fujisawa, and Ted Y. Furumoto, who had been connected in person with Yobun Shima in Tokyo. Shima and some of the relatives of the Asahi players came in touch with Norio Goto, who was connected both to the Asahi families in Canada and to scholars of Japanese Canadians in Japan. My connection with Shima through a public lecture I delivered on Japanese Canadian history in Kyoto in 2012 helped me get to know these other families of former Asahi members. Thus, through social networks and personal connections, families of return migrants and scholars of Japanese Canadian history quickly became acquainted with each other. These new connections opened a new chapter in the historical uncovering of the Asahi story in Japan.

One individual in Kaideima village in Shiga Prefecture started his investigation of the Asahi team's history in 2014 after he learned about the release of Ishii's film in the newspaper. His name is Satoshi Matsumiya, and he is a grandson of Sotojiro Matsumiya, who was an influential merchant on Powell Street in prewar Vancouver. Sotojiro's store, Matsumiya Shoten, was one of the biggest stores in the earlier history of the Japanese Canadian community on Powell (Sasaki 88–89). Sotojiro's son and Satoshi's father, Masuo Matsumiya, authored the book *Kaideima Monogatari* (The Kaideima story), a history of emigration from Kaideima. Masuo was a nisei born in Vancouver who was sent to Japan when he was young and received schooling in Hikone City near Kaideima (M. Matsumiya). After schooling, Masuo returned to Vancouver to help his father's store on Powell Street. Masuo and his family were deported in 1946 by the Canadian government's repatriation policy. He settled and retired in Kaideima and remained active in the local community of returned emigrants in Shiga. Satoshi was born in Japan, and he did not know the story of the Asahi until he learned about it through the media coverage of the movie *The Vancouver Asahi*. Satoshi compiled information about his grandfather's store and the Vancouver Asahi and self-published a book titled *Matsumiya Shoten to Bankuubaa Asahi Gun* in 2017.

Residents of Kaideima had resorted to sojourning after the village was hit by a massive flood in 1896 (Kobayashi, "Emigration to Canada"; S. Matsumiya). The villagers developed a "transnational migration circuit" between Kaideima and Vancouver and came to be the most influential group in the Japanese Canadian Powell Street community. Because the founding members of the Asahi team were dominated by migrants from Kaideima, Satoshi's village connection led to some major new findings about the early period of the team, including the identity of the first Asahi manager, Matsujiro Miyasaki.

## New Findings about the Asahi Team Members

Although Pat Adachi and Norio Goto did their best to gather records on the Asahi, substantial information about the team was missing several decades after the team's dissolution and the community's expulsion from British Columbia. In Adachi's 1992 book, those players who had stayed in Canada and stayed in touch with the community are described in detail, while many others appear only in the photographs, as their identifications and later lives were unknown. Goto's book also largely depended on Canadian sources, although his book is more detailed and descriptive than Adachi's book, as he used Japanese-language materials, such as the *Tairiku Nippo* newspaper, as well as English sources. For example, Goto's book contains correct kanji (Chinese characters) for many of the players' names as well as place names in Japan, which are sometimes misspelled in Adachi's books. However, Goto depended heavily on interviews with survivors and descendants in Canada, and regarding such questions as when or how their families emigrated to Canada, the interviewees sometimes remembered the facts incorrectly, or inaccurate stories had been passed on. Another challenge for writing a more comprehensive history of the Asahi was that many players' identities remained unknown, as they only appear in their last names or in photos unidentified.

When the Asahi team was inducted into the Canadian Baseball Hall of Fame in 2003 and the BC Sports Hall of Fame in 2005, medals were made for individuals affiliated with the team. However, many of these medals remained unclaimed, as the whereabouts of those individuals or their descendants were unknown. After relatives in Japan became reconnected, a great amount of information became available for the Japanese Canadian community looking for recipients of the unclaimed medals. Such information is very much appreciated by scholars and researchers of Japanese Canadian history as well.

The earliest remaining photograph of the Asahi was taken in 1915. Adachi could not identify two figures in this photograph, and four are missing their first names (Adachi, *Asahi: A Legend* 10). Among the original members, Adachi's book carries details about Tom Matoba, Teddy Furumoto, and the Kitagawa brothers. However, it explains little about other original members such as Yosomatsu Nishizaki and Sotaro Matsumiya. Nor does it give any information about Shima or Tabata, whose last names only are included in the caption.

When Yobun Shima became connected to scholars and Asahi families in Japan, his involvement prompted rapid progress in the discovery of new facts related to the Asahi. After his retirement from the Nippon Yusen shipping company, Shima started excavating his family history. His grandfather, Kiyosaburo Shima, was from Mie Prefecture. Kiyosaburo first migrated to Hawaii at the turn of the century and, from there, moved to Vancouver around 1907. After settling in Vancouver, he brought his wife and three sons from Japan to Vancouver. Yobun's father, the fourth son, Yoshio Fred, was born in Vancouver. The eldest son, Shoichi Shima, played on the Asahi team when it was founded. It turned out that it was Shoichi Shima who appeared in the front right end in the 1915 photograph of the original team.

Nothing except his last name had been known about Shoichi until Yobun provided information about his family. Shoichi played on the Asahi team until 1916, returned to Japan in 1917 to get married, and remigrated to Canada the following year with his wife. He stayed until 1925, when his family returned to Japan for good. While most family members, including Yobun's nisei father, returned to Japan in the 1930s, one brother, Hisao, remained in Canada. Hisao's family relocated to a self-supporting site after the attack on Pearl Harbor. Hisao's daughter, Yvonne Shima, later became an actress and lived in the United Kingdom until she retired as a result of a traffic accident. Yvonne appeared in the original 007 series, *Dr. No.* Since 2014, Yobun has been working hard to liaise between the Japanese Canadian community and the relatives of the Asahi members in Japan, trying to find other Asahi families to deliver the unclaimed medals. Thanks to his and others' efforts, several unclaimed medals have been presented to the relatives.

Another relative of the Asahi members discovered was Teruo Nakanishi. His grandfather, Kanekichi Nakanishi, from Hiroshima, was an influential entrepreneur and labor contractor in Canada (Ayukawa 21, 32). Kanekichi's son Ken played in the Asahi. Ken's brother and Teruo's father, Hajime, returned to Japan to become a diplomat. Ken also moved to Japan during the 1930s, while Kanekichi stayed in Canada. During the war Kanekichi was interned in New Denver, British Columbia, as he was suffering from tuberculosis. Kanekichi's sons both died during the war. Ken was conscripted to the Japanese army and was killed in action. Hajime perished in the atomic bomb dropped on Hiroshima. Teruo, who was in elementary school in 1945, survived the war because he and his mother had been evacuated from Hiroshima to a rural area. After a stable career in postwar Japan, Teruo retired. He often visits Canada to find out more about his grandfather, who once was a labor contractor at a gold mine in the Cariboo and the owner of pool bars on Powell Street, but who eventually passed away in New Denver, British Columbia.

Satoshi Matsumiya from Kaideima lives a few minutes away from Yaeko Miyazaki, a nisei deportee from Vancouver born in 1932. Yaeko is a daughter of Ihachi Miyazaki, who was the first manager of the Asahi. The first manager/coach of Asahi was Matsujiro Miyasaki, aka "Bashamatsu" (Adachi, *Asahi: A Legend* 11). Furumoto's novel speculates that he was called Bashamatsu because he was a very rigorous coach (*basha-uma* means a rigorous horse that leads a cart), pushing young players to "show the Japanese pride" (Furumoto, *Bankuubaa Asahi Gun* 21, 33). Although this may not be entirely untrue, Yaeko provided a different explanation (Miyazaki). Her father, Ihachi, ran a store and a freight business on Powell Street. Before he purchased an automobile, he used a horse and a cart to transport goods. Ihachi somehow did not like his name, and he preferred to be called Matsujiro, or Mattsan, hence the nickname "Bashamatsu." This solves the problem of different names, Matsujiro Miyasaki and I. Miyazaki, as captions of the same person differ between the 1915 photograph and the 1917 photograph in Pat Adachi's book (Adachi, *Asahi: A Legend* 10, 26).

Yaeko led a happy childhood as a daughter of an affluent business owner. Her father was a baseball fan, and her mother sewed uniforms for the team. When the war started, Yaeko was pulled out of Strathcona School in Vancouver and was interned in Lemon Creek camp in the interior of British Columbia. Yaeko was deported with her family in 1946. She could not adjust to the local school in Kaideima, so she started working without finishing school. She later got married and had children, and now she is happily retired in Kaideima. She speaks nisei *nihongo*, Japanese language with English words mixed in Japanese sentences.

Satoshi Matsumiya found the Miyazaki family tree in the local temple records in Kaideima. These records showed that Ihachi had an uncle named Matsujiro, who was sometimes called Ihachi. This kind of name switching had in fact often occurred in old-time rural Japan. Matsujiro (aka Ihachi), the uncle of the first Asahi manager, was the father of Masajiro Miyazaki, a famous Japanese Canadian doctor who settled in Lillooet, British Columbia, who was later awarded the Order of Canada for his contributions to the community through coroner and medical services. Dr. Masajiro Miyazaki, born in Kaideima in 1899, moved to Canada with his father in 1913 but lost touch with his father in Canada. The Miyazaki family temple records revealed that Matsujiro died at the age of eighty-three in 1946 in Shiga. Yaeko's family was close to Dr. Miyazaki, who assisted Yaeko's mother during a difficult labor delivering Yaeko. Yaeko's testimony clarified the identity of the first manager of the Asahi team, which was an alteration of the conventional Asahi history accepted for decades. Yaeko received the medal for Matsujiro Miyasaki from the BC Sports Hall of Fame.

Sotaro Matsumiya, another member of the earliest Asahi team, was also from Kaideima. The testimonies of Takashi, his grandson, revealed the life history of this young baseball player, whose later life had been unknown. Sotaro was born in 1899 and moved at the age of seven to Vancouver, where his father was working. Sotaro went to the Vancouver Japanese School and joined the Asahi team. He later worked in a British confectionery store in Vancouver until he moved back to Japan in 1923. He started a candy manufacturer, which was later merged with the Morozoff Corporation in Kobe. He joined the executive board of Morozoff and contributed to the development of the confectionery industry in Japan. Sotaro was very close to his grandchildren, but he did not tell them about the Asahi team before he passed away in 1975. Takashi now runs a café in Kobe. Takashi had preserved records related to his grandfather's life and had wondered why there were so many artifacts and photographs related to baseball and other sports. In March 2015, he and his sister, Mana, received Sotaro's medal of honor from the BC Sports Hall of Fame.

Through the Kaideima connection, one of the original Asahi members was newly identified. When a photo exhibit of the emigration of Shiga people was held in Hikone in 2011, one visitor realized that her father appeared in the 1915 Asahi photograph. He was Yozaemon Kondo, who played on the Asahi team in the first three years before returning to Japan. His descendants did not know about Kondo's affiliation with the Asahi team. The medal from the BC Sports Hall of Fame was presented to the family in March 2015.

The most famous among the original Asahi players are the Kitagawa brothers, Mickey Hatsujiro, Yotaro (Horii), and Eddie Eizaburo. Mickey was the first pitcher of the team, Yo was the catcher, and Eddie was well known for his extraordinary fielding skills (Adachi, *Asahi: A Legend* 17, 18, 23). Mickey and Eddie stayed with the team until 1931, and Eddie served as a manager of the team in the last two years of his service. Eddie married Muriel Fujiwara, a journalist in Vancouver. Muriel's letters to her brother, Wes, during World War II later gained a broad readership through their appearance, in slightly modified form, in Joy Kogawa's novel *Obasan*. Muriel's original letters were later compiled into a book edited by Roy Miki (M. Kitagawa). Eddie and Muriel are one of the most well-known couples in Japanese Canadian history. On the other hand, Eddie's brothers' lives were less known. Yo passed away in Canada in 1926 due to alcohol abuse (Goto, *Bankuubaa Asahi Monogatari* 39), and recent research in Kaideima revealed that Mickey Hatsujiro returned to Kaideima to take over the Kitagawa household shortly before the Pacific War broke out (K. Kitagawa). The medals of honor for the Kitagawa brothers had been kept by Eddie's descendants in Canada, but Mickey Hatsujiro's medal was handed to the heir of the Kitagawas, Kiyomi Kitagawa, in Kaidemima on April 10, 2015.

## Creation of the New Asahi Team

Although the movie *The Vancouver Asahi* was not commercially successful in Japan, its creation bore another unexpected fruit: The New Asahi Baseball Team was formed in Vancouver by Japanese Canadian children. The team collected enough donations to fund a trip to Japan in March 2015. The team visited and played against teams in Ashikaga City in Tochigi Prefecture (where the filming took place), Yokohama in Kanagawa Prefecture, Ohfu in Aichi Prefecture, Tenri in Nara Prefecture, and Notogawa in Shiga. The families of the original Asahi members gathered in Yokohama and Notogawa, and some of the unclaimed medals were presented during these visits.

The Yokohama reunion was attended by Chinami Kaminishi, a jazz singer and a relative of Kaye Kaminishi in Canada. Chinami is actively involved in the peace movement in Hiroshima through her music, and she has incorporated Kaye's Japanese Canadian experiences in her poetry and song lyrics (Kaminishi, *A Thousand Cranes*). Chinami heard the story from Kaye about his experience in wartime Lillooet, British Columbia, where one of the self-supporting Japanese Canadian relocation camps was located. Based on the story, she wrote "The Vancouver Asahi and the Bridge of Hope" (Kaminishi, *Bankuubaa Asahi Gun*). The same story of white residents and Japanese Canadians who established warm relationships through playing softball together is also told in Canada through books and a documentary film (Hotchkiss 179–180; Osborne).

## Conclusion

Japanese scholars of Japanese Canadian history and culture have long known that historical materials related to Japanese overseas migration remain to be discovered in Japan. However, because ex-migrants are reintegrated into the Japanese nation-state and are not organized, it is difficult to find individual return migrants other than through personal connections. Communities such as Kaideima and Hassaka in Shiga and Mio in Wakayama have produced many emigrants to Canada. However, these close-knit communities are not necessarily approachable to outsiders, and until recently, prefectural or municipal governments had not been enthusiastic about excavating or preserving the history of migrants. The stigma attached to the notion of emigration has discouraged former migrants from speaking about their experiences even to their children and grandchildren. But as the experiences of overseas Japanese are popularized through novels, TV, and movies, the atmosphere surrounding these ex-migrants has shifted toward the positive.

The generation who had direct contact with the migrant generation is now rigorously searching for their family history. If this chance is missed, it will be extremely difficult to gather information about the deportees from Canada in Japan as the generation who experienced migration and those who directly knew such people will be gone. The remarkable economic development in postwar Japan prevented further emigration, and the traumatic and dishonorable war memories have generated collective amnesia among the Japanese citizens about their nation's prewar overseas colonies and international migration (Oguma 343–348). It is only recently that the general public and the mass media in Japan have become interested in prewar overseas Japanese experiences. Family archives are mounds of treasure, but through generational transitions, artifacts get lost, and personal memories disappear. Under such circumstances, the task of preserving transnational Japanese and Canadian histories has gained urgency. The Asahi connection has provided a remarkable opportunity for researchers to access private archives.

The inclusion of return migrants expands the scope of Japanese Canadian historiography and the subjects considered in it. While nisei deportees were victims of racial expulsion from Canada, their lives after the deportation from their native country reveal stories of struggle and survival in their ancestral community in Japan, which involved simultaneous acceptance and alienation. For those who left Canada before World War II, the return to Japan brought them various fates. Some became part of Japan's imperial aggression in Asia and the Pacific. Some survived the war while others did not, as the war affected residents in Japan in more directly physical and violent ways than it did civilians living in Canada. The prewar returnees' lives, on the other hand, illuminate the migrants' agency in making choices over where to pursue their livelihood.

It is a task of historians concerned with human rights to retrieve voices of those who cannot speak for themselves and write for the rights of all who are destitute. The resurrection of the Asahi story in Canada and Japan reconnected families dispersed and distanced from each other by the ocean as well as by silenced memories of exclusion, deportation, and war. Digging up and narrating such "microhistories" of individuals remains an arduous task. But sharing such histories as the Kaminishis', for example, which connects Kaye's story of bridging racial gaps through baseball games and Chinami's singing about a thousand cranes in Hiroshima, may help give voice to the subjects of violence that transcend national boundaries.

## WORKS CITED

Adachi, Pat. *Asahi 100th Anniversary: The Legacy Continues.* Toronto: Self-published, 2016.

———. *Asahi: A Legend in Baseball—A Legacy from the Japanese Canadian Baseball Team to Its Heirs.* Etobicoke, ON: Coronex Printing and Publishing, 1992.

Ayukawa, Midge Michiko. *Hiroshima Immigrants in Canada, 1891–1941*. Vancouver: University of British Columbia Press, 2007.

Bangarth, Stephanie. *Voices Raised in Protest: Defending North American Citizens of Japanese Ancestry, 1942–49*. Vancouver: University of British Columbia Press, 2008.

Furumoto, Ted Y. *Bankuubaa asahi gun: Densetsu no "samurai yakyu chiimu" sono rekisi to eiko* [The Vancouver Asahi: History and glory of a legendary Samurai baseball team]. Tokyo: Bungeisha, 2008.

Gabaccia, Donna. "Is Everywhere Nowhere? Nomads, Nations, and the Immigrant Paradigm of the United States History." *Journal of American History* 86.3 (1999): 1115–1134.

Goto, Norio. *Bankuubaa Asahi Monogatari: Densetsu no Yakyuu Chiimu* [The Vancouver Asahi story: A legendary baseball team]. Tokyo: Iwanami Shoten, 2010.

———. *Shirarezaru Kanada Asahi Gun* [The little-known Canadian Asahi baseball team]. TV documentary, Tokyo Broadcasting System, 1994.

———. *The Story of Vancouver Asahi: A Legend in Baseball*. Trans. Masaki Watanabe. Self-published, 2016.

Hara, Hidenori. *Bankuubaa Asahi Gun: A Legend of Samurai Baseball*. 5 vols. Tokyo, Shogakkan Big Comics Superior, 2014.

Hotchkiss, Ron. *Diamond Gods of the Morning Sun: The Vancouver Asahi Baseball Story*. New York: Friesen, 2013.

Hsu, Madeline. *Dreaming of Gold, Dreaming of Home: Transnationalism and Migration between the United States and South China, 1882–1943*. Stanford: Stanford University Press, 2000.

Ishii, Yuya, dir. *Bankuubaa no Asahi* [The Vancouver Asahi]. Toho, 2014. DVD.

———. *Fune o Amu* [The great passage]. Shochiku, 2013. DVD.

Izumi, Masumi. "Japanese Canadian Exclusion and Incarceration." *Densho Encyclopedia*, 2013. http://encyclopedia.densho.org/Japanese%20Canadian%20exclusion%20and%20incarceration. 12 October 2016.

———. "The Japanese Canadian Movement: Migration and Activism before and after World War II." *Amerasia Journal* 33.2 (2007): 49–66.

———. "Reclaiming and Reinventing 'Powell Street': Reconstruction of the Japanese Canadian Community in Post–World War II Vancouver." *Nikkei in the Pacific Northwest: Japanese Americans and Japanese Canadians in the Twentieth Century*. Ed. Louis Fiset and Gail M. Nomura. Seattle: University of Washington Press, 2005. 308–333.

Jette, Shannon. "Little/Big Ball: The Vancouver Asahi Baseball Story." *Sport History Review* 38 (2007): 1–16.

Kage, Tatsuo. *Nikkei Kanada-jin no Tsuihou* [Expulsion of Japanese Canadians]. Tokyo: Akashi Shoten, 1998.

Kaminishi, Chinami. *Bankuubaa Asahi Gun to Kibou no Hashi* [The Vancouver Asahi and a bridge of hope]. Hiroshima: Chugoku Shinbun, 2015.

———. *A Thousand Cranes*. Green Leaf Label, 2013. CD.

Kawahara, Norifumi. *Kanada Nihonn-jin Gyogyou Imin no Mita Fuukei: Maekawa-ke "Koshashin" Korekushon* [Landscapes seen by a Japanese migrant fishing family: The Maekawa family's "old photo" collection]. Kyoto: Sanninsha, 2013.

Kitagawa, Kiyomi. Interview in Kaideima, Shiga, with Masumi Izumi, accompanied by Satoshi Matsumiya and Norio Goto. 10 April 2015.

Kitagawa, Muriel. *This Is My Own: Letters to Wes and Other Writings on Japanese Canadians, 1941–1948*. Ed. Roy Miki. Vancouver: Talonbooks, 1985.

Kobayashi, Audrey. *A Demographic Profile of Japanese Canadians and Social Implications for the Future.* Ottawa: Department of the Secretary of State, Canada, 1989.

———. "Emigration to Canada from Kaideima, Japan, 1885–1950: An Analysis of Community and Landscape Change." Diss. University of California, Los Angeles, 1983.

Kogawa, Joy. *Obasan.* Lester and Orpen Dennys, 1981.

Matsumiya, Masuo. *Kaideima Monogatari: Ume no Hana to Kaede, Hikone-shi Kaideima to Sono Imin Shi* [The story of Kaideima: Plum blossoms and maple, Kaideima village, Hikone City and its history of emigration]. Self-published, 1984.

Matsumiya, Satoshi. *Matsumiya Shoten to Bankuubaa Asahi Gun: Kanada Imin no Sokuseki* [Matsumiya General Store and the Vancouver Asahi: Footprints of Japanese immigrants in Canada]. Hikone: Sun Rise Shuppan, 2017.

Miki, Roy. *Redress: Inside the Japanese Canadian Call for Justice.* Vancouver: Raincoast, 2005.

Miyazaki, Yaeko. Interview in Kaideima, Shiga, with Masumi Izumi, accompanied by Satoshi Matsumiya and Norio Goto. 10 April 2015.

Oguma, Eiji. *Tan-itsu Minzoku Shinwa no Kigen: "Nihonjin" no Jigazo no Keifu* [The myth of the homogeneous nation]. Tokyo: Shinyosha, 1995.

Omatsu, Maryka. *Bittersweet Passage: Redress and the Japanese Canadian Experience.* Toronto: Between the Lines, 1992.

Osborne, Jari. 2003. *Sleeping Tigers: The Asahi Baseball Story.* 2003. Film. https://www.nfb.ca/film/sleeping_tigers_the_asahi_baseball_story. 12 October 2016.

Ozeki, Ruth. *A Tale for the Time Being.* New York: Viking, 2013.

Price, John. *Orienting Canada: Race, Empire, and the Transpacific.* Vancouver: University of British Columbia Press, 2011.

Roy, Patricia E. *The Oriental Question: Consolidating a White Man's Province, 1914–41.* Vancouver: University of British Columbia Press, 2005.

Sasaki, Toshiji. *Nihon-jin Kanada Imin-shi* [History of Japanese immigration to Canada]. Tokyo: Fuji Shuppan, 1999.

Shimokura, Howard. "The Last Living Asahi: Kay Kaminishi and His Life in Baseball." *Discover Nikkei*, 30 December 2015. http://www.discovernikkei.org/en/journal/2015/12/30/kaye-kaminishi-2.

Sunahara, Ann Gomer. *The Politics of Racism: The Uprooting of Japanese Canadians during the Second World War.* Toronto: Lorimar, 1981.

Thomson, Grace Eiko, curator. "Leveling the Playing Field: Legacy of Vancouver's Asahi Baseball Team." Japanese Canadian National Museum, Burnaby, British Columbia, Canada, 2005. Exhibition.

# 4

# A Journey to Freedom

## *Human Rights Discourse and Refugee Memory*

Vinh Nguyen

On April 30, 2015, hundreds of Vietnamese Canadians from across the country congregated on Parliament Hill in Ottawa, the nation's capital, to commemorate the fortieth anniversary of the end of the Vietnam War and to celebrate the proposed state-sponsored construction of the Memorial to the Victims of Communism.[1] Amid a sea of Canadian and South Vietnamese flags, former refugees denounced the current Vietnamese government for its human rights abuses, focalizing the "problem" of forced migration and asylum on the issue of *rights* over those of war, political ideology, and foreign intervention. Holding banners that read "Human Rights for Vietnam," "Vietnamese Boat People Refugees: Victims of the Communist Party of Vietnam," and "Vietnamese People around the World Determined to Fight for Freedom and Human Rights in Vietnam," they condemned Vietnam as a totalitarian state, antithetical to the liberal ideals of freedom and democracy.[2] This condemnation called for the liberation of Vietnamese people living in Vietnam while providing a rationale for the refugee exodus of the 1970s and 1980s, an explanation for the diaspora. That is to say, Vietnamese people are scattered across the globe because there were, and there continue to be, no human rights in their homeland.

This telling articulation demonstrates how Vietnamese diasporics remember their histories and negotiate their place within the Canadian national imaginary through a now-established discourse of human rights. Constituting a prominent segment of the Vietnamese Canadian community, those gathered in Ottawa utilized the language of rights to construct a migration narrative that charts the movement from communist oppression to capitalist freedom.[3] Such a refugee narrative allowed them to make sense of their displaced past and the ways it has shaped present forms of (trans)national belonging and affiliation. In particular, the commemoration was an occasion for former Vietnamese refugees to express how their act of refuge seeking was motivated and purposeful: to leave one's homeland is to call into question the political legitimacy of the governing body, to reject a sovereign power that cannot accommodate and protect its people. For them, asylum seeking is a political statement against the Socialist Republic of Vietnam, one that endures beyond the historical event and continues to press at the limits of Vietnamese nationhood. Such a statement reveals how Vietnamese refugees are not passive, helpless, or empty of history and politics, even when they are victims. The adoption of human rights discourse during the fortieth anniversary commemoration was one way for former refugees to vocalize anticommunist politics and, in the process, give meaning to their experiences of asylum seeking. In this way, human rights functions as an important framework for understanding the conditions of refuge(es), past and present.

This politicized reliance on human rights, an internationally recognized instrument of justice, also renders former Vietnamese refugees legible to the Canadian nation-state. As they criticize Vietnam for its rights infractions, what emerges is a free and grateful Vietnamese refugee who exemplifies the authoritarian rightlessness of Vietnam and the rights-possessing and rights-granting capacities of Western liberal states such as Canada.[4] As such, thankful refugees promoting human rights in their home countries are intelligible to and politically valuable for the asylum state because they expediently rehearse its exceptional qualities of benevolence and humanitarianism.

A week before the anniversary, the Canadian government showed its enthusiastic support for the commemoration event by passing Bill S-219, officially marking April 30 as the "Journey to Freedom Day." The bill recognizes and honors Vietnamese refugees' postwar exodus from Vietnam—their struggles and sacrifices in search of freedom—as well as Canada's role in resettling them. Such forms of state legitimation illustrate how minority projects of memorialization and activism can align with state interests, how they can be deployed to construct a particular understanding of the "good" of political asylum, and how the nation can act as premier advocate of human rights. The legal incorporation of refugee memories into national memory makes possible a narration of history that deemphasizes Canada's participation in the Vietnam War, a point that I will return to later in this chapter, in order to highlight its role as refugee "savior" when the fighting ended.

Employing the fortieth anniversary commemoration event in Ottawa as a point of departure, this chapter explores the entanglements of refugee discourse and human rights.[5] Since the legal inscription of "refugee" into the United Nations Convention Relating to the Status of Refugees in 1951, human rights have consistently been invoked to explain the idea of "persecution" central to the concept. In other words, our understanding of political refuge(es) requires human rights to give it meaning and legitimation. This is not surprising given the definition of "refugee" arose, in part, from Article 14 of the Universal Declaration of Human Rights, which states, "Everyone has the right to seek and to enjoy in other countries asylum from persecution." Defining persecution through "race, religion, nationality, political opinion or membership of a particular social group" ("Convention and Protocol"), the Convention forwards a notion of "refugee" that is largely based on escape from forms of authoritarian governance. Today, refugee law is one of the most important apparatuses of the international human rights regime—a project of sociopolitical organization and a moral ideology sponsored by major Western states. As James C. Hathaway and Michelle Foster state, "Refugee law may be the world's most powerful international human rights mechanism. Not only do millions of people invoke its protections every year in countries spanning the globe, but they do so on the basis of a self-actuating mechanism of international law that, quite literally, allows at-risk persons to vote with their feet" (1). While asylum seekers, policy makers, and practitioners call on human rights for purposes of legality, the mobilization of human rights by former refugees, as a form of activism and political visibility, necessitates an examination of the ways in which refugees have historically relied on the framework of rights to make various claims—for asylum, for recognition, for diasporic agency, and for community formation. Human rights, then, not only are the basis for claiming legal status as "refugees" but also critically operate as a force that sustains various collective identities and political projects in the long aftermath of forced migration.

## Vietnamese Refugees in Canada

The resettlement of over sixty thousand Southeast Asian refugees of the Vietnam War, including Vietnamese, Cambodian, Laotian, and Hmong, during an eighteen-month period from 1979 to 1980 is arguably the highlight of Canadian refugee and immigration history. This resettlement program, the largest single intake of refugees in Canada to date, was an unprecedented event in the wake of significant changes in immigration policy laid out by the 1976 Immigration Act. These changes, such as provisions for a humanitarian "designated class," which allowed the government to identify and expedite the resettlement of groups in need that do not fit neatly under the parameters of the Convention definition, and the private sponsorship program, which made it possible for ordinary civilians or groups to sponsor refugees, were crucial instruments in Canada's response to the Vietnamese "boat people" crisis. According to Molloy et al., the success of the "Indochinese" resettlement program was the direct result of hard work, political will, and collaboration between the Canadian people and the government. In recognition of their efforts, the UNHCR Nansen Refugee Award was bestowed on the "Canadian people" in 1986. This memory of Canadian humanitarianism permeates Canada's understanding of itself as a haven of refuge, its image as an exceptional nation-state on the international stage. Canada's response to Southeast Asian refugees has become the gold standard in relation to subsequent refugee crises. For example, when the image of Aylan Kurdi's lifeless body drew attention to Syrians fleeing geopolitical violence, Vietnamese refugees were recalled in the public sphere as a prime example of Canadian generosity, a moment in time when Canada stepped up to the challenge and showed the world that it was capable of ethical action and exerting national sovereignty through the granting of asylum.[6]

In the roughly three decades after the end of the Vietnam War, Canada accepted approximately two hundred thousand refugees from Southeast Asia for resettlement (Robinson). This history of successful humanitarianism is an important piece in the larger puzzle of Canadian nation-building, in a cultivated image of civility and peace-making. Dominant discourse tends to represent Canadian humanitarianism as an act of altruistic magnanimity, eliding issues of complicity in creating the conditions of violence and displacement, more of which I will discuss below. Thus, it is not surprising that the Canadian government is eager to support some members of the Vietnamese Canadian community, which now number over 220,000, as they gather to commemorate the war and its legacies. Such memory projects reiterate a narrative of humanitarianism that, while true on one level, also obscures the complexities of Canadian involvement in Vietnam and how refugees were perceived and received in a newly "multicultural" Canada.

Laura Madokoro, for example, reminds us that contemporary celebrations of Canadian generosity to refugees of the Vietnam War ignore "opposition to the resettlement efforts [at the time]—including from the National Citizens Coalition. . . . The historical narrative that is being produced is one of pure, righteous generosity" (n.p.). The state's investment in the work of Vietnamese diasporic commemoration is intimately tied to this production of a "pure, righteous generosity" central to Canadian (inter)national identity. At the same time, part and parcel of commemoration as nationalist labor is the ensconcing of a very specific, dominant Vietnamese Canadian identity, one that is strictly anticommunist, within Canadian culture, history, and politics. It is important to note here that this identity is not shared by all Vietnamese Canadians and that there is no "unified" Vietnamese Canadian community or identity. Yet the dominance of diasporic anticommunism, which stems from a history of war and migration, stifles divergent and dissenting identities, especially ones that may sympathize or desire reconciliation with the Vietnamese state. The work of commemoration is, at its core, a project of creating, defining, and demarcating the limits of identity and community.

## "Strong, Proud, and Free": The Fortieth Anniversary Commemoration

In Canada, the fortieth anniversary of what many Vietnamese in the diaspora call "the Fall of Saigon" or "Black April" was an especially momentous occasion. Not only was it a significant historical milestone but, as briefly mentioned above, it also coincided with the inaugural "Journey to Freedom Day" and what was supposed to be the "breaking ground" of the Memorial to the Victims of Communism.[7] The anniversary event began with a rally at the stretch of land between the Supreme Court of Canada and the Library and Archives Canada, the building site the then-government promised to Tribute to Liberty, a nonprofit organization behind the fund-raising for and construction of the memorial.[8] The site had enormous symbolic significance, situated between the national institutions of justice and memory. In attendance, alongside Vietnamese Canadians, were Polish and Hungarian former refugees, Korean War veterans, and various government ministers. This coming together of those who had fought and fled communism was a strategic display of Cold War solidarities—a shared history of loss and political commitment to anticommunism—that amplified the need for contemporary acts of memorialization. The official website of Tribute to Liberty states: "Memorials are essential parts of our national landscape: they serve as important markers for events and people that make up the diverse fabric of our nation. In Canada, over 8 million people trace their roots to countries that suffered under Communism. Since the beginning of the first Communist regime in 1917, immigrants from Communist countries have flocked to Canada in search of freedom and safety" ("Why a Memorial?"). The symbolic power of the proposed memorial was meant to exalt Canada as a "land of refuge," in which asylum facilitated refugee solidarity, creating the opportunity for victims to live together freely and unite against communism. On April 30, 2015, these human legacies of the Cold War gathered to remember communist atrocities and celebrate Canada's role as a welcoming country that provided shelter for those who suffered through such atrocities. In doing so, this group of actors resurrected Cold War memories in the present, (re)creating a Manichean world of refugee producers versus refugee havens.[9]

The chair of Tribute to Liberty, Ludwik Klimkowsk, in his official address told the crowd that their "journey was almost complete," because they were about to gain recognition and belonging in Canada through the memorial. For him, the memorial represents a national "home" for refugees, a place where they can educate the Canadian public about the oppressions and losses they experienced at the hand of communist regimes. Senator Ngo Thanh Hai, a Conservative Party politician behind the genesis of Bill S-219, pressed upon the audience that "freedom is not free," that it comes with a very heavy price, and that the next generation needs to remember this crucial history lesson.[10] The Canadian government officials who spoke, including former immigration minister Jason Kenny, made it clear that it was the Conservative Party who ushered Bill S-219 through Parliament, and it was going to be the Conservatives who would see the building of the memorial through to completion. Describing the crowd as "strong, proud, and free," Kenny made sure that these former refugees understood that Canada, and the Conservative government in particular, created the conditions for this gathering of free citizens. The rally had a strong memory imperative, with each major speaker inciting the crowd to keep various memories—of communist cruelty, of generational refugee suffering, of Canadian kindness, of the Conservative Party's commitment—alive, and toward different but overlapping political ends.

Vietnamese refugees did not fail to pick up on Kenny's point about Canada's humanitarian efforts. In the early afternoon, the Vietnamese contingent marched from the rally site to Parliament Hill with a leading banner that read, "Thank You Canada from Vietnamese Canadian Community." Individual participants held similar placards with "40 Years Thank You Canada Merci" and "Thank You Canada: We Support the Canadian Government's Journey to Freedom Act" written on them.[11] These expressions of gratitude emphasize Canada as a refugee savior, rescuing Vietnamese refugees from the ravages of war and the dangers of communism. In the American context, both Yến Lê Espiritu and Mimi Thi Nguyen have discussed how grateful Vietnamese refugees abet revisionist and nationalist accounts of the Vietnam War, while providing alibis for contemporary war-making in the name of liberation and rescue. For Espiritu, narratives of gratitude espoused by "good" refugees are utilized to turn the war into a morally "good" war and to offer evidence of the need for future American military intervention in foreign conflicts ("The 'We-Win-Even-if-We-Lose' Syndrome"; *Body Counts*). Nguyen calls the "rescue" of refugees that are produced from such interventions the "gift of freedom," whereby refugees become indebted to the United States through both war and refuge (*Gift of Freedom*).

While these arguments cannot be mapped neatly onto the Canadian context because of different historical relationships to the Vietnam War, the ideological function of refugee gratitude that Espiritu and Nguyen outline is instructive to thinking about the "value" that anticommunist Vietnamese refugees have to projects of Canadian nation-building, a point that I will return to later in the chapter. It is clear that expressions of refugee gratitude benefit the nation; it is also clear that gratitude allows Vietnamese refugees to have a "voice" at Parliament Hill, the literal and symbolic site of Canadian politics. It is with such expressions of gratitude that former Vietnamese refugees were able to articulate anticommunism through the language of human rights. As an expected and easily digestible discourse, gratitude opens up

**Figure 4.1** Vietnamese Canadians attending the commemoration of the fortieth anniversary of the "Fall of Saigon" on April 30, 2015, Ottawa, Canada. (Photo credit: Vinh Nguyen)

certain possibilities even as it constrains refugees to buttressing nationalist projects. That is to say, while gratitude affectively and politically limits refugee expression, it can, as a public platform, make other concerns such as memories of migration and critiques of homeland politics recognizable to the national mainstream. At Parliament Hill, gratitude for Canadian humanitarianism comingled with grievances about Vietnam's human rights record. Gratitude and calls for human rights reverberated throughout as speakers recalled the pain of losing one's country, asserted the presence of Vietnamese people in Canada, and urged others to remember their perilous journeys to freedom. Like the rally that preceded it, the ceremony at Parliament Hill sought to establish and share memory, not only within the Vietnamese Canadian community but also importantly in Canada's national imagination.

## Memories of Persecution

Steve J. Stern notes the intimate association between memory and human rights, arguing that memory is a cultural code word, a "language of experience and continuing struggle" (126) in the push for justice after state violence. For him, memory provides important moral lessons about the inviolability of human rights, where past violations are recalled so a more democratic future becomes possible. Following Stern, I suggest that the framework of human rights can enable, for those who have been violently displaced, who must seek protection outside their homelands, a structure for the process of remembering. If memory can fortify human rights, then human rights can provide an established mechanism, a sanctioned language for the recollection of difficult memories. It allows for what we might call a *refugee memory of persecution* that makes sense of past trauma, present existence, and future formations. To wit, the discourse of human rights has the potential to make a past experience of asylum seeking legible in the present as a way of affecting what is yet to come—it gives political narrative to individual and collective memory. For those gathered in Ottawa on April 30, 2015, this narrative was situated both in and beyond Canadian borders, moving between past and present, between Vietnam, Canada, and various global passages. Remembering, in this context, means summoning a lost country from the past (South Vietnam), producing a country in the present (Canada), and attempting to shape a country for the future (Vietnam). Viet Thanh Nguyen reminds us that refugee memories refuse "the progressive notion of time that belongs to the nation"; they are, instead, sites where the "imagination of the past, present, and future countries can occur simultaneously" (934). These real and symbolic "countries" scramble the discreteness of times and geographies, making possible a more transnational and temporally porous understanding of affiliation, activism, and justice.

The commemoration event in Ottawa illuminates how Vietnamese refugees continue to search for a "country" of refuge, how they continually seek asylum, which is revealed to be an ongoing process intimately tied to the unfinished fate of the homeland. While many Vietnamese refugees have found material refuge in Canada—and they show incredible gratitude for such a gift—their search for asylum continues because their homeland is without freedom. As Nguyễn Văn Phát, a representative from the Veterans Association, emphatically reminded the crowd, Vietnam is still not free, and its people do not enjoy the rights that those in the diaspora possess. The chair of the Commemoration Organizing Committee went further to state that the Vietnamese diaspora has a crucial role to play in promoting human rights in Vietnam, that they must actively petition the Canadian government to pressure Vietnam to enact free speech, release political prisoners, and move toward democracy. Such protests from the community suggest that asylum for refugees—understood as the movement toward rights—is incomplete if Vietnam is still without human rights. The reach and significance of asylum, then, expand to encompass those who left as well as those who stayed behind, refugees of the past and citizens of the present. In this way, it is not just refugees undertaking perilous boat journeys but also Vietnam and the Vietnamese people who require refuge from the lack of human rights.

The commemoration event was, in many ways, a political performance that revised the meaning of refuge, enacting the process of asylum seeking in the present moment. The invocation of human rights at the commemoration functions as a refugee claim, a call for freedom from oppression and persecution not just for individual refugees but for a whole nation. This linking of refugee experience to contemporary concerns over human rights actually constructs the "journey to freedom" as one that has yet to reach a final point of arrival. Such an understanding of refuge keeps a past of migration pertinent to the present, where the struggle for freedom is anything but over. According to Human Rights Watch, the situation is dire in Vietnam:

> Basic rights, including freedom of speech, opinion, press, association, and religion, are restricted. Rights activists and bloggers face harassment, intimidation, physical assault, and imprisonment. Farmers continue to lose land to development projects without adequate compensation, and workers are not allowed to form independent unions. The police use torture and beatings to extract confessions. The criminal justice system lacks independence. State-run drug rehabilitation centers exploit detainees as laborers making goods for local markets and export. ("Vietnam")

Forty years after the end of the Vietnam War, the past is not past, because the problem of rights has not been resolved. As a result, the question of Vietnamese refugees acquires contemporary immediacy—the past, and a memory of persecution, remains relevant to the presence of Vietnamese people in diaspora and their anticommunist political agendas. Even though many Vietnamese refugees are now free citizens of Canada and other nations, "refuge" for them and their communist homeland must be understood as open-ended and forthcoming. Thus, while the display of gratitude might suggest that the gift of refuge has been received, that the search for home and freedom is complete, the anticommunist pronouncements reveal how refuge remains in progress, how it functions as a political project that requires renewed acts of claiming rights.

Seen in this way, the trenchant anticommunism of the Vietnamese Canadian community is not so much an outdated politics of melancholic, first-generation immigrants but an embodied politics that attempts to negotiate the complexities of exile and asylum. Scholars such as Thuy Vo Dang ("Cultural Work") and Lan Duong and Isabelle Thuy Pelaud ("Vietnamese American Art") have pointed out how Vietnamese diasporic anticommunism can function as a discourse of community building, even while it problematically polices cultural identity. In her study of the Vietnamese American community in San Diego, Vo Dang writes, "Anticommunism becomes the vehicle for sustaining an identity and community in the present and serves as pedagogical tool for the younger generations of Vietnamese Americans" (69). In performing this work, anticommunist discourse relies on charges against the Socialist Republic of Vietnam of human rights infractions. It paints the Vietnamese regime as "backward" and devoid of human rights, not in line with other states in a modern, democratic international community. Such a government does not, in this depiction, have political legitimacy, and its country cannot be a viable place of habitation. This logic explains the need for flight and the importance of refuge; it gives reason for the diaspora. Through statements about the value of human rights and what happens when they are absent, a Vietnamese diasporic community is able to take shape. Refugee collective identity gains definition in relation to the presence or absence of human rights.

This community formation has its foundations in loss—and indeed, the commemoration event in Ottawa can be viewed as an important opportunity for members of the community to voice and highlight their difficult migration and the painful losses they have experienced. Nguyễn-võ Thu-hương rightly points out that loss is the dominant mode of expression in Vietnamese exilic communities. The appearance of human rights complaints alongside articulations of loss, however, speaks to the way these communities use loss to register criticism and grievance and, in the process, create a sense of communal purpose. Accordingly, loss acquires an edge of political critique when it is expressed alongside human rights; it is a form of mourning that calls for justice in the present, where the mode of expression is protest through loss. Although the remembrance of loss is not easily separable from calls for human rights, it is important to recognize that they are not the same. Loss, I suggest, is oriented toward victims and survivors while human rights discourse points a finger at a perpetrator—it puts pressure on the Socialist Republic of Vietnam to follow Western, putatively universal guidelines of moral conduct. Human rights discourse names a problem that requires engagement and address in the present; it complicates the view that Vietnamese diasporic communities are melancholic and backward looking. Instead, the compulsion to effect geopolitical change and to influence homeland politics through the diaspora emphasizes the political agency of those who have been exiled from home, who, at one point in time, fell outside the primary category of social and political organization. Not only is the past given meaning through a present appeal to human rights but refugees also become political actors who skillfully utilize the language of rights to make political demands.

## Bill S-219: Remembering Canada in and beyond the Vietnam War

While the material outcomes of their activism are debatable, what is clear is that, at certain strategic moments, some prominent Vietnamese refugees become legible and legitimate subjects within the schema of the Canadian nation-state. One prime example of this is the passing of the "Journey to Freedom Day Act" by the Canadian Parliament on April 23, 2015. The act officially dedicates "a national day of commemoration of the exodus of Vietnamese refugees and their acceptance in Canada after the Fall of Saigon and the end of the Vietnam War" ("Bill S-219"). Senator Ngo Thanh Hai describes it as a "way to mark this milestone year [the 40th anniversary in 2015], to thank Canada for saving our lives and to commemorate the Vietnamese refugees' new-found freedom" ("Statement by Senator Ngo"). Originally called "Black April Day," the bill was met with deep disapproval from Vietnamese authorities.[12] The prime minister of Vietnam, Nguyễn Tấn Dũng, wrote to then prime minster of Canada, Stephen Harper, expressing concerns that the bill "presents a distorted version of Vietnam's history and could damage the bilateral relations both countries have worked to build" (Mackrael). Shrugging off this concern, Harper and his immigration minister continued to support the bill, citing that it was an important move to honor and celebrate the sixty thousand Indochinese refugees who "risked their lives in search of freedom, and found it here in Canada" (qtd. in Mackrael).

Behind their support were the calculations of partisan and electoral politics. The commemoration in Ottawa occurred a few months before a key federal election in Canada, and, as a consequence, every government official who spoke during the event impressed on the crowd how Harper's Conservative government made this commemorative opportunity possible by creating the occasion and space for refugee remembrance. They described how the Liberal and New Democratic Parties opposed and hindered the progress of Bill S-219 into law, while the Conservatives ardently stood behind it. For Vietnamese Canadians in the crowd, the passing of the bill added a layer of significance to their gathering as it represented a major acknowledgment of their past and their presence. The granting of space and recognition to Vietnamese refugees and their human rights grievances on the anniversary thus allowed the Conservatives, as opposed to their centrist or left-leaning opponents, to be seen as the party that championed the quest for freedom of those fleeing communist regimes, including Vietnamese, Hungarian, and Polish ethnic groups. In doing so, the Conservative government could lay claim to human rights as its exclusive concern, an integral part of its platform. Capitalizing on the anticommunism of Vietnamese Canadians and other diasporic groups, the government sought to win votes, this time not by "voting feet" but through ideological support, national exaltation, and, most importantly, casted ballots on election night.

Party politics continued to play out after the 2015 federal election. Shortly after Justin Trudeau's Liberal Party took office in November 2015, the construction of the memorial was put on hold. Canadian heritage minister Mélanie Joly explained that "the way the project was handled under the Conservatives was 'too political, too divisive and ultimately far from its goal of remembering the horror of victims of communism'" (qtd. in Butler). The overhaul of the memorial project, which includes a new building site, design, and construction date, was a way for the Liberals to antagonize the Conservatives, to criticize their motives and management. Just as the Conservatives used Bill S-219 and the memorial to bolster its image with Cold War refugees-turned-Canadians, the Liberals used the memorial to distinguish themselves from the failings of the Conservatives. By doing so, they too politicized refugee memories for partisan interests. The change in government hence did not diminish official support for the memorial and the larger project of constructing Canada's reputation as a leader in human rights; there was no evident policy change with the change in leadership, only modifications to the plan. Political orientation aside, the government of Canada uniformly invests in forms of memorialization such as Bill S-219 and the Memorial to the Victims of Communism primarily as a means to reinforce an image of Canadian exceptionalism on the world stage.

As Vietnamese Canadians gathered to condemn the Vietnamese government and its human rights record on April 30, 2015, they simultaneously expressed patriotism for and gratitude to Canada, joining in the production of Canadian exceptionalism. Shouts and signs of "Thank You Canada" reverberated alongside slogans such as "Human Rights for Vietnam." Here, Canada is constructed as a torchbearer of rights, freedom, and democracy; its image as a leading advocate of international human rights is reaffirmed in the condemnation of Vietnam. Canadian exceptionalism requires such narratives of exaltation, where Canada is able to rise above other, less democratic nations, in order to maintain a sense of national identity. International human rights have historically been an important tool of Canadian nationhood, even if Canada was slow to embrace its tenets. Andrew Lui points out that when the Universal Declaration of Human Rights was being drafted in 1947 and 1948, "Canadian policymakers approached [it] with a mix of skepticism, indifference, and outright hostility. . . . [T]he Canadian government attempted to scuttle or delay its release as much as possible" (3). It was not until the country was experiencing the threat of internal violence and fragmentation with the Quebec separatist movement in the 1970s that it "enacted constitutional guarantees for individual human rights. . . . Human rights thus became a source of legitimacy from which the federal government could assert its authority by externally projecting a particular self-image of Canada as a just society that was undivided despite its diversity. Human rights concerns therefore played a key role in laying the contemporary foundations for Canadian federalism" (7). Much in the same way, the gratitude of Vietnamese refugees plays into the idea of Canadian national unity, a unity that is anchored to a concern for international human rights. Their "thank yous" are incontrovertible evidence of Canada's singularity, its position in the world order as a defender and protector of justice.

This exceptionalism is most evident in the wording of the Journey to Freedom Day Act, where Canada's role during the global hot war that was "Vietnam" is documented only as follows: "The Canadian Forces were involved in the Vietnam War with supervisory operations to support the aim of establishing peace and ending the Vietnam War by assisting in the enforcement of the Paris Peace Accords of 1973" ("Bill S-219"). This memory, which is a state-directed narrative, forgets that Canada was the chief arms dealer for the United States during the war, producing traditional and chemical weapons that enabled the fighting and killing of millions of Vietnamese civilians. Yves Engler writes, "As the U.S. military buildup in Vietnam grew, Canadian weapons sales to the U.S. doubled between 1964 and 1966. Between 1965 and 1973, Canada sold $2.5 billion worth of war materials to the Pentagon" (127). In addition,

> at least $10 billion worth of other war-related supplies, including arms components, resources to build arms, and, of all things, green berets, were sold to the US armed forces. Every B-52 which unloaded its munitions over civilian targets in North Vietnam—Acts which resulted in tens of thousands of civilian deaths—were made out of Sudbury's finest nickel. In the mid-1960s, unemployment in Canada fell to a record low level of under four per cent; not only did select war-related industries prosper, but a wide section of Canadian society shared in windfall profits stemming from America's war in Vietnam. (Ziedenberg 25)

The modern Canadian capitalist economy, one of the pillars of Canadian civil and political society, must be understood as being partially built on the deaths of war civilians, on militarized violence against third-world bodies. Moreover, the cultivated memory of Canada as an innocent peacekeeper during the war suppresses its role as a

> willing ally in the U.S. counter-insurgency efforts, sharing the same assumptions about the nature of the insurgency, the strategic geopolitical importance of Indochina, and the value of trade and investment in Southeast Asia to the world market system. Canada geared its peace-keeping duties to the interests of the West, and its record on the international commissions to which it was appointed was characterized by partisan voting, willful distortion of fact, and complicity in U.S. violations of both the Geneva and Paris agreements. (Levant 2)

Rather than being a neutral facilitator of peace, Canada played an active role in steering the war along toward a Western bloc victory. While it did not officially "fight" in the war, Canada was crucially involved in the maintenance of the war-making machine, propping up U.S. counterinsurgency efforts by providing military supplies and enacting its soft power.

The Journey to Freedom Day Act rewrites history in a way that washes the blood from Canadian hands. Anh Ngo argues that the act "erases the Vietnam War and Canada's complicity in it by shining the spotlight on the success of the Vietnamese refugees and Canada's compassion" (78). Through the act, Canada's involvement in the war is transformed into that of a peacemaker rather than an enabler of violence. In this context, the appearance of Vietnamese refugees within Canadian borders, and their expressions of gratitude during the commemoration ceremony sanctioned by the state, is further proof of Canadian benevolence, which becomes a national and naturalized characteristic. As Vietnamese refugees find a sense of identity through commemorative memories of persecution and demands for human rights, the Canadian nation fortifies itself as a haven of rights and freedoms.

While commemoration work is concerned with memory and remembrance, the "peaceable kingdom" image that Canada cultivates also requires strategic forms of forgetting for it to take shape.[13] The remembering of Vietnamese refugees in official state legislation such as Bill S-219 or public commemoration ceremonies including the fortieth anniversary are forms of "mimed" remembrance that forget some memories by way of remembering others.[14] In celebrating the extension of refuge to Vietnamese subjects displaced by war, Canada can turn away from the violence it has enacted within its own borders: the mass displacement and genocide of Indigenous populations in the early years of the nation's "founding" as well as contemporary forms of settler colonialism, and the relocation and internment of Japanese Canadians during the Second World War are but two examples. Furthermore, such celebrations of an exceptional time when Canadian borders were open to refugees from Asia obscure the times when the Canadian border was categorically shut to racialized others: the Chinese head tax, the Komagata Maru incident, the MV *Sun Sea* incident, and the MS *St. Louis* incident, to name a few. The narrative of Canadian benevolence and generosity, exemplified in the case of Southeast Asian refugees from the Vietnam War, has a larger function in relegating moments of national ungenerosity, of racism, violence, and failed humanitarian ideals, to the past and the margins of memory. The human rights grievances directed at Vietnam by former Vietnamese refugees cum Canadian citizens help obscure a less-than-spotless human rights record for Canada.

## Human Rights and the Question of Refugees

In his essay titled "Illegible Humanity," Bishupal Limbu inquires, "If social death is reserved for someone who is less than or other than human, where do we situate the refugee? Is the refugee included in the human? Can the refugee claim 'human' rights?" (278). He goes on to explain that "one cannot take for granted the transparency and self-evidence of the human when figures of apparent humanity such as the refugee remain illegible in the conceptual and representational scheme" (278). Similarly, Giorgio Agamben writes that "the figure that should have embodied human rights more than any other—namely, the refugee—marked instead the radical crisis of the concept. . . . In the system of the nation-state, so-called sacred and inalienable human rights are revealed to be without any protection precisely when it is no longer possible to conceive of them as rights of the citizen of a state" (92). While the refugee is our most stark figure of humanity, because he or she is stripped of the political-juridical rights of nationality and reduced to what Agamben calls "naked life," the refugee also calls into question human rights as a framework for social and political organization. Human rights, then, cannot guarantee humanity without the nation-state system and thus fail the refugee and the fundamental concepts of man and rights. The refugee's oscillation between "human" and "nonhuman" within this framework brings into sharp relief the limits of a world system based on rights, revealing how the "humanity" of human rights is not inalienable or universal but constrained by the prior existence of other political and legal categories of personhood.

I suggest, however—and the April 30, 2015, commemoration event in Ottawa demonstrates—that if in becoming a refugee a human loses rights and thus becomes less than human within the representational scheme of citizenship, rights, and nationality, then the regime of human rights is one legitimate recourse through which to (re)gain rights and, thus, humanity. Of course, this humanity defined through rights is a reenfoldment into what Liisa Malkki calls the "national order of things," or a liberal-capitalist status quo where nationalism reigns. The refugee accepts and proves the biopolitical power of state sovereignty to grant life and political subjectivity (or take them away). In becoming subjects (again), refugees are subjected to the terms of a structure that has been at the root of producing modern-day refugee crises. Following Chandan Reddy, we might call this humanity "with violence," whereby humanity is contingent on subscription to and acceptance of conditions of violence, displacement, and exclusion as part and parcel of social life. Yet history has shown that refugees can and do lay claims to human rights as a means of reentering the political-juridical order of the nation-state. Nationality's protection, however problematic, is often a coveted "gift" for those who find themselves in materially precarious and dire situations—who must fight to stay alive. Although this desire for reincorporation into the nation-state framework may be seen as a flattening of the critical potential of the refugee condition to challenge and reimagine political life, it is in many instances crucial for material survival and the possibility of surviving.

It is often easy for critics to dismiss refugees' subscription to and deployment of liberal ideologies and mechanisms such as freedom, human rights, and gratitude as politically naive or potentially complicit with normative structures of power. But to seriously engage how and why they call upon something like human rights reveals the complex forces, tensions, and negotiations at play in actually lived lives. While the concept of human rights is flawed and even violent in its constitution, it is at the same time a useful discourse for former refugees to make sense of their refuge seeking and to structure a narrative of their diasporic existence. The various agendas that these narratives support are, of course, not above critique; indeed, the conservatism and nationalism at play when Vietnamese refugees in Canada gather to commemorate the "Fall of Saigon" places limits around community and identity, serving particular ethnic and national ends. I have attempted in this chapter to re-present and analyze viewpoints and actions that do not necessarily reflect my own political commitments or beliefs; yet I insist that these commitments and beliefs deserve consideration for what they can tell us about the contexts in which Vietnamese refugees endeavor to find a place in history and politics.

If refugees are rendered socially dead, the Vietnamese Canadian case that I have discussed shows it is possible to recover life and legibility through human rights grievances, insofar as political possibilities in the present are still constrained by the "national order of things." Through human rights discourse, expressions of condemnation, grievance, and gratitude serve and support various ideological constructions of refuge, rights, and nation; they reveal the deep and intertwined link between refuge(es) and human rights. Vietnamese refugees, understood here more capaciously than in the UN legal definition, employ human rights to shed light on a past of forced migration and a future with rights and, in the process, a humanity that exists in the embodied present.

## NOTES

An earlier version of this chapter, titled "Commemorating Freedom: The Fortieth Anniversary of the 'Fall of Saigon' in Canada," appeared in *Canadian Review of American Studies* 48.3 (2018).

1. The author was present to observe this commemoration event. The subsequent descriptions of the scenes, activities, and speeches are taken from his field notes, photographs, and recordings.

2. The third banner was written in Vietnamese and read, "Người Việt Khắp Thế Giới Quyết Tâm Tranh Đấu Cho Tự Do & Nhân Quyền Tại Việt Nam."

3. I call them "prominent" in the sense that they subscribe to the dominant, anticommunist politics of Vietnamese diasporic communities, and as a result, they are most publically visible within the community as well as to the Canadian mainstream. Moreover, many of these members hold various leadership roles in Vietnamese Canadian community organizations and associations.

4. For a discussion of the grateful refugee, see my article "Refugee Gratitude."

5. Throughout this paper, I conflate "refugee" and "former refugee" intentionally and use them interchangeably. I do this because former refugees are often regarded as refugees in mainstream discussions through a discourse of "perpetual refugees" and, more importantly, to gesture to the situation whereby the condition or experience of being a refugee might not end when the legal designation is lifted. This points to the significance of "refugee" in putatively "post"-refugee life.

6. Public memory overwhelmingly remembers these refugees as being solely Vietnamese, forgetting that the sixty thousand resettled refugees also consisted of Cambodians, Laotians, and Hmongs. This is a symptom of the larger amnesia around the participation and suffering of non-Vietnamese peoples during and after the war. See Um.

7. At the time of writing, the construction of the memorial is still ongoing. Shortly after the Liberal Party took power after the 2015 federal election, the building site of the memorial was moved to the Gardens of the Provinces and Territories, close to Parliament but away from the previously agreed-upon location in between the Supreme Court and the Library and Archives Canada Building. In February 2016, the government conducted an online public survey to "offer feedback on the size, 'desired emotional reaction,' and 'visitor experience' of the monument" (Canadian Broadcasting Corporation) in a redesign effort. See also Butler.

8. The mission statement from the Tribute to Liberty official website reads, "Tribute to Liberty (TTL), established in 2008, is a Canadian charity whose mission is to establish a Canadian memorial to commemorate the victims of Communism. TTL is governed by a nine-member volunteer board of directors who represent key ethno-cultural communities in Canada affected by Communism. In September 2009, the National Capital Commission (NCC) granted approval to TTL to build a memorial called The Memorial to the Victims of Communism—Canada, a Land of Refuge in the National Capital Region" ("About Us").

9. For a thorough discussion of human rights' rise in prominence during the Cold War era, see Foot.

10. In Canada, Senator Ngo has been at the forefront of protesting Vietnam's human rights abuses, particularly its imprisonment of political dissidents and peaceful human rights activists. In a report commissioned by his office, the senator's work is described as follows:

> Since his appointment as Canada's first senator originally from Vietnam, Senator Ngo has consistently campaigned for human rights for Vietnam. First he visited different Vietnamese communities all over Canada, ensuring that the voices of the Vietnamese diaspora have not been forgotten. Senator Ngo tabled a "Million Hearts, One Voice" petition (spearheaded by Mr. Truc Ho) in the Senate to call on the Canadian government to request Vietnam's release individuals [*sic*] who have been engaged in peaceful activism for their country. Both Prime Minister Stephen Harper and Senator Ngo delivered a speech at the Toronto Tết Festival emphasizing Canada's unwavering stance on the values of the rule of law and fundamental freedoms while maintaining ties with Vietnam. (Office of Senator Thanh Hai Ngo 36)

11. The second placard was written in Vietnamese and read, "Cám Ơn Canada: Chúng tôi ủng hộ Đạo Luật Hành Trình Tìm Tự Do của Chính Phủ Canada."

12. The Vietnamese Canadian community at large was not unanimous in their wholesale support of the bill. Anh Ngo writes, "Vietnamese-Canadians took to websites, media, and a community listserv to also express their reluctance in supporting this bill in its entirety, proposing instead the date Canada officially committed to admitting 50,000 Indochinese refugees: July 27, 1979 (Senate Committee, April 1, 2015, p.6)" (65).

13. For an elaboration of the "peaceable kingdom" myth, see Ziedenberg.

14. I borrow this idea of a mimed remembrance from Nguyễn-võ. In the U.S. context, she writes that America remembers Vietnam by forgetting the very people "who were the main participants and victims of that history—Vietnamese from North and South, and Vietnamese diasporics including Vietnamese Americans . . . [America] mimes acts of remembering by way of an amnesiac memory" (158).

## WORKS CITED

"About Us." *Tribute to Liberty*. Web. 12 April 2016.

Agamben, Giorgio. "Beyond Human Rights." *Social Engineering* 15 (2008): 90–95.

"Bill S-219 (Historical)." *openparliament.ca*. Web. 26 June 2016.

Butler, Dan. "Victims of Communism Memorial to Be Moved, Joly Announces." *Ottawa Citizen*. 17 December 2015. Web. 10 April 2016.

Canadian Broadcasting Corporation. "Government Seeks Feedback on Memorial to Victims of Communism." *CBC* News. 2 February 2016. Web. 28 June 2016.

"Convention and Protocol Relating to the Status of Refugees." *United Nations High Commissioner for Refugees*. http://www.unhcr.org/3b66c2aa10. 17 September 2017.

Duong, Lan, and Isabelle Thuy Pelaud. "Vietnamese American Art and Community Politics: An Engaged Feminist Perspective." *Journal of Asian American Studies* 15.3 (2012): 241–269.

Engler, Yves. *The Black Book of Canadian Foreign Policy*. Black Point, NS: Fernwood, 2009.

Espiritu, Yến Lê. *Body Counts: The Vietnam War and Militarized Refuge(es)*. Oakland: University of California Press, 2014.

———. "The 'We-Win-Even-if-We-Lose' Syndrome: U.S. Press Coverage of the Twenty-Fifth Anniversary of the 'Fall of Saigon.'" *American Quarterly* 58.2 (2006): 329–352.

Foot, Rosemary. "The Cold War and Human Rights." *The Cambridge History of the Cold War, Volume III: Endings*. Ed. Melvyn P. Leffler and Odd Arne Westad. Cambridge: Cambridge University Press, 2010. 445–465.

Hathaway, James C., and Michelle Foster. *The Law of Refugee Status*. Cambridge: Cambridge University Press, 2014.

Levant, Victor. *Quiet Complicity: Canadian Involvement in the Vietnam War*. Toronto: Between the Lines, 1986.

Limbu, Bishupal. "Illegible Humanity: The Refugee, Human Rights, and the Question of Representation." *Journal of Refugee Studies* 22.3 (2009): 257–282.

Lui, Andrew. *Why Canada Cares: Human Rights and Foreign Policy in Theory and Practice*. Montreal: McGill-Queens University Press, 2009.

Mackrael, Kim. "Vietnam 'Hurt' by Senate Bill Commemorating 'Black April Day.'" *Globe and Mail*. 4 February 2015. Web. 10 March 2016.

Madokoro, Laura. "History as Rhetoric: Indochina and Contemporary Refugee Crises." *ActiveHistory*. 28 May 2015. Web. 1 September 2016.

Malkki, Liisa H. "Refugees and Exile: From 'Refugee Studies' to the National Order of Things." *Annual Review of Anthropology* 24.1 (1995): 495–523.

Molloy, James, et al. *Running on Empty: Canada and the Indochinese Refugees, 1975–1980*. Montreal: McGill-Queens University Press, 2017.

Ngo, Anh. "'Journey to Freedom Day Act': The Making of the Vietnamese Subject in Canada and the Erasure of the Vietnam War." *Canadian Review of Social Policy / Revue canadienne de politique sociale* 75 (2016): 59–86.

Nguyen, Mimi Thi. *The Gift of Freedom: War, Debt, and Other Refugee Passages*. Durham, NC: Duke University Press, 2012.

Nguyen, Viet Thanh. "Refugee Memories and Asian American Critique." *positions: asia critique* 20.3 (2012): 911–942.

Nguyen, Vinh. "Refugee Gratitude: Narrating 'Success' and Intersubjectivity in Kim Thúy's *Ru*." *Canadian Literature* 219 (2013): 17–36.

Nguyễn-võ, Thu-hương. "Forking Paths: How Shall We Mourn the Dead?" *Amerasia Journal* 31.2 (2005): 157–175.

Office of Senator Thanh Hai Ngo. "Vietnam Human Rights Report, 2012–2013." Ottawa.

Robinson, W. Courtland. *Terms of Refuge: The Indochinese Exodus and the International Response*. London: Zed, 1998.

"Statement by Senator Ngo on the Adoption of Journey to Freedom Day Bill in the Senate." senatorngo.ca. Web. 12 April 2016.

Stern, Steve J. "Memory: The Curios History of a Cultural Code Word." *Radical History Review* 124 (2016): 117–128.

Um, Khatharya. "The 'Vietnam War': What's in a Name?" *Amerasia Journal* 31.2 (2005): 134–139.

"Vietnam." *Human Rights Watch*. https://www.hrw.org/asia/vietnam. 17 September 2017.

Vo Dang, Thuy. "The Cultural Work of Anticommunism in the San Diego Vietnamese American Community." *Amerasia Journal* 31.2 (2005): 65–86.

"Why a Memorial? Why in Canada?" *Tribute to Liberty*. Web. 12 April 2016.

Ziedenberg, Jason. "Canada's Vietnam Legacy." *Canadian Dimension* 29.5 (1995): 24–28.

# PART II

## Impossible Subjects

*Race, Gender, and Labor*

# 5

# "Every Bombed Village Is My Hometown"

## *James Baldwin's Engagement with the American War in Vietnam*

YIN WANG

To scholars of the black freedom struggle, the American War in Vietnam marks a time of disillusionment and anguish that proves the U.S. government's disregard of the Geneva Accords, the inadequacy of civil political rights to bring African Americans justice, and the impracticality of asking the United Nations (UN) to stop American wars. When Lyndon B. Johnson signed the Voting Rights Act into law in 1965, he also began systemic bombing in North Vietnam and committed to an unprecedented expansion of the U.S. ground forces. Martin Luther King played a pivotal role in condemning the war's immoral basis and its worrisome consequences, while the Student Nonviolent Coordinating Committee (SNCC) became the most vocal antiwar organization after 1966. Grieved by the brutal murder of Samuel Younge Jr., a black veteran killed when trying to use a white bathroom at a gas station, the SNCC demanded that the federal government act immediately to address the escalating causalities in Vietnam and racial injustices in all American social domains. After Richard Nixon took office, civil rights workers continued to demand a cease-fire and threatened to report cases of racial injustice to the UN Commission on Human Rights. However, since the UN had already in 1947 declined to intervene in the subjugation of African Americans, grassroots activists developed their tactics in the "human rights phase" of the long civil rights movement for economic and social equality.[1]

This essay traces esteemed African American writer James Baldwin's engagement with the American War in Vietnam as an effort to understand the circumstances of rights deprivation in black America and to respond to the disproportionally low presence of black experiences in the mainstream

American memory of the Vietnam War.[2] Since 2014, James Baldwin's searing critique of the social, political, and juridical racisms against African Americans in the United States has undergone a phenomenal revival, largely because many the problems he addressed and challenged half a century ago remain unsolved or unsolvable.[3] However, while he has been generally cited and celebrated as a legendary icon in the mid-twentieth-century black freedom struggles, what has not always been carefully remembered is that he made quite different criticisms of the U.S. government and society at different points of time. His work in the 1950s was largely autobiographical, where he lays bare his experience of growing up in poverty with astonishing candor. In the words of Cheryl Wall, he employed "strategic American exceptionalism" to demand social change and was successful in a variety of respects.[4] Baldwin's memoirs about the civil rights movement and the following decades in the United States were much more pessimistic, sometimes to the extent of being bitter, as he combed the dynamics and the backlashes of the movement he observed during his extensive travels in the American South, on the West Coast, and in Western Europe. Since the late 1960s, his attacks on the U.S. government, his tension with Black Nationalist leaders, and his qualitatively uneven literary productions brought him out of public attention for a long time. Critics tend to assess his work as "the early Baldwin" and "the later Baldwin"; the common framing is that he became too politicized or that he became too eager to push forward his agenda, so that his work became repetitive and monotonous.

However, when exactly does "the later Baldwin" period begin? Baldwin's work had always been mobilized by political messages, but it was not until he condemned the Johnson administration's policies on Vietnam that he spoke more in the voice of a revolutionary than that of a reformer. What were the reasons for this change? How did he position himself and black America with regard to Vietnam? Since he began criticizing the U.S. war in Vietnam around 1966, a time when most of the general American public supported the war and believed they would win, how did he explain that opinion of the American majority (in square opposition to his own)? Moreover, as he continued to oppose the war well into the 1970s, with a persistent concern over the destruction American wars in Asia caused to black America, how did his novels produced in this period further reveal the rationales of his political pursuit?

This chapter looks at Baldwin's criticism of the U.S. government and society regarding the American War in Vietnam, with a focus on how he developed a new political vision for black America that is antiassimilation, antiorientalism, and (to borrow the term of Manning Marable) "tranformationist." My analysis develops along three axes. First, although he had been commonly viewed as a pacifist in the civil rights movement, Baldwin openly and unambiguously denounced the war before many civil rights groups, including even Dr. Martin Luther King, declared their position. His opposition to the American War in Vietnam revealed his identification with black power organizations in the late 1960s. By extending Malcolm X's opposition to the war, Baldwin juxtaposed black America, Native America, and Vietnam as internal and external colonies of the United States, subjected to economic-military oppression and deprived of the political right of self-determination. The second section of this chapter compares Baldwin's critique of the orientalist American lens on Asia and Asians during the Cold War and the concurrent Hollywood racism in misrepresenting and disrepresenting black American experience. Baldwin's analysis of the general American public's objectifying sympathy with Asians must be paired with his analysis of the American denial of black humanity and black struggle, so that we may gain a comparative view of how Asians and black Americans are displaced from their lives and worlds to become dehumanized symbols in war rhetoric (which circulates and causes influences beyond specific wars). Baldwin criticized the American mainstream media's coverage of Asians for being frequently premised on a patronizing, sentimental, and eroticizing outlook. Four years later, he almost made a parallel observation of Hollywood's representation of black women, where a similarly patronizing, sentimental, and eroticizing perspective not only dominates but distorts the life stories they proclaim to objectively present. Hence while sentimental representations of Asians stimulated Americans readers' sympathy and support for the "anticommunist war," sentimental cinematic representations of struggling black Americans suppressed and eclipsed the truth of their plight. The final section explores how Baldwin maps out the relationship between several American wars in Asia and the losses suffered by black America. In his essays and novels produced in the Vietnam War period, Baldwin brings to the fore how economic and juridical segregations in the United States have made working-class African American men the nation's unacknowledged precariats. That is, the American wars in Japan, Korea, and Vietnam took the most disadvantaged youths of the nation to kill and destroy Asian towns, bombing Asians to freedom. By teasing out the internal struggles of black veterans and their loved ones, Baldwin not only returns to his earlier thematic concentration on love as the only viable redemption for the American tragedy of race and racism but also indicates the need to move beyond the bipolar black/white model of race relations in grasping the evolving scenes of racial stratification in the United States.

## Addressing the American War in Vietnam "as an American Negro"

On Wednesday February 24, 1965, James Baldwin paid a public visit to the British philosopher Bertrand Russell at his house in London and exchanged thoughts with Russell on racial relations in the United States. It was less than three days after Malcolm X was shot to death at a public rally in Harlem. Baldwin was in London to launch a novel. When he was asked by the press to comment on Malcolm X's assassination, he told them while there might be just one man that committed the crime, "the entire Western white supremacy forged the bullet" (*No Name* 115). Having expressed on several occasions that antiblack racism was as pervasive in Europe as in the United States, Baldwin chose to frame the assassination not as an isolated incident in New York but rather as a brutal result of the fear of black political uprisings ingrained in the modern Western psyche.[5] His host, Bertrand Russell, was then devoting himself to opposing the global expansion of U.S. military power, for which he made persistent efforts to meet and correspond with Vietnamese artists, activists, scholars, and journalists who had witnessed the catastrophic U.S. military maneuvers on the ground. Although the conversation between Baldwin and Russell was not fully disclosed to the public, it could be said that they concurred in fighting the racial logic of America's power. In the next year, when Russell founded a "people's tribunal" against the U.S. war crimes in Vietnam, Baldwin was listed as one of the founding members, along with Jean-Paul Sartre and Simone de Beauvoir. Their idea was to set up an unprecedented independent international court of justice without the backing or intervention of any single nation-state.

James Baldwin published "The International War Crimes Tribunal" in the radical African American journal *Freedomways* in fall 1967 to publicize his support for Bertrand Russell. In a statement that bears clear imprints of Malcolm X's "The Ballot or the Bullet" speech, Baldwin declares his moral support for the cause and even proposes that the trial be held in Harlem. To this transnational antiwar movement, Baldwin provides an elucidation of the internal racial division of the United States under the facade of a unified nation:

> I speak as an American Negro. I challenge anyone alive to tell me why any black American should go into those jungles to kill people who are not white and who have never done them any harm. . . . I challenge anyone alive to convince me that a people who have not achieved anything resembling freedom are empowered, with bombs, to free another people whom they do not know at all. I challenge any American, and especially Mr. Lyndon Johnson and Mr. Hubert Humphrey and Mr. Dean Rusk and Mr. Robert McNamara, to tell me, and the black population of the United States, how, if they cannot liberate their brothers—repeat: *brothers*—and have not even learned to live with them, they intend to liberate Southeast Asia. I challenge them to tell me by what right, and in whose interest, they presume to police the world, and I furthermore want to know if they

> would like their sisters, or their daughters to marry any one of the people they are struggling so mightily to save. And this is not a rhetorical question. . . . I want an answer: If I am to die, I have the right to know why. (246–247; emphasis in original)

Echoing King's same-year statement on "the interrelatedness of racism and militarism and the need to attack both problems rather than leaving one" ("Dr. King"), Baldwin condemns the U.S. government for its use of the lowest racial caste of the country to prey on an exploited Asian colony. The question Baldwin asks is simple: How could those who have denied the humanity of their kin at home risk their lives to save a people whom they do not know? The answer is clear: The self-appointed crusaders are probably not being sincere, and they are probably not risking their own lives for such task. Countering the American propaganda of the Vietnam War as a noble crusade, Baldwin recast the scenario into one of an imperial nation dispossessing its disposable subjects to destroy a presumably weak enemy.

After questioning America's unfulfilled promise of liberating black men and women, he draws on the provocative comparison of black America, Native America, and Vietnam: "Long, long before the Americans decided to liberate the Southeast Asians, they decided to liberate me: my ancestors carried these scars to the grave, and so will I. A racist society can't but fight a racist war—this is the bitter truth. The assumptions acted on at home are also acted on abroad, and every American Negro knows this, for he, after the American Indian, was the first 'Vietcong' victim. We were bombed first" (248). Baldwin situates the American idea of liberation as an expansive catalogue of violence. In a time when the state propaganda framed Vietnamese peasants as potential communist spies or suicide bombers, Baldwin reminded readers that, for centuries, black Americans and Native Americans had been similarly smeared and unjustifiably mistreated as enemies to the nation. By comparing Native Americans and black Americans to "the first 'Vietcong' victim," Baldwin shows the American idea of war for freedom is not a new invention in the mid-twentieth century, and it must be viewed with discretion, especially its danger of generating lies and terror, within and beyond the U.S. border.

In addition, Baldwin emphasizes in the statement that the American decision of "liberating the Vietnamese" is meant to revoke the political decision the Vietnamese made for themselves—in this case, of building a communist society. He denounces the U.S. war in Vietnam as a war in contradiction to the principle of self-determination:

> The American War in Vietnam raises several questions. One is whether or not small nations, in this age of superstates and superpowers, will be allowed to work out their own destinies and live as

> they feel they should. For only the people of a county have the right, or the spiritual power, to determine that country's way of life. Another question this war raises is just how what we call the underdeveloped countries became underdeveloped in the first place. Why, for example, is Africa underdeveloped, and why do the resources of, say, Sierra Leone belong to Europe? Why, in short, does much of the world eat too little and so little of the world eat too much? (247–248)

While Malcolm X in his "Ballot or Bullet" speech criticizes the United States "minding somebody else's business way over in South Vietnam," Baldwin elaborates that argument to remind his readers of how U.S. hegemony, through the global Cold War, deprived "small nations" of their right to self-determination and therefore perpetuated colonialist exploitation in Africa and Asia. Baldwin's political turn, or radical turn, at this point can be seen as an effort to continue Malcolm X's vision of building a transnational coalition of black America and the third world.

Vietnam was being devastatingly bombed as members of the Russell Tribunal used various platforms to protest against the escalating warfare. Since its establishment, the campaign received mixed press coverage in Europe but was largely blocked out of public attention in the United States due to governmental intervention. Despite its intended imitation of the Nuremberg Tribunals, in the end it was carried out more as an event to attract broader attention than as a legal experiment that truly sought to try the heads of the United States as "war criminals." Sartre presided over the Stockholm session in April 1967 and announced in the verdict that the United States was launching a "genocide" against the Vietnamese. Both the Tokyo session in August and the Denmark session in November publicized an unprecedented amount of evidence of violence, committed individually and institutionally, by the U.S. military in Vietnam. While the verdicts reached predictable conclusions, the "trial" sessions released a large amount of unheard, horrendous evidence of wartime cruelty from Vietnamese and American testifiers. In the United States, the Johnson administration was angered by the tribunal's attempt to shame the U.S. military and ordered mainstream U.S. media, including the *New York Times* and *New York Magazine*, to minimize their coverage of the tribunal and spawn problematic images of Russell and his aides as deceived communist sympathizers.[6]

## The Figure of the Victim

In May 1970, Baldwin did a series of interviews with Turkish filmmaker Sedat Pakay in Istanbul, where he discussed how the general American public's views of Asia and Asians authorized Kennedy and Johnson to launch the war in Vietnam.[7] In the interviews, he located the general American public's tacit sanction of the war as a result of middlebrow Americans' views of Asians as a pitiable inferior race and of Asia as a premodern lawless land. He characterized middlebrow American readers of such stories as credulous, self-righteous, but in fact manipulated minds holding "the rest of the world" in contempt:

> American ignorance . . . is not the ignorance of the peasant. . . . What do you do with the people who are ignorant in the way Americans are ignorant? Who believe they can read, and read the *Reader's Digest*, *Time Magazine*, *The Daily News*; who think that's reading; who think they know something about the rest of the world because they think they are better than the rest of the world, better than the other countries in the world, and really cannot not [*sic*], really have no respect for language, because they cannot read, which means they cannot think. (Fortuny 437)

Baldwin compared the predominantly white, middle-class or lower-middle-class readers of popular anticommunist magazines to those "benevolent" readers of the sentimental novel *Uncle Tom's Cabin* a century ago. He explained that, in spite of their superficial condemnation of slavery or communism as an ultimate evil, the ignorant middlebrow American readers remained incapable of imagining the humanity of the oppressed, because the oppressed were always shown as submissive, inarticulate, infantile cardboard figures. Perhaps as a longtime beneficiary of United States Information Agency sponsorship, Baldwin had an insider's knowledge about the political infiltration of popular stories that the major consumers of American popular culture had no sensibility to detect. His diachronic analysis of self-centered white middlebrow American readers reveals clearly how reading habits of racial difference exacerbates racist ideologies.

Also in the interviews with Sedat Pakay, Baldwin condemned the propagandist framing of the war in Vietnam as a charitable mission to export the "American Way of Life" to Southeast Asia. Baldwin calls it "a new kind of totalitarianism which doesn't call itself that" (447) and a modern version of the so-called Manifest Destiny (446). Baldwin's view that the white-centered American middle class have unashamedly prided themselves on being rich, right, and willing to help "the lesser races of the world" (446) after the United States rose to the world's strongest superpower can be corroborated by Christina Klein's analysis of American popular culture from 1945 to 1961, a time when Asian subjects were vigorously represented along two complementary ideological axes that confirmed the United States as a global nonimperial power and the new center of the world: "the global imaginary of containment" and "the global imaginary of integration" (23). While the former "imagined the Cold War as a crusade against communism," Klein finds, the latter proposed "a model of sentimental education" that encouraged Americans to "look outward" and "forge intellectual and emotional bonds with the people of Asia and Africa" (23).[8] Baldwin suggested that the extraordinary success of Henry Luce's *Time-Life* empire determined the way American middlebrows looked at Asia and the war in Vietnam.[9] To his Turkish interviewer, Baldwin added that the mythical "American Way of Life" had never been made available to all Americans, let alone Asians: "Speaking as a black man, I know what this way of life costs these people who are not really considered to be part of it, who are considered to be a kind of fuel for it, a kind of beast of burden for it" (447). In other words, he presented the "American Way of Life" as the foundation of the American middlebrows' self-image and their phantasmic relationship to "the rest of the world."

From Baldwin's perspective, as American middlebrows assigned Asians the status of an inferior race through sentimental narratives of "Asia," they simultaneously enjoyed watching movies about black Americans as another inferior race struggling for accomplishment and recognition but often to little avail. The critical difference between these two cultural forces is that while stories about Asian subjects were overwhelmingly tragic and pitiable, cinematic representations of black American subjects were usually formulaic tragic romances that replaced the painful true stories on which the movies were based. This is what Baldwin argues in his essay collection *The Devil Finds Work*, that the numerous Hollywood movies centered on African American talents in the late 1960s actually "make black experience irrelevant and obsolete" (105). In the book, he analyzes how the biopic of Billie Holiday, *Lady Sings the Blues*, is a thoroughly problematic product in its betrayal of Holiday's autobiography and its reluctance to show the many compelling scenes of social injustice Holiday's autobiography has laid bare. He comments,

> [The off-screen Billie Holiday] was much stronger than this film can have any interesting in indicating, and, as a victim, infinitely more complex. . . . The film cannot accept—because it cannot use—this simplicity. That victim who is able to articulate the situation of the victim has ceased to be a victim: he, or she, has become a threat.
>
> The victim's testimony must, therefore, be altered. (114)

As a lifelong moviegoer and once a hired scriptwriter in Hollywood, Baldwin points out that commercial American films would not deal with Billie Holiday's experience with violence and exploitation in American society first and foremost because they wanted to comfort, rather than discomfort, the audience. These biopics and cinematic fictions (such as *Guess Who's Coming to Dinner?*) show black American talents failing as individuals, typically with unwise life decisions or lack of good luck, while in reality most of them were hit by deliberate suppression or destruction due to structural social factors. This is dehumanization; this is not so much dehumanization for sympathy (as the case with dominant representations of "Asians") as dehumanization for denial (in the long history of posttruth white nationalist contentions). It is worth noting that in the final pages of *The Devil Finds Work*, Baldwin predicts that such normative, purposeful blindness to the oppressed will one day prompt the racialized minorities under American governance—including the Vietnamese—to act with vengeance.

Baldwin's reference to both black Americans and Vietnamese in *The Devil Finds Work* is thought provoking. It transcends or progressively transforms traditional parameters of identity politics. The violence of institutional denial, as occasioned by the films he analyzes, binds people of the internal colony and the external colony under American rule. Together, they point to larger, structural problems of the Cold War–conditioned, transcontinental America that seems to be constantly fighting multiple wars—declared and undeclared—at once.

## Hardly Part of the Nation, Always Part of the War

Although Baldwin's essays and novels produced after 1965 have long been regarded as less successful than his earlier works, I would like to emphasize that they counter black American communities' experience with their loveless country with tangible, physical, category-defiant interpersonal love. For instance, *Tell Me How Long the Train's Been Gone* (1968) tells the story of a pair of black American brothers whose courses of life are changed by the Second World War. The older brother, Caleb, is a reticent, bitter black veteran and a minister willfully withdrawn from society after the Second World War. He has joined the army because of the poverty of his family and his record of some minor offense when he was underage. He is embittered by the segregation in the military and confused by the commands of blind slaughter they received and executed. The younger brother, Leo, is a black actor who has little faith in the U.S. government and the white-centered U.S. society. He lied to Harlem's draft board to escape military service and went off home to pursue his artistic career. On the day after the Japanese surrender, Leo and his white female lover are stopped by a jubilant old white woman who invites them to share her joy over the triumph. While Leo's mind is occupied by the atrocity of nuclear bombing, he suddenly finds them joined by several other excited passersby, who look at him with "a profound distrust" and examine his girl with "a disapproving wonder." The couple leaves before they have to endure more curious gazes in the small celebration on the street. Through their respective journeys, Caleb and Leo show different reactions to their position as racialized subcitizens in their native country.[10] Caleb fights in a war he does not believe in and turns to religion to seek relief from his self-reproach. Leo escapes a war he does not believe in, but the tacitly racist imperative of American patriotism allows him no escape in his native city. Although this novel addresses the Second World War rather than the Vietnam War, its date of publication suggests the allegorical function of the story.

As a son of Harlem, Baldwin did not perceive the destruction caused by the American War in Vietnam through newspaper headlines but felt and witnessed it through people he knew from Harlem and from similar communities. In *No Name in the Street* (1970), his first memoir about the civil rights movement, Baldwin recounts an indicative anecdote of his fight with a childhood friend who, in spite of his loss of a brother in the Second World War and his family's infinite struggle against poverty, supported the U.S. government's decision on fighting the war in Vietnam. Baldwin's confrontation against him reveals his angry disapproval and saddened pain for their community:

> I was astounded that my friend would defend this particular racist folly. What for? For his job at the post office? And the answer came back at once, alas—yes. . . . I told him that Americans had no business at all in Vietnam; and that black people certainly had no business there, aiding the slave master to enslave yet more millions of dark people, and also identifying themselves with the white American crimes: we, the blacks. . . . It wasn't, I said, hard to understand why a black boy, standing, futureless, on the corner, would decide to join the Army, nor was it hard to decipher the slave master's reasons for hoping that he wouldn't live to come home, with a gun; but it wasn't necessary, after all, to defend it: to defend, that is, one's murder and one's murderers. "Wait a minute," he said, "let me stand up and tell you what I think we're trying to do there." "*We*?" I cried, "what motherfucking *we*?" (17–18; emphasis in original)

While Baldwin fiercely reprimands the American War in Vietnam as "a racist folly" that pushes young black men from urban ghettos to a fatal war that causes countless deaths among Vietnamese and themselves, his friend sees the situation as an unfortunate yet profitable occasion for some unprecedented integration of black labor in the nation's social arena. As the only surviving child of his parents, Baldwin's old-time friend, now a low-ranking post office worker, exhausts himself in earning barely enough bread for his family and is sustained by his humble dream of getting his family out of the shabby apartment and darkly deteriorating neighborhood he was born into. To him, Baldwin's protest against the war sounds like a luxurious sentiment of idealism. On the other hand, Baldwin's long, vehement speech reveals his anxiety and his rage against this friend who, in his eyes, has unnecessarily traded himself for an illusory bait. Baldwin gives no time to his friend's explanation, it seems to me, not because he does not understand what his friend has to say or the daily humiliating battle he fights but because he knows too well what his friend has to say, and he does not want to listen to it. Baldwin's regrets about his rudeness to his friend later that night reveal his shame as a crowned celebrity and the distance he now has from his native community.

Finally, his 1974 novel *If Beale Street Could Talk* presents military service as a common but indescribable experience among black American men in Harlem, an experience that takes a large portion of their youth but does not guarantee better opportunities for them or their community.[11] Fighting wars in Asia becomes a common path to adulthood for children of the urban ghetto. The heroine Tish grows up seeing boys of her age in the community going to war. Her father has worked as a seaman to avoid being drafted for the Korean War, but black Americans of her generation are given far fewer employment opportunities to move upward financially. At the same time, returning black veterans can be found all the time at bars and on the street, usually drinking and chatting among themselves with distraught apprehension about their future, as many menial jobs have been taken by Puerto Ricans and other immigrants during their absence. This novel shows that "Latinization" of big American cities accelerates as more and more black American men depart—to wars, to prison, or under the needle. The competition and friction between black Americans and Caribbean migrant workers culminate in the novel with Tish's boyfriend, Fonny, being falsely identified and indicted as a rapist of a Puerto Rican migrant worker. When Tish's entire family strives to find the victim and begs her to drop the false accusation, she rejects their request and, at the brink of a total breakdown, insists her injury is the sum of all the cruelties she has undergone during her stay and must be paid back by American citizens on behalf of their country. The ending of Fonny serving as a scapegoat for his country—which has never offered him anything but the draft—evidences black America's peculiar vulnerability in a time of consumptive wars in foreign lands and systemic importation of low-paid laborers.

## Conclusion

This essay has examined James Baldwin's political opposition to and cultural analysis of the U.S. war in Vietnam. In his support of Bertrand Russell's civil tribunal against the U.S. war crimes in Vietnam, Baldwin advances Malcolm X's vision of building interracial and transnational coalitions to end the injustices endured by black Americans and peoples of the African diaspora. His parallel reference to black America, Native America, and Vietnam as internal and external colonies of the United States, as well as his exposition of the American War in Vietnam's contradiction to the principle of self-determination, reveals his philosophical affection for the black power movement. As for the general American public's racializing logic after the Second World War, Baldwin sees among Americans a condescending compassion toward the presumably vulnerable and pitiable "Asians" on the one hand and a persistent refusal to come to terms with black American precarity under the nation's racial stratification on the other. He takes the American majority's emotive support for the "Vietnam War" in the mid-1960s as the result of the state's propaganda success through nongovernmental avenues. At the same time, he hastens to take Hollywood's problematic representation and straight distortion of black Americans as revealing evidence of American popular culture's denial of black humanity after the civil rights movement. Finally, the fictional texts Baldwin published in the Vietnam War period flesh out the damages caused by America wars in Asia to black America. His cross-racial investigations of economic, political, juridical, and social injustices in the United States illuminate his commitment to racial politics based on transformative rather than self-interested principles.

## NOTES

1. Several other studies point to this same conclusion; see Anderson 562–564; Berg 81–96. See also Borgwardt, especially chapter 2, for an in-depth analysis of how "the doctrines of modern human rights" are derived from Franklin Roosevelt's plea for "four freedoms of the people" that "combined social and economic rights with more traditional civil and political rights as ideological weapons in an anti-Axis arsenal" (9). The UN's denial of DuBois and the NAACP as legible human rights advocates from the US reveals, to a considerable extent, the constrained frames of racial inequity in its human rights campaign.

2. On the critical value of rediscovering relevant documents and memories for understanding racial relations in the United States since the war, see Goodwin 12–31; Hoy 169–179; Loeb 105–108; Stur 1–15, 142–82; Wood 1–12.

3. Since the 2013 protests against the acquittal of George Zimmerman in the shooting death of black American teen Trayvon Martin, the Black Lives Matter movement has been active across the United States and, as of the writing of this essay, sustained by widespread discontent with police brutality against black Americans. In this period, references to James Baldwin in social media and in print are far too many to be counted, although the best-known representative examples may include Ta-Nehisi Coates's book *Between the World and Me* and Raoul Peck's 2016 documentary *I Am Not Your Nigger*. For essential overviews of the Black Lives Matter movement from 2014 to 2016, see Ransby; Harris.

4. In Wall's analysis, Baldwin used to deploy the collective pronoun *we* to refer to himself and the entire American citizenry, using "strategic American exceptionalism" to call for encompassing social reforms of the United States rather than simply raising an accusative finger as a victim; but he gave up this approach in the memoir, since "it had proved its in-effectiveness" (46).

5. As a rare case himself being an African American writer spending more than half of his life living in Europe, Baldwin was sensitive to Europeans' speculation on his political positionality and consistently resistant to simplistic categorization. For scholarly

examinations of his expatriate experiences in his fictional writings and activist commitments, see Tomlinson 137–139; Kramer 36–44.

6. See Mehta for more details about Russell's interaction with North Vietnam and the U.S. press management of his peace movement.

7. See Fortuny's account of the rediscovery and publicization of the interviews (434–436). This essay's excerpts of the interviews are based on Fortuny's transcriptions.

8. Such sympathy-based imaginative U.S.-Asia connection has also been viewed as a drive for American transnational adoption of Asian children throughout the Cold War. See Kim.

9. See Vials for an excellent analysis of its multivalent consequences.

10. For a more positive reading of the capacity of love in the novel, see Thompson.

11. This novel has also been taken as a key text with which Baldwin contributes to black American civil groups' calls for prison reform and for ending the massive U.S. incarceration of black males. See Plastas and Raimon.

## WORKS CITED

Anderson, Carol. "From Hope to Disillusion: African Americans, the United Nations, and the Struggle for Human Rights, 1944–1947." *Diplomatic History* 20.4 (1996): 531–564.

Baldwin, James. *The Devil Finds Work*. 1975. New York: Vintage, 2002.

———. *If Beale Street Could Talk*. 1974. New York: Vintage, 2002.

———. "The International War Crimes Tribunal." Originally published in *Freedomways*, 3rd quarter, 1967. Reprinted in *The Cross of Redemption: Uncollected Writings by James Baldwin*, ed. Randall Kenan. New York: Pantheon, 2010.

———. *No Name in the Street*. 1972. New York: Vintage, 2000.

———. *Tell Me How Long the Train's Been Gone*. 1968. New York: Vintage, 1998.

Berg, Manfred. "Black Civil Rights and Liberal Anticommunism: The NAACP in the Early Cold War." *Journal of American History* 94.1 (2007): 75–96.

Borgwardt, Elizabeth. *A New Deal for the World*. Cambridge, MA: Harvard University Press, 2007.

Coates, Ta-Nehisi. *Between the World and Me*. New York: Spiegel and Grau, 2015.

"Dr. King to Weigh Civil Disobedience if War Intensifies." *New York Times*. 2 April 1967.

Fortuny, Kim. "James Baldwin's 1970 Turkish Interviews: 'The American Way of Life' and the Rhetoric of War from Vietnam to the Near and Middle East." *Texas Studies in Literature and Language* 55.4 (2013): 434–451.

Goodwin, Gerald F. *Race in the Crucible of War: African American Soldiers and Race Relations in the "Nam"*. Diss. Ohio University, 2014.

Harris, Fredrick C. "The Next Civil Rights Movement?" *Dissent* 62.3 (2015): 34–40.

Hoy, Pat C. II. "The Beauty and Destructiveness of War: A Literary Portrait of the Vietnam Conflict." *A Concise Companion to Postwar American Literature and Culture*. Ed. Josephine G. Hendin. London: Blackwell, 2004.

Kim, Jodi. "'An' Orphan with Two Mothers: Transnational and Transracial Adoption, the Cold War, and Contemporary Asian American Cultural Politics." *American Quarterly* 61.4 (2009): 855–880.

Klein, Christina. *Cold War Orientalism: Asia in the Middlebrow Imagination, 1945–1961*. Berkeley: University of California Press, 2003.

Kramer, Lloyd. "James Baldwin in Paris: Exile, Multiculturalism and the Public Intellectual." *Historical Reflections* 27.1 (2001): 27–47.

Loeb, Jeff. "MIA: African American Autobiography of the Vietnam War." *African American Review* 31.1 (1997): 105–123.

Marable, Manning. *Beyond Black and White.* 1995. London: Verso, 2016.

Malcolm X. "The Ballot or the Bullet." *American RadioWorks.* 11 June 2018. http://americanradioworks.publicradio.org/features/blackspeech/mx.html.

Mehta, Harish C. "North Vietnam's Informal Diplomacy with Bertrand Russell: Peace Activism and the International War Crimes Tribunal." *Peace and Change* 37.1 (2012): 64–94.

Peck, Raoul, dir. *I Am Not Your Nigger.* Velvet Film, 2016.

Plastas, Melinda, and Eve Allegra Raimon. "Brutality and Brotherhood, James Baldwin and Prison Sexuality." *African American Review* 46.4 (2013): 687–699.

Ransby, Barbara. "The Class Politics of Black Lives Matter." *Dissent* 62.4 (2015): 31–34.

Stur, Heather Marie. *Dragon Ladies, Gentle Warriors, and Girls Next Door: Gender and Ideas That Shaped the Vietnam War.* Diss. University of Wisconsin–Madison, 2008.

Thompson, Clifford. "Tell Me How Long the Train's Been Gone." *Iowa Review* 29.2 (1999): 114–120.

Tomlinson, Robert. "'Payin' One's Dues': Expatriation as Personal Experience and Paradigm in the Works of James Baldwin." *African American Review* 33.1 (1999): 135–148.

Vials, Chris. "The Popular Front in the American Century: Life Magazine, Margaret Bourke-White, and Consumer Realism, 1936–1941." *American Periodicals* 16.1 (2006): 74–102.

Wall, Cheryl. "Stranger at Home: James Baldwin on What It Means to Be an American." *James Baldwin: America and Beyond.* Ed. Cora Kaplan and Bill Schwarz. Ann Arbor: University of Michigan Press, 2011. 35–52.

Wood, John A. *Veteran Narratives and the Collective Memory of the Vietnam War.* Athens: Ohio University Press, 2016.

# 6

# Matronly Maids and Willful Women

## *Migrant Domestic Workers in the Plural*

Christopher B. Patterson

In Mia Alvar's 2015 short story "Shadow Families" (published in *In the Country*), a group of "lucky" upper-class Filipina women living in Bahrain host weekly get-togethers and provide gifts for lower-class Filipina maids (*katulong*) also working in Bahrain. The lower-class women are spoken of as "helpers," the "janitress" and the "gardener," whom the higher-class Filipinas try to match up by finding them pen pals in Manila, feeling that "we owed them a chance at the life we enjoyed" (95). These "lucky" upper-class women take pity on these domestic servants, sending them home with leftovers and praying for them before bed, seeing them as remnants of their homeland, people who come from "farming provinces, like our fathers" and speak "Tagalog with country accents, like our mothers" (95). "Helping these helpers," as the women say, "felt like home" (95). Each helper becomes a symbol of their national pride, as a self-sacrificing matronly maid whom the upper-class migrants see as a "sweet, humble church mouse, who'd somehow strike us as child and granny all at once" (95).

The representation of Filipina maids has captured the attention of human rights groups, popular media, and academia.[1] In the Philippines, popular movies like *The Flor Contemplacion Story* have depicted migrant workers as martyrs and victims, while films like *The Maid* and *Ilo Ilo* in Singapore have reworked these victimized figures into third-world women who are vulnerable to first-world modernity and who can cure the traumas haunting the household. This discourse of heroism appears often in presidential speeches, such as when then-president Gloria Macapagal Arroyo, in 2002, called on "the work and reputation of the overseas Filipinos" to "confirm to the world that indeed, the Philippines is the home of the Great Filipino worker" (qtd. in Guevarra 3), or with the Philippine government's declaration of "Migrant Heroes Week" to celebrate the signing of the Migrant Workers and Overseas Filipinos Act of 1995 (Rodriguez 75). In Alvar's story, the migrant "helpers" are depicted as church mice stamped with the discourses of heroism and self-sacrifice but also as asexual, matronly women, who could be both "child" and "granny." Alvar's language here exposes the sexual and erotic (or nonerotic) dimensions that constitute the overseas migrants as matronly women who sacrifice themselves for the good of their family and their nation. While a "matron" can command authority, to be cast as "matronly" in fashion or figure has become less synonymous with respectability than with asexuality and ennui. In societies that value women according to their youthfulness, the matronly woman appears frumpy, matured, and concerned primarily with the household. If films about maids have often followed the identity-making of the state, literary texts such as Jose Dalisay's *Soledad's Sister* (2008) have sought to reflect overseas maids not as mere matronly figures but as women subjected to sexual norms that manage migrants and housekeepers.

The contemporary figure of the matronly maid can be traced to the 1970s, when the Philippines became one of the first Asian countries to aggressively export maids abroad by marking them as national heroes while accounting for their exploitation through religious symbols of martyrdom. Such migrants were made "emplowered" (employed and empowered) by brokerage companies to have pride in an ahistorical Filipina identity based on matronly affection and care, an identity that migrants are now expected to perform as condition of their employment (Guevarra). As Anna Guevarra reminds us, this vision of femininity is also that of a responsible neoliberal subject, whose "emplowerment" "fulfills the goal of producing 'responsible' (that is, economically competitive, entrepreneurial, and self-accountable) and therefore, ideal workers and global commodities" (8). While human rights discourses see such migrants as at risk of being sexually assaulted and trapped, migrant feminine identity neutralizes the so-called danger of sexual promiscuity by marking it as taboo. In what sense, then, can we speak of a sexual migrant maid? How can we see domestic workers as those who don't mind defaulting on their debts to the homeland, the host country, the family, and their prescribed roles?

This chapter considers how the figure of the "matronly maid" lays bare the failure of human rights to account for the exploitative use of migrants whose labor is predicated on the denial of basic rights (political and economic rights as well as social and sexual rights). As Leslie Bow wrote in 1999, Asian American cultural production has often placed Asia within a human rights framework that depicts Asian "homelands" as spaces characterized by totalitarian regimes, deploying "the rhetoric of human rights in order to critique methods of governmental repression" as well as violations "such as torture and detention without trial" (40). What have been omitted from this rhetoric are forms of neoliberal exploitation reserved for migrants who seemingly follow similar "self-making" trajectories that have characterized the Asian American model minority. The celebrated freedoms to travel overseas, to make money, and to find opportunity obscure the exploitative dimensions of overseas work that suffocate rather than bestow liberal freedoms.

To investigate the "matronly maid" figure, I examine its literary expressions in two short story collections, Kristiana Kahakauwila's *This Is Paradise* (2013) and Mia Alvar's *In the Country* (2015). Both collections have crossed a barrier in the popularity of the migrant worker, as both were published by Random House subsidiaries, and both have won numerous awards and accolades.[2] From each collection, I focus on one story that uses the first person plural *we* and third person plural *they* to resituate migrants into mobile sisterhoods that offer a support structure while also reinforcing expectations of matronly behavior. In doing so, these stories show how the figure of the migrant domestic worker is produced through a human rights discourse that sees care work as a sign of neoliberal benevolence, where capitalist exploitation is reframed as charity, and the matronly affection of migrant maids is reinterpreted as heartfelt gratitude. Whereas scholars have rightfully pointed out that migrants from the Philippines and the Pacific Islands have "competitive advantages" in domestic work by knowing English, can we also see conservative and religious sexual norms as marking domestic workers with a competitive edge? How crucial is "matronlyness" for the ongoing supply of affective labor?

## Domestic Work and the Neoliberal Entrepreneur

The trend toward overseas Filipina migrancy can be traced back to the early 1900s, in nursing campaigns that began in U.S. colonial schools in the Philippines, and in the mass exportation of Filipino workers to the United States, wherein the dependency on migrant labor remittances grew to become a mainstay of the Philippines and its diasporas. As Dawn Mabalon notes, the colonial education regimes in the Philippines and the Pacific Islands trained young women toward service, putting in place "domestic science curricula required for young girls in the Philippines—cooking, knitting, sewing, crocheting, and household sanitation—[that] sought to civilize them in the model of middle-class, white [V]ictorian womanhood or, at the very least, her perfectly trained servant" (35). Given this colonial history, Filipinas hold ideal characteristics for domestic work, as many are educated in nursing and housework, and many have "a stellar competency in the English language" (10). Neferti Tadiar has shown how this affective identity values servitude as a form of self-sacrifice built on Catholic notions of martyrdom and repayment of both spiritual and national debt, while Denise Cruz has pointed out how this figure came as a reaction to the fears of "coed" stereotypes of transnational Filipinas, who were seen (by Filipino men) as promiscuous, easily corrupted and inauthentic.

In the 1970s, the Philippines took the form of a "labor brokerage state," and its attempts to police Filipina migrant identity as "matronly"—through training regimes, advertisement campaigns, and films—marked a shift in previous representations of transnational Filipina femininity (Rodriguez). As Cruz observes, the representation of transnational Filipinas has "long, tangled roots in debates recurring throughout the twentieth century over who and what made a Filipina" (5). In the 1970s, this identity expanded as other markets for overseas work created a demand for domestic workers from the Global South; according to Guevarra, "women from Asia and Latin and Central America are viewed as imbued with an ideal docility, which employers attribute to cultures with a strong work ethic and values related to family, loyalty, and authority" (10). Whereas the turning point in the Philippines toward brokering women abroad occurred in 1974 when Marcos launched an overseas employment program, in the island states of Micronesia and the Marshall Islands, the change to exporting migrant labor came in 1986 with the implementation of the Compact of Free Association (COFA). This agreement gave COFA members the freedom to live permanently or come and go at will in the United States, so that by 2006 one out of every four Micronesians lived in the United States (Hezel and Samuel). Domestic helpers from Micronesia, like Filipinas, are characterized in the global market for maintaining explicit marks of colonial histories that befit service labor (use of English, Protestant notions of sexuality, rights to travel in the United States), while their darker remnants of colonial history (cancer, environmental degradation, military recruitment) remain obscured by their seemingly grateful attitudes. While women from these island states frequently go abroad to send home remittances, the men help make up the highest volunteer rate per capita in joining the U.S. military and also share in the military's highest casualty rate, higher than in any U.S. state (Letman).

The critical scholarship concerning migrant domestic workers has developed a counternarrative to human rights discourses, which see such migrants as a people "at risk" of gendered violence. In the 2000s, after abuses of foreign domestic workers began to make headlines around the world, human rights organizations like Human Rights Watch increasingly scrutinized domestic work as a form of modern slavery, creating new definitions, identities, and expectations for regulating fair treatment.[3] Amnesty International has documented abuses around the world, most notably in Singapore, Hong Kong, and the Gulf States. Since the targets of abuses are migrants, human rights organizations often label "at risk" migrants those who belong to countries where employers typically confiscate travel documents, invade workers' personal space, pay below the minimum wage, and put workers on call at all hours without giving them a day off (*Maid to Order*). But besides labeling and tracking abuses, human rights organizations have limited power in enforcing changes in local laws, and their attempts to combat contemporary forms of servitude are often stymied by employment-based visa structures.[4] These limitations leave domestic workers in need of adjusting to local views of gender, religion, race, and sexuality, and the restriction of domestic workers' reproductive, marriage, and sexual rights has led to cases of deportation, common for impregnated domestic workers, and jail time (*Swept under the Rug* 80). Implied in these laws is a regime of surveillance, where migrant domestic workers, unlike casual travelers or corporate jet-setters, are presumed to give up rights to privacy as a condition of entry.

Laws that attempt to police workers' sexual relationships are represented as benevolent for the domestic worker, as they line up with religious notions of sexuality and female purity that are also held sacrosanct in the workers' homelands (the Philippines, Indonesia, India, Micronesia). But such laws also reflect "an underlying fear that foreign women workers pose a sexual and social threat to families" (*Swept under the Rug* 81). This discourse sees these women, now free from the policing forces of their families, friends, nation-states, and religious institutions, as workers who must be kept pure by the laws and norms of the local host country. In the Asia Pacific, the matronly migrant maid contrasts with oversexualized local women, as well as migrant women working in massage parlors and brothels. Yet the maid also symbolizes a figure in need of rescue, one burdened by the inability of the home country to make it as a developed nation. Their migration is a sign that their people have undertaken a last recourse, a desperate attempt to stay afloat. In the game of global development competition, they are seen as the losers. Thus their positions as servers seem fitting, or worse, a sign of the benevolence of neoliberal policies. The fact that the workers' domination comes from nonwhite clients mark places that host migrants, like Bahrain, Hong Kong, Singapore, and Honolulu, with a veneer of multicultural fairness. Such spaces, as Vernadette Gonzalez points out, appear multicultural and tolerant, marking service workers as responsible for their own failure or as residual remnants of history ("Military Bases" 45). Their jobs, positions, and livelihoods are constructed as gifts within a neoliberal rescue narrative, a mode of temporary adoption that secures the space itself from being perceived within the domain of humanitarian crisis.

Given the limitations of human rights groups in effecting changes to local laws, attitudes, and prejudices, such groups are often co-opted into nations as rule-keepers or "umpires" that maintain an ideological sense of local space as fair, multicultural, and benevolent toward outsiders.[5] Human rights organizations can sometimes function as umpires within a logic that sees domestic and care work as benevolent in providing jobs, remittances, and cultural interactions to "subjects in need." Umpire logic sets human rights organizations as (free) watchdogs and lets the neoliberal state appear to give migrant populations the freedom to self-govern, to discipline and dominate themselves, so long as they do so within the terms of their employment and immigration laws (Guevarra 8). This "governing from afar" strategy rationalizes low wages and exploitative conditions as a cost of freedom and self-accountability. Service work then becomes shaped as a mode of humanitarian assistance through affective actions that construe migrants as objects of need and pity (having a live-in maid, sharing food, leaving tips). Indeed, benevolence becomes practiced in the everyday as workers are "given" more than they would typically earn in their hometown, and such excess of pay is evident in the amount of remittances sent home. Meanwhile, the workers' travel routes within so-called multicultural spaces make their exploitation and abuse seem exceptional to the otherwise benevolent provisions they receive.

## From Matronly Maids to the Willful Traveler

In human rights discourse, female migrants are subjected within moralistic battles over the representation of migrant femininity and sexuality. The human rights language of "forced," "free," "economic duress," and "bounded rationality" do not go far in questioning the supposedly universal rationality that sees some forms of affective labor (domestic work) as legitimate and others (sex work) as immoral and fraught with exploitation. Domestic workers secure forms of family and culture, resigning the migrant maid into a matronly role that supports the family unit, while the sex worker threatens this stability and opposes what Sara Ahmed refers to as the presumptions of universal happiness. As Nicole Constable argues, domestic work and sex work overlap in their associations with migrant work and intimacy, yet human rights and neoliberal discourses have obscured their similarities as affective "contributions" that both produce "intimate surplus labor" (46–47). The affective characteristics of domestic workers, of course, can be reconstituted as sexual acts and can broach the excesses of commodification, breaking apart the family unit as easily as supporting it. Representations of sex work (whether as trafficked or not) abound in human rights literature as well as in Asian American literature, where sex work is often placed as part of a traumatic family history that reinforces the host country as a benevolent space of rescue.[6] In turn, representations of "matronly" migrant domestic work remain as a symbol of neoliberal benevolence.

In the context of the religious (Protestant, Catholic, or Islamic) homeland, the victimization of maid work can be reframed into a transnational form of the "Madonna/whore" binary, where self-sacrificing domestic workers are mirrored against promiscuous sex workers. As Tadiar maintains, religious upbringing combined with traditional notions of curing and healing helps constitute the migrant maid through images of sacred women whose libidinal energies are proof of their "life-producing activity of loving performed by what can now be recognized as domestic labor" (724). Their potential as passionate healers is incorporated into value for capital, as a commodification of healing power similar to commodified traits of sex workers in the Global South, who are also marked as affective laborers capable of healing, passion, and intimacy. Thus, what remains crucial in differentiating migrant "helper" intimacy from the intimacy of sex work is matronlyness itself. Compared with the supposed traumas induced through sex work, domestic work appears benevolent insofar as it also appears nonsexual.

The lack of representation of contemporary male migrants also overlaps conveniently with the function of human rights organizations, which often see women as more "at risk" figures and on occasion deal exclusively with women out of mistrust of the men.[7] The nonappearance of men as subjects of rescue is thereby crucial to maintaining affective structures that expect gratitude and "life-force" from low-wage migrants. Where women are victims whom the Global North must be hospitable to, men must disappear or perhaps reappear only as "warriors" in the military or in jobs such as seamen that do not interact with the general public. As Teresia K. Teaiwa notes, "In the context of war, society has an ideological stake in the reification of female bodies when male bodies are being sacrificed heroically" (91). Gender is thus deployed as a regulatory mechanism to rationalize the positioning of migrants as cheap service workers while also lending credence to their inhabited space as providing "benevolence" through the "opportunities" of tourism, militarism, and the freedom to migrate (Gonzalez, *Securing*).

In Ahmed's reading of happiness, governmental and capitalist discourses point people toward recognizing happiness not only in objects but within social structures themselves—that of the family and in being bound with those of the same nation. Happiness for Ahmed involves "a way of being aligned with others, of facing the right way," so that "the points of alignment become points of happiness" (*Promise* 45). The given notion that the Global North brings benevolence to others is a pivotal point of human rights discourse, as providing the happiness of economic security functions as a means of rationalizing migrant labor. Opposing such structures are migrants who refuse to find happiness, refuse to accept sexual surveillance, and refuse to secure the happiness of family units via their sexual promiscuity. Ahmed calls these counterfigures "willful subjects": "willful women, unwilling to get along, unwilling to preserve an idea of happiness" (*Willful* 2). Ahmed's notions of willfulness allow us to trace how migrant helpers are cast as "matronly" (nonlibidinal) whose will is made subject to the whole both through the risk of human rights violations (deportation, domestic violence, abuse of contracts, predatory lending) and through disciplinary tactics that police sexuality (miscegenation, queerness, promiscuity). Ahmed uses the analogy of body parts to elaborate on the need to "secure" willful subjects as "hands" or "feet" and to see them not as sexual or thinking subjects but simply as extensions of their employers. "Willfullness" in this case "threatens the degeneration of the whole body; not to function would cause the whole body to become dysfunctional" (*Willful* 111). Willful subjects threaten the stability of the colonial order by seeking to act as the social body's head or libido. It is not that the "will" itself is threatening but that "freedom to will" can be given only to those within the bodily division of labor whose will is seen as supreme: the masters, the captors, the leisure class. Their freedom is predicated on the condition that they are released from the mere "function" of serving as the "hands" or "feet" that support the social structure. If migrant domestic workers are kept from playing "the head" of a neoliberal social space, then "matronlyness" reveals how they too are restricted from the libidinal body (i.e., the crotch), a position routinely inhabited not by migrants but by marriage and the family institution. Indeed, in the context of neoliberal benevolence, the leisure class trusts nonthreatening, nonsexual, and nonwillful migrant women as its hands, those "matronly maids" whose gratitude and sexual obedience help secure the hierarchical social body.

For the remainder of this chapter, I treat representations of the "matronly maid" that is constituted through comparisons to "willful women," who experience sexual pleasure and refuse to identify as subjects in need of rescue or protection. Migrant sisterhoods in these stories bond together through identifying (and vilifying) willful women who refuse the duty to reproduce social and gender norms. Indeed, while the "we" narrative of the stories I discuss exposes shared assumptions, it also reveals the ambiguous ways that human rights discourse can be invoked to identify victims who are in need of rescue. By revealing how "willful women" expose anxieties of sexual promiscuity and miscegenation, these stories allow us to see how global human rights subjects such as sex workers are similarly constituted as "others" to migrant domestic workers, who are expected to reproduce the standards for happiness defined by the Global North. The willful female migrants nonetheless refuse to reproduce or smile correctly; rather than show gratitude, they expect equality.

## Alvar's Baby

Mia Alvar's debut collection, *In the Country*, depicts diverse Filipino/a diasporic experiences, such as Filipino laborers in Saudi Arabia, Filipina teachers and maids in Bahrain, and Filipino exiles in America. The stories follow

Alvar's routes from her birth in Manila to growing up in Bahrain, attending Harvard and Columbia University in the United States, and returning to live in Manila. While the collection mostly concentrates on Filipino political figures and events, the collection's fourth story, "Shadow Families," which is about Filipina housewives who offer gifts to Filipina helpers, seems to take a lighthearted tone. Alvar's political dexterity emerges in the story's first-person plural narrative, which captures the Filipina housewives as smug wannabe royals. The story differs from previous conceptions of domestic workers in that it makes no serious attempt to authentically interiorize the maids' thoughts and motivations; nor does it cast them as martyrs. Rather, Alvar's story depicts the bourgeois desire to rescue these maids and questions how this desire reinforces sexual norms and produces the maids as others to cosmopolitan, upper-class migrants. By depicting these upper-class migrants from a shared gaze, Alvar's story lays bare assumptions that individual narratives would otherwise attempt to tone down or complicate through first-person narratives that emphasize the complexities of individuals imbricated within global capitalism. With no narrative burden to individualize the upper-class migrant's point of view, the plural narrative uncovers the crucial self-making that reconstitutes the upper-class housewives as sexual, intelligent, and charitable.

Alvar's story traces the ambiguous relationship of human rights and the migrant domestic worker when the "lucky" housewives mentioned at the outset of this chapter encounter the office cleaner Baby, a *katulong* who seems to "walk on air" in her translucent heels and straps. Unlike the other migrant helpers, Baby refuses to act thankful for the housewives' gifts but instead receives their hospitality as "her birthright" (100). Rather than act matronly, Baby provocatively flirts with the housewives' husbands and later accuses the husbands of attempting to touch her whenever they drive her home. While these charges may or may not be true, Baby's attitude toward the husbands, who almost all work in Bahrain's oil industry, is to feel "tickle[d]" rather than offended (101). "If you're gonna touch, touch," Baby says between laughs, "Don't pretend you want a cigarette" (101). As Baby's accusations appear after every ride home, the group of upper-class housewives become concerned for their own position as caretakers of their husbands, thinking that "even the least jealous wife among us couldn't resist questioning her designated driver afterward" (103).

Baby's visible sexuality contests narratives of migrant feminine obedience. Her danger is not so much in departing from the Philippines nation but in the shame she brings as a representative of that nation who has "the potential to circulate as unauthorized and inauthentic" (Cruz 193). Indeed, Baby's sexual promiscuity and accusations upset the safety of the family unit, challenging the matronly maid figure as a simplistic symbol of Filipina language, religion, and culture, a figure that has been accepted into the intimate spaces of domestic work. Baby claims she forgot her Tagalog, and when Baby mysteriously disappears, the women wonder about their own class security: "Just how far up did we live," they ask, "from the slop sink and the soil?" (108). With Baby's disappearance, the housewives realize that class movement does not merely go up—from the island provinces to the wives of successful Filipino men—but can, at any moment, also plummet downward.

Baby is later rediscovered on the street wearing a "black abaya" and living in an apartment for Muslims. Immediately the housewives begin to frame Baby's newfound freedom as a form of "descent": "Losing Baby to a world of mosques and abayas and possible polygamy set off a more desperate alarm, as if one of our children had woken with a fever and was speaking in tongues" (109). The "lucky" women assume that Baby is a second or third wife of a Bahraini and seek immediately to provide rescue. While losing Baby to prostitution (her mother's profession) seems at the bottom of the ladder of success that the housewives have climbed, the thought of mixed marriage (and perhaps mixed children) represents an altogether different descent, a "world of mosques and abayas" where the lucky women have little understanding or influence. With Baby's disappearance, the housewives cannot help but expose their own interests in policing the *katulong*'s sexuality and cultural purity, thus replacing the role of the church, family, and nation that these migrant women have all but escaped. When Baby finally reappears at her old flatmate's wedding pregnant, she claims that the father of her child is one of the housewives' husbands. "While you were cooking in your kitchen," Baby says, "rip[ping]" with laughter, "while you were shopping in the mall, while you were in the Philippines—where did you think he was?" (112). Confronted with their greatest fear, the first-person plural narrative responds, "We didn't try to catch her eye just then, or ask who *you* and *he* were" (112).

Alvar's refusal to individualize the group of housewives through the story's group narrative keeps the story from reiterating a narrative of personal journeys, one that might turn the housewives into lifelong victims who have somehow "earned" their upper-class status (through personal adversity and personal traumas). Their personal stories remain untold, leaving only their status as upper-class housewives who seek to manage and influence the helper. As Baby never reveals the father of her child, the housewives' suspicion for their husbands remains a shared rather than an individual anxiety. They all knowingly conform to the anxieties of monogamous, heterosexual marriage and, in turn, endeavor to take revenge against Baby by threatening to report her pregnancy to the Bahraini police, leaving her with the choice of either prison or repatriation. Tellingly, their successful attempt to deport Baby simultaneously maintains their identities as charitable women, as they take it upon themselves to "rescue" Baby from her trespasses: "Even the so-called playground of the Gulf had no room for an unwed mother" (116).

When the housewives fail to manage Baby themselves, they appeal to the higher power of the Bahrain immigration laws: "The only law that could contain her," they declare, "was the one that ruled us all" (116). Bahrain's laws policing women's bodies line up uniformly with the sisterhood's interests in maintaining their social power, as such laws "renewed our awe and obligation toward our hosts" (116).

Alvar's story exposes the multiple hegemonic forces of family, religion, and local laws to which migrant workers are subjected. In Bahrain's capital city, Manama, the "playground" of the Middle East where Saudis and Egyptians mix to gamble, drink, and trade with sex workers, migrant domestic workers are subject to puritanical notions of family, sexuality, and miscegenation. In remaining hidden, domestic workers are more subject to placement agents using legal loopholes to ensure contracts limit worker movement, and to weak inspection systems that make it nearly impossible for workers to take legal action (Buhejji). That most employers confiscate employee passports makes legal recourse even more unlikely. As in many Gulf States, employers rely on the *kafala* system that restricts migrant workers' abilities to change employers and enables employers to revoke sponsorship at will, triggering deportation. Due to the hidden nature of migrant labor and the need to adjust to local cultural norms, human rights organizations like Human Rights Watch are limited to seeing human rights violations in terms of trafficking or forced labor. In places such as Bahrain, the exploitation of migrant workers seems a norm in itself from which the lucky women of Alvar's story unknowingly benefit as it increases their own security and safety in the family.

## Kahakauwila's Migrant Hotel Workers

If Alvar's "Shadow Families" provides a glimpse into how some upper-class migrants see migrant workers, Kristiana Kahakauwila's titular story from her collection, *This Is Paradise*, attempts to provide the shared perspective of Micronesian helpers who clean hotels in Honolulu, Hawaii. While Alvar's collection captures the diversity of the Filipino/a diasporic experience, Kahakauwila's showcases the diversity of Hawaii not as a multicultural paradise but as a colonial territory of ongoing rivals and prejudices that include diasporic Chinese ("Wanle"), queer sons ("The Old Paniolo Way"), and indigenous Hawaiians ("Thirty-Nine Rules for Making a Hawaiian Funeral into a Drinking Game"). The most ambitious of these stories, "This Is Paradise," focuses on three separate groups of women, who, as in Alvar's "Shadow Families," all speak in a first-person plural voice. The first group are young local surfer women, the second are middle-aged and upper-middle-class women, and the third are hotel maids who have migrated from Micronesia. The story follows these three groups as each observes the promiscuous and careless freedom of Susan, a white tourist wearing a polka-dot bikini, who conjures sexual anxieties in every group and who, in the end, is assaulted and killed by a man sporting prison tattoos.

"This Is Paradise" represents the migrant helpers as matronly women with whom tourists feel comfortable and who are expected to clean up their condoms and pornography. Unlike in Alvar's story, Kahakauwila's "we" narrative takes for granted the maids' matronly affections, which appear boundless and seem to disregard the colonial histories that brought them to work in Honolulu. The maids instead appear as magical healers and as the least judgmental of all the women. Whereas the two other female groups see Susan as a dangerous, young, and foolish tourist, the matronly maids see her as one of their own children, their "eldest daughter," as they say: "This girl, like our girls, is the type a mother can depend on to do things: drive Grandmother to a doctor's appointment, cook breakfast for Papa, dress and feed the babies before school. We smile back at her. We feel as if we can trust her" (12). Despite the unlikelihood that each of the maids (whose number cannot be determined) has a similar eldest daughter, this passage repeats much of the same gendering labor that produces matronly maids: reframing the sexual, effervescent energy of a young woman into recognizable labor power. The same woman who dresses scantily and seeks adventure, the maids know, can be incorporated into becoming a woman who can be trusted to "cook breakfast for Papa" and "dress and feed the babies" (12).

If the maids themselves show little awareness or concern over the colonial histories that brought them to the Hawaiian Islands, the bikini that Susan wears tells of this very past. As Teaiwa points out, the bikini was originally named after Bikini Atoll, a site in the Marshall Islands where the United States tested twenty-five nuclear bombs from 1946 to 1958. The story's focus on the maid's reactions to Susan's bikini externalizes the implicit narrative of the suit, as Teaiwa puts it, to "manifest both a celebration and a forgetting of the nuclear power that strategically and materially marginalizes and erases the living history of Pacific Islanders" (87). The bikini is also a prominent feature of the exotic brown beach woman, a figure commonly seen in tourist advertisements in island states in both the Philippines and Hawaii. For Gonzalez, the sexualized bikini-clad brown body entices American soldiers in their routes to conquer and marks the tourist space as one in need of American security and protection (*Securing* 13). Furthermore, the bikini-clad body also serves to distract from the matronly maid, who is meant to remain barely visible, unexciting, and nonenticing. Desexualized, the domestic worker serves a moralistic, quasi-religious purpose, one produced through a history of colonial religious training. Yet their function serves the same imperial structure, as the matronly maid's asexual but comforting nature and ability to nurture provide legitimacy to the tourist. The domestic worker shows happiness where one might expect anger and provides a symbol of moral virtue that affirms and approves of a tourist's pleasures.

While Kahakauwila's story illuminates the contemporary struggles of Hawaiian locals and natives in dealing with tourism, poverty, and the buying up of private land, the representation of Micronesian maids as potential victims of U.S. atomic testing and military recruitment remains hidden by the maids' obligation to implicitly give approval to tourists and local Hawaiians, thus providing legitimacy to colonial power. For Teaiwa, U.S. colonial logic responds by gendering and domesticating such representations so that "the female body is appropriated by a colonial discourse to successfully disguise the horror of the bomb" (92). Indeed, the first-person plural narrative here does not mock the group but solidifies the migrants as matronly maids. The maids' collective narration makes them more indistinguishable than the other two narrative groups—the "successful" women and the surfers—who are consistently identified as individuals even as they speak in a shared voice. The successful women are individualized by differing life choices and careers: Paula is a detective who never chose to live off the island, Kiana is a journalist, and the others are identified as a lawyer and a business consultant. Similarly, the young surfer women are differentiated by the parts of the islands they come from: Cora is from Kailua (which makes her "naïve"), and Lanie is "a Nanakuli girl and likes to pretend she's tougher" (24). While the young women visit clubs searching for appropriate men to dance with, the successful women lounge at quiet bars wondering if passing men are single, wishing they could "have the husband and the babies and the home" (30). In contrast, the matronly maids possess a natural group cohesion of sameness and typicality.

In Alvar's "Shadow Families," the first-person plural narration exposes the group's shared interests in maintaining their social position through shared attempts to "rescue" lower-class Filipina migrants, while in Kahakauwila's "This Is Paradise," the groups of local Hawaiian women do so by pining for what they collectively lack: a good husband and children. Indeed, in a story where heterosexual marriage seems like the only route to happiness (even more than financial success), the migrant maids are depicted not so much as victims to be rescued but as subjects who provide rescue to clients through their affective labor, a commodified product of their "less developed" origins. Their matronly identity speaks to their function of care and affection that allows the separate groups in the story to mourn the death of Susan, the promiscuous white tourist. When the maids discover Susan's body on the beach, they conduct an act of mourning that sees Susan beyond the limiting and insulting language of the two local groups:

> We form a circle around her, protecting her even though she is beyond our protection. . . . She is older than even our eldest girls, and, on any other day, we could have called her haole, foreigner, a white woman independent and capable of caring for herself. But in these few minutes before the police come running down the beach with a

> first-aid kit and walkie-talkie, this girl is a child. She is helpless. She is in need of a mother, and that's a job at which we are experts. . . . We are here, we tell the unmoving girl. All us mothers are here. (38–39)

In contrast to Alvar's story, which employs plural narration to expose shared prejudices, this narrative's first-person plural voice swallows up the individuality of these maids while foregrounding their "motherly" powers. The matronly maids thus see Susan as their child, and their first reaction when they see her dead body is to cover her nudity and to protect and rescue a willful woman whose frenetic energy has been reduced to a childish helplessness.

Only upon seeing these maids mourn for the deceased Susan can the other two female groups appropriately reconnect to the "natural" purposes of female life. The career women are struck with a sense of guilt for not helping Susan: "We should have done something," they collectively say (42). The surfer women see the maids standing in a circle near Susan's body, "stand[ing] sentinel, very still and very tall," to protect Susan's exposed body from the news cameras and tourists. Ahmed's discussion about the will is useful for us to think through the disciplinary techniques for migrant women. Ahmed writes that "willfulness" helps understand how "power relations can be secured 'willingly,'" and "once secured, the will is not easy to apprehend as will" (*Willful* 16). Through this act of covering the "willful woman's" body in death, as she refused to do herself in life, the maids' encircling is understood as a mournful act that erases Susan's sexuality and adventurous attitude as an integral part of her selfhood. Indeed, the maids' efforts also succeed in guilting the surfer girls into performing their own islander ritual with flowers purchased from a nearby Safeway (45). In inspiring others to forgive, the maids' desire to sexually police Susan becomes symbolic of their natural morality. For these matrons, the distractions of success and tourism have not gotten in the way of the things that provide them happiness: marriage, children, and group comfort. The facts that Micronesian migrancy is partially the product of military technology (the atomic bomb) and that their husbands and sons may be serving in the U.S. military for want of other work seem like distant counterpoints to the women's matronly majesty.

## Defaulting on Happiness

The first-person plural narrative in both Alvar's and Kahakauwila's stories refuse to individualize group prejudices toward "willful women," revealing how migrant female sexuality remains under surveillance by multiple groups: the employers, the locals, and groups of migrant women themselves. In "This Is Paradise," the first-person plural narratives capture how global capital forces have managed to exploit migrant life-force by reinterpreting religious notions of sexuality into labor productivity. This process is made to seem natural through the maids' plural point of view, which sees libidinal and willful force as fuel for service labor. In Alvar's "Shadow Families," the envisioned "sisterhood" among diasporic Filipinas is displaced by a crucial desire for upper-class migrants to see domestic workers as matronly servants in need of humanitarian rescue, producing an imagined sisterhood of intimacy and interdependence that helps sustain an otherwise blurred power structure. In interviews, Alvar states how the tenuous bonds between maids and clients in the Philippines were tightened once abroad, as if class structures suddenly did not exist or were made inconsequential. As Alvar says of the "wives of engineers" and the "maids and nannies in 'Shadow Families,'" "in Bahrain they bond as friends over shared customs, nostalgia, and a mutual awe and fear of the Bahrainis whom they regard as the true upper class" (Nelson). Alvar's character, Baby, seems like a victim of the "true upper class" given her deportation and sexual promiscuity, yet if we read her not as a human rights subject but as a "willful woman," the story proffers a counterpoint to how "helpers" are expected to act and reveals how domestic workers respond to their matronly identities. Baby's trespasses cause anxiety, while her appearance helps mark the "obedient" and "happy" maids as exactly that: workers whose labor involves creatively reinterpreting and delivering matronly performances in order to match a construct produced through colonial encounters and incorporated into global structures of exchange. Baby's visible sexuality threatens to expose the "matronly maid" figure as partially a performative gesture required for migrant domestic labor, a crucial transgression that the sisterhood must punish.

Like Baby's sexuality, the matronly maids of "This Is Paradise" continue to see Susan's sexualized body as something in need of covering up. Indeed, all three groups of women seem to understand Susan's murder as a reminder of the dangers of becoming willful. In both stories, willfulness excludes but also produces difference. It sets individuals apart from the sisterhoods and carries "the possibility of not being reduced to thing, of not being compelled by an external force, including the will of others, enshrined in or as law" (Ahmed, *Willful* 143). As apart from the "we" narrative structuring both stories, the (singular) "she" of the willful woman exposes the freedom enabled by migration, the danger of losing one's culture, and the notion that travel for women is dangerous and must be done in groups. As Constable argues, domestic workers in spaces such as Hong Kong often spend their time off participating in nightlife activity "motivated largely by a desire for fun, friends, relaxation, and an escape from the narrow identity of 'domestic helper'" that intersects with work in the wider sex industry (52). Such representations allow us to reconceive of migrant work not through concerns of "duress" and "benevolence" but as a desire for travel, access, and sexual pleasures.

By walking away from the typical norms promising happiness, both Baby and Susan become "willful wanderers" who are "opposed to the figure of the wife," as Ahmed puts it (*Willful* 15). As wanderers, they teach those around them "what it is to be the woman other women hope not to become" (Alvar 119). Their wandering away from family is read by "migrant sisterhoods" as a failure. They produce anxieties that question the viability of the "matronly maid," and in both stories, reactions to willfulness can be interpreted politically as a reflexive desire to maintain given hierarchies of affective labor. If willfulness continues to be seen as a deviation from the group, then willfulness becomes political the moment it becomes recognized from being an aberration to being a passed-on legacy. This potential lies in the "will" as a shared desire for freedom, an "inheritance" as Ahmed calls it, or to use Tadiar's terms, a reclamation of one's "life force." It is the expectation that migrant maids perform as "matrons" rather than as "willful women" that allows us to comprehend the Pacific Islands and the Philippines as part of what Walden Bello calls an American "transnational garrison state" where male military labor and female service labor are reshaped as benevolent provisions for safety, security, and "uplift" (311). The surveillance, regulation, and punishment accorded to the willful migrant woman are a beckoning reminder that in an age defined by the presumed "rise of Asia," there are those who rise and those who remain in servitude.

## Acknowledgments

This chapter was formed through the workshops, discussions, and lectures at the 2015 Summer Institute in Asian American Studies. Many thanks to its organizers, Pin-chia Feng, Shyh-jen Fuh, Guy Beauregard, Hsiu-chuan Lee, and Chih-ming Wang. I'd also like to thank the summer institute's speakers, Cathy Schlund-Vials and John Erni, whose ideas on human rights inform the basis for this project. Conversations with Vernadette Gonzalez, Oscar Campomanes, R. Zamora Linmark, Francisco Benitez, Ferdinand Lopez, and M. Evelina Galang were crucial during the revision process, as was the intellectual activity hosted by the Centre for Cultural Studies at the Chinese University of Hong Kong. Thank you finally to Y-Dang Troeung, my partner and challenger.

NOTES

1. See, for example, Parreñas; Guevarra; Rodriguez.

2. Alvar's book won the 2016 PEN/Robert W. Bingham Prize for Debut Fiction; Kahakauwila's was short-listed for the William Saroyan International Prize for Writing and was named a 2013 Barnes & Noble Discover Great New Writers Selection.

3. See *Maid to Order*; *Swept under the Rug*.

4. Human Rights Watch, for example, is limited to seeing only violations of domestic workers' human rights that rise to "the level of forced labor and debt bondage" (57).

5. Chua Beng Huat writes of "umpire" as a managerial, seemingly neutral neoliberal mode of governance wherein state and international forces act as "autonomous, neutral

umpire[s] that allocate[s] resources equally and adjudicate[s] disputes among the races" (345). I have previously expanded on "umpire" as a neocolonial form of governance that seems to "exist outside of history" and acts in the name of "overcome[ing] the imperial violence and capitalist exploitation that defined all of history before it" (15); see Patterson.

6. See, for example, Tan; Kingston.

7. Most microfinance organizations, for example, take on only female clients.

## WORKS CITED

Ahmed, Sara. *The Promise of Happiness*. Durham, NC: Duke University Press, 2010.

———. *Willful Subjects*. Durham, NC: Duke University Press, 2014.

Alvar, Mia. *In the Country: Stories*. New York: Alfred A. Knopf, 2015.

Bello, Walden. "Conclusion: From American Lake to a People's Pacific in the Twenty-First Century." *Militarized Currents: Toward a Decolonized Future in Asia and the Pacific*. Ed. Setsu Shigematsu and Keith L. Camacho. Minneapolis: University of Minnesota Press, 2010. 309–322.

Bow, Leslie. "The Gendered Subject of Human Rights: Asian American Literature as Postcolonial Intervention." *Cultural Critique* 41 (1999): 37–78.

Buhejji, Hana. "Bahrain's 'Third Millennium Slavery.'" European Commission. 2011. https://ec.europa.eu/europeaid/sites/devco/files/article-hanabuhejji_en.pdf. 5 April 2015.

Constable, Nicole. "Reproductive Labor at the Intersection of Three Intimate Industries: Domestic Work, Sex Tourism, and Adoption." *Positions* 24.1 (2016): 45–69.

Cruz, Denise. *Transpacific Femininities: The Making of the Modern Filipina*. Durham, NC: Duke University Press, 2012.

Dalisay, Jose Y. *Soledad's Sister: A Novel*. Manila: Anvil, 2008.

Gonzalez, Vernadette V. "Military Bases, 'Royalty Trips,' and Imperial Modernities: Gendered and Racialized Labor in the Postcolonial Philippines." *Frontiers: A Journal of Women Studies* 28.3 (2007): 28–59.

———. *Securing Paradise: Tourism and Militarism in Hawai'i and the Philippines*. Durham, NC: Duke University Press, 2013.

Guevarra, Anna R. *Marketing Dreams, Manufacturing Heroes: The Transnational Labor Brokering of Filipino Workers*. New Brunswick, NJ: Rutgers University Press, 2010.

Hezel, Francis X., and S. E. Samuel. *Micronesians Abroad*. Pohnpei: Micronesian Seminar, 2006.

Huat, Chua B. "The Cultural Logic of a Capitalist Single-Party State, Singapore." *Postcolonial Studies* 13.4 (2010): 335–350.

Kahakauwila, Kristiana. *This Is Paradise: Stories*. London: Hogarth, 2013.

Kingston, Maxine Hong. *The Woman Warrior*. New York: Alfred A. Knopf, 1976.

Letman, John. "Micronesians in Hawaii Face Uncertain Future: COFA Agreements Provide US Regional Control in Exchange for Limited Access to America." *Al Jazeera*. 3 October 2013. http://www.aljazeera.com/humanrights/2013/10/micronesians-hawaii-face-uncertain-future-201310191535637288.html. 5 April 2015.

Mabalon, Dawn B. *Little Manila Is in the Heart: The Making of the Filipina/o American Community in Stockton, California*. Durham, NC: Duke University Press, 2013.

*Maid to Order: Ending Abuses against Migrant Domestic Workers in Singapore*. New York: Human Rights Watch, 2005.

Nelson, Sara. "Mia Alvar on Miracle Workers, Mothers and Being a Citizen of the World." *Omnivoracious*. 29 June 2015. http://www.omnivoracious.com/2015/06/mia-alvar-on-miracle-workers-mothers-being-a-citizen-of-the-world.html. 5 April 2016.

Parreñas, Rhacel Salazar. *Servants of Globalization: Migration and Domestic Work*. Palo Alto, CA: Stanford University Press, 2001.

Patterson, Christopher B. "Role-Playing the Multiculturalist Umpire: Loyalty and War in Bioware's Mass Effect Series." *Games and Culture* 10.3 (2015): 207–228.

Rodriguez, Robyn. *Migrants for Export: How the Philippine State Brokers Labor to the World*. Minneapolis: University of Minnesota Press, 2010.

*Swept under the Rug: Abuses against Domestic Workers around the World*. New York: Human Rights Watch, 2006.

Tadiar, Neferti X. M. "Himala (Miracle): The Heretical Potential of Nora Aunor's Star Power." *Signs* 27.3 (2002): 703–742.

Tan, Amy. *The Joy Luck Club*. New York: G. P. Putnam's Sons, 1989.

Teaiwa, Teresia K. "Bikinis and Other S/pacific N/oceans." *Contemporary Pacific* 6.1 (1994): 87–109.

# 7

# (De)humanizing Labor

## *Southeast Asian Migrant Narratives in Taiwan*

Grace Hui-chuan Wu

Since the late 1980s, the increased presence of Southeast Asian migrant workers in Taiwan has made visible strategies the local government has taken to counter labor shortages and sustain economic viability in the global market. Expressly, in 1989, Taiwan began importing Southeast Asian migrant workers for national infrastructure projects. This "opening up" of Taiwanese labor markets intersected with growing corporate demands for cheap, low-skilled workers; five years later, in 1992, the Taiwanese government passed the Employment Service Act, which extended the regulated importation of Southeast Asian migrant labor into the private sector. As of February 2018, there were 676,875 Southeast Asian migrants (2.9 percent of Taiwan's total population) working in manufacturing and service industries (specifically domestic work and caregiving); these workers hail mainly from Indonesia (38 percent), Vietnam (31 percent), the Philippines (22 percent), and Thailand (9 percent) (Ministry of Labor).

Taiwan's migrant worker policy, as labor studies scholar Liu Mei-chun notes, is designed to create unequal power dynamics between local employers and foreign low-skilled workers as a means of "stabiliz[ing] relations of production" and weakening local labor unions (77), making apparent structural discriminations against foreign blue-collar workers. Notwithstanding some revision, the restrictions on transfers between employers and the maximum duration of stay for low-skilled foreign workers have accordingly subjugated Southeast Asian migrant laborers to exploitation.[1] The brokerage system, which adds to migrant workers' financial difficulty, makes this group particularly vulnerable to human rights violations.[2] Unpaid overtime, no days off, hazardous working conditions, abuses, sexual assaults, and restrictions on individual freedom of movement and other basic rights are common predicaments. In addition to exploitation in the workplace, Southeast Asian migrant workers are doubly excluded in Taiwan's nationalist politics because of their race and class; they do not enjoy the rights of local workers and, unlike high-skill foreign workers, they can never become citizens (Tseng 32–46). Under such circumstances, running away and seeking illegal employment become at times the only alternatives to defy unjust regulations.

Situated adjacent this neoliberal imaginary, the call for rethinking migrant workers' rights in Taiwan cannot be understood simply as isolated human rights abuses and as a matter of local redistribution of social justice; instead, these rights considerations are inextricably linked to a concomitant effect of global capitalism. Transnational migration has brought a new challenge to the actualization of humanity due to the increased discrepancies that exist between citizen and noncitizen rights.[3] Southeast Asian labor migration exemplifies the "inhuman conditions" of global capitalism and the insufficiency of human rights discourse to fully achieve humanity in the age of globalization since "humanity is generated by inhuman techniques" (Cheah 230). The paradox, which Pheng Cheah explicates by showing how the humanity of Philippine migrant workers is generated by a set of competing inhumane biotechnologies from both labor-exporting and labor-receiving countries, highlights the making of the subject of human rights as a by-product of individual and political struggles. The imbrication of the human and the inhuman elucidates the exploitative nature of the new global division of labor and enables us to understand human rights not in the celebratory mode of progress and democracy but in the form of "interminable political negotiations" and "resistance" to the dehumanizing force of global capitalism (Cheah 264, 265).

Crucial to the difficult invention and articulation of migrant workers as the subject of human rights is the social imaginary of what constitutes humanity in the Taiwanese context. In tracing the social formation of human rights in the Western tradition, Lynn Hunt has argued that "new kinds of reading (and viewing and listening) created new individual experiences (empathy), which in turn made possible new social and political concepts (human rights)" (62). Her reading of epistolary novels in relation to the invention of human rights shows the significant position literature plays in rights articulation and comprehension. At the juncture of migration, human rights, and globalization, the capacity to empathize with Southeast Asian migrant workers and further advocate for institutional reforms is the key to challenging inequality embedded in the uneven socioeconomic development within and modernization of Asian countries. Such capacities presage a set of connected questions: How does literature in Taiwan imagine and articulate labor migrants as human beings? How does literary work reshape human rights discourses at the local level and make the inhumanity of global capitalism visible? Last, but certainly not least, how might literature enable new social relations to Southeast Asian migrant workers that do not necessarily reproduce the racial hierarchies of the world economic order?

This chapter attempts to answer these questions through a comparative reading of literary works by both Southeast Asian migrant workers in Taiwan and Ku Yu-ling, an award-winning Taiwanese writer. My juxtaposition of two different modes of authorship is guided by questions concerning who has the right to speak and is driven by the consideration of how such articulations enable a two-part evaluation of human subjects (as legible figures) and human rights (in a local context). Lucie Cheng, former director of the UCLA Asian American Studies Center and founding editor of *4-Way Voice*, a newspaper for Southeast Asian migrant workers and immigrants in Taiwan, maintains that ethnic media is essential to the realization of "liberating humanism" and "multiculturalism" in Taiwan (130). Her emphasis on equal access to public media for minority groups like (im)migrants accentuates the role of representations in shaping social relations between people of different languages and cultures and construes articulation as active political engagement. Correspondingly, life writing by Southeast Asian migrant workers in Taiwan, including pieces in *Tao: Women de baodao, tamen de lao* (Escape: Our island, their prison), offers insights into the migrants' experiences and their visions of human rights. Yet the right to speak does not promise equality and social justice; as Sophia A. McClennen and Joseph R. Slaughter point out, "as often as cultural forms make human suffering visible they distort perceptions in ways that make it possible to disenfranchise and abuse others" (8).

My reading of Southeast Asian migrant narratives, predicated on the ways in which literary forms enable and disenable social inclusion, speaks to the conflicting forces of oppression and liberation in cultural representations pertaining to human rights; to that end, I examine the literary birth of Southeast Asian migrant workers as human subjects in Taiwan. Situating Southeast Asian migrant narratives produced in Taiwan via globalization, I approach this burgeoning ethnic literature from a transnational perspective that foregrounds its points of intervention in the production of basic human rights for inter-Asia migrant workers and militates against a singular reading of such work as national literature. In doing so, I accentuate the underlying tension between citizenship and human rights in these stories; this tension undergirds a characterization of Southeast Asian migrant writing as counternarratives that challenge the dominant representation of labor migrants as purely economic beings. This chapter's analysis opens with a consideration of a twenty-six-letter column collection by Southeast Asian migrant workers (published in 2012 under the collective identity of *Taopao wailao*, or "runaway migrant workers") entitled *Tao: Women de baodao, tamen de lao* (henceforth referred to as *Escape*). I explore how labor migrants appropriate the language of slavery to describe their experiences and the limits of such narrative strategies. I propose that such figurations of slavery and accounts of suffering circumscribe the agency of migrant workers.

The chapter then turns to Ku Yu-ling's two acclaimed books on Southeast Asian migrant workers, *Women* (2008; published in English as *Our Stories* in 2011) and *Huijia* (*Return Home*, 2014), with a focus on her narrative style in the tradition of literary reportage, a genre to which the books belong. My reading of Ku's stories shows that the narrative form she employs engages intensively with the question of social justice and alternative development. This attentiveness to literary forms extends from McClennen and Slaughter's emphasis on the interlocking relation between cultural forms and human rights, especially their argument that "much of the imaginative and social work that literature does is . . . done through the *forms* of stories that enable forms of thought, forms of commitment, forms of being, and forms of justice" (11). The juxtaposition of two forms of narrative—readers' letters and literary reportage—demonstrates the laboring and paradoxical process of writing migrant workers into being. When the local law in Taiwan is complicit with the uneven world economic order and indifferent to structural exploitation, how literary production in Taiwan discloses such inhumane conditions and imagines alternative futures is crucial to bridge the gap "between the imagination of human rights and the state of their practice" (McClennen and Slaughter 4).

## The Disenabling Effect of Literary Humanitarianism

In *Escape*, an anonymous runaway migrant laborer who has worked in Taiwan for three years with thirteen different employers recalls how often she cried on a lonely bed, thinking, "If I were to put all my hardship and bitterness together, those materials would be more than enough to build a slavery museum" ("Nuli" 50–51). The term *slave* (*nuli*), which the writer uses to summarize her working experience in Taiwan and which the editors chose to title this readers' letter, evokes an analogy between the history of slavery in the United States and elsewhere in the Americas and the experiences of Southeast Asian migrant workers in Taiwan.[4] This analogy is concretized as the writer describes all the mistreatment that she has received, ranging from sleep deprivation and movement restriction to verbal and physical abuse, when she works as a caregiver for a newly rich family. The daily insults and violence involved in taking care of the family's grandmother, a job that the writer again equates with "being a slave," eventually become unbearable and trigger her escape ("Nuli" 54). As the letter ends with her retelling of the day of her departure and her concern for the grandmother's current well-being, the narrative explicates why being a runaway is the only choice left for survival. The contrast between bondage and freedom connoted in the writer's past and present circumstances further reconfigures her former working conditions as a form of servitude that compromises her humanity, a quality that she obviously possesses in her display of her concern for the grandmother and in her aspiration for freedom and self-determination. Her letter is thus both a testimony of human rights abuses in the workplace and an affirmation of her human subjectivity.

The narrative "Nuli"—which, along with the other letters, originally appeared in *4-Way Voice* in Vietnamese and then was translated into Mandarin and published in *Escape*—showcases the workers' predicaments for Chinese-language readers. The letters consistently detail the reasons why labor migrants run away (including exploitative brokerage systems, hazardous working conditions, sexual assault, physical abuse, discriminatory treatment, deprivation of liberty, and deportation threats) and recount subsequent police raids that at times cause the unnecessary deaths of undocumented workers. In one of the collection's forewords, Lin Feng-zheng suggests that the anthology's purpose involves a "conscience call" (or "responsibility" in Chu Shi-ying's language) to rethink how Taiwanese treat migrant workers (21, 19); in another foreword, Zhu Tian-xin depicts the anthology as a "mirror" to reflect on "the values that Chinese people cherish, democracy, civilization, and human rights" (12). The stories' affective power, as the forewords show, relies on seeing labor migrants as victims of slavery, of human rights abuses, of human trafficking, and of other forms of institutional inequality.[5] The corresponding language of slavery reinscribes the runaway migrant writers as the subject of human rights rather than subject to law enforcement.

Even as this reinscription demands global revisions of labor migration policies in Taiwan, the embodied experiences of human rights violation substantiated by those migrant writers are subjected to specific forms of truth claims. Zhu Tian-xin's and Chu Shi-ying's forewords narrate personal experiences of working with Southeast Asian migrant workers; filled with care and marked by respect, these forewords relegate the suffering and pain endured by migrant writers to the periphery as spectacles. For instance, Zhu characterizes the relationship with her grandfather's migrant caregiver, Lê Thị Mai, as tough but not exploitative, stressing a long-standing friendship with Å Mai. Alternatively, Chu expresses his shock as a potential employer when he discovers that labor migrants do not always enjoy the freedom to have weekends off or to have cellphones. The contrast between benevolent and callous employers replicates Harriet Beecher Stowe's *Uncle Tom's Cabin*, which distinguishes kind and cruel masters; however, what remains ambiguous is an overall critique of capitalist-driven migrant labor. Likewise vexed is the extent to which Zhu's and Chu's accounts inadvertently undermine the experiences documented in *Escape* as a universal condition of Southeast Asian migrant workers in Taiwan.

Moreover, the representation of labor migrants as slaves and fugitives subjugates migrant workers to specific discourses of human rights and the international human rights regime. The strategic employment of slave rhetoric in *Escape* regarding the working conditions of labor migrants in Taiwan effectively identifies foreign workers as victims of abuse and exploitation and thus requiring protection.[6] The narrative of victimization, however, also evokes too readily the need for outside intervention, ignoring the workers' specific understanding of and demand for human rights.[7] Casting migrant workers as slaves links migration to human trafficking, which results more often in criminalizing undocumented workers and enforcing border control than in providing help or services.[8] As Zhang Jun-mei points out in her discussion of the 2005 Thai workers' riot in Kaohsiung, the historical formation of the connection between slavery and human rights, translated within a Taiwanese context, reroutes the public discussion from exploitation and inequality to foreign relations and national image, flattening out the possibility of revolution to abolish discriminatory migration policies. The concerns about Taiwan's reputation regarding its human rights practices, like Zhu's mirror metaphor noted above, make the experiences of migrant workers a simple reflection of Taiwan's democracy and modernization. Only by helping Taiwanese people improve international relations and achieve their full humanity can the workers' experiences matter and can migrant workers speak.

Even though the narratives in *Escape* do not textually embody letter format with proper salutations and addressees, the editor of the book and of *4-Way Voice*, Zhang Zheng, describes these stories as "readers' letters" (34), and the jacket states that it is a book of "twenty-six letters of confession from runaway foreign laborers." The literary conceit of readers' letters gestures to a division between the private and the public that makes personal experiences available to a general reading public.[9] The form of readers' letters turns the personal complaints and suffering of labor migrants into public knowledge of enslavement and rights violations and encourages the readers to respond to these private tellings. Nevertheless, the shift of readership returns the public discourse of exploitation to the private experience of labor migration since the formal structure of addresser and addressee arguably reinstates an identity-based form of reading. The migrants' telling of suffering was originally published in *4-Way Voice* in their native languages to engender solidarity with other labor migrants; when translated into Mandarin, the collection's focus changes, inviting Chinese-language readers to witness and sympathize with the workers' pain. This readerly reconfiguration transforms Southeast Asian migrant worker life writing into testimony, creating an "uneven power dynamic between a privileged reader and an unfortunate victim-turned-storyteller" (Rickel 87). This reading practice, which Jennifer Rickel broadly defines as literary humanitarianism, positions nonmigrant readers as the agents of human rights while relegating migrant workers to humanitarian recipients/dependents. Although the original formal structure breaks down the division between the private and the public, the impossibility of the Chinese-reading audience (as the substituted audience of those narratives) to cross the boundaries between witnesses and victims reiterates uneven power dynamics vis-à-vis established human rights regimes.

Consequently, the use of slave rhetoric and characterization of victims in collections such as *Escape* render impossible migrant workers' agency save for the possibility of fugitive subjectivity. Echoing such a logic, when labor migrants exercise their rights to freedom and self-determination, embodied by their undocumented status, they are further subjugated to laws that criminalize, detain, and deport them. While the impossibility of construing their self-determination as a positive right illustrates the difficulty for government authorities and people in Taiwan to treat labor migrants as full human beings, the narrative of slavery further circumscribes migrant workers' subjectivity as victims without agency. Since Taiwan adopted the United Nations Convention against Transnational Organized Crime and the Protocols Thereto (2009) into its local law to eliminate human trafficking, the language of victimization further embeds migrant workers within the context of a state more invested in foreign relations and border control than in human rights.[10]

While migrant worker activists and advocates in Taiwan have tactically deployed the language of slavery in the hope of protecting migrant workers' rights, antitrafficking law tends to reinforce border control rather than enable labor migration policy reform.[11] Social activist and writer Ku Yu-ling, whose work I will turn to shortly, argues that "anti-slavery is anti-forced labor" ("Examining" 13). The claim highlights a link between labor migration and slavery and appeals to antitrafficking legislation as a motor for policy reform. Yet, as Ku states, antitrafficking campaigns have become sites of political struggles in Taiwan. Migrant worker activists soon realized this fact and then shifted their focus from antitrafficking to anti–forced labor in 2005 ("Examining" 13). The need to differentiate anti–forced labor from antitrafficking points to the contradictions between two different and often opposing forces underlying the institution of antitrafficking law—"one to stop female prostitution, and another to stop labor exploitation" (Vance 935). These contradictions show how the issue of labor migration is implicated in a hierarchy that prioritizes women's right to sexual self-determination (as antitrafficking typically targets prostitution) over migrant workers' right to economic equality in the workplace.[12]

The narratives of forced labor in *Escape* recapitulate the conflicting relationship between migrants and citizens when nation-states still serve as the institutional actors of the law and juridical regimes of human rights. My reading does not suggest that life writing by labor migrants at this historical moment is self-centered and lacking an understanding of political consciousness. Rather, the drive to write and share personal experiences through the ethnic newspaper *4-Way Voice* demonstrates an act of community building. Yet such a vision of sociality and community is built on a certain understanding of "authentic" experience and voice that leaves the issue of identity politics intact and arguably sustains the division between labor migrants and Taiwanese people. The limits of self-representation in *Escape* to create a new social formation that transcends cultural and racial differences thus point to the problem of an identity-based humanitarian reading practice and the necessity to visualize the subject of human rights not as an abstraction but as an embodiment of particular social, cultural, and historical contexts.

## Alternative Developments

Whereas the 1948 Universal Declaration of Human Rights (UDHR) conceives of human beings, regardless of their gender, race, religion, or nationality, as the primary bearers of human rights, Renata Salecl contends that the nondiscrimination principle requires "active forgetfulness" to disregard the history of the conception of human rights and its subject as such, and thus the universal ideas of human rights "are in themselves empty" (164).[13] The abstraction inherited in human rights discourse, a disembodied and disembedded subject when put into legal practice, often creates a "fundamental and irresolvable tension between national sovereignty and human rights discourse" that calls for further elaboration and expansion (Yeatman 1511). The shift from "the narrative of the declaration of human rights as natural endowments with that one of the production of human rights as fully political and historical constructions," as Riccardo Baldissone asserts, "opens towards the production, claim and exercise of further rights" and suggests that "all human beings are acknowledged not simply as bearers, but as producers of human rights" (93).[14] The emphasis on seeing human subjects as "narrative beings" and "authors" of human rights couples individual agency with narration and creativity, reorienting the claim to rights as a positive act of production and ramification rather than an affirmation of aggression and violation (Baldissone 92; Gregg 87). The production approach allows a rethinking of how literature negotiates, configures, normalizes, and potentially challenges human rights.

The literary shift from the bearers to the producers of human rights takes a distinctive form in Southeast Asian migrant writing in Taiwan. Ever since the publication of "Run Away," a short piece on the unequal treatment of labor migrants and the labor movement in Taiwan that won the China Times Literary Award for literary reportage in 2005, Ku Yu-ling's stories of Southeast Asian migrant workers have often been categorized as literary reportage. Ku's engagement with the genre of literary reportage highlights what has been at stake in the knowledge production of Southeast Asian migrant workers in Taiwan. "I could not bring myself to treat these workers and their life stories as part of a sterile thesis that often relegates them as a mere index like A310 or C409," and "I cannot imagine de-contextualizing their stories and their lives by reducing them into a few lines of observation, analysis, and conclusion," Ku writes in the postscript of the English translation of *Women*, henceforth referred to as *Our Stories* (327). Her concerns about institutional violence practiced against labor migrants and their subjugation to the dominant discourse illustrate how the existing framework of representation fails to treat them as full human beings. Unlike most life writing by Southeast Asian migrant workers, such as the texts included in *Escape*, whose characters/narrators appear to be only victims of workplace violence and fugitives who are always already deprived of basic human rights, Ku's stories of labor migrants with personal histories parcel out their struggles for agency in a disenabling social context. By interweaving literary reportage with stories of individual development as an operating technique to unravel the stories of migrant workers in both *Our Stories* and *Huijia* (henceforth referred to as *Return Home*), Ku's narratives enable a reading of situated subjectivity that explores the conflicts between the private and the public, the individual and the nation-state.

A mixture of oral history, reportage, and ethnography, Ku's stories are concerned about the interplay of the domestic and the foreign and the interlocking relationship between global capitalism and dehumanization in inter-Asia labor migration. In *Our Stories*, Ku asks her readers to rethink and redefine the linguistic, social, and cultural boundaries that differentiate foreign workers from Taiwanese people by appealing to shared experiences of migration, both domestic and international, and the dream of socioeconomic mobility. The interwoven narratives of Ku's parents (an interethnic marriage between a mainland Chinese man who immigrated to Taiwan after 1945 and a Taiwanese woman whose family has settled on the island for several generations) and an interracial marriage (between a Taiwanese factory worker and a Philippine migrant laborer) represented in *Our Stories*, for instance, illuminate shared histories of poverty, displacement, and migration between foreign workers and Taiwanese people. While *Our Stories* explores the lives and ongoing struggles of Philippine migrant workers in Taiwan, *Return Home* explores the promises and shadows of migration for Vietnamese workers after their stay in Taiwan. The text narrates the challenges awaiting returnees and traces their life changes over a span of four years between Ku's two trips to Vietnam in 2009 and 2013. Imbricating accounts of life overseas and at home, *Return Home* shows how inter-Asia labor migration unsettles a progressive narrative of mobility and development. The juxtaposition of *Our Stories* and *Return Home*, a seemingly full circle of departure and arrival, encapsulates the disenabling effects of labor migration.

Ku's deployment of the genre of literary reportage shows not only her investment in the struggles of labor migrants as a social activist but also her vision of literature as a medium to construe a form of human rights claims and social justice that hinges not necessarily on the liberal subject but on a social collective. The development of the genre of literary reportage has long been associated with the history of social and political movements in Taiwan since the 1930s, particularly with left-wing politics, even though it was not until the lifting of martial law on Taiwan proper in 1987 that literary reportage began to flourish and play an important role in social and political mobilization.[15] The leftist writer Chen Ying-zhen, who has helped popularize the genre by publishing the journal *Renjian* (*Human World*), has remarked that literary reportage should "observe the people, life, labor, environment, and social history of Taiwan from the perspective of the marginalized" and should "record, witness, and critique from that observation" (qtd. in Shiu 22). Ku's focus on the struggles of labor migrants in Taiwan and her detailed descriptions of their life experiences in *Our Stories* and *Return Home* echo Chen's concerns for the underprivileged and for social inequality. Yet her choice to make migrant workers her writing subjects extends beyond Chen's emphasis on "*Taiwan de ren*" (Taiwanese people, defined by nationality), and it is through multiple forms of marginality (including citizenship, race, and class) that Ku offers social critiques of local migrant labor policies and global capitalism.

The convergence of multiple identities in Ku's writing reconfigures the subject-object relationship in literary reportage and enables new social formations. Ku has repeatedly claimed, "I've lived with, fought with, and borne uncertainty with these people [migrant workers] in the last twenty years of my life," and "my writing does not go through the whole process of interviewing people, going to remote areas, and bringing stories back, which is often involved in literary reportage" ("My Labor Movement"). Her idiosyncratic approach to migrant workers' narratives, which she identifies as "being there" (*wo zai chang*), shows her long-term engagement in activism and her efforts to write migrant workers into being ("My Labor Movement"). Ku deploys both a third-person subjective narration with the narrator as the implied author and a first-person narration that tells her personal stories. As Ku writes herself in the narratives, she revises the convention of literary reportage in Taiwan—the use of a singular point of view.[16] Her presence in the narratives recreates her sense of "being there" in the struggles of labor migrants in everyday life and in social movements. Ku's interlaced narrative voices show her awareness of her own embeddedness in making the experiences of migrant workers visible. Her texts' hybrid narrative modes not only suggest the impossibility of sustaining the binary of objective and subjective reporting but also break the boundaries of class, race, culture, and nationality that Ku's stories intend to critique.

Ku's experimental reportage provides a different framework to understand the relationship between personal suffering and public sharing. Consider for instance Ku's narration of Vina in *Our Stories*, where Ku uses third-person narration to describe why Vina has to give up the college education she has dreamed for and work as a caregiver in Taiwan at the age of eighteen. Ku concludes her objective description of Vina's development and work experience, particularly Vina's intense relations with her employers, with the following sentence: "Why does the legal system allow people to behave like beasts and force workers to be slaves?" (*Women* 148; translation mine).[17] Here the authorial voice functions as a social commentary that reorients the readers' interpretations of and responses to Vina's suffering, denouncing the institutional violence that implicates both employers and migrant workers. The formal structure of the third-person narrator, a surrogate witness, in literary reportage mediates and reroutes the victim-witness relationship in Ku's stories of exploitation. Such intervention disrupts an easy identification between the character and the readers and unsettles a humanitarian reading practice built on sympathy and compassion. Ku's narrator is the figure of a social activist who demands institutional change, not sentimental identification with the abused and the exploited.[18] The triangular relationship between the characters, the narrator, and the readers transforms the narrative space from the personal to the political. Unlike the runaways' confessions collected in *Escape*, which appeal to the readers' understanding of their conundrum and thus return the telling to interpersonal reconciliations, Ku's narratives create a discursive space that allows for multiple forms of identification, mobilization, and alliance.

As Ku's narrative voice disrupts forms of humanitarian reading that prioritize the readers' agency, her incorporation of the fragmented stories of migrant workers' individual growth further opens up the possibility of making labor migrants the producers of human rights. Ku's use of developmental narratives as a frame to tell the experiences of labor migrants highlights the tension between the individual and the nation-state underlying the myth of labor migration. Depicted in certain discourses as national heroes, Southeast Asian migrant workers in labor-exporting countries such as the Philippines, Vietnam, and Indonesia bring home remittances that help sustain their countries' economies.[19] Yet those remittance heroes, who call home only to "tell them the good things and send them gifts," "have nowhere or no one to turn to" in difficulty, as Joy and Vina point out (Ku, *Our Stories* 142). The discrepancy between personal experience and public discourse shown in Joy's and Vina's comments suggests how the master narrative of labor migration fails to tell a story of identification and consolidation and instead tells one of alienation both at home and abroad. In *Return Home*, the unfinished project of modernizing homes—including fully equipped bathrooms without water and sewage and new refrigerators without electricity—becomes a way to figure the difference between house and home. Ku's description of newly built houses with modern facilities in contrast with the difficulties in reconnecting with family members after returning underlies what has been missing in the grand narrative of overseas workers as national heroes.

The myth of migration and the awareness of compromised rights enable Southeast Asian migrant workers to imagine an alternative community in Ku's narratives. The twenty-two-year-old Vina does not go back to the Philippines and attend college as her father wishes; instead, she learns to organize overseas Filipino workers to speak for the politically oppressed at home and to fight against injustice. "Living and working overseas as a migrant worker has opened up a whole new world for her. Unexpectedly, she embarked upon a different life path from what she expected when she was still in the Philippines" (Ku, *Our Stories* 176). Vina's developmental narrative cannot be contained by the master narrative of individual growth and economic development delineated by the Philippine nation-state; nor does her story conform to an enduring narrative of exploitation. Her displacement allows her to understand the contradictions embedded in the discourse of industrial modernization and to further challenge its dehumanizing forces.

The twists of individual development rearticulate what it means to be human. "Vina's dreams are wandering between borders," Ku writes; "she may remain active in the indigenous people's movement even after her return. Or perhaps, she may move to another country after Taiwan, to continue the Filipino migrant workers' struggle elsewhere" (*Our Stories* 202). The narrator's speculation about Vina's future and her vision of Vina as a transnational social activist break the division between fiction and reality underlying the convention of literary reportage, and invite the readers to take part in a form of imagining that refutes a humanitarian reading of sympathetic identification.[20] Meanwhile, in *Return Home*, the Vietnamese worker Kim Yên, who was seriously injured in a car accident when she worked in Taiwan, refuses to let her disability define who she is and starts to fight against oppression in her homeland. Ku's insistence on seeing Vina's and Kim's resistance to being incorporated in the grand narrative of labor migration enables the articulation of alternative futurities. The claim to have the right to "dream" about the social collective good and to place that right above the realization of economic rights subverts the integration of the individual and the nation-state, undergirding the notion of development, fictional and real. Ku's texts thereby ask readers to acknowledge migrant workers' agency to determine and assign new content to human rights—the right to imagine and invent alternative social formations.

Taken together, Ku's narratives of migrant workers' formation in *Our Stories* and *Return Home* challenge and renegotiate the ways in which the rights to development are narrowly understood in the economic sense and are appropriated by the state as biopolitical technologies of governance.[21] The friction between the individual and the state opens up the possibility of a different understanding of modernity in Asia, an understanding that "problematizes a Cold War version of positivist epistemology—a positivism whose modernity and authority is linked to rapid industrialization, and its attendant values and structures of feeling," as Amie Parry observes in her reading of *Our Stories* (178). The labor migrants' becoming in Ku's narratives registers more of their intervention in reshaping the dehumanizing forces of global capitalism than their subjugation. The stories foresee the growth of a social collective "wandering between borders" in all forms (Ku, *Our Stories* 202), including the lines that divide the readers from the migrant workers and the social activist and writer, Ku Yu-ling. Such border crossing initiates opportunities to build transnational social movement networks and reenvision what constitutes human rights and humanity.

*Escape*, *Our Stories*, and *Return Home* have articulated the dynamics between texts and readers to forge new social relations and collectively historicize incongruities between labor migration, globalization, and human rights. As an emerging ethnic literature in Taiwan, Southeast Asian migrant narratives, which cannot be narrowly defined by the writer's ethnicity alone, have become a site of convergence to rethink boundaries in all forms and to envision new social imaginaries. These texts cannot right what has been violated and retrieve what has been lost along the way for labor migrants. What they can do is to tell seemingly sporadic and incoherent stories of individual formation to register moments of transformation and consolidation and thereby envision new possibilities for social change. When read together, these texts challenge readers to actively engage in such alternative social imaginaries and disentangle Taiwan's racial (re)formation from the global division of labor and the world economic order. The double development of a suffering person in need of protection (in *Escape*) and a migrant subject in hopes of charting his or her own life trajectory (in *Our Stories* and *Return Home*) does not envision the articulation and actualization of human rights in a singular form. It instead evokes two different sets of power dynamics between the giver and the recipient of human rights. The possibility of "liberating" foreign workers from enslavement by appealing to antitrafficking campaigns and abiding by global and regional human rights laws without unsettling preexisting social, economic, and racial inequalities in the Taiwanese context foreshadows the intimate relationship between human rights regimes and global capitalism. It is in the shadow of such intimacy that the right to envision alternative social collectives, locally and globally, shows what it means to be human.

## NOTES

1. On discrimination against foreign blue-collar workers in the Employment Service Act, see D. Liu 614–25; Ku, "Bojiao" 95–105; Ma 97–101; Hsia 336–349.

2. For a critique of the brokerage system, see Lan, "Legal Servitude." For Taiwan's labor migration policy and human rights violation, see Sun.

3. Sociologist Alison Brysk defines the gap between citizen and human rights as a "citizenship gap"—"a lack of political mechanisms to ensure individual membership,

power holders' accountability, and respect for human rights in a globalizing world system" (246). The systematic exploitation of Southeast Asian migrant workers in Taiwan through discriminatory migration policy depends on the "citizenship gap" to generate national economic development.

4. This chapter generally follows the Hanyu Pinyin system used in academia in the United States. In some cases, the Wade-Giles system is used in the transcription of Taiwanese names if those names are commonly known in this form.

5. Zhu notes that words like "runaway, slave, adventure, drifting, criminal, and falling into" keep popping up in *Escape* (14). Those keywords explicitly show the contrast between freedom and incarceration, connecting the workers' experiences to that of forced labor.

6. In the discussion on policy reforms—for example, Taiwan's proposed Long-Term Care Services Act—the term *bloody forced labor* (*xuehan nugong*) is used to emphasize the systematic exploitation of migrant workers in Taiwan.

7. I do not suggest that such "outside" support and intervention are unnecessary. I am instead concerned about the advice from the annual human rights reports issued by the U.S. Department of State and the local government's subsequent action to engage with U.S. antitrafficking propaganda, which often result in local law enforcement.

8. See Lan, *Global Cinderellas* 50–58.

9. Here I borrow Joseph Slaughter and Jennifer Wenzel's idea about the division between the private and the public in the epistolary novel and letter writing.

10. The implementation of antitrafficking law in Taiwan, heavily influenced by U.S. antitrafficking law, has focused on forced prostitution, as Ku Yu-ling and Cheng Keng-liang show, even as the exploitation of migrant workers also constitutes a violation of antitrafficking law.

11. See K. Cheng 98–103; Zheng.

12. For antitrafficking campaigns and the hierarchy of human rights in Taiwan, see K. Cheng 90–100.

13. See Moore for a critique of a disembodied subject.

14. On individual narration and human rights, see Ward 3–5; Slaughter, *Human Rights* 1–44.

15. For the link between social movements and literary reportage, see Shiu 10–29.

16. Both C. Lin's and Shiu's studies of the history of reportage in Taiwan suggest that there is a bifurcation of subjective/objective narrative modes.

17. Agnes Khoo inserts the first- and third-person plurals in her English translation of Ku's text to foreground the function of the narrative voice as a social commentator, while the original text adopts a third-person narrator.

18. Ku's narrator is different from Joseph Slaughter's reading of the figure of the humanitarian subject (aid workers) in Henry Dunant's *A Memory of Solferino*. According to Slaughter, such aid workers invite the readers to take a philanthropic position ("Humanitarian Reading").

19. For analysis of migrant workers as new national heroes, see Rodriguez; Guevarra. See also Christopher Patterson's essay in this collection for a critique of this discourse as it pertains to the Philippines.

20. For discussions of the generic divide between fiction and journalism, see C. Lin; Shiu.

21. On the relation between the narrative of development and biopower, see Cheah 183–229, 239–266.

**WORKS CITED**

Baldissone, Ricardo. "I and Another: Rethinking the Subject of Human Rights with Dostoyevsky, Bakhtin and Simondon." Ward 83–100.

Brysk, Alison. "Conclusion: From Rights to Realities." *Globalization and Human Rights*. Ed. Alison Brysk. Berkeley: University of California Press, 2002. 242–256.

Cheah, Pheng. *Inhuman Conditions: On Cosmopolitanism and Human Rights*. Cambridge, MA: Harvard University Press, 2006.

Cheng, Keng-liang. "Whose Human Rights: Human Rights with Hierarchy of Marriage and Nation-State in Human Trafficking Prevention Movement." *Applied Ethics Review* 53 (2012): 83–108.

Cheng, Lucie. "Searching for Migrant Voices in the Media." *Transborder and Diaspora: Immigrants and Migrant Workers under Globalization II*. Ed. Hsia Hsiao-chuan et al. Taipei: Taiwan shehui yanjiu zazhishe, 2008. 129–158.

Chu Shi-ying. "Niwo gongtong de zeren" [Our shared responsibility]. Taopao wailao et al. 15–19.

Employment Service Act. *Laws and Regulations Database of the Republic of China*. 7 October 2015. https://law.moj.gov.tw/Eng/LawClass/LawAll.aspx?PCode=N0090001. 25 February 2016.

Gregg, Benjamin. *Human Rights as Social Constructions*. Cambridge: Cambridge University Press, 2012.

Guevarra, Anna Romina. *Marketing Dreams, Manufacturing Heroes: The Transnational Labor Brokering of Filipino Workers*. New Brunswick, NJ: Rutgers University Press, 2009.

Hsia, Hsiao-chuan. "Quanqiuhua xia de Taiwan yimin/yigong wenti" [The problem of immigrants and migrants in Taiwan under globalization]. *Taiwan de shehui wenti 2005*. Ed. Qu Haiyuan and Zhang Liyun. Taipei: Juliu, 2005. 328–367.

Hunt, Lynn. *Inventing Human Rights: A History*. New York: Norton, 2007.

Ku Yu-ling. "Bojiao de weiziyou shichang: Jianxi Taiwan wailao zhengce de sanda maodun" [A crippled pseudo-liberal market: Analyzing the three main paradoxes in Taiwan's foreign labor policy]. *Taiwan renquan xuekan* 2.2 (2013): 93–112.

———. "Examining the Way 'Anti-Trafficking' Has Been Constructed in Taiwan." International Conference on Human Rights Protection and Practice in Taiwan, 3 October 2008, National Cheng Kung University, Tainan. 25 August 2008. Web. 7 September 2016.

———. *Huijia* [Return home]. New Taipei City: INK, 2014.

———. "My Labor Movement and My Writing." Ed. Zuodushou. 14 September 2010. Web. 11 April 2016.

———. *Our Stories—Migration and Labor in Taiwan*. Trans. Agnes Khoo. Selangor, Malaysia: Strategic Information and Research Development Centre (SIRD), 2011.

———. *Women: Yidong yu laodong de shengming jishi* [Our stories: Migration and labor in Taiwan]. New Taipei City: INK, 2008.

Lan, Pei-chia. *Global Cinderellas: Migrant Domestics and Newly Rich Employers in Taiwan*. Durham, NC: Duke University Press, 2006.

———. "Legal Servitude and Free Illegality: Control and Exit of Migrant Workers." *Taiwan: A Radical Quarterly in Social Studies* 64 (2006): 107–150.

Lin, Chi-yang. "Taiwan baodao wenxue de xugou xushi guiyue" [The convention of fictional narratology of literary reportage in Taiwan]. *Wenshi Taiwan xuebao* 6 (2013): 26–48.

Lin, Feng-zheng. "Huhuan Taiwan ren de liangxin" [Call for Taiwanese people's conscience]. Taopao wailao et al. 20–21.

Liu, Dorothy. "The 1992 Employment Service Act and the Influx of Foreign Workers in Taiwan and Translation of the 1994 Implementary Provisions." Trans. Mingde Li and Judy DeMarsh. *Pacific Rim Law and Policy Journal* 5.3 (1996): 599–636.

Liu, Mei-chun. "'Lianjia wailao' lunshu de zhengzhi jingjixue pipan" [A political-economic critique of the discourse of "cheap foreign labor]. *Taiwan shehui yanjiu jikan* 38 (2000): 59–90.

Ma, Cai-zhuan. "Taiwan waiji laodongli de xiangqian—jieji yu xingbiehua" [Taiwan's intertwined migrant labor power—class and gender]. *Taiwan laogong jikan* 16 (2013): 92–103.

McClennen, Sophia A., and Joseph R. Slaughter. "Introducing Human Rights and Literary Forms; or, the Vehicles and Vocabularies of Human Rights." *Comparative Literature Studies* 46.1 (2009): 1–19.

Ministry of Labor. "Waiji gongzuozhe—chanye ji shefu waiji laogong renshu" [Foreign workers—the number of foreign workers in industry and welfare]. 17 April 2018. https://www.jiemian.com/article/2202237.html.

Moore, Alexandra Schultheis. *Vulnerability and Security in Human Rights Literature and Visual Culture*. New York: Routledge, 2016.

"Nuli" [Slaves]. Taopao wailao et al. 50–55.

Parry, Amie Elizabeth. "Inter-Asian Migratory Roads: The Gamble of Time in *Our Stories*." *Inter-Asia Cultural Studies* 13.2 (2012): 176–188.

Rickel, Jennifer. "'The Poor Remain': A Posthumanist Rethinking of Literary Humanitarianism in Indra Sinha's *Animal's People*." *Ariel: A Review of International English Literature* 43.1 (2012): 87–108.

Rodriguez, Robyn. "Migrant Heroes: Nationalism, Citizenship and the Politics of Filipino Migrant Labor." *Citizenship Studies* 6.3 (2002): 341–356.

Salecl, Renata. "See No Evil, Speak No Evil: Hate Speech and Human Rights." *Radical Evil*. London: Verso, 1996. 150–169.

Shiu, Wen-wei. "Zaixian Taiwan tianye de jiti jiyi—cong shehui yundong yu zaixianlun kaochaxia de Taiwan baodao wenxue shi" [Representing the collective memory of fieldwork in Taiwan—a history of literary reportage in Taiwan from the perspective of social movements and representation]. *Baodao wenxue duben*. Ed. Xiang Yang and Shui Wen-wei. 2002. Taipei: Eryu wenhua, 2012. 8–45.

Slaughter, Joseph. *Human Rights, Inc.: The World Novel, Narrative Form, and International Law*. New York: Fordham University Press, 2007.

———. "Humanitarian Reading." *Humanitarianism and Suffering: The Mobilization of Empathy*. Ed. Richard Ashby Wilson and Richard D. Brown. Cambridge: Cambridge University Press, 2009. 88–107.

Slaughter, Joseph, and Jennifer Wenzel. "Letter of the Law: Women, Human Rights, and Epistolary Literature." *Women, Gender, and Human Rights*. Ed. Marjorie Agosín. New Brunswick, NJ: Rutgers University Press, 2001. 289–311.

Sun, You-lian. "Yidong zhong de boxue: Taiwan wailao renquan pouxi" [Exploitation in migration: An analysis of migrant workers' rights in Taiwan]. *Taiwan renquan xuekan* 2.2 (2013): 113–128.

Taopao wailao, et al. *Tao: Women de baodao, tamen de lao* [Escape: Our island, their prison]. Ed. Zhang Zheng et al. Trans. Luo Yi-wen et al. Taipei: Shibao, 2012.

Tseng, Yen-Fen. "Yinjin waiji laogong de guozu zhengzhi" [The nationalist politics of the importation of foreign workers]. *Taiwan shehui xuekan* 32 (2004): 1–58.

Vance, Carole. "States of Contradiction: Twelve Ways to Do Nothing about Trafficking While Pretending To." *Social Research: An International Quarterly* 78. 3 (2011): 933–948.
Ward, Ian. "Literature and Human Rights: Interdisciplinary Reflections on the Law, the Language and the Limitations of Human Rights Discourse." Ward 1–8.
Ward, Ian, ed. *Literature and Human Rights: The Law, the Literature, and the Limitations of Human Rights Discourse*. Berlin: De Gruyter, 2015.
Yeatman, Anna. "Who Is the Subject of Human Rights?" *American Behavioral Scientist* 43.9 (2000): 1498–1531.
Zhang, Jun-mei. "Nuli chuan" [Slave ships]. *Zhongshi luntan*. 26 August 2005. Web. 15 March 2016.
Zhang, Zheng. "Taiwan liuwang suoyin" [Exile index in Taiwan]. Taopao wailao et al. 30–34.
Zheng, Shi-ying. "Paohu haishi yapo—zaisi 'fan renkou fanyun'" [Protection or oppression—rethinking antitrafficking]. *NPOst*. 26 May 2014. Web. 2 May 2016.
Zhu, Tian-xin. "Yingzhao niwo de jing" [A mirror of our reflection]. Taopao wailao et al. 6–14.

# 8

# Factories, Farms, and Fisheries

## *Human Trafficking and Tethered Subjectivities from Asia to the Pacific*

Annie Isabel Fukushima

In 1998, Kil Soo Lee, a Korean, opened the Daewoosa garment factory in American Samoa. Lee brought migrant laborers from Vietnam and China to work in the factory. Complaints of trafficking circulated in media networks as early as 2000. The Daewoosa factory trafficked two hundred workers from Vietnam and China to work alongside approximately fifty Samoan workers in American Samoa. Court records and media coverage of the case illuminated to the public how this employer starved the workers, threatened deportation, restricted the workers' movement, and even beat them. One witness described the beatings: it was like "watching a film where the people are being brutally beaten to the point of like a massacre" ("Servitude in American Samoa"). In 2001, Lee was charged in Hawaii federal criminal courts on violations including involuntary servitude, extortion, and money laundering. Lee was convicted in 2003 and sentenced in 2005 to forty years in prison.

Narratives like the Daewoosa case shed light on human rights violations and the failures to facilitate human rights in Asia-Pacific. Visible trafficking narratives are bound to facilitate a kind of witnessing in dualities: victim/criminal, illegal/legal, and citizen/noncitizen. These dualities reify how some subjects are viewed through colonial frames, wherein those who fail to further a narrative of citizenship, legality, and victimhood are socially dead. In this chapter, I argue that one cannot separate understanding rights in the Pacific from the modern colonial economic condition of settler logics. I will ground this argument by seeking to understand human rights violations circulating from Asia to American Samoa to Hawaii to California on the west coast of the continental United States.

The U.S. presence in the Asia-Pacific region is bound to militarisms and the modern colonial economic system. Plantations in the Pacific grew in the mid-1800s due to the U.S. Civil War (1861–1865)—a war that disrupted the provision of supplies, leading to the establishment of plantations in Samoa, Fiji, Tahiti, northern New South Wales, and Queensland (Lal et al.). In 1898, the United States annexed Hawaii. During the nineteenth century, Hawaii became a central part of a Pacific trade of goods and people (Rosa 226). President William McKinley signed the Tripartite Convention (1899) a year after the annexation of Hawaii, placing west Samoa under the U.S. Department of the Navy. Encompassing the processes of settler colonialism was a legitimization of U.S. presence in the region through civil rights claims, furthering an ideal of American democracy (Fujikane and Okamura). Hawaiians, Kanaka Maoli, were granted citizenship with the United States and, for some indigenous Hawaiian scholars, were seen as "second class native-Americans" (Trask 83). This contrasts with the American Samoan experience, where U.S. law supplants indigenous laws, thereby normalizing U.S. law above Samoan law in American Samoa. Joanne Barker's *Sovereignty Matters: Locations of Contestation and Possibility in Indigenous Struggles for Self-Determination* describes the thwarted relations of U.S. protectionism and Samoan identity of *fa'asamoa* (Samoan language, culture, and way of life) and *fa'amatai* (Samoan chiefly system). The Treaty of Berlin (1899) divided the Archipelago into American Samoa (East) and the independent nation of Samoa, and the Tripartite Convention (1899) placed West Samoa under U.S. military control. The trial of Ipu (1900) reinforced U.S. law over Samoan law when the last sovereign of Manu'a, Tutuila Manu'a Elisala, was forced to sign a deed of cession of Manu'a. U.S. notions of protectionism over American Samoa are deeply defined by a power relationship and colonial difference, where independent Samoans have difficulties entering an American Samoa that enacts its own laws, has its own power of taxation, and controls its own borders. The mixing of languages in American Samoa, including Samoan and American English; the territorial status of American Samoa; and U.S. military presence—all are constant reminders of how colonial relations shape the Pacific. Not only are U.S. military occupancy and economic presence in the region a part of settler colonialisms; so too are the migrant laborers who come from multiple parts of Asia. Asian migrant laborer presence in Asia-Pacific is bound to a legacy of labor migration and labor exploitation (i.e., the coolie trade). In the twenty-first century, these labor exploitive flows are often called human trafficking. How a society may come to know who and what counts as the human and the trafficked person discursively circulates in the media and in the law shaping dominant perceptions of Asian victimhood and criminality. The intervention I make in this chapter is to examine how the circulation of victimhood as human rights discourse (notably in the media and the law) produces a tethered subjectivity. When I use the term *tethered subjectivities*, I am referring to the dualities in (self-)perception of migrant identities that discursively and in practice circulate and are reified through the law, social relations, and politics. As I argue in this chapter, such tethered subjectivities cannot be delinked from narratives of settler colonialism.

Human trafficking is legally defined in the United Nations' Palermo Protocol to Prevent, Suppress and Punish Trafficking in Persons Especially Women and Children (2000). Article 3 of the protocol defines human trafficking as follows:

> "Trafficking in persons" shall mean the recruitment, transportation, transfer, harbouring or receipt of persons, by means of the threat or use of force or other forms of coercion, of abduction, of fraud, of deception, of the abuse of power or of a position of vulnerability or of the giving or receiving of payments or benefits to achieve the consent of a person having control over another person, for the purpose of exploitation. Exploitation shall include, at a minimum, the exploitation of the prostitution of others or other forms of sexual exploitation, forced labour or services, slavery or practices similar to slavery, servitude or the removal of organs.

Although slavery is deeply tied to colonial legacies, the coloniality of the present has largely been absent in discussions of human rights and human trafficking. This chapter examines language and content from court documents, explores media representation in the form of press releases and news articles, and draws on secondary sources such as Virginia Lynn Sudbury's *Sweatshops in Paradise: A True Story of Slavery in Modern America* to conceptualize the subjectivities produced in antitrafficking narratives. An important theoretical intervention of this chapter surrounding human rights is that subjects such as trafficking subjects (i.e., trafficked persons, traffickers, and antitraffickers) are reproduced through a tethered subjectivity—the dualities by which rights-based subjects are defined, which are reified through a discourse and practice regarding appeals for citizenship. The call for a citizenry is deeply bound to notions of who has the right to have rights, naturalizing settler-colonial logics that further a socially dead status of those whose subjectivity is bound to criminality, illegality, and noncitizenship. To witness the dualities to which Asian migrants are bound even in the context of human rights violations in the Pacific and North America is to reconcile the multiple forms of violence that materialize when settler-colonial logics are operationalized as normal, the everyday. Although a tethered subjectivity is bound to (settler) colonialism and global capitalism, this chapter offers a methodology of witnessing an analytical category I have argued elsewhere as having social, political, and material consequence (Fukushima). To witness beyond dualities requires enactments of new forms of witnessing. Therefore, I draw on Gayatri Chakravorty Spivak's notion of ritual hacking to witness on the side of those who are oppressed (Lugones) as a decolonial modality of witnessing. I will examine *United States v. Kil Soo Lee* (2005), *EEOC v. Global Horizons, Inc.* (2014), and the story of Sonny in California. From Samoa to California, these cases collectively construct how tethered subjectivities across contexts produce socially dead subjects who are deeply defined by eventfulness and ongoing modern colonial economic systems. To conclude, I offer an exemplar of witnessing on the side of the oppressed by challenging the very discursive terrain of colonial systems. By tracing various cases from the Pacific to the west coast of the continental United States, this chapter offers a practice of witnessing, appealing to readers to contend with the multiple sites and contexts where such modalities of seeing are materialized.

## Theoretical Framing: Tethered Subjectivities

The subjectivities shaping transnational economies and rights violations are multiple. Feminist and antiracist genealogies, where feminists theorize intersectionality, the multiplicity of subject locations, the enactments of oppositional consciousness and practices, the need for historical and contextual specificity, and the imaginaries and material implications through which objects become subjects—all are central to understanding tethered subjectivities (Alarcon; Alexander; Hooks; Lugones; Mohanty; Moraga and Anzaldúa; Sandoval). A tethered subjectivity is a naming of the process through which experience is categorically reified, preventing communities from seeing multiple forms of subjectivities beyond those that one is bound to regarding legality, citizenship, and victimhood.

In human rights discourse and practice, tethered subjectivities encompass how diasporic subjects are legally, socially, and politically bound to dualities of victim/criminal, illegal/legal, and citizen/noncitizen. Tethered subjectivities produce the terms of legibility that enable diasporic migrant laborers to be propelled into visible status as victims of human trafficking. To be seen is to be able to name events as trafficking. The terms of legibility and the markers of eventfulness are political, social, and discursive. As I argue, a tethered subjectivity—how one is politically, socially, and legally bound—reproduces social death.

## *United States v. Kil Soo Lee*: Social Death and Citizenship Denied in American Samoa

To see beyond tethered subjectivities—an untethered subjectivity—one must ritually "hack" witnessing. There are two threads of action this paper sutures throughout: first, the naming of a tethered subjectivity that is produced through rights discourse and, second, ritually "hacking" the process of witnessing to enable an untethered subjectivity. Gayatri Chakravorty Spivak writes, "To suture thus the torn and weak responsibility-based system into a conception of human dignity as the enjoyment of rights one enters ritual practice transgressively, alas, as a hacker enters software. . . . The point is to realize that democracy also has its rituals, exaggerated or made visible, for example, when in our metropolitan life we seek to make politically correct manners 'natural,' a matter of reflex" (559). To ritually hack how one is bound means finding new ways of witnessing. Robyn Wiegman's *Object Lessons* frames a relational understanding of the epistemological and affective political claims of subjectivities that bridge the imaginary to materiality in social justice fields. Theorizing tethered subjectivities enables one to name a phenomenon in human rights. This is the first step toward radically undoing, as appealed for by Wiegman (12), the field of human rights discourse and its regimes of witnessing. Moving toward new visions and practices begins with witnessing how tethered subjectivities are produced. The case of Kil Soo Lee in American Samoa is illustrative of how human rights appeals in antitrafficking discourse reify how subjects are bound. As we will see, the consequence for those whose legibility relegates them to invisibility is social death. Social death renders groups functionally ineligible for personhood (Cacho).

As American Samoa was removed from the United Nations' list of nations to be decolonized (2001), trafficking in the archipelago made headline news. Allegations leading to court hearings surrounding the case of Kil Soo Lee propelled American Samoa into the public eye of the media. It was found that Kil Soo Lee—the Korean owner of the Daewoosa garment factory—was trafficking women from Vietnam and China. In 1998, Lee established the Daewoosa garment factory in American Samoa and brought migrant laborers from Vietnam and China to work in the factory. By 2000, the labor violations occurring in the Daewoosa factory were well documented through complaints including a web video interview of a Ms. Nga and a Ms. Dung. The abuses included false promises, food deprivation, long hours of work, and wages owed (*Report*). Although all the crimes occurred in American Samoa, Kil Soo Lee's case was brought to trial in Hawaii. In 2003, Kil Soo Lee was convicted and sentenced in Hawaii courts to 480 months in prison under Title 18. His crimes included extortion, money laundering, conspiring to violate the civil rights of others, and holding workers in involuntary servitude in his garment factory.

In 2006, Kil Soo Lee drew on the colonial and geopolitical history of American Samoa to appeal his case due to a "lack of jurisdiction and improper venue" (*United States of America v. Kil Soo Lee*). His appeals claiming that Hawaii did not have jurisdiction over his case failed. Kil Soo Lee was charged with federal crimes, where the U.S. federal government has territorial rights over American Samoa, including all places and waters, from continental to insular. Here the nation-state that was called to uphold rights was the colonial one, reifying the U.S. nation-state as benevolent rescuer and upholder of rights. This narrative was furthered in how rights were (re)imagined and rearticulated in the everyday aspects of the case.

The lead attorney for the case, Virginia Lynn Sudbury, published the story of Daewoosa in her book, *Sweatshops in Paradise: A True Story of Slavery in Modern America* (2012). In *Sweatshops in Paradise*, Sudbury narrates how when speaking with former employees of the Daewoosa factory, Christa, Adeline, Dale, Dung, and Nga, it was essential that she convey to the workers their rights. Sudbury describes the moment she educated the workers about their rights, stating, "I drew a teeny little speck over to the west" (Sudbury 10). She then said to the group, "Here in Vietnam something may be illegal. But here, in the big United States, we all have *rights*." Sudbury then describes to the reader, "I wrote RIGHTS in big letters." She recalls how she impressed upon the group of workers the notion of "Lots of rights! We can all think any way we like and express our opinions. We can hangout out with anyone we want. If someone treats us badly, we can complain against him or her. And no one can make us work without giving us wages. Do you understand?" Sudbury's account furthers universal notions of human rights, where one is eligible for these rights simply because one is human. This universal notion of human rights is legitimized through the law, and it is claimed when things are not going well (Donnelly 10–15). The location of truth and universal rights reifies how it is located in the West, or the Global North, and embodied in the knowledge holder of the United States and its citizens. The questioning and emphasis of "Do you understand?" compels the reader to see the diasporic subject, the migrant laborer, as not always knowing and not always understanding, where truth claims and truth enactments are arbitrated in the West. "Do you understand?" also draws attention to the normalization of global designs arbitrating who is the upholder of rights—the Global North—and the Global South in Asia is perceived as unknowing, implicating Asians as backward and uncivilized.

In human trafficking narratives, what counts as human is the victim. As Julietta Hua's research illustrates, "human rights concerns like [human] trafficking are not just about providing aid to those in need; they are also about the very ways we have come to know and understand what and who counts as human" (xvi). In order to ritually hack the witnessing of what can be named as rights, the human—and human rights violations—requires a new practice of seeing, a kind of seeing that allows for witnessing how human rights appeals reproduce social death (see Patterson; Cacho; Cho).

How trafficking subjects circulate reifies their socially dead status. Social death is bound to notions of citizenship—to be a part of the living, one must be legally recognized where denials of legal recognition are social death. The naturalization of migrants into citizenship status, the desire to be naturalized, and the status one has in papers is constantly renarrated in antitrafficking stories where a central aspect of coercion is connected to the question, "Has someone taken your passport?" Being documented as an "alien" in territories like American Samoa reifies the power of citizenship. In American Samoa, non-American Samoans and non-U.S. citizens have to carry their alien ID card with them at all times. "Failure to do so [is] a misdemeanor" (Sudbury 32). Nga, a Vietnamese migrant and former employee of the Daewoosa factory, testifies to how citizenship served as the backdrop to her trafficking experiences in American Samoa.

> I work at the compound in Daewoosa. I live at the compound in Daewoosa, at the female section. The meal is rice and potatoes, rice and some noodles and sometimes with some chicken. Since I got here, I do not know where my passport is. . . . I arrived at the airport, and I gave it to Mr. Lee. . . . On January 14, I lost the card [ASG alien ID card]. . . . I went to the entrance and gave the card to the security guard, and when I came back, I didn't know where it was. Neither did the security guard. . . . I went to report it to Mr. Lee, and I asked him about it, and he said we'll wait until the hearing, and we'll sort it from there.

Nga is translated as slipping into describing her card as "lost." To lose something in a rights violation, such as rape, means to lose one's sense of security, safety, and rights to one's own body. The loss Nga experiences surrounds security; her security was lost where it was taken by another person. However, when cross-examined, Nga was asked about losing her own card. She responded, "I go to the gate, and if I don't give my card, then I won't be able to be let out" (Sudbury 32–33). She once had an opportunity to leave at will; now the loss has a double meaning—Nga lost her card, and she lost her freedom to leave. The questioning from Kil Soo Lee's defense team suggests Nga's own responsibility for her card—she lost it; it was her agency and actions that led to the loss. However, this dual meaning of loss in Nga's testimony—something taken, something she no longer has—also reinforces how trafficked diaspora narratives are tethered to citizenship. Nga is denied rights to personhood through the withholding (passport as taken) of identity. Nga is bound to legibility through citizenship/noncitizenship. She was undocumented, unidentified, unknowable on paper and to the institutions, and her appeals for her legibility as a victim of human trafficking required documenting her and understanding how her loss of identification was tied to her trafficking experience. For Asian diaspora laborers in American Samoa, their recognition depends on a normalizing of colonial presence, appeals for human rights denied through the establishment of citizenship, and a call for a path to citizenship.

For homogenized Vietnamese migrant laborers, mostly women in the Lee case, their socially dead status is also ritualized in legal representation. The public never knows the migrant workers' pasts except in relation to how they matter for the legal case of human trafficking. The legal records did not discuss the genealogies of where the case occurred, nor is there ever a deeper understanding of diaspora histories. Instead, how the diasporic laborers mattered was always in relation to the Daewoosa factory. The image of the bloodied workers and the worker whose eye was gouged out came to dominate how the case circulated in the media—reproducing how migrant laborer diasporas are bound to a story of victimhood. Depersonalized and desocialized, the social death an enslaved person experiences is one from which they can never be brought to life again (Patterson 38).

Although the real names of Dung and Nga and other women exploited in the Daewoosa factory circulated, they are referred to as "victim," "trafficked," and a homogeneous two hundred, reinforcing how the witness is called to see the subjectivities of transnational trafficked subjects as a homogenized other. The Daewoosa factory workers were described as experiencing indentured servitude, forced to labor, imprisoned in the factory. Those who resisted were beaten and threatened with deportation. The civilians, two missionary men, and a police officer witness the scene of the Vietnamese women behind barbed-wire fences "crying for food and help" (Trott 10). The public sees the many faces crying for help, a delinked imagining of plural and diverse experiences.

The politics and social implications of settler colonialism are marginalized in the dominant media deployments of the Kil Soo Lee case. When Samoans and Samoa appear, Samoans are portrayed as complicit in the violence. Samoan police were described as furthering the abuse of the workers, and Samoan workers were regularly described as beating the Asian migrant workers. Regardless, only two Samoans were convicted as traffickers. Samoa serves as the backdrop, the site of violation. The rights of Samoans, who were also employees in the factory; their pressures; their relationship to colonial capitalism, which led to the emergence of the Daewoosa factory; and the invisibility of how U.S. law presided over a case that occurred in Samoa were obscured.

It is unsettling to see a story about rights violations, about human trafficking, as also a story about the naturalization of colonial relations between the United States and American Samoa. The layers of rights, rights violations, and the obfuscation of rights cannot be easily reconciled where Vietnamese and Chinese diasporic migrant workers were both victims of labor violations and complicit in settler colonialisms, where Samoans were used as mediators, as go-betweens in a colonial system, even though Samoan land was ceded to the United States. In witnessing rights violations in American Samoa, the United States has the face of both an ally, as an attorney advocating for rights, and a producer of systems of exploitation where the demands for cheap and affordable products necessitate and create these systems. Eventfulness marks the trafficking victim's subjectivity, whereas the colonial context and the settler realities are deemed uneventful in the media. What follows next is a discussion of the case of *Equal Employment Opportunity Commission (EEOC) v. Global Horizons* (2011) and the eventfulness that reinforces colonial logics.

## *EEOC v. Global Horizons*: Uneventfulness and Settler Colonial Realities

Human rights narratives make visible events of rights violations. Elizabeth Povinelli discusses eventfulness through the examination of Le Guin's "The Ones Who Walk Away from Omelas," the story of a child in a broom closet in Omelas, where happiness depends on keeping the child, whom everyone knows about, suffering in the closet. In her analysis of the child in the broom closet, Povinelli points to how one may contend with the suffering. It is not through the eventful, catastrophic, or sublime but rather the "ordinary, chronic, acute, and cruddy" (511). To contend with the tethered subjectivities migrants are bound to surrounding victimhood, legality, and citizenship in an antitrafficking narrative, one must look to how uneventfulness, the ordinary, and the chronic are normalized in human rights narratives through the imagining of the trafficking experience, the rights violation, as eventful. *EEOC v. Global Horizons, Inc.* is a case that is marked by (un)eventfulness in the settler context of Hawaii.

In 2011, charges were brought against Global Horizons regarding the trafficking of migrant workers in their farms. Global Horizons, a labor contracting company, supplied approximately five hundred workers for companies such as Mac Farms, Kauai Coffee, Kelena Farms, and Captain Cook Coffee. The laborers were brought to the United States as guest workers. Companies like Global Horizons depend on U.S. guest worker programs, which recruit international laborers to work in the United States on a temporary basis. The heritage of the guest workers, or contract laborers, may be traced to the coolie laborer in the postslavery era. Contract laborers, indentured laborers such as the coolie, who worked on U.S. plantations were legal workers who were in essence what Lisa Yun refers to as "mobile slaves"—workers who were contracted but whose contract could be sold to other employers (133). A later version of guest worker was the bracero. Braceros were Mexican workers who were recruited to fulfill labor shortages in the U.S. agricultural industry during World War II (Cohen; Griffith). The imported laborers came soon after the establishment of the Fair Labor Standard Act (FLSA; 1937), which created minimum wage standards and protected overtime pay. The FLSA created exempt categories regarding who would receive overtime pay in which agricultural workers were left out, reinforcing the normalization of the historical mistreatment of guest workers in a quasi-slave system.

Allegations of human trafficking were brought against two top officials of Global Horizons: the chief executive, Mordechai Orian, and the company's director of international relations, Pranee Tubchumpol. In 2012, the courts dismissed the criminal charges. After years of investigation, the charges were suddenly dropped (Zimmerman). The difficulties of investigating and prosecuting a human trafficking case in the criminal context are due to the length of time required to investigate a case (ranging up to three years), coordination among multiple law enforcement entities (local law enforcement, Defense Security Service, Federal Bureau of Investigation, Homeland Security Investigations, and Immigration and Customs Enforcement), and misreporting (Bales and Lize; Nichols and Heil). During the ten years after the implementation of the federal Trafficking Victims Protection Act (2000), less than three hundred cases were prosecuted, in spite of the estimates at the time that 17,500 people were trafficked in the United States alone (U.S. Department of Justice Civil Rights Division). Case dismissal—a trafficking case that never becomes visible as a trafficking conviction—is the norm. But it is through the scripts of the spectacle of suffering that victimhood is narrated as eventful (Chouliaraki). The case of the EEOC started off as a quasi-event of human trafficking—an event that was and never was human trafficking.

Two years later, the EEOC filed charges of civil rights violations against Global Horizons, and the everyday work abuses, hostile work environment, and racist discrimination in the workplace took the stage as eventful (even if, one could say, such is the norm in low-wage labor). The condition of victimhood was centralized not through the trafficking but rather through claims of a hostile work environment, disparate treatment, and a pattern and practice of retaliation. In 2014, U.S. District Judge Leslie E. Kobayashi approved settlements between the EEOC and four Hawaii farms totaling $2.4 million for about five hundred Thai farmworker victims of national origin discrimination and retaliation.[1] The settlement included monetary relief, options for jobs and benefits, housing, other reimbursements of expenses, and sweeping injunctive relief remedies—a $1.2 million settlement from Del Monte Fresh Produce.[2] Judge Kobayashi found that "Thai workers were often paid less, made to work less desirable and more demeaning jobs and denied breaks, yet worked longer hours than non-Thai farm workers. Food, housing and living conditions were also deplorable for the Thai workers" (EEOC v. Global Horizons, "Federal Judge").

The case spoke to the ongoing racist ideologies shaping transnational economies and labor recruitment. In the summary judgment, one can see how everyday racist ideologies shaped what eventually became an eventful case. The Thai laborers were recruited to work on Hawaii farms. Records show the racist attitudes toward the laborers:

> Global Horizons has admitted that Mordechai Orian, its chief executive officer, "specifically sought Thai nationals to fulfill the farm labor contracts believing that Thai workers would be easier to exploit than workers from other national origins and/or races," and Global Horizons "selectively recruited impoverished, uneducated Thai workers who couldn't speak English, and had no family or contacts in the U.S. so they couldn't escape or question Global [Horizons]." [Hostile Work Environment CSOF at 1.] Orian believed that, in general, "Thai people, they are good people, nice people. And they just follow. . . " [Noh Decl., Exh. 1 at Nos. 64.] Specifically, Orian believed that, as workers in the United States Department of Labor ("Labor Department") H–2A guest worker program, the Claimants would "just follow." [ Id. at No. 65.] Orian previously hired workers from Mexico, China, and Nepal, but he had problems with those workers because they often disappeared. Orian stated that he believed that Claimants would not leave. [Id. at Nos. 66–69.] Orian has stated: "That's why we decide to go with Thailand, because the ration-ratio at that time of people who be absconded [sic] was 3 percent, 2 percent compared to 80 percent, 90 percent, 100 percent from other countries . . . " [Id. at No. 70 (alteration in original).] He also stated, "you just go to countries. You know it's going to be easier and they're going to stay on the job. . . . That's why Thailand." (EEOC v. Global Horizons)

"That's why Thailand" is a reminder that twenty-first-century labor violations in the current modern global economic system are deeply tied to recruitment practices that depend on racist and racialized understandings of groups of people. The civil rights claims, hostile work environment, disparate treatment, and patterns and practices of retaliation in the case are all reminders that, while the case was uneventful as human trafficking, it was eventful as a civil rights case. Although Global Horizons was not convicted for trafficking, the civil case that followed the criminal claims points to the racism in labor recruitment in Asia-Pacific.

Haunting the civil rights appeals of the Global Horizons case is the need to contend with settler-colonial realities. The settler-colonial context itself in a human trafficking case is commonly treated as uneventful. Appeals for corrections of rights violations further this; Olophius Perry, district director for the EEOC's Los Angeles District Office, is quoted as saying, "Foreign workers should be treated as equals when working in the U.S., not as second class citizens. All workers foreign and U.S. are protected under the law and have the right to complain of such employment abuses which poison the moral fabric of our society" (EEOC, "EEOC Files"). Democratic ideals further what is considered eventful in U.S. media and what is uneventful in settler-colonial logics—the illegal annexation of Hawaii and the colonial relations that place U.S. law above Samoan law relegate ongoing occupations to the ordinary and the chronic. While the laborers themselves are also recruited, a settler-colonial narrative makes invisible why migrant laborers from Asia continue to be exploited in Samoa and Hawaii.

## Conclusion: From Samoa to the Continental United States

In 2000, the United Nations passed the Protocol to Prevent, Suppress and Punish Trafficking in Persons Especially Women and Children, supplementing the United Nations Convention against Transnational Organized Crime. The internationally accepted and recognized definition of human trafficking sustains how the human is recognized, while the eventfulness of policies and experiences of abuse are wrapped in a discourse and practice that reproduce how subjects are tethered to dualities. The testimonial narratives of trafficking subjects are part of the discourse and practice that further whose stories matter and whose events speak to a public. Therefore, while laws and events of abuse are perceived to be eventful in antitrafficking narratives, by paying attention to uneventfulness, the mundane, and the normal, how language matters is made apparent.

To close, I end with the story of Sonny, whose journey bridges the contexts explored in this chapter of Asia, Samoa, and Hawaii as connected to the continental United States. Sonny was a fisherman from Indonesia who was contracted to work for two years in Hawaii. Sonny's journey led him from Indonesia to Australia to Fiji and then to American Samoa, where he boarded a fishing ship that eventually enabled his travels to San Francisco and indigenous lands of the Ohlone and Miwok, among other tribes who peopled the region. Sonny's story was depicted on public radio on January 15, 2014, in a story entitled "Human Trafficking: A Fisherman's Story" (Day). Sonny's experience of being defrauded began after he arrived in American Samoa. After a couple of weeks of waiting without food in American Samoa, he finally boarded a ship that was not the one named in his contract. Sonny experienced a variety of rights violations, including food deprivation, the taking of identifying papers (legal documents), long work hours from 2:00 P.M. to 3:00 A.M. every day, and a hazardous work environment that led to a damaged finger. If he left and broke his contract, he would face a $1,000 fine—four months of wages. Although he feared the consequences, Sonny fled his employers when the ship docked in San Francisco. From Indonesia to the islands in the Pacific and eventually the Americas, Sonny's journey reflects the physical transnational linkages of geographies, politics, and economies that produce a tethered subjectivity in human rights framings of violations such as human trafficking. As fair-trade and slave-free goods are a central aspect of the twenty-first-century human rights endeavor to abolish what has been colloquially referred to as "modern-day slavery," the site of Asia-Pacific as a violator regularly makes headline news. Since 2000, story after story has captured the trafficking of Indonesians and other Southeast Asians in the Thai fishing industry (Fault Lines; Htusan and Mason).

But Sonny, like the employees of the Daewoosa factory and Global Horizons, is also a socially dead subject, whose resurrection is through victimhood, vulnerability as a noncitizen subject, and the illegal means through which he jumped ship to leave his trafficking experience. He is also eventful only as a trafficking story—no other aspects of his story are visible. Therefore, Sonny is tethered to dualities surrounding victimhood, legality, and citizenship. How does one untether the subjectivities that produce Sonny, the workers of the Daewoosa factory and Global Horizons, and the many other incidents that connect Asia across the Pacific to the United States?

There is a seemingly insignificant moment in Sonny's testimonial: his refusal to tell his story in English. In the radio interview, the listener hears Sonny's voice through an interpreter but also his voice echoing in the background. A hum of voices, from Sonny to interpreter to the interviewer, collectively narrates Sonny's story. Sonny's refusal to speak in English is captured by the narrator: "Though he speaks English, he wants to make sure all of the details are right" (Day). The details can be right only in Sonny's native language, and through the translation the listener is held at a distance from Sonny. The listener trusts the female voice translating Sonny's experiences. The listener hears Sonny occasionally slip into English. For example, when asked how much he was paid as a fisherman in Indonesia, Sonny speaks in Indonesian, and the interpreter states, "About one-hundred fifty dollars, every month." The listener hears Sonny echo after the translator in English, "Every month." At this moment, the listener is reminded of his ability to speak in English and his refusal to be interviewed entirely in English. Sonny forces the listener to experience what Maria Lugones has referred to as "faithful witnessing"—witnessing on the side of those who are oppressed. Sonny's commitment to being interviewed in Indonesian forces the listener to hear his story in Indonesian, his native language—to hear the listener's own limitations and to reconcile how a story about "rights" cannot always be done through Western frames, in English. As Sonny inhabits the eventfulness of being trafficked, he describes the mundane details of what it was like to fish, how he loves fish, and his reunification with his daughter. While it matters that he has a work visa and is on a path toward citizenship, where he is able to apply for his green card, this information is not narrated through Sonny. Instead, the interviewer, who also serves as the narrator, describes his recovery of his humanity through legal status. This is not to say that legal relief does not enable recognition; rather, as long as the denial of recognition and rights is reserved for those who lack citizenship, it will also be a preoccupation in antitrafficking endeavors. Sonny's voice, which is marked by slippages between Indonesian and English, underscores a desire to move beyond a simple the trafficking story where Sonny was reunited with his daughter. Accordingly, "the ship's captain was never prosecuted—and Sonny's not interested in pursuing it. He now works in a liquor store in San Francisco where he makes $13 an hour, with no plans at all to return to sea" (Day). Whereas assumptions of rights, justice, and prosecution have been deeply tied together in antitrafficking discourse, Sonny rejects these assumptions, even though his interview began with his reflection on the fishing industry: "I like it, being a fisherman. . . . I especially like fishes. And the income is pretty good." No matter how much he liked it, Sonny found his economic survival taking him elsewhere, and the appeals to live beyond a trafficking story simply mean living a life beyond it.

Ongoing U.S. colonialities in American Samoa, Hawaii, and California are all too often met with silence in human rights discourse. The context of California and indigeneity is invisible in how trafficking is circulated. California and the United States have a legacy of abuse that normalized slavery during the antebellum period. In California, the Act for the Government and Protection of Indians was passed in 1850, but "protection" was a misnomer. Through the language of protection, the United States held indigenous children in servitude until the age of thirty (Anderson; Johnston-Dodds).

A tethered subjectivity is the consequence of modern colonial economic systems that sustain categorical constructions and visions of the colonial state. Current transnational economies depend on the furtherance of a tethered subjectivity that reifies how trafficking subjects are witnessed through dualities surrounding victimhood/criminality, citizen/noncitizen, and illegal/legal. Ritually hacking the process of witnessing tethered subjectivities means grappling with invisibility and the paradox surrounding how subjects are bound. In human rights endeavors, one must contend with the paradox of the advocates of human rights (the Global North) who also in their endeavor to speak to rights violations normalize another kind of rights violation—settler-colonial presence in the Asia-Pacific region as well as in the continental United States. How one witnesses human rights violations is through a resurrection of the socially dead for the living as a human rights spectacle as "other." To untether subjectivities requires not merely new positionalities but rather enacting new ways of witnessing rights violations.

## Acknowledgments

I would like to extend my warmest appreciation to Guy Beauregard, Cathy J. Schlund-Vials, and Hsiu-Chuan Lee for their incredibly generous feedback that helped further the deep analysis in this chapter. In addition, I am grateful to the audience members who engaged with my piece at the Association for Asian American Studies and copanelists Guy Beauregard and Chris Patterson, where we continued to engage in the subjects of human rights from Taiwan to Florida. And thank you to Hediana Utarti, Susan French, and members of the Freedom Network USA; your work on the ground in a struggle for a more just and human-rights-possible world is inspiring.

## NOTES

1. The four farms are Mac Farms of Hawaii, Kauai Coffee Company, Kelena Farms and Captain Cook Coffee Company.

2. Mac Farms of Hawaii will pay $1.6 million, Kelena Farms will pay $275,000, Captain Cook Coffee Company will pay $100,000, and Kauai Coffee Company will pay $425,000, according to settlement agreements.

## WORKS CITED

Alarcon, Norma. "The Theoretical Subject(s) of This Bridge Called My Back and Anglo American Feminism." *The Postmodern Turn: New Perspectives on Social Theory*. Ed. Steven Seidman. Cambridge: Cambridge University Press, 1994. 140–152.

Alexander, M. Jacqui. *Pedagogies of Crossing: Meditations on Feminism, Sexual Politics, Memory, and the Sacred*. Durham, NC: Duke University Press, 2005.

Anderson, Kat M. *Tending the Wild: Native American Knowledge and the Management of California's Resources*. Berkeley: University of California Press, 2005.

Bales, Kevin, and Steven Lize. "Investigating Human Trafficking: Challenges, Lessons Learned, and Best Practices." *FBI Law Enforcement Bulletin* 76 (2007): 24–32.

Barker, Joanne. *Sovereignty Matters: Locations of Contestation and Possibility in Indigenous Struggles for Self-Determination*. Lincoln: University of Nebraska Press, 2005.

Cacho, Lisa Marie. *Social Death: Racialized Rightlessness and the Criminalization of the Unprotected*. New York: New York University Press, 2012.

Cho, Grace M. *Haunting the Korean Diaspora: Shame, Secrecy, and the Forgotten War*. Minneapolis: University of Minnesota Press, 2008.

Chouliaraki, Lilie. *The Spectatorship of Suffering*. London: Sage, 2006.

Cohen, Deborah. *Braceros: Migrant Citizens and Transnational Subjects in the Postwar United States and Mexico*. Chapel Hill: University of North Carolina Press, 2011.

Day, Leila. "Human Trafficking: A Fisherman's Story." *KALW*. 28 September 2015. http://kalw.org/post/human-trafficking-fisherman-s-story#stream/0. 25 May 2016.

Donnelly, Jack. *Universal Human Rights in Theory and Practice*. Ithaca, NY: Cornell University Press, 2003.

EEOC (Equal Employment Opportunity Commission). "EEOC Files Its Largest Farm Worker Human Trafficking Suit against Global Horizons, Farms." Press release. 20 April 2011. https://www.eeoc.gov/eeoc/newsroom/release/4-20-11b.cfm.

———. "EEOC v. Global Horizons." 19 March 2014. www.slideshare.net/civilbeat/eeoc-v-global -horizons.

———. "Federal Judge Finds Global Horizons Liable for Discriminating, Harassing, and Retaliating against Hundreds of Thai Farm Workers in EEOC Suit." Press release. 24 March 2014.

Fault Lines. "A Trafficked Fisherman's Tale: 'My Life Was Destroyed.'" *Al Jazeera*. 5 March 2016. http://www.aljazeera.com/indepth/features/2016/03/trafficked-fisherman-tale-life-destroyed-160303122451399.html. 25 May 2016.

Fujikane, Candace, and Jonathan Y. Okamura, eds. *Asian Settler Colonialism: From Local Governance to the Habits of Everyday Life in Hawai'i*. Honolulu: University of Hawaii Press, 2008.

Fukushima, Annie Isabel. "Anti-violence Iconographies of the Cage: Diasporan Crossings and the (Un)Tethering of Subjectivities." *Frontiers: A Journal of Women's Studies* 36.3 (2015): 160–192.

Griffith, David. *American Guestworkers: Jamaicans and Mexicans in the U.S. Labor Market*. University Park: Pennsylvania State University Press, 2006.

Hooks, Bell. *Yearning: Race, Gender, and Cultural Politics*. Boston: South End, 1990.

Htusan, Esther, and Margie Mason. "Thousands of Indonesian Fishermen Rescued after Slave Island Probe." *Associated Press*. 17 September 2015. http://www.huffingtonpost.ca/2015/09/17/ap-investigation-prompts-rescue-of-more-than-2-000-slaves-plus-arrests-lawsuits-legislation_n_8153672.html. 25 May 2016.

Hua, Julietta. *Trafficking Women's Human Rights*. Minneapolis: University of Minnesota Press, 2011.

Johnston-Dodds, Kimberly. *Early California Laws and Policies Related to California Indians*. Sacramento: California Research Bureau, 2002.

Lal, Brij V., Doug Munro, and Edward D. Beechert, eds. *Plantation Workers: Resistance and Accommodation*. Honolulu: University of Hawaii Press, 1993.

Lugones, Maria. *Pilgrimages/Peregrinajes: Theorizing Coalition against Multiple Oppressions (Feminist Constructions)*. New York: Rowman and Littlefield, 2003.

Mohanty, Chandra Talpade. *Feminism without Borders: Decolonizing Theory, Practicing Solidarity*. Durham, NC: Duke University Press, 2003.

Moraga, Cherríe, and Gloria Anzaldúa. *This Bridge Called My Back: Writings by Radical Women of Color*. New York: Kitchen Table; Women of Color, 1983.

Nichols, Andrea J., and Erin C. Heil. "Challenges to Identifying and Prosecuting Sex Trafficking Cases in the Midwest United States." *Feminist Criminology* 10.1 (2015): 7–35.

Patterson, Orlando. *Slavery and Social Death: A Comparative Study*. Cambridge, MA: Harvard University Press, 1982.

Povinelli, Elizabeth A. "The Child in the Broom Closet: States of Killing and Letting Die." *South Atlantic Quarterly* 107.3 (2008): 509–530.

*A Report on What Is Happening with Imported Asian Labor by Daewoosa Samoa in American Samoa*. Perf. Nga and Dung. PCS TV, 2000. Waitogi TV.

Rosa, John P. "Beyond the Plantation: Teaching about Hawai'i before 1900." *Journal of Asian American Studies* 7.3 (2004): 223–240.

Sandoval, Chela. *Methodology of the Oppressed*. Minneapolis: University of Minnesota Press, 2000.

Spivak, Gayatri Chakravorty. "Righting Wrongs." *South Atlantic Quarterly* 103.2–3 (2004): 523–581.

Sudbury, Virginia Lynn. *Sweatshops in Paradise: A True Story of Slavery in Modern America*. iUniverse, 2012. Kindle edition.

Trask, Haunani-Kay. *From a Native Daughter: Colonialism and Sovereignty in Hawaii*. Honolulu: University of Hawaii Press, 1993.

Trott, Wardlaw. Opinion. *United States v. Kil Soo Lee*. No. 05-10478 D.C. No. CR-01-00132-SOM Opinion. Appeal from the United States District Court for the District of Hawaii. Susan Oki Mollway, District Judge, 2006.

U.S. Department of Justice Civil Rights Division. "Report on the Tenth Anniversary of the Trafficking Victims Protection Act." 29 October 2010. https://www.justice.gov/sites/default/files/crt/legacy/2010/12/14/tvpaanniversaryreport.pdf. 25 May 2016.

Wiegman, Robyn. *Object Lessons*. Durham, NC: Duke University Press, 2012.

Wong, Brad. "Servitude in American Samoa." *Seattle Post-Intelligencer*. 16 November 2003. https://www.seattlepi.com/news/article/Chapter-1-Servitude-in-American-Samoa-1129763.php. 18 June 2019.

Yun, Lisa. *The Coolie Speaks: Chinese Indentured Laborers and African Slaves of Cuba*. Philadelphia: Temple University Press, 2007.

Zimmerman, Malia. "Exclusive: Global Horizons CEO Speaks Out about Human Trafficking Allegations—and the Justice Department's Decision to Drop the Charges." *Hawaii Reporter*. 24 July 2012. 25 May 2016. http://www.hawaiireporter.com/exclusive-global-horizons-ceo-speaks-out-about-human-trafficking-allegations-and-the-justice-departments-decision-to-drop-the-charges/.

# PART III

## Reading at the Limits

*The Aftermaths, Afterlives, and Aesthetics of Human Rights*

# 9

# Reframing Cambodia's Killing Fields

## *The Commemorative Limitations of Atrocity Tourism*

Cathy J. Schlund-Vials

Did not confess. Torture him!
Hit him in the face.
We must apply pressure, absolutely.
Beat them all to death.
Smash them to pieces.

—Kaing Guek Eav (aka "Comrade Duch"),
Directions to Torturers at S-21 (44)[1]

"Cambodia's Genocide Museum Becomes Battleground for *Pokémon Go* Players"

—August 9, 2016, headline in *Southeast Asia Globe*

S-21 [Tuol Sleng Prison] "is not a game." It is a crime against humanity and it is everyone's responsibility to prevent such atrocities from re-occurring to harm our children.

—Youk Chhang, Documentation Center of Cambodia (*Southeast Asia Globe*)

Based on the highly successful *Pokémon* series, Niantic's *Pokémon Go*—developed for iOS, Android, and Apple Watch devices—was released in Australia, New Zealand, and the United States in July 2016; one month later, *Pokémon Go* increased its global reach when it became downloadable to smartphone users in Central America, South America, Europe, East Asia, and Southeast Asia. Consistent with the rest of the franchise, players of *Pokémon Go* located, captured, and trained cartoon creatures imbued with special powers (e.g., pyrokinesis, hydrokinesis, electrokinesis, or venomous capacity).[2] Given the game's zoological registers and fantastical dimensions, it is not surprising that "adaptive enhancement," "evolution," and setting figure keenly in the *Pokémon* gaming universe; specifically, as a means of "leveling up," organisms augment existing abilities or mature into more powerful versions of their previous form. Once "trained," players strategically use their assembled menagerie to battle other Pokémon (in designated "gyms" or assigned "arenas").

Accessing the search logics of an exotic safari, the cultivating dimensions of animal husbandry, and the spectacular registers of a gladiatorial battle, *Pokémon Go* is a free-for-all, free-to-play, location-based, real-time augmented game that preternaturally places virtual lifeforms in everyday environs. Accordingly, *Pokémon Go* utilizes a smartphone's data usage and GPS mobile capabilities; these resources enable players to "find" their imaginary targets in publicly accessible spaces such as local businesses, national parks, built monuments, museums, churches, and governmental centers. As is the case with other "free" mobile games, *Pokémon Go* profits from extra data charges and in-app purchases (for instance, players can increase the likelihood of capturing more animals by buying additional pokéballs or enhance their ludic experience by unlocking various bonus perks, both at cost). Credited with reinvigorating franchise interest and increasing foot traffic to various sites, *Pokémon Go* from the outset enjoyed considerable success: one week after its summer 2016 release, the app was downloaded twenty-one million times, making it the most popular mobile game in the United States (Makuch). Such widespread usage was matched by *Pokémon Go*'s astonishing profitability: one month after its initial release, *Pokémon Go* earned $200 million and set a "speed" record as the fastest game to achieve fifty million downloads outside the United States. More recently, as of March 2018, *Pokémon Go* had 752 million downloads, and its revenues totaled $1.2 billion (*Venture Beat*).

Notwithstanding its status as a global phenomenon, despite its sizeable commercial success, and in the face of its "all ages" appeal, *Pokémon Go* was—soon after its 2016 release—at the center of several controversies involving commemorative sites, memorials, and museums. Because the app exploited open-access locales, *Pokémon Go* players could (and did) pursue their digital conquests in somber places such as Arlington National Cemetery (the final resting place of U.S. war dead), the Auschwitz-Birkenau State Museum (previously a notorious World War II–era Nazi concentration camp, wherein 1.3 million individuals were detained and 1.1. million people perished), and the U.S. Holocaust Memorial Museum. As public sites, each was troublingly demarcated by the *Pokémon Go*'s producers as "pokéstops," places in which players could cybernetically connect with one another and capture additional Pokémon. Incongruously, these Janus-faced places—originally aimed at engendering justice-oriented remembrance within a rights-recognizable present—were involuntarily transformed into multipurpose sites wherein tourists-turned-players could vicariously experience past state-dictated abuses while furthering their gameplay progress in real time.[3]

In response, Arlington National Cemetery employed social media, solemnly tweeting, "We do not consider playing 'Pokemon Go' to be appropriate decorum on the grounds of ANC. We ask all visitors to refrain from such activity" (O'Brien). Following suit, the U.S. Holocaust Memorial Museum issued a public statement condemning the game and its players, grimly stressing that it "was not appropriate in . . . [a] memorial to the victims of Nazism" ("Auschwitz Museum"). Finally, Pawel Sawicki, the official spokesperson for the Auschwitz-Birkenau State Museum, asked that Niantic remove the site from its list of viable *Pokémon Go* platforms, forcefully reminding the game's producers that it was "disrespectful to the memory of victims of the German Nazi concentration and extermination camp on many levels and it is absolutely inappropriate" ("Auschwitz Museum"). To ameliorate these institutional disputes, Niantic created a website so that users and others could report "sensitive locations"; upon notification, such sites were systematically and swiftly removed. At high-profile memorial locations like the abovementioned Arlington National Cemetery, the Auschwitz-Birkenau State Museum, and the U.S. Holocaust Memorial Museum, signs were posted at entry points and ticketing counters prohibiting visitors from playing *Pokémon Go* on site.

As the opening epigraphs from *Southeast Asia Globe* and Youk Chhang (director of the Documentation Center of Cambodia) make clear, these debates over the collision of the ludic and the commemorative were not limited to the United States or Europe; nor, as this chapter maintains, are the stakes involving what is "sacred" and "profane" simply a matter of dominant mores, socially acceptable behavior, or individualized judgment.[4] Indeed, soon after *Pokémon Go*'s Southeast Asian release, Cambodia's Tuol Sleng Genocide Museum and the nearby Cheoung Ek Center for Genocide Crimes were available to players as pokéstops. To add insult to injury, the Tuol Sleng Genocide Museum was the problematic setting of two virtual "gyms," fixed locations meant to facilitate—via game-circumscribed rule—*Pokémon Go* battles between different players. One of these gyms was stationed in a place gruesomely known as "The Gallows," named after a device used by the Khmer Rouge to hang and torture prisoners detained at Tuol Sleng Prison, upon which the same-named museum was established (Millar and Connor). Survivors of Cambodia's Khmer Rouge past (like Chhang and former Tuol Sleng Prison inmate Chum Mey) alongside human rights activists and academics predictably decried the game's inclusion of the Tuol Sleng Genocide Museum, which presently functions as the nation's primary site of genocide commemoration and contains one of the most significant atrocity archives about the Democratic Kampuchean era.[5]

While *Pokémon Go*'s opportunistic use of such contemplative sites—as commentators, critics, and curators repeatedly note—hits a decidedly inappropriate chord, and whereas the ensuing denunciations by and large make common sense within a prima facie human rights domain, the polemics concerning the ludic and the commemorative inadvertently yet evocatively lay bare a peculiar parallel between memorializing large-scale loss and touristic encounter. As now-recognizable settings of mass violence and human catastrophe, places like the Auschwitz-Birkenau State Museum and Tuol Sleng Genocide Museum have become "must-see" stops for those engaged in what Malcolm Foley and J. John Lennon provocatively characterize as "dark tourism"; such destinations are marked by "the presentation and consumption (by visitors) of real and commodified death and disaster sites" (198). Though understood within the field of cultural geography as a subgenre of mainstream tourism, "dark tourism" (aka "macabre tourism," "heritage tourism," "thanatourism," "doom tourism," "morbid tourism," or "atrocity tourism") is, as will soon be clear, increasingly popular and exceedingly profitable (Stone and Sharpley).

To that end, as the 1.4 million visitors who annually travel to Auschwitz-Birkenau highlight, genocide tourism is—in the twenty-first century—a thriving global business ("Attendance Record"). From Vietnam's War Remnants Museum to Thailand's Death Railway, from Rwanda's Kigali Genocide Museum to Taiwan's National Human Rights Museum, and from London's Imperial War Museums to New York City's 9/11 Memorial and Museum, twentieth-century histories of state-authorized violence and twenty-first-century accounts of large-scale loss have been fervently curated, ardently commemorated, and vigorously cultivated in the purposeful and unintended service of atrocity tourism.[6] With regard to Cambodia, "dark tourism" and religious tourism have emerged as particularly significant industries: on top of the estimated seven hundred thousand tourists who visit the Tuol Sleng Genocide Museum and the Choeung Ek Center for Genocide Crimes in Phnom Penh each year, approximately two million make their way to Angkor Wat, a multitemple UNESCO World Heritage Site in Siem Reap.[7]

In addition to the Tuol Sleng Genocide Museum and the Choeung Ek Center for Genocide Crimes, atrocity tourism figures prominently in the post–Khmer Rouge, postconflict remaking of Cambodia; legislative and administrative plans remain underway to rehabilitate key sites in Anlong Veng (a district in Oddar Meanchey Province), situated near the Thai border. To wit, Anlong Veng was, until the late 1990s, a Khmer Rouge stronghold and postregime home to Pol Pot (Saloth Sar, "Brother Number One"), Ta Mok (the regime's highest-ranking general), Son Sen (who oversaw Democratic Kampuchea's secret police—the Santebal—and was Tuol Sleng Prison's first warden), and Khieu Samphan (former Khmer Rouge head of state). Currently, tourists traveling to the northern Cambodian district can visit Pol Pot's grave (which is remarkably unadorned and nondescript), Ta Mok's mausoleum, and the foundational remnants of Pol Pot's bunker/house; as final destinations, the "intrepid" atrocity tourist can make a relatively easy trek to Ta Mok's mountain and town domiciles. In 2000, the Cambodian government (under Prime Minister Hun Sen, a former Khmer Rouge soldier) included Anlong Veng on its list of planned sites for "historical tourism" connected to the Khmer Rouge; the commitment was reiterated in 2006 (at the start of the hybrid UN/Khmer Rouge Tribunal, known officially as the "Extraordinary Chambers in the Courts of Cambodia" or by the acronym "ECCC"). In 2010—the year in which the UN/Khmer Rouge Tribunal issued its first guilty verdict against former Tuol Sleng Prison head warden Kaing Guek Eav—the Cambodian government issued a development contract that contained provisions to rehabilitate roads and restore relevant Khmer Rouge structures (e.g., homes of leading figures, meeting places, and cemeteries; Little and Muong).

Situated against Cambodia's macabre historical backdrop and set within an ever-growing atrocity tourist landscape, debates concerning the "appropriateness" of *Pokémon Go* prompt an expanded reconsideration of the possibilities—and even more important, the limitations—of "atrocity tourism" in the ethical recollection of human rights violations and the remembrance of those lost. While it is easy to dismiss such digital play along the lines of "crassness," the didactic mission of sites dedicated to commemorating mass loss—predicated on remembrance, guided by a "never again" impulse, and circumscribed by teleologies of rights progress—often conflict with the spectacularization of violence that serves as primary draw and appeal for out-of-town and out-of-country visitors. Thus, on the one hand, *Pokémon Go*'s ludic logics as sightseeing game analogously cohere with the dramatic presentation of "unimaginable" histories of mass loss and genocide. Accordingly, the Manichean representation of such histories—situated along an axis of clearly delineated perpetrators and victims—uncannily replicates the binaried relationship between player and platform. On the other hand, the inability of *Pokémon Go* players to appropriately commemorate through solemn witnessing and quiet contemplation lays bare a troubling "memory failure" consistent with an affective disconnect between tourist and victim.

Such disconnects presage the remaining focus of this chapter, which considers a site that, in its overt focus on perpetrators, eschews victim commemoration in favor of criminal prosecution: Tuol Sleng Genocide Museum. As this chapter makes clear, the politics that brought the Tuol Sleng Genocide Museum into being were less about remembering those lost and more indicative of contemporaneous state-driven agendas. Accordingly, while the Tuol Sleng Genocide Museum is ostensibly intended to commemorate those detained, the museum is—as a close reading of specific exhibits accentuates—paradoxically focused on "memorializing the actions of the Khmer Rouge" (Tuol Sleng Genocide Museum). Concomitantly, those who visit the museum (expressly foreign tourists) become capitalist consumers of Democratic Kampuchean atrocities, a point substantiated by the site's emphasis on perpetrators, the availability of survivor-guided tours, and the ubiquity of on-site souvenir stands. Through tactical juxtaposition and comparative reframing, what becomes apparent is the extent to which the critique of consumptive practices vis-à-vis *Pokémon Go* strategically disremembers the commercial dimensions of contemporary atrocity tourism. As the conclusion of this chapter brings to light, the Tuol Sleng Genocide Museum and its companion site, the Choeung Ek Center for Genocide Crimes, operate as vexed memorials to a genocide that has—due to a paucity of Khmer Rouge defendants and in the absence of victim reparation—yet to be juridically or affectively reconciled.

## Curating Atrocity: Tuol Sleng Genocide Museum

Despite its international reputation as a primary site of human rights violation and authoritarian brutality, the Tuol Sleng Genocide Museum sits inauspiciously on 113 Boeng Keng Kang 3 (in the Tuol Svay Prey subdistrict of southern Phnom Penh); it is surprisingly commonplace in its architecture and distressingly mundane in appearance. However, the swell of *tuk* drivers by the museum's entrance, coupled with the unmistakable presence of foreign tourists and the loud bustling of vendors, brings into focus the site's status as a frequently visited Phnom Penh landmark. To be sure, the Tuol Sleng Genocide Museum is expectedly unwelcoming: the five-building compound is surrounded by a high metal fence that prevents a clear street view. A pictorial sign at the front gate instructs those who enter to refrain from loud talking or laughter, which—in tandem with its titular emphasis on genocide—signals the museum's unavoidable thanatouristic registers. The exhibits contained therein—including rooms marked by bloodstained floors, rusted shackles, oxidized implements of torture, and ghostly black-and-white detainee photographs—are starkly distinguished from the orderliness of Tuol Sleng's manicured square lawns and swept concrete sidewalks.

The Tuol Sleng Genocide Museum's presentist focus on large-scale mass loss and profound human rights contravention is ineludibly distinct from and inextricably connected to its past uses. Formerly Chao Ponhea Yat High School, the facility was repurposed into a maximum-security detention center roughly four months after the Khmer Rouge April 17, 1975, takeover of the nation's capital (which signaled the start of the disastrous Democratic Kampuchean regime). To briefly summarize, between 1975 and 1979, over the course of three years, eight months, and twenty days, the authoritarian Khmer Rouge oversaw the deaths of an estimated 1.7 million Cambodians (roughly 21–21 percent of the country's extant population) due to starvation, famine, forced labor, torture, illness, and execution. Guided by an overriding desire to enact an agricultural revolution, propelled by a zealous commitment to classlessness, and driven by the violent impulse to bring the country to "year zero," the Khmer Rouge systematically emptied the nation's cities, prohibited religion, proscribed currency, and forbade the use of affective family names for siblings, mothers, and fathers (Kiernan 80).

The Khmer Rouge singled out those unable to work (due to illness or age), targeted those ideologically "out of pace" (e.g., individuals from the middle and upper classes), and ruthlessly weeded out those connected to the ancien régime and so-designated "enemies of the people": teachers, lawyers, judges, civil servants, doctors, artists, returning Cambodian ex-patriots (who were fellow leftists), Cambodian Muslims (the Cham), Khmer Khrom (Cambodians living in the Republic of Vietnam), and ethnic Vietnamese Cambodians. When the invading Vietnamese army "liberated" Cambodia in early January 1979, the majority of Cambodia's teachers (three-quarters) had died or fled the country (Kiernan 80). Nine judges remained; 90 percent of Khmer court musicians and dancers were dead; and, out of an estimated 550 doctors, only 48 survived (Munro). Faced with ongoing famine, lack of medicine, no infrastructure, and persistent political uncertainty, approximately 510,000 Cambodians fled to neighboring Thailand, and 100,000 sought refuge in close-by Vietnam (Southeast Asian Resource Center). Between 1980 and 1985, almost 150,000 Cambodians came to the United States, facilitated by the passage of the 1980 Refugee Act, and others would eventually find asylum in France and Australia, among other countries (Southeast Asian Resource Center).

As synecdochical site and indexical milieu, the Tuol Sleng Genocide Museum's function during and after the Democratic Kampuchean era (as detention center and memorial) concomitantly reflects violent regime agendas, renders visible governmentally supported rights violations, and amplifies their unassailable human costs. Known by Khmer Rouge leaders as "Security Prison 21" or "S-21," the jail featured a slogan that concurrently epitomized both Democratic Kampuchea's mission and Tuol Sleng's panoptic charge: "Fortify the spirit of the revolution! Be on your guard against the strategy and tactics of the enemy so as to defend the country, the people, and the Party" (Chandler 2).[8] S-21's primary objective involved "guarding against the strategy and tactics of the enemy," and those detained were alleged traitors to "the country, the people, and the Party" (Chandler 2). As prisoner photographs, hundred-page confessions, and a paucity of survivor accounts reveal, S-21 was not only a detention center for "enemies of the people"; it was also a torture facility, repository complex, and execution site. Under the exacting management of former math teacher Kaing Guek Eav, S-21 would infamously be branded by workers outside the prison as *konlaenhchoul min daelcheng*, "the place where people go in but never come out" (Chhang).

Despite the disciplinary single-mindedness of Tuol Sleng's administrative agenda, those brought to S-21 were, at first, not charged with specific crimes. Instead, detainees were accused of engaging in general prerevolutionary behavior. As Im Chan, a sculptor and former Tuol Sleng prisoner, relates, "When they arrest you there are no charges, they just say 'You have known a modern life. You used to go to the cinema, the restaurants, the bars. If we leave you, then you will tell the youth stories and they will want some" (qtd. in Maguire 26–27). In turn, these "past lives" were used in allegations of treason and mostly comprised accusations involving anti–Khmer Rouge political memberships. After hours, days, and months of torture (including waterboarding, electrocution, starvation, and beatings), prisoners would admit to covert activities involving the American Central Intelligence Agency (CIA) and the Soviet Komitet Gosudarstvennoy Bezopasnosti (KGB), which conveniently coincided with the regime's antagonist politics in relation to the United States (the embodiment of Western imperialism) and Vietnam (whose principal ally was the USSR).

The prison's reputation as a "killing machine" is most salient in its staggering prisoner/execution ratio, which outmatched the losses endured by those in Cambodia's numerous "killing fields."[9] Of the twelve to fourteen thousand detained at S-21, a little more than two hundred survived their imprisonment (approximately 2 percent of the total prison population; "Khmer Rouge"). Most of Tuol Sleng's inmates were detained between 1977 and 1978, as tensions between Vietnam and Democratic Kampuchea rose and fighting between the two countries intensified. For the majority of S-21's prison population, Choeung Ek Killing Field (located approximately 14.5 kilometers south of Phnom Penh) would serve as execution site and final resting place. According to eyewitness accounts and S-21 records, up to three hundred detainees were taken each night to the former Chinese graveyard and unceremoniously executed (Choeung Ek Center for Genocide Crimes).

After an eleven-month military campaign, the Vietnamese army triumphantly entered Phnom Penh on January 7, 1979, signaling the end of both the Cambodian-Vietnamese War and the Democratic Kampuchean era. The next day, on January 8, two Vietnamese photojournalists found Tuol Sleng Prison, purportedly after following the odor of rotting corpses to the recently abandoned site (Chandler 6). Armed with the initial intent to photograph the Vietnamese-orchestrated "emancipation" of Cambodia, the two came across fourteen recently killed prisoners and five still-living children (including two infants). No prison personnel were present, and the jail was in disarray (Dunlop). Indeed, twenty years would pass until the prison's head warden was identified, arrested, and placed in Cambodian custody. Furthermore, thirty-one years would elapse before Kaing Guek Eav—the first Khmer Rouge official to face the UN/Khmer Rouge Tribunal—was found guilty of war crimes and crimes against humanity ("Press Release").[10]

Despite S-21's contemporary notoriety—as the horrific epicenter of Khmer Rouge atrocity and human rights violation—the photographers who located S-21 were originally unaware of its use. As David Chandler notes,

"The purpose of the compound was unclear . . . although the single-story building, littered with papers and office equipment, had obviously been used for some sort of administration. In rooms on the ground floor of the southernmost building, the two Vietnamese came across corpses of several recently murdered men. Some of the bodies were chained to iron beds. The prisoners' throats had been cut. The blood on the floors is still wet" (3). Notwithstanding preliminary uncertainty, what quickly became apparent—first to the photographers and subsequently to the occupying military force—was the presence of various "evidences" (in the form of aforementioned forced confessions, prisoner photographs, and human remains). Almost a year later, Vietnamese occupiers and their in-country allies discovered Choeung Ek killing field, which carried even more gruesome proof of Khmer Rouge–directed mass violence. As investigators labored to document, archive, and categorize forensic evidence, they systematically unearthed 129 mass graves filled with bleached bone, tattered clothing, and fractured skulls. Taken together, Choeung Ek killing field at present contains the remains of an estimated 8,985 regime victims (Choeung Ek Online).

To be sure, Tuol Sleng Prison and Choeung Ek killing field were and remain potent sites for remembrance that on the one hand render visible the unimaginable bounds of Khmer Rouge atrocity. On the other hand, the story of how each site was "rehabilitated"—by way of politicized recovery work—underscores a more complex project fixed to Vietnamese occupation and regime change. To wit, during the Vietnamese-ruled People's Republic of Kampuchea (PRK) era (1979–1989), Tuol Sleng and Choeung Ek figured keenly in post–Democratic Kampuchean nation-building efforts, which depended on vilifying the former regime through allegations of genocide and depictions of war crimes. Admittedly, the National Liberation Front and the Democratic Republic of Vietnam had, before the formation of Democratic Kampuchea, been allies of the Khmer Rouge. In the aftermath of Democratic Kampuchean authoritarianism, the People's Republic of Kampuchea had to substantially distance and differentiate—via the public sphere—Khmer Rouge totalitarianism from Vietnamese communism.[11]

Hence, amid politicized shift and political reorganization, to remember the killing fields era was from the outset determined by domestic nation-building efforts. And, as a brief history of the People's Republic of Kampuchea accentuates, the still-forming state of in-country remembrance collided with a post-Vietnam conflict politics; such politics were necessarily forged within the context of a vexed Cold War relationship with the United States and the United Nations. Domestically, even with the January 7, 1979, Vietnamese takeover of Phnom Penh, the Khmer Rouge still held strongholds in the country's northwest provinces (namely the previously mentioned Anlong Veng district) and continued to wage skirmishes against the occupying army. Internationally, the newly installed People's Republic of Kampuchea was under attack from the former regime's high officials, who, until 1989, were recognized as the nation's rightful rulers. Recently ousted Khmer Rouge leaders including Pol Pot, Khieu Samphan, Foreign Minister Ieng Sary, and Social Minister Ieng Thirith claimed that they and their countrymen were victims of a "war of aggression against Democratic Kampuchea." Central to such accusations of "aggression" was the increasingly disputed claim of genocide (Maguire 67).

As Peter Maguire productively recounts, Samphan (who, like Sary and Thirith, was, after 2007, in UN custody for crimes of genocide) vociferously (and ironically) declared that during the eleven-month war between the Khmer Rouge and the Vietnamese, "more than 500,000 Kampucheans have been massacred and more than 500,000 others have died from starvation" (67). To buttress in-state authority and assert international sovereignty, the People's Republic of Kampuchea directly engaged the genocide question and initiated trial proceedings against former Khmer Rouge leaders. In August 1979 (eight months after the Vietnamese takeover and four years after the establishment of Tuol Sleng Prison) the People's Revolutionary Tribunal tried Pol Pot and Ieng Sary in absentia for crimes of genocide, which began with the allegation that three million Cambodians perished during the Khmer Rouge era. Further, the People's Revolutionary Tribunal utilized so-categorized evidences found at Tuol Sleng Prison and gathered 995 pages of survivor testimony that confirmed acts of torture and orders of execution authorized by the authoritarian Democratic Kampuchean regime.[12]

On August 19, 1979, Pol Pot and Ieng Sary were expeditiously found guilty by a ten-person jury and sentenced to death. As Maguire maintains, notwithstanding "a great deal of legitimate evidence, such as the testimony of S-21 survivors Ung Pech [the first director of the Tuol Sleng Genocide Museum] and [the previously mentioned] Im Chan," the "indictment's strange categories of criminality, the short duration of the trial, and the absurd defense combined to create the impression of primitive political justice" (66). Such "strange categories" included accusations of state-authorized cannibalism and spectacular charges of executions involving pools of water filled with crocodiles.[13] Moreover, attorneys assigned to Pol Pot and Ieng Sary categorically refused to represent their clients due to the assumption they were—in light of genocidal crimes—morally indefensible (Maguire 67). Responding to such unorthodox legalities, the United Nations subsequently delegitimized the People's Revolutionary Tribunal because it did not adhere to the standards of international law.

Despite the People's Revolutionary Tribunal's "strange categories" and eccentric jurisprudence, the genocide case against the Khmer Rouge was undermined more profoundly by post–Vietnam War realpolitik. In the immediate aftermath of the American War in Vietnam, the United States maintained a strict anti-Vietnamese policy, composed of embargos, epitomized by trade restrictions, and marked by antithetical alliances with the Khmer Rouge. Given its indubitable anti-Vietnamese politics, the Chinese-supported Khmer Rouge—in the face of anticommunist agendas—became a Cold War ally of the United States. Between 1980 and 1986, the United States funneled $85 million in aid to the Khmer Rouge through the euphemistically named Kampuchea Emergency Group, countering Soviet-backed Vietnamese humanitarian efforts in the region (Maguire 70). Such nonmilitary support was matched by the United Nations, which (under the Security Council sway of the United States and China) refused to recognize the authority of the People's Republic of Kampuchea on the grounds that the Vietnamese were an oppressive—not redemptive—force.

Within this politicized Cold War climate, the national and international acceptability of the People's Republic of Kampuchea, as Rachel Hughes argues, "hinged on the exposure of the violent excesses of Pol Pot exemplified by S-21 and the continued production of coherent memory of the past . . . of liberation and reconstruction at the hands of a benevolent fraternal state" ("Abject Artifacts" 26).[14] On one level, fundamental to the People's Republic of Kampuchea's legitimizing agendas were the calculated restaging and recollecting of Khmer Rouge atrocity, which was emblematically configured through the Tuol Sleng Genocide Museum and the Choeung Ek Center for Genocide Crimes. On another level, the repurposing of Tuol Sleng Prison and Choeung Ek killing field from Democratic Kampuchean torture center and execution locale into built Khmer Rouge atrocity memorials signaled a particular "memory war" waged on the terrain of Cambodian human rights remembrance. Tellingly, amid a context of a nascent governmentality (wherein the production of loyal subjects was integral to state stability) and international back-and-forth, the People's Republic of Kampuchea appointed Vietnamese colonel and "war crimes expert" Mai Lam to oversee the rehabilitation of the Khmer Rouge jail and killing field.

Lam had previously curated Saigon/Ho Chi Minh City's aforementioned War Remnants Museum (hitherto "The House for Displaying War Crimes of American Imperialism and the Puppet Government"), which was intended to bolster anti-American support for a newly reunited Vietnam. Under Lam's supervision, the Tuol Sleng Genocide Museum and the Choeung Ek Center for Genocide Crimes (aka the Choeung Ek killing field memorial) were quickly opened to the public in 1980 (Chhang). Until 1993, most of their visitors included Cambodians and tourists from other communist countries (Vietnam, the Soviet Union, Hungary, Laos, and Poland). The tourist demographic dramatically shifted after the country ceased to be under communist rule. Most present-day museum visitors and memorial sightseers hail from Japan, France, Germany, South Korea, the United States, and Taiwan (Chhang). Despite changing visitor profiles and the passage of more than three decades since both sites were made public, what persists is the degree to which each location replays—through body corpus exhibits (for example, prisoner photographs, inmate remains, and detainee confessions)—the horrific dimensions of the Khmer Rouge body politic.

As a close reading makes clear, both places continue to embody Colonel Mai Lam's original curatorial program, which was principally concentrated on a state-sanctioned prosecutorial agenda against the previous Democratic Kampuchean regime. At the same time, the Tuol Sleng Genocide Museum and the Choeung Ek Center for Genocide Crimes remain significant in light of contentious politics, regime changes, and contemporary Cambodian genocide remembrance. Such prosecutorial presentations—originally connected to the People's Republic of Kampuchea and People's Revolutionary Tribunal but relevant to the workings of the present-day UN/Khmer Rouge Tribunal—underscore a juridical mode of collected memory fixed to Vietnamese-oriented statecraft and contemporaneous understandings of human rights. As Hughes argues, "the presentation of physical evidence" at both the Tuol Sleng Genocide Museum and the Choeung Ek Center for Genocide Crimes evoked (and continues to bring to mind) a "*legal* functioning of evidence: evidence of *genocide* (universally-defined) [that] necessarily motions to universal (*international*) laws" ("Memory and Sovereignty" 272; emphasis in original). Correspondingly, Lam's curatorial focus on war crimes, made plain in graphic depictions of atrocity and the prevalence of perpetrator-driven exhibits, foments a distinct narrative wherein the Vietnamese are cast as emancipators, human rights activists, and antigenocide saviors.[15]

Understandably, this specific Vietnamese-centric narrative has largely fallen out of favor in the post–People's Republic of Kampuchea era. Three years after the Vietnamese-occupied state collapsed (in 1989), Cambodia endured a series of leadership transitions that included UN intervention (during the "United Nations Transition Authority in Cambodia" period, or UNTAC, which took place between 1992 and 1993), state-level coup (via the 1997 overthrow of then–prime minister Norodom Ranariddh led by the Cambodian People's Party and Hun Sen), and tribunal formation (which commenced in 2003 but was solidified in 2006–2007 with the public arrest of former Khmer Rouge officials Khieu Samphan, Nuon Chea ["Brother Number Two"], Ieng Sary, and Ieng Thirith). Despite these political shifts, and in the face of changing juridical dynamics, Cambodia's killing fields era remains largely unreconciled. To date, only three Khmer Rouge leaders have been convicted of crimes against humanity (Guev, Samphan, and Chea); of the two other officials facing the tribunal, Ieng Thirth was deemed incompetent to stand trial due to Alzheimer's diagnosis, and Ieng Sary passed away during detention. It is unlikely that further prosecutions will be sought given that many in the Cambodian government are former Khmer Rouge. Moreover, while there is an apparatus for victims to pursue juridical claims (via a complainant process), there are no state- or internationally sanctioned monies for individual reparation or collective recompense (in the form of a funded museum, education program, or memorial).

## The Limitations of Atrocity Tourism and the Possibilities of Asian Americanist Critique

Situated adjacent to this unsettled imaginary, wherein human rights abuses committed during the Khmer Rouge era are juridically limited (to a few perpetrators) and inadequately commemorated (via the absence of victim-focused memorials), sites like the Tuol Sleng Genocide Museum and the Choeung Ek Center for Genocide Crimes unescapably accrete greater significance. For better or worse, both sites—as popular destinations for willing and accidental "atrocity tourists"—are imbued with the insurmountable task of remembering Cambodia's genocidal past while attending to communal, familial, and individual loss. The privileging of perpetratorhood over victimhood underscores the degree to which the Khmer Rouge—as an authoritarian, rights-violating regime—has by and large occupied a space of nonprosecution; and the impulse to emphasize criminality over commemoration is very much tied to an incomplete and tragic nonprosecution of those most culpable.

By way of conclusion, and in the interest of bringing the argument full circle, this chapter ends with the recent conclusion of the UN/Khmer Rouge Tribunal and returns to the commemorative conundrum engendered by the recent *Pokémon Go* controversy. On November 15, 2018, the Extraordinary Chambers in the Courts of Cambodia issued a final verdict for both Khieu Samphan and Nuon Chea; both former Khmer Rouge officials were found guilty of genocide and sentenced to life imprisonment. Set against a backdrop of overdue prosecution and situated within a context of juridical belatedness, the ruling was quite historic; after all, one of the major points of tribunal contention was whether nor not what happened in Cambodia was indeed "genocide" given that the Khmer Rouge—with a few exceptions—targeted not an ethnic/religious affiliation but a class-oriented status (i.e., the middle class and urban denizens). Correspondingly, the genocide verdict was predicated not on the 1.7 million who perished under the regime's reign but instead on the Khmer Rouge slaughter of Cambodia's Muslim Cham minority and Vietnamese (Beech).

Notwithstanding the significance of the verdict, reporters and commentators focused on the tribunal's worth, measured in terms of cost and validity. Regarding the former, as *New York Times* correspondent Seth Mydans presciently summarized in an April 10, 2017, article, "After spending more than a decade and nearly $300 million, the United Nations-backed tribunal prosecuting the crimes of the Khmer Rouge has convicted just three men." And, in terms of the latter, the tribunal's legitimacy was called into question roughly one month after the genocide ruling with the revelation that Nuon Chea's defense lawyer, Victor Koppe (a Dutch national), had not been a member of the bar in the Netherlands since 2015. As a nonregistered attorney, he was deemed ineligible according to the Cambodian bar and was summarily dismissed by the tribunal.[16] The implications of Koppe's dismissal remain unclear, though the controversy has opened the door for further debate and possible defendant appeal (Wallace).

Such open-endedness is perhaps a fitting juridical end to the Khmer Rouge era, which—despite wholesale acknowledgment and tribunal emphasis—continues to pivot on criminality and perpetratorhood. Correspondingly, if integral to the Tuol Sleng Genocide Museum (along with the Choeung Ek Center for Genocide Crimes) is the affective and evidentiary reiteration of Khmer Rouge atrocity, then the apolitical presence of *Pokémon Go* underscores the genocidal "memory work" that remains unfinished. As de facto critical analytic, the seeming incommensurability between "collection" game and "collective" remembrance offers a way to consider both the limitations of atrocity tourism and the possibilities of Asian Americanist critique. Regarding the former, the emphasis on barbarism over compassion bespeaks the incomplete contours of Cambodia's juridical imaginary vis-à-vis the Khmer Rouge era. In terms of the latter, it is through the acknowledgment of nonreconciliation—what Lisa Lowe eloquently characterizes in *Immigrant Acts* as a "tireless reckoning" with the violent past—that makes possible a potentially restorative understanding of human rights outside the very limited purview of state-sanctioned justice and state-authorized tribunal.

## NOTES

1. These directives were drawn from Case 001 proceedings (involving Kaing Guek Eav) from the Extraordinary Chambers in the Courts of Cambodia (ECCC). Quoted in Cruvellier.

2. Created by Satoshi Tajiri, *Pokémon* debuted on the Nintendo Game Boy system on February 27, 1996 (in Japan). Based on Tajiri's childhood fascination with insect collection, the franchise has grown considerably to encompass multiple media modes, including playing cards, television shows, full-length films, and several digital platforms. Tajiri is currently the CEO of *Game Freak*, a popular gaming magazine. Illustrator Ken Sugimori provided the franchise's artwork and is Tajiri's close collaborator. Pokémon characters assume diverse forms; among the most popular are Charmander (a small orange lizard with a flamed tail), Squirtle (a turtle that shoots water from its mouth), Bulbasaur (a plant-based character known for his retractable vines), and Pikachu (a chubby yellow rodent that conducts electricity). Each character has evolved equivalents: Charmander's more powerful form is Charmeleon; Squirtle becomes Wartortle; Bulbasaur evolves into Ivysaur. The antecedent form for Pikachu is Pichu; Pikachu's evolved form is Raichu.

3. The 9/11 Memorial in New York City, the Los Angeles Museum of the Holocaust, the Vietnam War Veterans Memorial in Washington, DC, and the Hiroshima Peace Memorial, among others, were also pokéstops.

4. Known as "DC-Cam," the Documentation Center of Cambodia is a nongovernmental organization (NGO) dedicated to researching and recording the Democratic Kampuchean era (1975–1979). The center is presently home to the largest archive about the Khmer Rouge period; to date, DC-Cam's archive contains 155,000 documents and over 6,000 photographs. DC-Cam has played a major evidentiary role in the UN/Khmer Rouge Tribunal.

5. There is presently no state-sanctioned memorial about the Khmer Rouge period. The Tuol Sleng Genocide Museum and the Choeung Ek Center for Genocide Crimes are run by JC Royal, a Japan-based enterprise.

6. The War Remnants Museum (Saigon/Ho Chi Minh City) was originally named the "Museum of American War Crimes" and highlighted various atrocities committed by U.S. troops during the American War in Vietnam (1959–1975). The "Death Railway" (Siam-Burma Railway) is a 258-mile railroad that connects Ban Pong, Thailand, to Thanbyuzayat, Burma; railroad construction commenced soon after the Japanese takeover of Burma in winter 1942 and was completed on September 15, 1943. An estimated 180,000–250,000 Southeast Asian civilians were forced to work on the railroad in addition to 61,000 Allied prisoners of war. Approximately 90,000 civilians and 12,000 prisoners of war perished. Rwanda's Kigali Genocide Museum commemorates the 500,000–1,000,000 Tutsi who were killed during a 100-day period (April 7–mid-July, 1994). Taiwan's National Human Rights Museum is focused on the Chinese Nationalist Party (KMT) and its authoritarian rule between 1949 and 1992, wherein those critical of the regime were forcibly detained and tortured; this particular era is known as the "White Terror Period." London's Imperial War Museums feature exhibits connected to atrocities, conflicts, and wars involving Britain and its colonies; the museum's focus commences with World War I and extends into the present. Finally, New York City's 9/11 Memorial and Museum commemorates the 2,977 victims of September 11, 2001, terrorist attacks wherein two planes collided into New York City's World Trade Center and one crashed into the Pentagon in Washington, DC. A fourth plane attack against Washington, DC, was thwarted (the plane crashed in Shanksville, Pennsylvania).

7. It should be noted that both the Tuol Sleng Genocide Museum and the Choeung Ek Center for Genocide Crimes are considered "haunted" places due to the violent nature of prisoner deaths. The overt display of bone represents a violation of Theravada Buddhism, Cambodia's dominant religion. Cremation is privileged in Theravada Buddhist funeral rites. It is therefore not surprising that the majority of those who visit both sights are foreigners. In 2010, the ECCC began hosting field trips to both sites as a means of educating a population that was largely born after the dissolution of the Khmer Rouge regime in 1979; in its inaugural year, the ECCC-supported initiative brought twenty-seven thousand Cambodians to both sites.

8. The name "S-21" also reflects the first initial of the Khmer Rouge's internal security apparatus (the Santebal) and the radio code used by the prison's first director, Son Sen.

9. The term *killing machine* is taken from Rithy Panh's 2003 documentary film, *S-21: The Khmer Rouge Killing Machine.*

10. On July 27, 2010, Kaing Guek Eav was found guilty of war crimes and crimes against humanity. He was originally given a sentence of thirty-five years; the actual verdict was nineteen years, a number that took into account the former head warden's arrest in 1999 and subsequent detention. Eav appealed the verdict, seeking a full acquittal of all charges. On February 3, 2012, Eav's appeal was denied, and he was given a life sentence.

11. These dynamics are divergently explored in Schlund-Vials.

12. The number "three million" was from the outset contested. Those who opposed the Vietnamese occupation within the international community claimed that the number was exaggerated for political purposes. To date, the accepted number of those who perished is 1.7 million, which is based on the mapping and cataloguing of mass graves.

13. In *Enemies of the People* (directed by Rob Lemkin and Thet Sambath), released in 2010, Khmer Rouge perpetrators confess to eating victims' gallbladders as per orders from cadres.

14. Before his work at S-21, Colonel Lam oversaw the curatorial program of the formerly named Exhibition House of Aggression War Crimes (aka American Atrocities Museum) in Ho Chi Minh City, which served an analogous political function vis-à-vis the South Vietnamese.

15. Judy Ledgerwood persuasively argues that the rehabilitation of such sites coincided with a particular "metanarrative" of Vietnamese liberation. I draw from this reading but maintain that the emphasis on perpetrators foreshadows a twenty-first-century preoccupation with atrocity tourism.

16. Koppe had been a member of the defense team since 2007.

## WORKS CITED

"Attendance Record." Auschwitz-Birkenau State Museum. http://auschwitz.org/en/visiting/attendance. 21 June 2018.

"Auschwitz Museum Says 'No' to Pokemon Go." 13 July 2016. *CBS News*. https://www.cbsnews.com/news/auschwitz-museum-no-pokemon-go. 11 June 2018.

Beech, Hannah. "Khmer Rouge's Slaughter Is Ruled a Genocide." *New York Times*. 15 November 2018. https://www.nytimes.com/2018/11/15/world/asia/khmer-rouge-cambodia-genocide.html?action=click&module=RelatedCoverage&pgtype=Article®ion=Footer.

Chandler, David. *Voices from S-21: Terror and History in Pol Pot's Secret Prison*. Berkeley: University of California Press, 1999.

Chhang, Youk. "The Poisonous Hill That Is Tuol Sleng." Documentation Center of Cambodia. http:/d.dccam.org/Database/Index1.htm. 7 June 2018.

Choeung Ek Center for Genocide Crimes. http://killingfieldsmuseum.com/s21-vitcims.html. 14 February 2018.

Cruvellier, Thierry. *The Master of Confessions: The Making of a Khmer Rouge Torturer*. New York: HarperCollins, 2014.

Dunlop, Nic. *The Lost Executioner: A Journey into the Heart of the Killing Fields*. New York: Walker, 2005.

Foley, Malcolm, and J. John Lennon. "JFK and Dark Tourism: A Fascination with Assassination." *International Journal of Heritage Studies* 2: 198–211.

Hughes, Rachel. "The Abject Artifacts of Memory: Photographs from Cambodia's Genocide." *Media, Culture, and Society* 25: 23–44. London: Sage Publications.

———. "Memory and Sovereignty in Post-1979 Cambodia: Choeung Ek and Local Genocide Memorials." http://opus.macmillan.yale.edu/workpaper/pdfs/GS26.pdf. 18 June 2018.

"Khmer Rouge Survivor Testifies." *BBC News*. 29 June 2009. http://news.bbc.co.uk/1/hi/world/asia-pacific/8123541.stm. 30 December 2017.

Kiernan, Ben. "Recovering History and Justice in Cambodia." *Comparativ* 14 (2004): 76–85.

Ledgerwood, Judy. "The Cambodian Tuol Sleng Museum of Genocidal Crimes: National Narrative." *Museum Anthropology* 21.1 (1997): 82–98.

Lemkin, Rob, and Theth Sambath, dir. *Enemies of the People*. Old Street Films, 2009.

Little, Harriet Fitch, and Vandy Muong. "Dark Tourism in Anlong Veng." *Phnom Penh Post*. 9 August 2015. https://phnompenhpost.com/post-weekend/dark-tourism-anlong-veng. 4 May 2018.

Lowe, Lisa. *Immigrant Acts: On Asian American Cultural Politics*. Durham, NC: Duke University Press, 1996.

Maguire, Peter. *Facing Death in Cambodia*. New York: Columbia University Press, 2005.

Makuch, Eddie. "Pokemon Go Becomes Most Popular Mobile Game in U.S. History." *Gamespot*. 14 July 2016. https://www.gamespot.com/articles/pokemon-go-becomes-most-popular-mobile-game-in-us-/1100-6441797/. 10 June 2018.

Millar, Paul, and Logan Connor. "Cambodia's Genocide Museum Becomes Battleground for Pokémon Go Players." *Southeast Asia Globe*. 9 August 2016. http://sea-globe.com/tuol-sleng-pokemon-go. 20 May 2018.

Munro, David I., dir. *Year Zero: The Silent Death of Cambodia*. Nar. John Pilger. London: ATV Network Limited, 1979.

Mydans, Seth. "11 Years, $300 Million, and 3 Convictions: Was the Khmer Rouge Tribunal Worth It?" *New York Times*. 10 April 2017. https://www.nytimes.com/2017/04/10/world/asia/cambodia-khmer-rouge-united-nations-tribunal.html.

O'Brien, Sarah Ashley. "Pokemon Go Players Unwelcome at Arlington, Holocaust Museum." *CNN Money*. 13 July 2016. http://money.cnn.com/2016/07/12/technology/pokemon-go-holocaust-arlington/index.html. 9 April 2018.

Panh, Rithy, dir. *S-21: The Khmer Rouge Killing Machine* (*S-21, la machine de morte Khmère rouge*). *Institut national de l'audiovisuel*, First Run Features, 2003.

"Press Release: Kaing Guek Eav Convicted of Crimes against Humanity and Grave Breaches of the Geneva Conventions of 1949." Extraordinary Chambers in the Courts of Cambodia. 26 July 2010.

Schlund-Vials, Cathy J. *War, Genocide and Justice: Cambodian American Memory Work*. Minneapolis: University of Minnesota Press, 2012.

Southeast Asian Resource Center. "Removing Refugees." (Report). 5 June 2018.

Stone, Philip, and Richard Sharpley. "Consuming Dark Tourism: A Thanatological Perspective." *Annals of Tourism Research* 35.2 (2008): 263–271.

Tuol Sleng Genocide Museum. http://www.tuolslenggenocidemuseum.com. 20 June 2018.

Wallace, Julia. "Lawyer's Status Throws Genocide Conviction into Doubt." *New York Times*. 16 December 2018. https://www.nytimes.com/2018/12/16/world/asia/cambodia-lawyer-khmer-rouge-genocide.html.

10

# Reclaiming Home and "Righting" Citizenships in Postwar Sri Lanka

## *Internal Displacement, Memory, and Human Rights*

Dinidu Karunanayake

Survival itself . . . can be a crisis.

—Cathy Caruth

Musing over the last and most critical phase of the civil war of Sri Lanka between the government forces and the Liberation Tigers of Tamil Eelam (LTTE), Sri Lankan American poet Indran Amirthanayagam identifies two destinies that awaited civilians who fled their home spaces in Kilinochchi and Mullaitivu, the two last LTTE strongholds in the North, before "liberators"—the government forces—appeared to militarily vanquish the enemy and bring an official end to war.[1] During the mass exodus, they find a momentary and elusive form of refuge in a nearby jungle within the firing range of heavy artillery exchanged between the two belligerents. Some, in their attempt to move to "liberated" areas, walk into the cross fire and perish. Others who make it to the safety net laid by the "liberators" eventually find themselves in refugee camps, which—despite their function as asylum spaces—bear the physical markers of carceral sites (Amirthanayagam 51–52). Both groups, the poet claims, receive the same treatment, as the heavily secured detention camps for internally displaced persons (IDPs) have come to resemble a living form of death and annihilation.[2] Amirthanayagam's censorious view that liberation by military means is encoded with ambiguity and aporia invites a critical interrogation of the putative humanitarian ideals that laid the ideological groundwork behind the Sri Lankan government's military offensive and its nomenclature "Humanitarian Operation." With similar undertones, in the opening epigraph, Cathy Caruth theorizes that survivors invariably find their postviolence existence in an enigmatic relationship with trauma: "It is not only the moment of the event, but of the passing out of it that is traumatic; that *survival itself*, in other words, *can be a crisis*" (9). Building on the scholarship of Sigmund Freud, she forcefully articulates the afterlife of a traumatic encounter that makes a survivor relive the trauma long-windedly. Survival does not put a closure to a horrific chapter but is a continuum, a slippage between life and death.

These two viewpoints undergird the weight under which internally displaced survivors of war lumber in a postwar scenario. While the state controls their corporal movement, traumatic imprints of multiple losses have taken control of their psyches. Keeping these two lines of inquiry as points of entry, this chapter investigates postwar experiences of IDPs of the Sri Lankan civil war. It charts the crisis of citizenship and human rights encountered by Sri Lankan IDPs, equivocal state measures to rehabilitate them, and questions pertaining to the efficacy of humanitarian interventions by the international human rights regime.[3] Through a reading of two projects premised on memories and testimonies of IDPs—*Handmade: Stories of Strength Shared through Recipes from the Women of Sri Lanka*, a cookbook published in 2015 by Palmera Projects, a nonprofit grassroots NGO based in Australia; and *The Incomplete Thombu*, an art project by Thamotharampillai Shanaathanan published in 2011 by Raking Leaves, a nonprofit grassroots NGO based in Colombo, Sri Lanka, with a global outreach—the chapter shows that the two projects engineer a creative platform for their IDP participants to negotiate statelessness and dispossessed citizenship with recourse to memory, an approach that is uncommon in both postwar state legislature and mainstream activism of international nongovernmental organizations (INGOs). The essay concludes with a proposal for rethinking or "righting"—to invoke Gayatri Chakravorty Spivak's sense of the word—the "etic" application of the Universal Human Rights discourse in non-Western contexts like Sri Lanka through the concept of mnemonic citizenship.

## Historical Premise: Internal Displacement and Humanitarianism in Crisis

Internal displacement in postcolonial Sri Lanka is an ethnically and class-nuanced crisis. Since obtaining independence from the British Empire in 1948, the nation-state of Sri Lanka has customarily favored the majoritarian Sinhalese Buddhist community over the Tamil, Muslim, and Burgher ethnic minorities, which is manifest in such landmark legislative decisions as the 1948 Ceylon Citizenship Act, the 1949 Ceylon (Parliamentary Elections) Amendment Act No. 48, and the 1956 Official Language Act. With Buddhism, the religion of the Sinhalese majority, being accorded "the foremost place" by the Constitution (3), the state administration has unfailingly remained a Sinhalese Buddhist prerogative. The state has concurrently been complicit in communal violence perpetuated against the minorities in 1956,

1958, 1977, and 1981, thus functioning as a "technology" of displacement and disenfranchisement (Daiya 131–133) in the case of Tamils. But nothing could match what happened during the 1983 Black July riots that resulted in a prolonged period of internal displacement.[4] The present-day crisis of war-induced internal displacement originated from the expulsion of 75,000 Muslims from the Northern Province in October 1990 by the LTTE.[5] The official conclusion of the civil war in May 2009 escalated this crisis to unprecedented proportions, displacing around 300,000 people in the formerly war-torn Northern and Eastern Provinces of the country. As of October 2009, 270,000 IDPs were being held in "internment camps" in the north, with the largest camp, Menik Farm, holding over 220,000 people, making it the country's second biggest town and one of the largest IDP sites in the world.[6]

## Noncitizens in Limbo and the Failure of Rights

The postwar state sees IDP subjects as an extension of the "collateral damage" of its otherwise successfully accomplished humanitarian mission. Unlike refugees who flee sites of violence across national borders and thus become eligible for legal protection under the Refugee Convention, IDPs are at the mercy of their nation-states, which are often complicit in creating or sustaining the conditions of displacement (Brun, "Local Citizens" 376; Amirthalingam and Lakshman, "Financing of Internal Displacement" 402; Norwegian Refugee Council 3). They are depicted simultaneously as lacking agency, vulnerable to being shifted and relocated against their will, "remaining perpetually strangers and outsiders," and as posing potential threats to national security (Daley 894). The predicament of being "outsiders" while dwelling inside their land of origin is succinctly conveyed by the following lamentation by a Muslim IDP in the North Western Province of Sri Lanka: "We are in Puttalam, but the government says that we are the guests here; 'you cannot demand anything'. The north says, you belong here, but you are not in your territory so we cannot help you. . . . So [we are] people [who] are in between" (Brun, "Local Citizens" 386). This account underscores a fundamental dilemma encountered by IDPs vis-à-vis their right to citizenship. The loss of home, and thereby a legal claim to a specific geopolitical space to be territorially rooted in, has resulted in a situation where the displaced subject can conveniently be disowned by the state. The subject's minoritarian position—here, being Muslim—further facilitates the state's disavowal.

If citizenship is "a mechanism for allocating rights and claims through political membership" (Brysk and Shafir 3), IDPs' exclusion from the nation-state makes them "noncitizens" who cannot claim what Hannah Arendt calls "a right to have rights" (294). This situation lays bare the paradoxical crisis of the "inalienable" nature of rights, as pointed out by Arendt in her 1951 *Origins of Totalitarianism*. Despite their so-called inalienable nature, rights depend on nation-states, for "the moment human beings lacked their own government and had to fall back upon their minimum rights, no authority was left to protect them and no institution was willing to guarantee them" (Arendt 288). Rights are unenforceable when people are no longer citizens of a sovereign state.[7] In the present-day neoliberal national politics, inclusion and exclusion are inflected not only by nationalist sentiments but also by neoliberal interests that have seeped into modern democracies. IDPs who cannot productively contribute to the national economy can conveniently be positioned outside the parameters of the nation's "healthy" population.[8] Internal displacement is a sociopolitical form of disability inflected by ethnic and capitalist associations. From a neoliberal point of view, there is no "return on investment" since IDPs continue to be an impending economic and security burden. For instance, speaking at the Sixtieth Session of the Executive Committee of the UN High Commission for Refugees in Geneva, Minister of Disaster Management and Human Rights Mahinda Samarasingha defended the postwar state's legislative decisions to rigidly limit the mobility of IDPs, highlighting the government's "responsibility to guarantee the human rights of the entirety of the Sri Lankan population" ("Govt Aware"). Invocation of human rights for military ends, as manifested in this instance, attests to a contradiction germane to the rights discourse, as pointed out by Wendy Brown, that human rights are not only defenses against power but also tools of domination (459).

The Sri Lankan state's failure to protect IDP rights calls for INGO interventions. INGOs have for the most part taken upon themselves the responsibility to hold the state accountable for human rights violations and to bring visibility as well as solutions to the IDP crisis. The INGO work for IDPs, however, does not end with the mission of helping the subjects in need but is used to cement the indispensability of Western humanitarianism. For example, an October 2009 report published in the *Forced Migration Review* questions, "If the humanitarian community does not assist the IDPs, who will?" ("Sri Lanka" 5). This rhetorical question embodies the ethos of the human rights regime, which figures itself as the last hope available to the IDPs in the Global South.

## "Enough Reality for the West"? "Speechless Emissaries" and Etic Invocations of the Rights Discourse

Being the self-proclaimed sole representative of the IDPs' welfare crystallizes INGOs' wish to become the "voice" of the subaltern community. As Bo Schack, senior protection officer of the United Nations High Commission for Refugees (UNHCR), Colombo, puts it, an important function of the UNHCR in Sri Lanka is "to carry the voice of the displaced" (104). Popular Western reading practices tend to acknowledge nonfictional journalistic accounts that "give a voice to the voiceless" in the illiberal Global South, disclosing humanitarian intimacies expressed by the morally shocked West toward the pain of the other.[9] Such intimacies are undeniably characterized by an imbalanced dynamic of power that positions the Western benefactor above the non-Western beneficiary, in turn elevating the West to a moral high ground. Therefore, while recognizing the value of INGO humanitarian work, it is also important not to disregard the West's figuring of an ethical superiority at the expense of the rightless community.

Writers and scholars have critically examined the West's equivocal representations of non-Western subjects of human rights. Liisa H. Malkki maintains that the term *refugee* in its Western-centric dominant usage denotes "an objectively self-delimiting field of study of anthropologists" and thus "an epistemic object in construction" ("Refugees and Exile" 496–497). In humanitarian universalism, the refugee becomes "an object of concern and knowledge for the 'international community,' and for a particular variety of humanism" whereby they cease to be individuals with unique identities but become "pure victims in general," hence, "speechless emissaries" (Malkki, "Speechless Emissaries" 378). The evacuation of specificity and identity is part of "dehistoricization" that denies the subjects the capacity to continue as "historical actors." Not only do they become "mute victims"; this process also "strip[s] from them the authority to give credible narrative evidence or testimony about their own condition in politically and institutionally consequential forums" (Malkki, "Speechless Emissaries" 378). Using a feminist lens, Maroussia Hajdukowski-Ahmed concurs with Malkki and identifies a gradual erosion of agency experienced by refugee women in their identity formation under the purview of hegemonic state and nonstate mediations. She calls it a process of "de-selving" in which they are being treated as "blank pages, as if they had no education, no occupation, or no life before" (39).

If the very interventions to uplift perilous human conditions perpetuate further damage in an epistemic sense, such attempts—notwithstanding their altruistic ambitions—fall short of productivity. The accounts by Malkki and Hajdukowski-Ahmed present a collective critique leveled against the West's imposition of its own values as the "universal standard" to make observations, judgments, and adjudications about non-Western subaltern bodies and their spaces. Since the inception of the Rights of Man, critics have contested the universality of "man" centric to universal rights, with some concluding that it is "an exclusive category" (Maslan 361).[10] It is a "*certain* conception of the human" that is not necessarily shared by all humans (Balfour and Cadava 286). The notion of "man" in the universal human rights discourse then is an "exclusive" view of the modern human being that runs the risk of not being applicable to all humans universally and non-Western subjects in particular.

Read from the perspective of comparative rhetorician LuMing Mao, this is an "etic" way of invoking the rhetoric of human rights. An etic viewpoint undergirds an "outsider's" way of approaching an alien culture and its language without paying careful attention to subtle valences and nuances that give shape and identity the culture and language in question. According to Mao, the Western rhetorical tradition that sustains a "language of opposition" encourages rhetoricians to use it as the universal standard to identify deficiencies in non-Western traditions.[11] Rhetoric of universal human rights follows a similar direction especially when rights are called on by the West on behalf of the Global South, or "sent abroad, along with medicine and clothes, to people deprived of medicine, clothes, and rights" (Rancière 307). Within the "rhetorical universals" of human rights, the conflict-ridden Global South is cast as "deficient" in energy, guidance, and wherewithal to achieve equal humanity on its own. Western interventions that promise to restore the lost humanity are marked by such a "language of opposition"—one rooted in Orientalist thinking—and are often governed by etic understanding of local culture, hence becoming attempts "from above." Against this backdrop, Mao proposes "reflective encounters"—a hybrid rhetorical methodology grounded in an "etic/emic" approach. When studying non-Western rhetorical traditions "on their own terms," one has to move from the etic approach to the emic approach so as to comprehend material and conditions native to those traditions (Mao 417–418). The etic/emic approach not only produces "reflective encounters" between the Western and non-Western rhetorical traditions and generates new levels of understanding but also occasions a productive interrogation of the Western (dominant) tradition, its privileged position, and its representations of the other (Mao 418). This model, when applied within a human rights discourse, responds to Malkki's and Hajdukowski-Ahmed's discontent with the Western epistemological formations of the refugee. The two projects I wish to turn to now bear testimony to how displaced lives can be chronicled in more epistemologically accountable ways.

## *Handmade*: Handcrafting Memories and Reclaiming Identities

*Handmade: Stories of Strength Shared through Recipes from the Women of Sri Lanka* probes postwar legacies and human rights through the concept of food. Printed as a cookbook by Palmera,[12] it assembles recipes recollected by thirty-four internally displaced women from the Northern and Eastern Provinces, the regions most severely affected by the civil war. The participants were asked to narrate from memory familiar recipes that they would prepare on a daily basis or for special occasions. The women's narrative accounts are inevitably steeped in testimonies of the civil war capturing memories of loss and displacement.[13] The narration of everyday cuisine impels them to lament their inability to prepare the food during the war and in the postwar period. It also enables them to ruminate on their resilience, in particular to talk about how they made culinary compromises by using substitute ingredients or prepared comfort food to live through psychologically testing times. The Palmera editorial team has chronicled those anecdotes alongside the recipes, interspersed with graphic photographs of the cuisine prepared in a test kitchen.

*Handmade* presents itself as more than a cookbook as explicit in its focalization of women's hands, which produce the food. The cover depicts a pair of weatherbeaten hands cracking open an *ariyatharam*, a sweet made of ground rice—a gesture that welcomes the reader into a culinary world of creativity and labor. Hands signify labor, both in domestic and public spaces, that women undertake for the upkeep of their families. On the other hand, hands symbolize self-defense, strength, dexterity, and, by extension, ability. In this sense, hands are a metonym for survival while the food they prepared during war and its aftermath becomes what Marianne Hirsch and Leo Spitzer call "testimonial objects"—artifacts that "carry memory traces from the past" (353). *Handmade*, read as a project premised on women's storytelling, emphasizes the legitimacy of oral testimony in envisioning an archive of war, one that is constituted mainly by mnemonic components rather than empirical evidence. The recipes narrated by the women function as "anchors" of memory imbued with nostalgia for a prewar, predisplacement past. Among many examples provided in the cookbook, the account by a participant named Rajini is a good case in point. She "vividly recalls Pallai, a lush green land, rich with vegetables—thick, furry, lime-colored okra; glossy black and green eggplant; and an abundance of purple yam" (Palmera 212). Rajini's bond with her arable land and memories of its luscious cultivations help her imaginatively transport herself to a temporality that is not maimed by violence.

Rajini's account reveals a nostalgic passage of memory unbolted by culinary memory. Critics have deliberated on multiple capacities enabled by nostalgia and food. For instance, writing about South Asian diasporic citizenships in Anglo-America, Anita Mannur recognizes that food functions as an "intellectual and emotional anchor" allowing an immigrant to look into "the desire to simultaneously embrace what is left of a past from which one is spatially and temporally displaced" ("Culinary Nostalgia" 11–12). Such yearnings for culinary-scapes, Mannur states, can be charted in "culinary nostalgia." Nostalgia, however, is not always considered a dynamic exigency. As Mieke Bal points out, it is a "specific coloring of memory" that has often been denounced as unproductive, escapist, sentimental, regressive, and romanticizing, as it is a search for "an idyllic past that never was" (xi). Leo Spitzer opines otherwise and uses Maurice Halbwachs's position that nostalgia's provision of an "escape from the present" is one of its merits to argue for its productive impact on a survivor's memory. He maintains, "As a 'retrospective mirage' constructed through hindsight, nostalgic memory thus serves as an important comparative and, by implication, animating purpose. It sets up the *positive* from within the 'world of yesterday' as a model for creative inspiration, and possible emulation, within the 'world of the here-and-now'" (92). Spitzer illustrates how nostalgic memory is useful to the community of Central European refugees who use nostalgic memory "as a creative tool of adjustment, helping to ease their cultural uprootedness and sense of alienation." "Creatively reconfigured," it is a "source thorough which they built a new communal culture and constructed a new collective identity to serve their changed needs" (Spitzer 92).

Spitzer's observation of nostalgia can be yoked with Mannur's "culinary nostalgia" in order to analyze *Handmade*'s mediation of IDP memories. By no means can experiences of a diasporic subject and an IDP be considered equal pairs for comparison. Therefore, it is with a critical awareness of fundamental differences pertaining to class privilege, education, capital, social networking, mobility, and state protection that figure in the two contexts in relatively oppositional ways that I invoke Mannur's and Spitzer's scholarship. A racially marked diasporic subject and an IDP, however, do share a few paradigmatic traits. Both often find themselves in "in-between" locales where their identities and subjectivities are far from fixed. As such, both are searching for more stable identities with recourse to nostalgic memories of an original home/land. Both a diasporic subject immigrant and an IDP walk under the weight of their racial and ethnic minoritarian position in a sociopolitical climate that privileges the will of the racial and ethnic majorities. Furthermore, just as much as food provides a language for Asian Americans to negotiate their othered position in the American imagination (Mannur, *Culinary Fictions* 13), it provides a language for IDPs to articulate their subjectivities in postwar Sri Lanka.

Mannur and Spitzer delineate the forging of community and citizenship away from original sites of home, ones held together by nostalgic memories. For Mannur, culinary trajectories offer potent avenues to inquire into matters of survival and resilience of minoritarian subjects, thus forming "culinary citizenship"—that is, "a form of affective citizenship which grants subjects the ability to claim and inhabit subject positions via their relationship to food" ("Culinary Nostalgia" 13). The participants of *Handmade* constantly use their relationship to food to give meaning to their present-day existence. Take, for example, the following account by a woman who presents a comparative temporal observation:

> In the days before the war we made our own rice flour, grinding the rice ourselves. Now we rely on packaged food and flours. We do not have the facilities to make the foods we used to make. . . . We had our

> own cows and fresh milk. Vegetable were in vast supply. Green mangoes and green bananas abounded, rice was so cheap. [Now f]resh fruits are expensive. Now we have processed foods, sodas, biscuits, Milo and juice. In those days children didn't get as sick. We used a lot of herbal medicine like curry leaves. [Now] *Kurakkan maa* is low in stock. There is no *saamai* rice for diabetic people. Now they are just given medicines. (Palmera 115)

Beneath her lamentation on the erasure of arable lands, animal husbandry, and prosperity that mark the pre-IDP life is a self-recognition of subjectivity anchored to a specific geopolitical history. This cannot simply be dismissed as an escapist account. It features a collective voice. Spitzer reminds us that nostalgic memory, by devising a bridge between a "self-in-present" and an image of a "self-in-past," contributes to the reconstruction and continuity of individual and collective identity (92). Along these lines, the woman's account explains the constitution of her community's identity as one informed by predisplacement memories.

Some culinary memories enable alternative realities. Confined in heavily guarded IDP camps, the women's mobility is scrutinized and regulated, but their memories are not. One participant of *Handmade*, for instance, narrates how food preparation helped her temporarily take her family to "another, more joyful world, outside of the camps" (Palmera 46). The woman forges emancipation through culinary creativity and "resettles" her family in a territory of her own design. The affective relationship she cultivates with food allows not only her family to carve out, claim, and inhabit identitarian positions (Mannur, *Culinary Fictions* 29). This is a form of citizenship that is constructed outside national, legal, and political boundaries. Hence, it is shielded from the intrusive eyes of the state and interference of its military apparatus. Identitarian positions facilitated by culinary citizenship allow displaced subjects to fixate themselves on specific historical and geopolitical locations via memory and to complicate popular notions of displacement. The women's narratives accompanying their recipes in *Handmade* unravel possibilities of defining citizenship as one that is not necessary coeval with territorial inhabitance in the nation-state but one that can actively and creatively function in a mnemonic domain as well.

The cookbook's presentation of a dozen close-ups of hands that are making, holding, or offering the visually appealing food is a subversive move. For Mannur, dominant culinary cultural politics conveniently mask labor practices underlying food production.[14] Foregrounding the women who create the food, *Handmade* acknowledges not only the culinary tradition but also the displaced women who produce it. Whereas refugee women are conventionally "socialized to silence their own experience, needs, and pain" since they have to undertake multiple employment and caregiving functions

(Hajdukowski-Ahmed 47), culinary power elevates the displaced women to positions of agency. Along these lines, *Handmade* recognizes the indomitable spirit with which the women survived the war and their memories before, during, and after the war.

## *The Incomplete Thombu*: Returning Home through Mnemonic Cartography

For the postwar state and the international human rights regime, repatriation or reterritorialization is the "preferred" and "durable" solution for displacement. The development projects launched by the government with INGO aid to revive the formerly war-torn Northern and Eastern Provinces, namely Uthuru Vasanthaya ("Northern Spring") and Negenehira Navodaya ("Eastern Revival"), primarily focused on demining, reconstruction, resettlement of IDPs, housing, infrastructure improvement, regional economy, education, and transportation.[15] The state and nonstate actors follow the position that resettlement or returning home is accomplished once IDPs return to physical structures that can be rebuilt if destroyed or renovated if damaged. Implicit in the postwar state's account above is a notion of a "closure" to all the sociopolitical and economic issues pertaining to the civil war, a closure that is coeval with the defeat of the LTTE. The Ministry of Defense, for instance, in a 2011 report, makes claims about the government's successful handling of the IDP crisis, among other things:

> Today, Sri Lankans of all ethnicities, living in all parts of Sri Lanka, are free from LTTE terror and no longer live in a state of fear. Democracy is restored in the North and the East, the electoral process has been resuscitated after decades, internally displaced persons have been resettled in their homes, infrastructure is being restored, the economy has been revived, former armed groups have been disarmed and have joined the political process, child soldiers conscripted by the LTTE are back with their families, and other cadres who surrendered are being reintegrated into civilian life after rehabilitation. Sri Lankans have begun the process of rebuilding their lives and their country. (3)

This report, however, has factual discrepancies. According to the Internal Displacement Monitoring Centre, an estimated 73,700 were living as IDPs as of July 2015. On the other hand, many Tamils cannot return to their former home spaces even after the areas have been "liberated" and demined because they fall under military jurisdictions of "high security zones."[16]

Set against this backdrop, Shanaathanan's 2011 art project, *The Incomplete Thombu*, probes an alternative methodology of reclaiming home for an

IDP. Having lived in Jaffna throughout the civil war, he has an emic perspective on the changing cultural and political landscape of the North. He gathered eighty internally displaced subjects representing the Sinhala, Tamil, and Muslim communities in the North and assigned them the task of remembering home and sketching a ground plan of what constitutes "home." The participants' immediate focus was on the nonexistent or inaccessible material structures of houses. But they also included other memorable landmarks such as shrines, wells, specific trees, orchards, and roads in their illustration as components of home. Equally important, they narrated specific memories of people anchored in their map. Shanaathanan then commissioned a surveyor to draw a professional plan based on each sketch. Third, he produced a monochrome artistic rendition with basic drawing material—pencil, sketch pen, or pastel—in response to original drawings. *The Incomplete Thombu* presents the drawings from the three stages layered on each other, accompanied by an English-language translation of the oral accounts given by each subject while taking part in the project.

Shanaathanan calls this activity "memory architecture" because to him, the damaged, bullet-ridden, and erased buildings are representative of those who dwelled in them (personal interview). Destruction of familiar surroundings, especially their architecture, Robert Bevan writes, can not only cause "a disorienting exile from the memories they have evoked" but also endanger one's collective identity (13). Shanaathanan's project then curates "perilous memories"—both "precarious and endangered memories in need of recuperation" and "memories that continue to generate a sense of danger" (Fujitani et al. 3)—in the case of IDPs whose historical subjectivities linked to their former homes and communities do not receive much import in the postwar state's mandate. IDPs become instruments of postwar metanarratives in that they are seen as the living proof of the state's humanitarian warfare against the LTTE.[17] In *The Incomplete Thombu*, the oral testimonies accompanying the hand-sketched plans constitute a mnemonic archive that supplements officialized archives of war. The artist's lexical use of "thombu" harks back to the colonial archive shaped by historical violence. Derived from the Greek word *tomos* ("large book"), *thombu* is a word coined by the former Dutch colonizer to refer to a public land registry (Raking Leaves).[18] Shanaathanan's summoning of a colonial vocabulary in naming the compilation of postwar memories mirrors a paradigm of power between the Dutch colonizer and the postwar Sri Lankan state. The title, *The Incomplete Thombu*, suggests that similar to the former colonial ruler's inadequate understanding of Ceylonese citizenship, the postwar state has a limited view of IDP experiences, which it sees as territorially defined.

Quite the contrary, the IDP participants of Shanaathanan's project unpack the notion of home as a concept that cannot be confined in one definitional possibility. The sketching activity encourages them to deliberate on different meanings of home. For instance, one participant says, "Home means brothers, sisters, relatives and friends. In Jaffna we lived very closely in neighboring streets. Now we are scattered all around Sri Lanka, after being expelled from our home town in 1990. I came back to Jaffna after my stay in Kurunegala. But I am alone here. I miss my neighbourhood. I do not think that we can recover the social network we once had" (Shanaathanan 18). For another, "A home means blood connection" (Shanaathanan 57). For some participants, home is a sentiment anchored in nostalgic prewar memories: "I lost all my toys that I'd keep since I was a child and all the glass bangles that I had kept in wooden boxes. I have since rebuilt my house but there are no toys and bangles to call it home" (Shanaathanan 74). These accounts reveal that home is not merely a physical structure but a composite, kaleidoscopic entity that holds memories, emotional bonds, nostalgic attachments, and community together. Once the multidimensional pieces that hold home together are disseminated, it is not easy to reassemble them into the home's original shape. Even if IDPs are able to return to their former land, they become "stranger[s] on [their] own street," to echo one participant (Shanaathanan 80). In this light, postwar state and nonstate endeavors to rebuild and resettle IDPs fall short of bringing the lives of IDPs back to how things were before.

The IDPs' discontentment—or the feeling of "incompletion"—stemming from their inability to reclaim home contests the state's stance about the military conclusion as a closure to the ethnic conflict. Whereas the mainstream postwar discourse catalogues war survivors as either displaced or resettled, Shanaathanan considers refugeeness a state of flux—or as Malkki calls it, "a matter of becoming" ("Speechless Emissaries" 381)—that involves a perpetual struggle with location and identity, dispossession and belonging, here and there. As such, their identities are always in the making as some cannot come to terms with loss and simply move on while others refuse to forget. The following account exemplifies this dilemma: "The anxiety, longing, suffering and temporariness is my reality. Recently we were allowed to see our property. I did not go because I do not have the heart to see it. Afterwards I came to know that it is empty and without a roof. The only thing that survived was a *murungai* tree near the well" (Shanaathanan 50). The reflection evinces the impossibility of closure for an IDP burdened by the weight of trauma etched in memories of lost home spaces. Trauma, "a blow . . . to the tissue of the mind" (Erikson 183), imprisons survivors to history (Caruth 5).[19] Since the traumatic event is not "fully assimilated" at the time but experienced belatedly, the subject experiences it in "repeated *possession*" (Caruth 5). Similarly, Bessel A. van der Kolk and Onno van der Hart (via L. L. Langer) see trauma as a "permanent duality" between the present and the past. In the postwar era, the topic of the psychological impact of war on IDPs has, for the most part, woefully fallen through the cracks of the mainstream state and nonstate interventions, which focus primarily on infrastructure development.[20] Jane Derges, in her examination of postconflict recovery in Sri Lanka, writes that for many survivors, "it was ultimately unhelpful to focus exclusively on their experience of past trauma, which they felt powerless to 'come to terms with' or address in a satisfactory way" (115). More than recovery, she adds, being able to continue with life in a practical sense is a problem for them (Derges 115). In this light, Shanaathanan's project is both a metacommentary on the incompleteness of the state and nonstate mandates that fail to recognize the mental health of the IDPs and an endeavor to attend to this gap by alternative means—thorough artistic curation of trauma.

Psychologists and theorists of trauma have emphasized the significance for a trauma survivor to integrate and assimilate traumatic memories through narration. Pierre Janet through his groundbreaking experiments in the late nineteenth and early twentieth centuries distinguished between ordinary/narrative memory and traumatic memory. Whereas ordinary memory is integrated with other experiences and thus becomes an aspect of social life, traumatic memory has no social component, nor is it flexible or variable (van der Kolk and van der Hart 163). To Dori Laub, narration and survival are mutually dependent (63). "Avoiding traumatic memories leads to stagnation in the recovery process," writes Judith Lewis Herman (176). Distressingly, in the case of postwar Sri Lanka, the state's adamant prohibitions geared toward survivor memories that contest the state's humanitarian warfare do not grant a safe space for the IDPs to engage with their memories.[21] The commemoration of the dead in the former war zones is strictly scrutinized as Tamils are prohibited to pay tribute to their fallen relatives who were members of the LTTE.[22]

Against the backdrop of these official commandments, *The Incomplete Thombu* facilitates a narrative platform for the IDPs to voice their officially repressed memories and act on them. The following testimony by a subject whose father was killed while in the service of the LTTE is particularly noteworthy at this juncture. The only tangible object that embodied the memory of the father was a photograph presented to the family by the LTTE as a token of honor. But "when we were displaced in the last phase of the civil war, we were afraid to carry the portrait with us. So we carefully buried it near the coconut tree. When we were allowed to resettle in our house we found that the photograph was missing. When we were displaced we lost all our photo albums. Now we do not have a single photograph of our father" (Shanaathanan 27). The surviving family members are not eligible to commemorate the father, who was an enemy of the state. Family photographs, Marianne Hirsch writes, are instrumental in bridging transgenerational distance and separation and in facilitating identification and affiliation (38). As such, the loss of the father's photograph in the above testimony is not only a material erasure but also the dispossession of the key to a temporal and affective premise. Shanaathanan's art project, however, opens an avenue for them to recognize and commemorate the memory of the father. By narrating the loss of the photograph amid many other losses, the subject acts on the officially and nationally taboo memory and, in this fashion, carves out an archival space for it. Thereby a relationship is forged with the nonexistent subjectivity of the historically nontraceable relative.

This enabling capacity of memory reveals an extension of the performative power of memory. In a manner similar to culinary citizenship, in which nostalgic memory is mediated to forge subjectivity in *Handmade*, here traumatic memories are invoked to revamp the missing links. Shanaathanan's project allows the participant to perform memories, first in a literal sense by sketching them out and second by constructing subjectivities in relation to those memories. Not only do such "acts of memory" allow them to invent an "imagined community"; they also encourage the subjects to renegotiate their lived condition by transcending their default status as "speechless emissaries." This is a mnemonic form of citizenship that permits them to reclaim and inhabit currently nonexistent and inaccessible homes. It both "reselves" and "rehistoricizes" the subject, to revisit Malkki's and Hajdukowski-Ahmed's call. Shanaathanan reveals that the participants commended the "therapeutic" nature of his approach, which was distinctly different from state and nonstate "interrogation methods" (personal interview). In this fashion, the project also lays a stepping stone toward a psychological intervention aimed at healing.

## "Righting" Rights and Mnemonic Citizenships

In tune with Arendt's position that the fundamental deprivation of human rights is primarily evident in "the deprivation of a place in the world which makes opinions significant and actions effective" (293), it is safe to say that the crisis of IDP rights—their loss of subjectivity, which makes them a liability in the postwar state's agenda and "mute victims" in the Western nonstate humanitarian perspective—is fundamentally a crisis emanating from the loss of home and community. When belonging to one's community is threatened, Arendt adds, "something much more fundamental than freedom and justice . . . is at stake" (293). Accordingly, measures geared toward restoration of IDP rights must begin with enabling the displaced subjects to reclaim home, which is not coeval with mere resettlement or repatriation. Such measures must also be engineered to rebuild and foster communities for individuals to reforge their fractured social and cultural networks. The postwar state's maintenance of IDP internment camps for the sake of national security further alienates the individuals and exacerbates the human rights crisis. Its resettlement endeavors are further tainted by postwar militarism, which precludes the repatriated subjects from reconnecting with their social and cultural roots. On the other hand, the human rights regime's involvement has brought about positive changes by making legible human rights violations that continue unabated in the postwar era. However, its top-to-bottom approach has often failed to grant equal humanity to IDPs. It would not be an overstatement to say that the IDP crisis has in fact augmented the INGOs' humanitarian ethos. These dynamics of rights activism are questioned by Palmera's *Handmade* and Shanaathanan's *The Incomplete Thombu*. By means of their participant-centric methodology, both projects organically utilize the performative power of memory in empowering capacities. Both projects make repressed trauma "narratable," which critics recognize as a crucial step toward healing. Revamped selfhood enables the participants to renegotiate their existence as agentive subjects and envision a state of belonging vis-à-vis home, place, and culture. It is a position informed by mourning, for only through mourning can the traumatized subject "feel autonomous" (Herman 188, 205, 133). This newfound subjectivity elevates them to a level where they are judged no longer by their default status as "mute victims" but by their own actions and opinions.

Mnemonic citizenship holds that the humanitarian accountability of the West does not end with their financial and material support of IDPs. It also extends toward the act of cultivating an epistemologically responsible encounter with the subject, one where the benefactor has to acknowledge intricacies of the beneficiary's cultures, identities, histories, and subjectivities that are very much alive and active in mnemonic domains. In this sense, *Handmade* and *The Incomplete Thombu* call for what Mao terms an "etic/emic" approach that pushes the etic invocations of the Western human rights discourse toward an emic framework. Such a model lays the groundwork for a "just membership," which Seyla Benhabib sees as the core principle of a cosmopolitan theory of justice (3).[23] It also offers a way to think through the inherent "perplexities" of what Spivak calls "righting wrongs," a process that in postwar Sri Lanka remains unsettled.

## Acknowledgments

I am grateful to the editors of this collection, Cathy J. Schlund-Vials, Guy Beauregard, and Hsiu-chuan Lee, for their valuable comments. I thank Evan Fackler, Tyler Groff, Nalin Jayasena, Anita Mannur, and Sammani Perera for their feedback at different stages of writing this chapter.

### NOTES

1. Ethnic fissures between the Sinhalese and Tamil communities can be traced back to the late British colonial era. After Ceylon (to be renamed "Sri Lanka" in 1972) obtained independence from the British Empire in 1948, violent, ethnically nuanced clashes erupted between the majoritarian Sinhalese and minoritarian Tamils in 1956, 1958, 1977, and 1981. The civil war between the Sri Lankan government and the LTTE

officially broke out in 1983 in the wake of the "Black July" riots—the state-sanctioned pogrom of Tamils. Where the government had been following a mandate favoring the Sinhalese Buddhist majority population over the ethnic minorities, Tamils, Muslims, and Burghers (Dutch descendants), the LTTE claimed to represent the interests of the Tamil community. After twenty-six years of warfare punctuated by several unsuccessful cease-fire agreements made in 1985 (followed by the failed deployment of an Indian peacekeeping force), 1994, and 2002, the government forces declared victory over the LTTE on May 18, 2009, by killing the LTTE leader Velupillai Prabhakaran, thus bringing an official closure to the civil war.

2. Here, I follow the definition by the Office of the United Nations High Commission for Human Rights that identifies IDPs as "persons who have been forced to flee their homes suddenly or unexpectedly in large numbers, as a result of armed conflict, internal strife, systematic violations of human rights or natural or man-made disasters; and who are within the territory of their own country" (Deng 3).

3. I understand the "international human rights regime" in line with Seyla Benhabib's use of the phrase in reference to "a set of interrelated and overlapping global and regional regimes that encompass human rights treaties as well as customary international law or international 'soft law'" (7). The soft law pertains to international agreements that are not treaties and hence not covered by the Vienna Convention. In this chapter, "mainstream" human rights activism is understood as mediations by powerful actors of the international human rights regime, specifically, international nongovernmental organizations (INGOs) such as the United Nations Human Rights Council (UNHRC), United Nations High Commissioner for Refugees (UNHCR), Amnesty International, and Human Rights Watch. They are well funded by the global/international humanitarian community, receive visibility locally and internationally, and have a wider scope of influence by virtue of their ties with nation-states as well as other INGOs.

4. In the absence of official statistics about the victims of the violence that was programmed and systematically executed by Sinhalese mobs with the state's patronage, sources vary in their calculation of casualties. Robert Muggah puts the figure of Sri Lankan and estate Tamils' internal displacement at 15,000, while V. Suryanarayan says nearly 100,000 Tamils were displaced within Colombo alone. With reference to the UNHCR data, Muggah further notes that an estimated 130,000 Sri Lankan Tamils sought de facto refugee status in India between 1983 and 1985. Sri Lankan refugees in Tamil Nadu exceeded 210,000 by 1987. Sri Lankan Tamils with better social networks and financial status sought refuge in the West, and between 1983 and 1999, at least 256,000 sought asylum in Western Europe (Muggah 142).

5. See Brun, "Reterritorializing the Relationship" 20; Amirthalingam and Lakshman, "Financing of Internal Displacement" 405.

6. See Amirthalingam and Lakshman, "Impact of Displacement" 29; "Sri Lanka: A Question of Rights" 4; and Wassel 8.

7. In *The Origins of Totalitarianism*, Arendt delves into the "perplexities" inherent in the figuring of the "abstract" human being in the Declaration of the Rights of Man and Citizen—the 1789 charter outlining human freedom and "inalienable rights" every man inherits for being human—that emerged against the backdrop of the French Revolution. Arendt takes issue with the conceptualization of "an 'abstract' human being who seemed to exist nowhere" as the source and the ultimate goal of those rights (288). No authority or laws were enacted to protect them because "all laws were supposed to rest upon them" (287). However, the refugee crisis laid bare the dependence of rights on nation-states.

8. Julie Avril Minich writes that the nation is configured as "a whole, nondisabled body" whose health must be safeguarded against "external pollutants," which include immigrants, citizens labelled *with* disabilities and diseases, and those marked by racialized and sexual minoritarian identities (2). For a postwar nation, IDPs are a potential "pathogen" or "parasite" that feeds on its healthy national body for sustenance, adding "dead weight" to its economy.

9. A case in point is Rohini Mohan's 2014 nonfictional account *The Seasons of Trouble: Life amid the Ruins of Sri Lanka's Civil War*, which is supposedly based on her reporting of the Sri Lankan war to Western media conglomerates such as the *New York Times* and *CNN-IBN*. The book was hailed as a successful humanitarian intervention by Western critics. Jon Lee Anderson of the *New Yorker* called it "a modern tragedy of truly epic proportions. Haunting and unforgettable," while Adrian Chen of *Slate* viewed it as a "remarkable feat of empathy." *The Economist* admired it for "giving voice to the voiceless" ("Giving Voice").

10. For example, in 1791, Olympe de Gouges interpreted "man" literally as a gendered term, thus excluding women. In 1844, Karl Marx saw "man" as a bourgeois subject (Maslan 361).

11. Mao observes that the Western rhetorical tradition relies on a "deficiency" model according to which non-Western cultures lack rhetorical traditions. It also identifies Western-centric "rhetorical universals" that can be applied across other cultures (401). This deficiency model has "pitfalls," Mao claims, as it standardizes the Western rhetorical tradition as the only rhetorical tradition in the world (407). The etic use is premised on a Western/Oriental duality and is imposed by the West on non-Western cultures from outside without recognizing nuances and intricacies inherent in the latter.

12. Palmera, an Australia-based grassroots NGO that uses crowdsourcing, perceives itself as a "for-purpose" organization with a humanitarian mission. It has launched a number of small-scale projects in northern and eastern Sri Lanka with the objective of bolstering self-sufficiency and entrepreneurship among women. It also provides farmers with training in business, banking, horticulture, farming, and water management to improve rural economies severely affected by the civil war.

13. My understanding of testimony is informed, on the one hand, by Dori Laub's recognition of the threefold levels of witnessing in the context of the Holocaust experience, namely "the level of being a witness to oneself within the experience" (the IDPs are witnesses to themselves through the course of survival), "the level of being a witness to the testimonies of others" (the participants see their own accounts in conversation with others in the final project), and "the level of being a witness to the process of witnessing itself" (the IDPs are not only narrators but also witnesses to the process of their memories being sketched out) (61–62). On the other hand, I follow Judith Lewis Herman's stance that trauma story, in its telling, becomes a testimony. Herman, via Inger Agger and Soren Jensen, sees testimony as constitutive of a private dimension that is confessional and spiritual and a public dimension that is political and juridical (181). Testimony transforms the trauma story into a "new story" that enables the survivor as it replaces the former narrative about "shame and humiliation" with one about "dignity and virtue" (Mollica, qtd. in Herman 181).

14. Situated within the South Asian diasporic culinary tradition, Mannur's critique is levied against the West's celebration of ethnic cuisine via "multiculturalism" while denying the racially marked creator of the food equal humanity in the white-dominant public space: "What makes CTM (chicken tikka masala) acceptable on British tables when the same Indian bodies that produce CTM are not welcome to sit at the table with

the British?" (*Culinary Fictions* 4). Mannur's critique can be productively applied to Western reading and viewing practices pertaining to understanding "ethnic" food from conflict-ridden regions in the Global South that are challenged through cookbooks and food documentaries.

15. According to a "performance report" published by the Ministry of Economic Development, 320 projects with an estimated value of Rs. 12,284.49 million were approved for 2010 under the Uthuru Wasanthaya development program. Together with INGO-funded programs, the state prides itself in achieving a 93.6 percent progress in all development projects in the North. Areas covered by these projects include infrastructure development, demining, resettlement, housing, water supply, agriculture, irrigation, education, and restoration of livelihood, among others (24–26). With a total investment of Rs. 5,311.62 million for 2010, Negenahira Navodaya focused on areas such as demining, reconstruction and rehabilitation of infrastructure facilities, development of livelihood for resettled people, transportation, fisheries, irrigation, and education in the Eastern Province (37–38). Foreign-funded programs totaling an allocation of Rs. 4651.53 million had similar areas of interest (39).

16. High security zones are spatial units established by the armed forces in areas that were deemed vulnerable to higher risks of incursion or infiltration by the LTTE. Originally designed to protect the government forces from LTTE artillery attacks in Jaffna of the Northern Province, high security zones expanded throughout the North and the East to give protection to transport corridors, military encampments, and villages (Muggah 155). Robert Muggah, in his study of relocation failures throughout the war, recognizes high security zones as a direct cause for displacement, dispossession of property, and restrictions of mobility of certain populations, thus preventing individuals and households from returning or resettling (155).

17. I owe this insight to Yến Lê Espiritu's position about refugees of the Vietnam War. She writes that in the U.S. political imaginary, Vietnamese refugees have become "an antidote to the 'rescue and liberation' myths and memories" (1).

18. The Dutch ruled Sri Lanka from 1658 to 1796 before the British imperialism.

19. Caruth identifies posttraumatic stress disorder (PTSD) as "a symptom of history": "The traumatized . . . carry an impossible history within them, or they become themselves the symptom of a history that they cannot entirely process." To be traumatized is "to be possessed by an image or event." It cannot simply be called "a distortion of reality" (5).

20. In addition to the astounding lack of official data available in the public domain, trauma and psychological disorders experienced by IDPs and war-affected communities in Sri Lanka have not received sufficient coverage. The first comprehensive study focusing on adult Muslims affected by conflict-induced prolonged displacement in northwestern Sri Lanka was conducted in 2011. It found an 18.8 percent prevalence of any common mental disorder among the study population with somatoform disorder (14.0 percent) followed by other depressive syndromes (7.3 percent) (Siriwardhana et al. 4).

21. The postwar state has named May, the month in which the government forces eliminated the LTTE, "War Heroes Commemoration Month" to celebrate and pay "tribute to the memory and recognition of invaluable services of War Heroes to the Nation" ("National War Hero"). Those who are not cast as "heroes"—in particular, Tamil civilians and IDPs—are thus officially excluded from these commemorative practices.

22. See "Sri Lanka Bans Remembrance"; "Sri Lanka Blocks Tamil Memorials"; Aneez and Sirilal. Even with the end of the Rajapaksa regime in 2015, the situation has not progressed ("Jaffna Fears Remembering").

23. Benhabib argues that a cosmopolitan theory of justice needs to be driven by a vision of just membership rather than just distribution on a global scale (3).

## WORKS CITED

Amirthalingam, Kopalapillai, and Rajith W. D. Lakshman. "Financing of Internal Displacement: Excerpts from the Sri Lankan Experience." *Disasters* 34.2 (2010): 402–425.

———. "Impact of Displacement on Women and Female-Headed Households: A Mixed Method Analysis with a Microeconomic Touch." *Journal of Refugee Studies* 26.1 (2012): 26–46.

Amirthanayagam, Indran. "Equal Treatment." *Uncivil War.* Toronto: TSAR, 2013.

Anderson, Jon Lee. "Visiting Sri Lanka's Ghosts." *The New Yorker.* 13 January 2011. https://www.newyorker.com/news/news-desk/visiting-sri-lankas-ghosts.

Aneez, Shihar, and Ranga Sirilal. "Tamils Say Barred from Commemorating War Dead, Sri Lanka Denies." *Reuters.* 18 May 2014. http://www.reuters.com/article/us-sri-lanka-war-celebrations/tamils-say-barred-from-commemorating-war-dead-sri-lanka-denies-idUSBREA4H09B20140518. 22 August 2017.

Arendt, Hannah. *The Origins of Totalitarianism.* New York: Harcourt, Brace, 1951.

Bal, Mieke. Introduction. *Acts of Memory: Cultural Recall in the Present.* Ed. Mieke Bal, Jonathan Crewe, and Leo Spitzer. Hanover, NH: University Press of New England, 1999. vii–xvii.

Balfour, Ian, and Eduardo Cadava. "The Claims of Human Rights: An Introduction." *South Atlantic Quarterly* 103.2/3 (2004): 277–296.

Benhabib, Seyla. *The Rights of Others: Aliens, Residents, and Citizens.* Cambridge: Cambridge University Press, 2004.

Bevan, Robert. *The Destruction of Memory: Architecture at War.* London: Reaktion, 2006.

Brown, Wendy. "'The Most We Can Hope For . . .': Human Rights and the Politics of Fatalism." *South Atlantic Quarterly* 103.2/3 (2004): 451–463.

Brun, Cathrine. "Local Citizens or Internally Displaced Persons? Dilemma of Long Term Displacement in Sri Lanka." *Journal of Refugee Studies* 16.4 (2003): 376–397.

———. "Reterritorializing the Relationship between People and Place in Refugee Studies." *Geografiska Annaler* 83 (2001): 15–25.

Brysk, Alison, and Gershon Shafir. "Introduction: Globalization and the Citizenship Gap." *People out of Place: Globalization, Human Rights and the Citizenship Gap.* Ed. Alison Brysk and Gershon Shafir. New York: Routledge, 2004. 3–9.

Caruth, Cathy. "Trauma and Experience: Introduction." *Trauma: Explorations in Memory.* Ed. Cathy Caruth. Baltimore: Johns Hopkins University Press, 1995. 3–12.

Chen, Adrian. "The Overlooked Books of 2014." *Slate.* 3 December 2014. http://www.slate.com/articles/arts/books/2014/12/underrated_books_overlooked_fiction_nonfiction_and_comics_of_2014.html. 2 May 2017.

Daiya, Kavita. *Violent Belongings: Partition, Gender, and National Culture in Postcolonial India.* Philadelphia: Temple University Press, 2008.

Daley, Patricia. "Refugees, IDPs and Citizenship Rights: The Perils of Humanitarianism in the African Great Lakes Region." *Third World Quarterly* 34.5 (2013): 893–912.

Deng, Francis M. *Internally Displaced Persons: Compilation and Analysis of Legal Norms.* New York: United Nations, 1998.

Derges, Jane. *Ritual and Recovery in Post-conflict Sri Lanka.* London: Routledge, 2013.

Erikson, Kai. "Notes on Trauma and Community." *Trauma: Explorations in Memory.* Ed. Cathy Caruth. Baltimore: Johns Hopkins University Press, 1995. 183–199.

Espiritu, Yến Lê. *Body Counts: The Vietnam War and Militarized Refuge(es).* Oakland: University of California Press, 2014.

Fujitani, T., et al. Introduction. *Perilous Memories: The Asia-Pacific War(s).* Ed. T. Fujitani, Geoffrey M. White, and Lisa Yoneyama. Durham, NC: Duke University Press, 2001. 1–29.

"Giving Voice to the Voiceless." *The Economist.* 18 November 2014. https://www.economist.com/blogs/prospero/2014/11/sri-lankas-civil-war. 22 May 2017.

"Govt Aware of Hardcore LTTE Members among IDPs—Samarasinghe." *The Island.* 29 September 2009. http://www.island.lk/2009/09/29/news27.html. 22 July 2017.

Hajdukowski-Ahmed, Maroussia. "A Dialogical Approach to Identity: Implications for Refugee Women." *Not Born a Refugee Woman: Contesting Identities, Rethinking Practices.* Eds. Maroussia Hajdukowski-Ahmed, Nazilla Khanlou, and Helene Moussa. New York: Berghahn, 2008. 28–54.

Herman, Judith Lewis. *Trauma and Recovery.* New York: Basic Books, 1992.

Hirsch, Marianne. *The Generation of Postmemory: Writing and Visual Culture after the Holocaust.* New York: Columbia University Press, 2012.

Hirsch, Marianne, and Leo Spitzer. "Testimonial Objects: Memory, Gender, and Transmission." *Poetics Today* 27.2 (2006): 353–383.

Internal Displacement Monitoring Centre. "Sri Lanka IDP Figures Analysis." http://www.internal-displacement.org/countries/sri-lanka. 22 March 2018.

"Jaffna Fears Remembering Tamil War Dead." *BBC News.* 27 November 2015. http://www.bbc.com/news/world-asia-34934250. 22 August 2017.

Laub, Dori. "Truth and Testimony: The Process and the Struggle." *Trauma: Explorations in Memory.* Ed. Cathy Caruth. Baltimore: Johns Hopkins University Press, 1995. 61–75.

Malkki, Liisa H. "Refugees and Exile: From 'Refugee Studies' to the National Order of Things." *Annual Review of Anthropology* 24 (1995): 495–523.

———. "Speechless Emissaries: Refugees, Humanitarianism, and Dehistoricization." *Cultural Anthropology* 11.3 (1996): 377–404.

Mannur, Anita. *Culinary Fictions: Food in South Asian Diasporic Culture.* Philadelphia: Temple University Press, 2010.

———. "Culinary Nostalgia: Authenticity, Nationalism, and Diaspora." *MELUS* 32.4 (2007): 11–31.

Mao, LuMing. "Reflective Encounters: Illustrating Comparative Rhetoric." *Style* 37.4 (2003): 401–425.

Maslan, Susan. "The Anti-human: Man and Citizen before the Declaration of the Rights of Man and of the Citizen." *South Atlantic Quarterly* 103.2/3 (2004): 357–374.

Minich, Julie Avril. *Accessible Citizenships: Disability, Nation, and the General Politics of Greater Mexico.* Philadelphia: Temple University Press, 2014.

Ministry of Defense, Democratic Socialist Republic of Sri Lanka. *Humanitarian Operation: Factual Analysis: July 2006–May 2009.* Colombo, 2011.

Ministry of Economic Development. "Performance Report." 2010. https://www.parliament.lk/papers_presented/21092012/performance_report_ministry_of_economic_development_2010.pdf.

Mohan, Rohini. *The Seasons of Trouble: Life amid the Ruins of Sri Lanka's Civil War.* London: Verso, 2014.

Muggah, Robert. *Relocation Failures in Sri Lanka: A Short History of Internal Displacement and Resettlement.* London: Zed, 2008.

"National War Hero Commemorative Month Begins." *Sri Lanka Army.* http://www.army.lk/news/national-war-hero-commemorative-month-begins. 22 July 2017.

Norwegian Refugee Council. *Internally Displaced People: A Global Survey*. 2nd ed. Oslo, Norway: Earthscan, 2002.

Palmera. *Handmade: Stories of Strength Shared Through Recipes from the Women of Sri Lanka*. Sydney: Palmera Projects, 2015.

Raking Leaves. "Book Projects." http://www.rakingleaves.org. 17 July 2017.

Rancière, Jacques. "Who Is the Subject of the Rights of Man?" *South Atlantic Quarterly* 103.2/3 (2004): 297–310.

Schack, Bo. "Integrating Protection and Assistance: Working with Internally Displaced Persons in Sri Lanka." *Refugee Survey Quarterly* 19.2 (2000): 101–109.

Shanaathanan, Thamotharampillai. *The Incomplete Thombu*. Colombo: Raking Leaves, 2011.

———. Personal interview. 4 August 2015.

Siriwardhana, Chesmal, et al. "Prolonged Internal Displacement and Common Mental Disorders in Sri Lanka: The COMRAID Study." *PLOS ONE* 8.5 (2013): 1–8.

Spitzer, Leo. "Back through the Future: Nostalgic Memory and Critical Memory in a Refuge from Nazism." *Acts of Memory: Cultural Recall in the Present*. Ed. Mieke Bal, Jonathan Crewe, and Leo Spitzer. Hanover, NH: University Press of New England, 1999. 87–104.

Spivak, Gayatri Chakravorty. "Righting Wrongs." *South Atlantic Quarterly* 103.2/3 (2004): 523–581.

"Sri Lanka: A Question of Rights." *Forced Migration Review* (2009): 4–5.

"Sri Lanka Bans Remembrance of Tamil Tigers." *Al Jazeera*. 25 November 2013. http://www.aljazeera.com/news/asia/2013/11/sri-lanka-bans-remembrance-tamil-tigers-20131125123443185221.html. 20 July 2017.

"Sri Lanka Blocks Tamil Memorials amid War Parade." *BBC News*. 18 May 2014. http://www.bbc.com/news/world-asia-27462326. 22 July 2017.

Suryanarayan, V. "Remembering 1983." *The Hindu*. 24 July 2003. http://www.thehindu.com/2003/07/24/stories/2003072401511000.htm. 22 August 2017.

"Universal Declaration of Human Rights; International Covenant on Economic, Social and Cultural Rights; International Covenant on Civil and Political Rights and Optional Protocol." *The International Bill of Rights*. New York: United Nations, 1988.

van der Kolk, Bessel A., and Onno van der Hart. "The Intrusive Past: The Flexibility of Memory and the Engraving of Trauma." *Trauma: Explorations in Memory*. Ed. Cathy Caruth. Baltimore: Johns Hopkins University Press, 1995. 158–182.

Wassel, Todd. "Protecting Housing Rights for IDPs in Sri Lanka." *Forced Migration Review* (2009): 6–8.

# 11

# Toward an Aesthetics and Erotics of Nonsovereign Rights in Okinawa

MAYUMO INOUE

In his lecture on January 26, 1976, Michel Foucault illustrated the constitutive collusion between disciplinary and sovereign powers administered by the state and called for an invention of "a new right": "The right of sovereignty and disciplinary mechanics are in fact the two things that constitute—in an absolute sense—the general mechanisms of power in our society. Truth to tell, if we are to struggle against disciplines, or rather against disciplinary power, in our search for a nondisciplinary power, we should not be turning to the old right of sovereignty; we should be looking for a new right that is both antidisciplinary and emancipated from the principle of sovereignty" (*"Society Must Be Defended"* 39–40). As is well known, in his subsequent lecture course now published as *Security, Territory, Population*, Foucault adds yet another mechanism of power that aims to regulate and normalize the aggregate flow of obediently productive bodies to his notion of sovereign and disciplinary state powers. With the gradual advent of regulatory power, the "triangle" that has "population as its main target and apparatuses of security" reactivates the necessity for both sovereign and disciplinary powers of the state even more acutely (143). As Foucault goes on to argue, this "governmentalization of the state" is determined by and is an attempt to regulate politico-economic forces internal and external to its limit (145). More specifically, Foucault discusses "police" as an assemblage of legislative, economic, diplomatic, police, and military apparatuses that would ensure the maintenance of both "the space of inter-state competition" and the intrastate political order and productive force. Such interstate police and intrastate policing constitute the global field of politico-economic power (410).[1]

Situated within this global field of inter- and intrastate power, Foucault's call to critically reinvent "rights" against or outside the parameters of the political fiction that circuitously legitimates both the sovereign power of the state and the nativist foundation called the citizen resounds with a sense of urgency.[2] How might we interrupt what he calls "the subject-to-subject cycle" that the state-sponsored rights discourse often institutionalizes in order to stabilize the subordinating relations between the nation-state and the citizen (*"Society Must Be Defended"* 43)?

I begin my essay on the possibility of "human rights" in the territory known today as Okinawa by way of Foucault's discussion of a new right that is nonsovereign, nondisciplinary, and, by extension, nonregulatory precisely because, as I argue below, the desire to imagine Okinawa as somehow a prepolitical substrate where cultural uniqueness precedes discourse and power obscures its production as a site to discipline, regulate, and at times enforce the deaths of differently racialized lives of people who inhabit its islands. To put the matter more simply, Okinawa has never been a prepolitical entity whose presence as territory or community is uncontestable.[3] Rather, its archipelago was constituted as a racialized space of disciplinary and regulatory extraction within the imperial world through a series of interstate diplomatic treaties, wars, and events. These include the Treaty of Amity and Commerce between the United States and Ryukyu in 1854, Meiji Japan's disposition of Ryukyu and the founding of Okinawa Prefecture between 1872 and 1879, the establishment of the United States Military Government of the Ryukyu Islands in 1945 (the U.S. Civil Administration of the Ryukyu Islands from 1950), and the archipelago's so-called reversion to Japan in 1972.[4] Each time the space we now refer to as Okinawa is constituted as "Ryukyu" or "Okinawa," the space is effectuated as the quasi-nation form that mediates the global flow of politico-economic forces that are internal and external to its limit and serves as a space of "policing" in the Foucauldian sense within the interstate space of capitalist and military powers.

To discuss the issue of human rights critically in Okinawa today thus necessarily entails a critique of the triangulation of sovereign, disciplinary, and regulatory powers across the global space, the powers that need to be mediated locally by the nation-state form. That is to say, a critically viable reimagination of human rights—more or less equivalent to Foucault's invocation of "new right"—requires us to call into question the intimate collusion or homology between U.S. imperialism's active production of local nation-state forms in East Asia and local nationalist desires to govern themselves by positing their own "populations" as the target and apparatus of discipline, control, and death.[5] This essay attempts to offer an interpretation of two aesthetic texts—a film and a poem—that labor to articulate an emergent notion of rights. From the outset, their explorations of such rights by way of humor, erotics, and images necessarily call into question the centrality of the state as the primary purveyor of protective rights for the very bodies it seeks to discipline, regulate, and at times kill.

## Male Detective and Sex Workers in *Let Him Rest in Peace*

In a certain sense, it is not surprising that a sustained critique of the interstate policing of lives in Okinawa appears in a filmic work that at once adheres to and extends the generic protocols of hard-boiled fiction. Director Sai Yoichi's early feature-length film *Let Him Rest in Peace* (*Tomoyo shizukani nemure*, 1985) narrativizes a former medical doctor's attempt to expose the local developer's scheme to turn the fictitious municipality of Tamari in northern Okinawa into a tourist site by way of bribing the local police and leaders. The film's politically allegorical dimension is further foregrounded as Sai decides to shoot the scenes of Tamari in Henoko, an actual coastal community in Nago city that has been partially occupied by the U.S. Marine Corps' Camp Schwab since 1956 and has been the proposed site for the new U.S. Marine Corps base since 1996. Moreover, since the film's central plot revolves around the protagonist's attempt to save the rundown residential hotel for female prostitutes from closure, *Let Him Rest in Peace* also problematizes the U.S. military's extralegal management of its sexual labor regime and the local population's disavowal of the latter as a threat to the health of the race.

Released approximately ten years before both the U.S. Department of Defense's 1995 East Asia strategy report, which called for fortifying U.S.-led bilateral and multilateral security initiatives in East Asia, and the U.S.-Japan joint publication of the SACO (Special Action Committee on Okinawa) final report, which used the rhetoric of "reduced burden on Okinawa" as part of its attempt to legitimize new base construction in northern parts of the island including Henoko, *Let Him Rest in Peace* offers a prescient critique of both multilateral militarism and local developmentalism, two discourses that, despite their seeming opposition, remain subtended by the logic of a racialized local population as the participant in and object of inter- and intrastate policing. While Okinawa's broadly popular anti–land expropriation struggle in the early to mid-1950s against the ruling American military apparatus eventually gave an impetus to the islands' "reversion" to Japan in May 1972, that very reversion effectuated a further proliferation of the legal protocols and diplomatic conventions instituted in Okinawa by the United States across the territory of Japan that now includes the Okinawa Prefecture. These protocols and conventions include the U.S. military's virtually free use of its bases in Japan, the transportation of nuclear weapons into and out of Japan, the implementation of the Special Measures Laws that allow extralegal expropriation of land for further base construction, and the increasingly seamless operation of the U.S. military and Japan's Self-Defense

Forces.[6] As we will see, the film unfolds its critique of such a logic of population, race, and racism through an aesthetic exploration of nonfoundational rights that arise at the limit of linguistic articulation and imagist vision.

Sai's film follows the grammar of hard-boiled fiction in order to index instances of quasi-negativity that continue to slip away from the statistical and panoptical gaze of the state and capital in postreversion Okinawa. Because its protagonist, Shindo Takeshi (played by Fuji Tatsuya), is a former university medical doctor who was fired after making a mistake in surgery, he can perform the role of a disempowered hero who is intellectually astute enough to critique both the police and the local developer, marginalized enough to be ironic about these institutions, and able to control his physical strength so as to resort to minimal violence only when necessary. Shindo thus initially seems to embody quite well the various aspects of a typical hard-boiled male hero: his critical distance from corporate capitalism, phantasmic identification with other outlaws, and skepticism toward collective forms of labor as the target of discipline and control. Shindo's detective work in and around the police station or the developer's building at night and his often taciturn recognition of the injustice wrought on ordinary people in Tamari/Henoko reveal a certain movement of thought that emerges at the limit of his speech and vision. As if to echo Deleuze's interpretation of Foucault's critique of stratified power, the film deploys "blind word" and "mute vision" until it reveals a disjunctive border between incomplete articulation and finite vision, a limit at which a certain critical thought could arise (*Foucault* 65). It is in the gaps of language and the lacunae of vision where the film's male and female characters begin to sense forces that are irreducible to the types of knowledge that are formalized as mutually "exterior" strata of power. As Deleuze further writes, "if seeing and speaking are forms of exteriority," thinking addresses itself to an outside of such strata that does not yet have its form in words or vision (87).

But if the critical kernel of hard-boiled fiction as a genre can be found in its ambivalent relation to the logic of economic rationality, which the genre's hero usually despises and occasionally partakes in, and to the themes of sexuality and affectivity that are often condensed in the disavowed figure of femme fatale, *Let Him Rest in Peace* deforms these conventions.[7] First, the film significantly widens the thematic parameter of the genre by implicitly treating militarism as a constitutively transnational form of sovereign power that becomes palpable only as a micropolitics in and of Tamari/Henoko. The seemingly local matrix of race, gender, and class materializes in the town's landscape within the larger flow of power and capital on a transnational scale, spatially figuring and configuring these subjects in places such as bars, hotels, a police station and its detention facility, and the military base. While the film shows the presence of the U.S. Marine Corps in Okinawa only once in its lengthy title sequence, it tacitly demonstrates that the entire physical environment of Tamari/Henoko is constituted as a militarized environment, constructed to guarantee the efficient and free movement of the U.S. military within Okinawa and across the globe. Second—and crucially—this militarized landscape is contiguous to the red-light district of Tamari/Henoko, which U.S. soldiers frequent in order to engage in "R&R," or "rest and recuperation," and to somehow reproduce themselves as valuably masculinized military personnel. If Shindo's car that approaches Tamari/Henoko on the arching military road at the beginning of the film delineates the spatial delimitation of militarized space, his retracing of this infrastructural line partially deforms the very line, indicating the possibility that many others might also produce such a lineation that gradually deviates from the norms of the line and draws its own tangential flight from it.

Shindo's encounter with the female sex workers and the men who seek to survive economically in Tamari/Henoko hint that such tangents of flight can be drawn at multiple locations in the township of Tamari/Henoko. A gendered division of labor into the base and the bars is mediated by one group of people whose passive wish to overcome their dependence on the military economy now only amounts to their subservience to developmental capitalism. More specifically, the presence of U.S. soldiers and female prostitutes—both of whom are predominant as so-called outsiders—occurs in relation to the figuration of a mainstream local population. Such a figuration concurrently emerges as an agent of local economic development, which in turn becomes the ineluctable target of biopolitical discipline and control. As sociologist Tomoyoshi Doi's appositely Foucauldian study on the postwar legislation of the tripartite categories of population—"U.S. military personnel," "Ryukyuan residents," and "resident non-Ryukyuans"—tells us, the U.S. military's occupying apparatus in Okinawa implemented a two-pronged administrative mechanism whereby its Ryukyu Command regulated the movement of its own personnel in and out of the occupied territory and the United States Civil Administration of the Ryukyu Islands (USCAR)—the military's civil administrative branch—oversaw the border control for "Ryukyuan residents" and "resident non-Ryukyuans" since 1954 ("Bei tochika"). As Doi sums up the consequence of such a pairing of the interstate space of war and the intrastate space of economic development, "the legislative structure that managed the 'resident non-Ryukyuans' came to constitute a political realm in which two lines of force intersected, i.e., one that instituted the thorough separation between the occupiers and the occupied and the other that governed the local residents as they were produced as the 'national' subjects'" ("Bei tochika"). As Doi points out elsewhere, despite stark material and political differences between the occupying U.S. military personnel and the local "Ryukyuan" population, both entities gradually constituted themselves as the groups that were differently engaged in and regulated by what Foucault calls "inter-state police" (Doi, "Amami henkanji";

Foucault, *Security, Territory, Population* 410). That is, the U.S. military's global mission to forcibly "police" those who do not adhere to its protocols of productivity and docility is reflected by local "Ryukyuan" elites' desire to manage a nation-state form that could discipline its labor force and aggregate such docile bodies as a population.[8]

Female sex workers in Okinawa thereby constitute a limited figuration of people only against whom the more majoritarian categories such as the Ryukyuan men and women and American military personnel can be stabilized. Their labor as sexual workers was legally prohibited and covertly demanded by the U.S. military, which sought to regulate its soldiers' hygiene and heteronormativity at once. Meanwhile, these women's racialized status as outsiders in Okinawa—as many were from Amami Island and elsewhere—was considered to be a threat to the reproduction of the local "Ryukyuan" population. To be more specific, the U.S. occupying apparatus made prostitution strictly illegal *and yet* instituted (between 1956 and 1958 and from 1962 to 1972) the "A-sign" system whereby it distributed the official signs of operational approval (which proclaimed "Approved for Patronage of U.S. Forces Personnel") to bars and restaurants in order to monitor the sanitary conditions of businesses that offered food or sexual entertainment. By doing so, the U.S. military apparatus tacitly made known that it sought to manage its own de facto regime of militarized sex work that it at once required and disavowed, as Kikuchi Natsuno and others have pointed out. By effectively transferring the military's need to "reproduce" the soldiers' masculinized bodies into the individual sex workers' willingness to commodify their own bodies, the U.S. military was able to both obscure its own sexual politics from public purview and control sexually transmitted diseases at these women's own cost (Kikuchi 154–166). On the other hand, denigrating discourses of these female sex workers also came from local political organizations such as the Okinawa Women's Federation (Okinawa Fujin Rengo, established in 1948). Setsu Taketomi, the federation's chairperson, argued in 1949 that the women who worked in food businesses and dance halls and catered to U.S. military servicemen might also "spoil the harmonious family life" of the local population. When Taketomi held a roundtable discussion with political leaders in the same year, some participants proposed the establishment of a special district for sex workers, which would then serve as a "protective wall" for more mainstream local residents (cited in Kikuchi 175–176).

In *Let Him Rest in Peace*, protagonist Shindo's task as the doctor-cum-detective is to help release from prison his old friend Sakaguchi Ryuichi, who owns the residential hotel—symbolically named Free Inn—and refuses to sell it to local developer Shimoyama Corporation. As the film skillfully equivocates the larger political scheme in which Shimoyama Corporation is also enmeshed, its viewers are constantly unsure whether the town of Tamari/Henoko is the proposed site for a U.S. military base or for tourist development. However, as if to resonate with Doi's analysis about the coconstitutive relation between U.S. militarism and local developmentalism, Shindo's amateur detective work in Tamari/Henoko reveals how the logic of policing and the apparatus of police discipline bodies and regulate populations, ultimately compromising people's desires, which are now articulable only according to the protocols of either militarism or tourism. This makes Shindo implicitly sympathetic to local police detective Tokuda Otomatsu, who is by nature sincere and hardworking but suffers economically and receives a bribe from Shimoyama Corporation. At the same time, he also grows sympathetic to the female sexual workers who live at the Free Inn as he learns about their precarious status and movement in Okinawa.

In a certain sense, the three men—Shindo, Sakaguchi, and Tokuda—and the female workers are aligned through their inarticulable mutual sympathy precisely because their respective precariousness as doctor, hotel owner, detective, and sexual workers illuminates both the fragility and the flexibility of the law and judicial apparatus that seek to produce them as economic subjects. While Tokuda initially appears to be a villainous police detective who often stretches the limits of the law to show his power vis-à-vis the disempowered including the female workers, the law's very flexibility that he partially embodies discloses its lack of moral foundation. At the same time, female prostitutes are construed as such precisely because, in U.S.-occupied Okinawa, laws flexibly made their labor illegal *and* regulated their very labor through the codes of hygiene and medicine. While the film's overall posture toward the law remains ambivalent as it could be both a site of tactical justice and a space where injustice is naturalized, the film's characters seek to draw their tangential lines of flight from the loop that structurally interlocks the sovereign individual with its "inalienable" rights, the sovereign state that seeks to act as such rights' sole arbiter, and the same state's judicial apparatus that aims to discipline and regulate those who live therein.[9] It is on these tangents of flight that Shindo and others express their yearnings to be free by way of sympathetic humor and tacit expressions. Such yearnings manifest through the instances of what Deleuze calls "a blind face and a mute vision" (*Foucault* 65).[10]

As the film progresses, Shindo learns to become friends with the female workers, who tell him of their life narratives, which are often interspersed with moments of sarcasm, oddly humorous speech patterns, and references to instances in life that are irreducible to their professional status. Of these women, two are particularly notable for their different indications of covert antagonism toward the apparatuses that produce and police them. First is Akai Shima (played by Baisho Mitsuko), who is Sakaguchi's lover and the owner of a bar named Kendo in Tamari/Henoko. As she fears the possible closure of her bar, Akai recounts to Shindo how she was able to save enough money as a bar hostess because of her frugality and cautiousness. The second figure is Kosaka Yukie (played by Miyashita Junko), from whom Shindo learns the reality of her and other women's labor in Tamari/Henoko. In their first exchange at Kendo, their respective lines of tangential flight from power intersect and vibrate through the forces of humor. When Shindo buys Kosaka and two other women drinks in order to ask whether Sakaguchi's neighbors are unreasonably hostile to him, his curt speech frightens her, and she can only offer a timid, truncated answer: "They are, yes." After a series of awkward exchanges between the two, Shinjo decides to imitate her speech somewhat humorously: "I'm also a good guy [like Sakaguchi], yes." Such a transformation of nervousness localized within the individual body into a humorous vibration that flits across multiple bodies arguably makes the hard-boiled hero and the sex workers in Tamari/Henoko temporarily *asubjective*, no longer delineating their limits as gendered and classed subjects but emerging as the singularities in mutual sympathy.[11] But if their amity proliferates in such unpredictable moments of humor, Shindo also resists this peculiar friendship's slippage into the realm of typically heterosexual romance premised on the logic of penetrative violence. In the film, he takes a measured distance from women's touch as if he fears he might devalorize this time-space of humor that reverberates its "facts of the surface" (Deleuze, *Logic of Sense* 197). When Shindo meets Kosaka again late at night in the lobby of the Free Inn, where he now stays as a paying guest, he sits at a relative distance from her and listens to her talking to Akai about the day's work:

> Kosaka: "My customer noticed I didn't get wet and told me to use my mouth. Three times. I might get a whiplash tomorrow."
> Akai: "Did you get paid properly?"
> Kosaka: "No, the third time was a giveaway. Did everyone get home yet?"
> Akai: "You were the last one."
> Kosaka: "I have to go to bed now. My elder son has to bring a lunchbox to kindergarten tomorrow. Have to get up at seven."

As the scene switches between two women's POV shots—Akai watching Kosaka and Kosaka watching Shindo—the film foregrounds the bond between two women that often materializes as their silences that permeate the intervals of their sentences. But in this scene, Shindo is also invited to join their exchange of sympathy not as an active and intrusive and thus penetrative interlocutor but as someone who witnesses their exchange through his quietly passive exposure to their words. But importantly, Shindo's face as yet another surface of reception and expression is in turn reflected as an image on Kosaka's face. The dark space of the hotel lobby envelops their bodily and facial surfaces that are passively and passionately exposed to one another. In such a touch of faces as surfaces, Akai and Shindo are affectively made aware that Kosaka's sudden reference to her elder son's "lunchbox" does not intend to valorize motherhood over sex work but rather indicates that her subjectivity, which is in constant transit between these two modes of labor, is and should be open to other possibilities. The darkness of the lobby invites the three figures to produce a thought about such possibilities, heretofore unknown yet virtually available hopes that vibrate their bodies humorously, inviting them to draw their tangential lines of escape from the perimeter of power.

Shindo's careful rejection of sexual intimacy with women who barely get by as sex workers in Tamari/Henoko also corresponds to his similarly sympathetic attitude to some of the men in town. However, this attitude usually expresses itself through homosocial competitions that do not preclude physical contact. As such, the film initially seems to fit quite squarely within the gendered grammar of hard-boiled fiction that is "conventionally organized along both homosocial and heterosexual axes. The relationships that fall along the homosocial axis alternate between collusion and competition, with an emphasis on the latter" (Breu 14–15). But if, as Christopher Breu indicates in his analysis of Dashiell Hammett's *Red Harvest*, homosocial relations are replete with "(usually implicit) homoerotic longing" and "[the] simultaneously erotic and homicidal embrace [between two men] encapsulate[s] the contradictory impulses that structure the homosocial national space" (74, 75), Shindo's relation with Takahata Jiro (played by Harada Yoshio), a former boxer now employed as the manager of Shimoyama Corporation, enfolds within this rubric of homosocial competition a more clandestine logic of homosexual touch. Such a touch between Shindo and Takahata deforms the delimited forms of their masculine subjectivities that are endowed with relative degrees of power and, perhaps precisely because of this, often self-consciously subservient to the institutional forms that employ them. With such an implicit and occluded homosexual longing, they begin to retrace the limits of the wounds that have already traced them as the subjects, allowing themselves to open a space on their skin that does not strictly belong to one body or the other.

The film's climactic scene, which depicts the duel between Shindo and Takahata, does not fully lead to their ejaculatory confirmation of masculine heroism but rather hints at the exhaustion and interruption of such gendered heroism. Ostensibly, this boxing match marks a pivotal point in the film where the structure of power sustained by homosocial bonds between men begins to collapse. That is, Takahata regains his outlaw position, which was lost decades ago. He now willingly hands Shindo a key to unlock the safe that contains the records of bribes that Tokuda received from Shimoyama Corporation. Shindo subsequently confronts Tokuda with these records, eventually prompting Tokuda to release himself from his debt-based bondage to

Shimoyama and to release Sakaguchi from prison. This then leads to Sakaguchi's feigned attempt to murder Shimoyama on the street, which provokes the latter to kill Sakaguchi. The film ends with Shimoyama's arrest and the demise of his plan to forcibly buy up lands and houses in Tamari/Henoko. While this transfer of power from the network of male political and business elites to such a confluence of outlaw men might help halt the structure of militarism or developmentalism, it still risks replicating the same form of male-centered representational politics whereby men speak for their women and negotiate only with those endowed with more power. The punches traded between Shindo and Takahata nevertheless seem at times less a confirmation of their masculinity and more an exchange of mutual caresses that could undo such a gendered self-image. At the end, these punches-as-caresses interrupt the rhythm of the duel and make the two men literally faint on the floor.

Such an implicitly homoerotic antieconomy of touch in the film resonates with Fred Moten's discussion of Amiri Baraka's ambivalent attraction to a certain "outness" in Cecil Taylor's alleged homosexuality and his deviation from the traditional notion of musical harmony in jazz ensemble. Moten discovers a certain "sexual cut" in Taylor's music and poetry as a "syncope" that interrupts the regular flow of rhythm, connects heretofore unrelated notes, and eventually induces an experience of swoon or faint in the hearer's body. Moten then redirects this "sexual cut" to Baraka's interpretation of Taylor's music, which tries to protect the poet from the same peril and promise of sexual cut that is offered by the man of the same race. As Moten asks, "how does out, the outness of the sexual cut within the same sex, sound?" The homoerotic cut of Tayler's music "invaginates" or internally interrupts the heterosexist logic of race and racial reproduction and brings to light a different kind of "fecundity," one that is premised on the notion of syncopation. What happens as a result of such an improvisational syncopation in music, dance, or poetry is a certain experience of clinical "faint" or "shock" that temporarily deprives people of their previously acknowledged sense of subjectivity: "Syncope is a strange word. It pivots from the clinic to the art of dance, tilts toward poetry, finally ends up in music. In each of these fields, syncope takes on a definition. At first there is a shock, a suppression: something gets lost, but no one says what is won" (Catherine Clement, qtd. in Moten 164).[12] Moten's homoerotic syncopation of Baraka's self-consciously black subjectivity into the proximity of Tayler's syncopating ensemble envisages a chromatic invention of new people who, temporarily freed from the binary logic of racial colors, begin to define themselves through a proliferation of a color that becomes increasingly invisible and hauntingly audible: blue.[13] Moten then links the emergence of this "blue" in its musical iteration and irruption as "blues" to a happenstance moment of occult universality partially indexed in Baraka's notion of "blues people": "a subalternity without origin and possible everywhere, a subalternity of universality, a subalternity of ensemble" (164).

Similarly, the punches exchanged between Shindo and Takahata often perform their soundings of a sexual cut, temporally interrupting the formation of male representatives who might speak for their women and could only negotiate with the dominant power. The invisible sounds of these punches as caresses and cuts proliferate and connect these men's bodies paradoxically as the subjectivities that have already swooned. That is, they no longer relate to one another as subjects (e.g., the developer's employee or the former doctor). The punches as touches rearticulate their relations not at the nexus of male subjectivities but at an erotic knot of singularities. Despite its narrative affirmation of an alternative homosocial bond that risks replacing or replicating its more corrupt counterpart, the film cannot ultimately disavow this communal and potentially communist formation brought on by an improvisational production of nonsubjects that are syncopated through humor or homoerotics.[14] In the film, as the sympathetic humor produced mainly by women touches men like Shindo, the invisible sounds of erotic touches exchanged between men reach women. *Let Him Rest in Peace* engages in the production of what may be called queer surfaces. Faces, retinas, and hands reflect and reverberate the sensual profiles of others that are in excess of the mutually constitutive grids of race, gender, and class that discipline and regulate them as subjects.

## Poetic Refusal and Biopolitics

The syncopation of nonpenetrative humor and homoerotic cut in *Let Him Rest in Peace* underscores the ways in which the antimilitary political imagination in Okinawa can unhinge itself from a biopolitical imaginary of racialized population, a notion that ultimately tethers any counterhegemonic race-based movement to the very grid of races and its politics of recognition and distribution from the dominant center. Efforts in scholarship and cinema by Foucault, Doi, and Sai can usefully illuminate how antiwar and anticolonial imaginations can critically exit what Foucault calls "the subject-to-subject cycle" whereby "a subjected—understood as meaning an individual who is naturally endowed (or endowed by nature) with rights, capabilities, and so on—can and must become a subject, this time in the sense of an element that is subjectified in a power relationship" set in place by the state (*"Society Must Be Defended"* 43). As this cycle extends itself to include regulatory control of population, sovereign power's emphasis on those endowed with normative "capabilities" is tied to this power's production of a race that is somehow "purer and healthier" (255). Of course, the terms of enforced life predicated within a race-based regulation of a population not only creates "ceasuras within the biological continuum" of humans but also "expose[s] its own race to the absolute and universal threat of death" (259).

Sai's 1985 film's attempt to imagine a space of viability for both female sex workers and covertly homoerotic men in the midst of Henoko/Tamari is thus a prescient critique of the logic of biopolitics and its foundation in the logic of racialization. If so, the film unwittingly presages a series of recent key studies by scholars such as Shinjo Ikuo, Tokuda Masashi, and Doi Tomoyoshi who have used Foucault's works on biopolitics, racialization, and gender relations in their own pioneering studies of the historical construction of the nation-form in Okinawa.[15] In literature and visual arts, there is also a corresponding attempt to oppose both the ongoing multistate militarization of Okinawa and the uncritical sentiment of nativism that traps the nation's viability within the compromised framework of global capital and local nation-states.

## Conclusion

If we return to Foucault's call to invent "a new right" that critically interrupts the interlocking juncture of sovereign, disciplinary, and regulatory powers, we are made aware that such an effort to interrupt this circuit requires an aesthetic and erotic disarticulation of the biopolitical terms of life and death enforced by the state. Moreover, imperial politics' increasing focus on the category of identity as the constructed—that is, fictive yet material—substrate on which disciplinary and regulatory powers are effectuated and naturalized has in fact fortified its deployment of sovereign power to kill those who fail to live up to the normative notions of race, be they dominant or subordinate racial groups. As Foucault astutely argues in the final lecture of *"Society Must Be Defended,"* "if the power of normalization wished to exercise the old sovereign right to kill, it must become racist" (256).

But since Foucault's work after his 1976 lecture makes relatively scant references to the notion of rights, one must glean from a number of his contemporary texts a glimpse into a method that might allow us to both critically and practically undo the complicitous cycle between the state's subjectivation of both dominant and marginalized identities and the rights-based claims that presuppose and authorize the state's legitimation of these identities.[16] In fact, in his 1984 essay titled "What Is Enlightenment?" we find Foucault calling on us to engage in an experimental form of historical or genealogical inquiry into the ways in which the regime of truth has been stabilized. Here, Foucault relocates the terms of argument concerning "enlightenment" from a certain Kantian focus on the legitimate limits of knowledge to one that looks at the historically legitimated limits of knowing. Foucault's critical double take on such historically contingent limits of cognition corresponds with his earlier attempt to undo the cycle that has formed between the allegedly sovereign subjects who outsource their "inalienable" rights to the state and the sovereign state that now acts as the sole arbiter of such rights, which then authorizes itself to discipline an individual and regulate a racialized population according to the norms of capital. In Foucault's 1984 essay, an ongoing project of "enlightenment" is reformulated as an attempt to both historically analyze and practically transform the imposed limits of such juridical, medical, and cultural codes that subjectivate the bodies and the populations within the larval network of the nation-states:

> This philosophical ethos may be characterized as a limit attitude. We are not talking about a gesture of rejection. We have to move beyond the outside-inside alternative; we have to be at the frontiers. Criticism indeed consists of analyzing and reflecting upon limits. But if the Kantian question was that of knowing what limits knowledge has to renounce transgressing, it seems to me that the critical question today has to be turned back into a positive one: in what is given to us as universal, necessary, obligatory, what place is occupied by whatever is singular, contingent, and the product of arbitrary constraints?
>
> The point, in brief, is to transform the critique conducted in the form of necessary limitation into a practical critique that takes the form of a possible transgression. . . . But if we are not to settle for the affirmation or the empty dream of freedom, it seems, to me that this historico-critical attitude must also be an experimental one. ("What Is Enlightenment?" 45–46)

The type of "limit attitude" Foucault seeks to incite among those who wish to critique the state-dependent notion of rights relates to an aesthetic comportment perhaps best characterized by syncopation, one that articulates singular senses within a body and singular bodies across the socius. Its tactile, sonorous, and sexual event happens as an incision on the delimited contour of the racialized subject within the nation-state, interrupting the heterosexist schema of racial reproduction and the gendered grid of ironic men and humorous women.

Sai's *Let Him Rest in Peace* inscribes their syncopating beats within the interstate space of politics-as-policing wherein the individual state continues to act as the sole purveyor of rights toward the subjects who are produced and codified through the very state's grid of race, gender, and class. In the present moment—when the proponents of the U.S. Marine Corps' new base construction in Henoko seek to justify it through the rhetoric of global security and a portion of oppositional politicians and activists slip into the logic of race that is tethered to the very norm of biopolitics that construes them as the target of sovereign, disciplinary, and regulatory powers—an aesthetics of syncopation and its differential erotics in Okinawa continue to invigorate the politics of experimental genealogy, that is, an anarchical opening to "the singularity of events outside of any monotonous finality" (Foucault, "Nietzsche, Genealogy, History" 139). What Foucault calls "a new right" perhaps materializes in such a moment of practical struggle for an anarchy of human rights. An aesthetics of syncopation and a politics of critical genealogy crisscross, opening up a space in which a claim made for individual and collective survival is decathected from the structure of feeling or the grid of knowledge that sustains the cycle of sovereignty forged between the nation-state and its invariably racialized citizen subjects.

## NOTES

1. See, for example, the essays collected in *War, Police and Assemblage of Intervention* (Bachmann et al.), which offer historical analyses of the ways in which the logic of "policing" has come to traverse both multinational warfare and intranational biopolitics whose target is aggregated as "population."

2. Giorgio Agamben's "Beyond Human Rights" implicitly takes up this question asked by Foucault and argues how "rights . . . are attributed to the human being only to the degree to which he or she is the immediately vanishing presupposition . . . of the citizen" (20).

3. On the production of the culturalist entity called "Okinawa" within the pre-1945 spatial domain of Japanese imperialism, see Matsumura.

4. As Shinjo Ikuo, professor in the Faculty of Law at Ryuku University, insightfully argues, the Treaty of Amity and Commerce between the United States and Ryukyu in 1854 did not constatively confirm the status of Ryukyu as a modern sovereign nation-state but rather performatively produced such a political form as a constitutive entity within the transnational space of imperial governmentality (2). For analyses of post-1945 U.S. production of essentialized Ryukyu culture and race, see Kano; Tanaka.

5. Wendy Brown astutely criticizes radical democratic theorists' attempt to adjudicate their critique of the liberal capitalist state and their vindication of identity-based rights politics that seeks protection from the very state. For Brown, it remains problematic that these theorists end up replicating "the sovereign subject of liberalism whose need for rights is born out of subjection by the state, out of an economy not necessarily bound to human needs or capacities, and out of stratifications within civil society . . . all of which may be attenuated but at the same time codified by the rights advocated by the 'radical democrats'" (11).

6. On the legal origin of Japan's Special Measures Laws in the U.S. military decrees instituted in occupied Okinawa, see Shinjo Ikuo, "Okinawa mondai." On the secret U.S.-Japan agreements to allow the United States to freely use its bases and store nuclear arms in Japan after they negotiated the terms of Okinawa's reversion in 1972, see Nishiyama; Gabe.

7. See Breu's reading of Dashiell Hammett's *Red Harvest* (1929) where the critic recognizes the quintessential hard-boiled protagonist's conscious critique of and unconscious cathexis to instrumental rationality (57–58).

8. While I cannot discuss specific local capitalists and their desires in this paper, it remains a task to critically analyze the ways in which the current anti–Henoko marine base movement can remain skeptical of the "all-Okinawa" ideology that subsumes antimilitarism into the elite discourse of local developmentalism and neoliberalism. On this, see the published conversation among Moriteru Arasaki, Seishu Sakihara, and Hiroji Yamashiro (esp. 93–100).

9. For example, at the end of the film, Sakaguchi manages to have Shimoyama arrested by provoking the latter to kill him.

10. This is why, for Deleuze, "Foucault is uniquely akin to contemporary film" (*Foucault* 65).

11. I use the term *singularity* here to mark a point in the social field of power where the dialectical complicity of the so-called universal and the so-called particular is unworked or interrupted.

12. See Jean-Luc Nancy's formulation of this syncopation as "incision," "beating, "breath cut off," and "beating heart" (230, 234, 240, 242).

13. My thought on Baraka's notion of "blue" draws on Akira Mizuta Lippit's meditation on the same notion in "Out of the Blue" (32).

14. As Moten argues, "here a certain relation between syncopation and orgasm, the little death that is marked for us already in the gesture and dance of shopping, syncope, and jazz. And there the syncope is a homosexual affair" (165).

15. For Shinjo Ikuo's exploration of homoerotic sociality and ethics that continues to be disavowed in the cofigurative nationalisms of the United States, Japan, and Okinawa, see his groundbreaking collection of essays titled *Okinawa o kiku* (2010). See also Tokuda for the eugenic politics espoused by Iha Fuyu (1876–1947), the local intellectual leader often known for his democratic localism.

16. The concepts Foucault himself developed include the "right of the governed" (1977) and the "independence of the governed" (1979). For an important discussion of the necessarily collective dimension of Foucault's notion of "the right of the governed," see Chevallier 178–183.

## WORKS CITED

Agamben, Giorgio. "Beyond Human Rights." *Means without Ends: Notes on Politics.* Trans. Vincenzo Binetti and Cesare Casarino. Minneapolis: University of Minnesota Press, 2000.

Arasaki, Moriteru, Sakihara Seishu, and Yamashiro Hiroji. "Minshu undo no atarashi chihei wo tsukuro" ["Creating a new horizon for popular movement"]. *Okinawa wo koeru* [Beyond Okinawa]. Ed. Moriteru Arasaki. Tokyo: Gaifusha, 2014.

Bachmann, Jan, Colleen Bell, and Caroline Holmqvist, eds. *War, Police and Assemblages of Intervention.* Abingdon, U.K.: Routledge, 2014.

Breu, Christopher. *Hard-Boiled Masculinities.* Minneapolis: University of Minnesota Press, 2005.

Brown, Wendy. *States of Injury: Power and Freedom in Late Modernity.* Princeton: Princeton University Press, 1995.

Chevallier, Philippe. "Michel Foucault and the Question of Right." *Re-reading Foucault: On Law, Power, and Rights.* Ed. Ben Golder. Abingdon, U.K.: Routledge, 2013. 171–187.

Deleuze, Gilles. *Foucault.* Trans. Seán Hand. Minneapolis: University of Minnesota Press, 1988.

———. *The Logic of Sense.* Trans. Mark Lester and Charles Stivale. New York: Columbia University Press, 1990.

Doi, Tomoyoshi. "Amami henkanji ni okeru zaioki amami jūmin no chii mondai ni kansuru noto" ["A note concerning the status of Amami residents in Okinawa during the reversion of the Amami Island"]. *Okinawa Prefectural Archives Bulletin of Study* 17 (2016): 29–43.

———. "Bei tochika no zaioki amami jumin (jo)" ["Resident Amami Islanders in U.S.-occupied Okinawa (1)"]. *Okinawa Times.* 17 December 2012.

Foucault, Michel. "Nietzsche, Genealogy, History." Trans. Donald F. Bouchard and Sherry Simon. *Language, Counter-memory, Practice: Selected Essays and Interviews*. Ed. Donald F. Bouchard. Ithaca, NY: Cornell University Press, 1980. 139–164.

———. *Security, Territory, Population: Lectures at the Collège de France 1977–1978*. Trans. Graham Burchell. New York: Picador, 2007.

———. *"Society Must Be Defended": Lectures at the Collège de France, 1975–1976*. Trans. David Macey. New York: Picador, 2003.

———. "What Is Enlightenment?" Trans. Catherine Porter. *The Foucault Reader*. Ed. Paul Rabinow. New York: Pantheon, 1984. 32–50.

Gabe, Masaaki. *Okinawa henkan toha nandattanoka—Nichibei sengo kosho no nakade* [What was the Okinawa Reversion? Within the U.S.-Japan postwar negotiations]. Tokyo: NHK Books, 2000.

Kano, Masanao. *Sengo Okinawa no Shisozo* [Intellectual landscape in postwar Okinawa]. Tokyo: Asahi Shinbunsha, 1987.

Kikuchi, Natsuno. *Posutokoroniarizumu to jendā* [Postcolonialism and gender]. Tokyo: Seikyusha, 2010.

Lippit, Akira Mizuta. "Out of the Blue (*Ex-nihilo*)." *Ex-Cinema: From a Theory of Experimental Film and Video*. Berkeley: University of California Press, 2012. 15–37.

Matsumura, Wendy. *The Limits of Okinawa: Japanese Capitalism, Living Labor, and Theorizations of Community*. Durham, NC: Duke University Press, 2015.

Moten, Fred. *In the Break: The Aesthetics of the Black Radical Tradition*. Minneapolis: University of Minnesota Press, 2003.

Nancy, Jean-Luc. "Sublime Offering." Trans. Jeffrey Libbrett. *A Finite Thinking*. Ed. Simon Sparks. Stanford: Stanford University Press, 2003. 211–244.

Nishiyama, Takichi. *Okinawa Mitsuyaku—Joho hanzai to nichibei domei*. Tokyo: Iwanami Shoten, 2007.

Sai, Yoichi. *Tomoyo shizukani nemure* [Let him rest in peace]. Tōei Central Films, 1985.

Shinjo, Ikuo. "'Okinawa mondai' toiu brakku horu: 'Fukki' to nanpo doho engokai" [A black hole called the Okinawa problem: "Reversion" and Nanpo Doho Engokai]. Japan's Post-war Amnesia: The 6th Conference: Rewriting Modern and Contemporary Japanese Intellectual History. Waseda University. 21 December 2012. Conference presentation.

———. *Okinawa o kiku* [Listening to Okinawa]. Tokyo: Misuzu Shobo, 2010.

Shinjo, Ikuo, and Tetsushi Marukawa. "'Sekaishi' no nakano Okinawa o kangaeru: Shi no kyodotai kara ikani nigeruka, do hikikaesuka" [Thinking Okinawa within world history: How can we escape or turn back from a community of death?]. *Tosho Shinbun* no. 3180 (October 25, 2014).

Shinjo, Takekazu. *Ototo, matawa ninin sankyaku* [Brother, or three-legged steps]. Naha: Asurasha, 2013.

———. *Shisho no umi* [The ocean of death and life]. Naha: Asurasha, 2011.

———. "Taredemo nai monono shi—hi-okinawa jin sengen" [A poem written by one who is anonymous: A non-"Okinawan" declaration]. *Asura* 36 (2014): 66–68.

Tanaka, Yasuhiro. *Fukei no sakeme: Okinawa, senryo no ima* [Rupture of landscape: Okinawa and the contemporary reality of the occupation]. Tokyo: Serika Shobo, 2010.

Tokuda, Masashi. "Jinshushugi no shinen: Iha Fuyu ni okeru yuseigaku to teikoku saihen" [The abyss of racism: Eugenics and the reformation of empire in Iha Fuyu]. *Gendai Shiso* 44.2 (2016): 160–183.

U.S. Department of Defense. *United States Security Strategy for the East Asia-Pacific Region*. Washington, DC: Department of Defense, Office of International Security Affairs, 1995.

# 12

# Figuring North Korean Lives

## *Reading at the Limits of Human Rights*

Christine Kim

In January 2015, stories circulated throughout the Western media about North Korean defector Shin Dong-hyuk, subject of the bestselling memoir *Escape from Camp 14: One Man's Remarkable Odyssey from North Korea to Freedom in the West* (2012), which detailed his life in and escape from the notorious political prison. In particular, Shin had admitted to multiple inaccuracies in his narrative. Faced with this controversy, Shin and Blaine Harden, the author who had written and published Shin's story after conducting extensive interviews, claimed that while certain details were altered, the heart of Shin's story remains unchanged. Harden summed up the dilemma as follows: "From a human rights perspective, [Shin] was still brutally tortured, but he moved things around" (Shoichet and Park). Yet given that Shin's story of being the only person to have ever been born into Camp 14 and to have escaped it had made him a highly visible spokesperson for North Korean survivors of state atrocities, such troubling admissions cannot easily be dismissed. Much of the story that Shin told in *Escape from Camp 14* reappeared in his deposition before the United Nations Human Rights Council, where he was the first witness to appear in the UN's video of select survivor testimony.

As one of three hundred people whose testimonies contributed to the 2014 report produced by the UN Commission of Inquiry on Human Rights in the Democratic People's Republic of Korea (DPRK), Shin's account carried much political weight. As one news story notes, "Shin was something of an activist poster-boy, giving speeches around the world, penning editorials and picking up awards. The US-based Human Rights Watch described him as the world's 'single strongest voice on atrocities taking place in North Korea.' Shin has acknowledged that the damage his retractions have done meant he 'may not be able to continue' his activist work" ("UN Dismisses"). The critique of Shin's story raises larger questions about the credibility of North Korean testimonials and poses significant potential repercussions for other human rights advocates speaking out against the DPRK. Because the UN was not given access to either North Korea or the bordering areas of China, its report on the DPRK relied heavily on witness and victim testimony; consequently, what is at stake is not just the authenticity of one individual's story but also the validity of an entire case that has been built against North Korea for its human rights violations.

I open with the Shin controversy because it underscores matters of audience, legibility, and recognition that bring to light the limitations of human rights and accentuate how the subject of human rights is constructed within these discourses. Without minimizing the potential damage for advocacy groups working on behalf of North Koreans, we must be mindful of how Shin's desire to alter and even embellish details of his account speaks to a situation that is not unique to him. It is therefore worth investigating Shin's story for what it reveals about the politics of voice and the polemics of representation as they are enacted on a global stage via cultural fantasies of North Korea as a place unlike any in the world. While North Korean refugee narratives accentuate violence, grinding poverty, and difficult circumstances that merit global attention, as Andrei Lankov points out, "The real story of the average North Korean refugee is depressing, but hardly dramatic enough for the average media audience."[1] It is in this regard that we can see most clearly how Shin was able to become a human rights star and capture mass audiences with his story. Predictably, *Escape from Camp 14* presents a view of North Korea that is quite extreme in terms of the conditions it depicts. These "extreme" characterizations, which converge on individual inhumanity, familial indifference, and East-versus-West depravity, bring into focus the essentializing impulses that undergird contemporary human rights politics.

## Inhumanity and *Escape from Camp 14*

Unlike other memoirs such as Lucia Jang's *Stars between the Sun and Moon: One Woman's Life in North Korea and Escape to Freedom* (2014), Hyeonseo Lee's *The Girl with Seven Names: A North Korean Defector's Story* (2015), and Jang Jin-sung's *Dear Leader: My Escape from North Korea* (2014) that speak about family ties and witnessing wide-scale poverty and starvation, *Escape from Camp 14* is unique precisely because of the subject's affective focus, which pivots on the absence of meaningful familial and filial relationships. Relationships with family members were emotionally distant and physically violent; of his mother, we are told that while Shin was completely dependent "upon her for all his meals," he would nevertheless "stea[l] her food" and "endur[e] her beatings" and "saw her as competition for survival" (Harden 16). The concept of love was foreign, and Shin could claim to feel it for his mother only years after he fled North Korea, while living in the United States, where he "learned that a civilized child should love his mother" (Harden 16). While the aforementioned testimonials illustrate the horrors of North Korea and showcase the *regime* as cruel and inhuman, only *Escape from Camp 14* presents its *subject* as inhuman. Shin does this by drawing attention to what he describes as a limited range of emotions: "I did not know about sympathy or sadness. . . . They educated us from birth so that we were not capable of normal human emotions. Now that I am out, I am learning to be emotional. I have learned to cry. I feel like I am becoming human" (Harden 190). This passage showcases how the regime damaged his humanity and reinforces the alienness of North Korea; Shin establishes by way of evidentiary account why he had been and was such an effective human rights advocate for North Koreans. As an individual whose affective capacity to experience his tragedy was curtailed because of profound human rights violations, Shin through self-characterization offered a compelling human rights subjectivity built on his very inhumanness.

Admittedly, there is a set of highly gendered and culturally specific assumptions at work in the notion that to be human requires the demonstration of affect and the performance of feeling. *Escape from Camp 14*'s definition of the human through affective performance is from the outset framed in terms of failed maternal affection. Here, the Freudian idea that the mother's withheld affection for the male child produces trauma figures keenly; it has been inserted into the geopolitical context of escaping North Korea, producing in the process a narrative in which Shin escapes maternal monstrosity via the embrace of the West. The root of Shin's humanity is accordingly traced back to a nonmaternal mother. As significant counterpoint, the West fulfills this "maternal vacuum"—as a place of freedom and a space of love, contrasting sharply with North Korea's dystopic, putatively unfeeling registers.

In analyzing Shin's testimony vis-à-vis the shape and moralizing tone of human rights discourse, it is difficult to ignore that effective advocacy such as Shin's speaks to the need for human rights even as it erases individual subjectivity. Shin's story, wherein brutal details of prison camp survival are situated alongside an account involving how he subverted a familial plot (comprising his mother and brother) to escape Camp 14 without him, illustrates the gravity of the North Korean human rights situation. However, these accounts do so at the expense of transforming Shin into the figure of the refugee rather than showing him as an individual who has fled North Korea. In *Escape from Camp 14*, Shin confesses that he was initially afraid to admit to anyone that he had betrayed family members because he "was terrified of a backlash, of people asking me, 'Are you even human?'" (Harden 47). His reluctance to describe his own role in the execution of his mother and brother demonstrates an understanding of how the human rights victim must inspire sympathy, an imperative that may even trump accuracy if the story is to engage its readers. The ability to affectively move audiences while instantiating empathy for the North Korean subject, whether it be a UN Commission or the reader of a testimonial, simultaneously demonstrates the power and limitation of human rights discourse. In assuming refugeeness, Shin's self-characterization relies on a world outside North Korea as a means of establishing a contradictory site of asylum; such human rights counterpoints influence Shin's testimony, which draws on audience expectations about North Korea through received notions of authoritarianism, totalitarianism, and violation.

For the remainder of this chapter, I locate stories of North Korean survivors in two different contexts. First, I examine the historical moment in which contemporary discourses of human rights emerged by focusing on the UN's Declaration of Human Rights (1948), the UN Convention Concerning the Status of Refugees (1951), and UNESCO's statements on race (1950–1967) as constitutive of a political archive of post-WWII thought. By turning to these documents, I ask how we might understand human rights as a racialized project and interrogate how North Korea is located within its parameters. Second, I situate North Korean life writing such as *Escape from Camp 14* within this discourse and consider how such human rights texts construct their humanitarian subjects. This subgenre of writing illustrates the conceptual limitations of the human and what this means for the kinds of rights and recognitions that can be imagined for the inhuman. By highlighting the failure of human rights discourses via the figure of the refugee from a totalitarian regime, I argue that North Korea provides an opportunity for understanding how the legacies of the Cold War shape what we understand to be the subject of human rights.

## Postwar Humans

On December 10, 1948, the UN General Assembly adopted the Universal Declaration of Human Rights (UDHR). The drafting committee for the document consisted of René Cassin (France), Charles Malik (Lebanon), Peng Chung Chang (China), and John Humphrey (Canada) and was chaired by Eleanor Roosevelt (United States), who "was recognized as the driving force for the Declaration's adoption" (United Nations). Motivated by the Holocaust and the aftermath of WWII, "the international community vowed never again to allow atrocities like those of that conflict happen again. World leaders decided to complement the UN Charter with a road map to guarantee the rights of every individual everywhere" (United Nations). Since then, human rights discourse has become familiar and widespread, perhaps even what Joseph Slaughter calls "normative" when he observes that "we are now living in the Age of Human Rights" (2). And yet, how are we to read this assertion of international human rights and dignity given that it occurs as the conditions for the Korean War and multiple other wars in Asia were being set? In what ways are these discourses of human rights unable to imagine either the Asian as a figure or North Korea as a nation-state to be the subject of human rights? Situated adjacent to such discourses and polemics, narratives by North Korean defectors exemplify the parameters of contemporary Western "rights" imagination and demonstrate what Jodi Kim calls "the protracted afterlife of the Cold War" (4). Within this context, North Korea functions alternately as a metaphor for the inhuman and as a metonym for Asian incivility.

The preamble to the UDHR unequivocally asserts a belief in human equality and declares a firm commitment to human rights defined in terms of four freedoms: freedom of speech, freedom of religion, freedom from persecution, and freedom from want. Such freedoms are not limited to individual subjectivity but are instead universalized as "the foundation of freedom, justice and peace in the world" and "the highest aspiration of the common people" (UDHR). This is crucial because while the document is not legally binding, it represents the principles and aspirations of the UDHR in 1948. The preamble, as well as the UDHR proper, is marked by a deep desire to ensure that the previous violations that had occurred in Europe would never be replicated. However, it is free from any sense of urgency with respect to addressing ongoing violations or conflicts that were being seeded as the document was being drafted. This tone and the objectives of the UDHR make it evident that the universal subject entitled to freedoms is not imagined to be Asian.[2] While the Korean War (1950–1953) is the most pertinent example of conflict in Asia that lies outside the UN's understanding of the world in 1948, I want to emphasize that the Korean War is one moment in a much longer process wherein Asia is separated from the West and its project of human rights. The UN and the United States sought to define and protect human freedoms even as the United States was, as Jodi Kim points out, "install[ing] governments and economic systems favorable to U.S. interests in the name of 'democracy' and 'collective security.' Just as the 'civilizing mission' of nineteenth century European colonialism had provided the ideological cover for conquest, this 'democratizing mission' provided the rhetorical justification for the United States in its effort to establish and maintain imperial control over Asia" (19). As both the first product of the Cold War and arguably its final visible legacy, North Korea represents the limits of human rights as conceptualized by the UDHR. As Kim argues, we must be aware of the Cold War "not solely as a historical epoch or event" but also as "a knowledge project or epistemology, which is always also a pedagogy, and

[ask] how it continues to generate and teach 'new' knowledge by making sense of the world through the Manicheaean logics and grammars of good and evil" (8). Analyzing North Korea as it is positioned within human rights discourses requires an understanding of the actions taking place within the nation-state and a consciousness of the Cold War analytics through which we view that space.

This project of imagining the subject of human rights in Western terms is extended further by the 1951 UN Convention Concerning the Status of Refugees, a document meant to address the status of refugees and determine the eligibility of asylum for stateless persons, which explicitly limits obligations to vulnerable persons through its temporal and spatial qualifiers. Until the 1967 Protocol was introduced, the scope of the protections afforded to refugees was limited to those affected by events occurring before January 1, 1951. Moreover, signatories were given (and continue to have) the option of limiting their obligations to those persons affected by events that had either taken place only in Europe or included and extended beyond Europe. These qualifiers underscore the fact that, like the UDHR, the 1951 Convention was produced in response to the events and aftermath of WWII and was initially borne out of a desire to safeguard the Western subject.

The Convention also establishes a distinct narrative of refugeeism by defining the refugee through his or her relationship to fear. The refugee is explicitly described as a person who, "owing to well-founded fear of being persecuted for reasons of race, religion, nationality, membership of a particular social group or political opinion, is outside the country of his nationality and is unable or, owing to such fear, is unwilling to avail himself of the protection of that country; or who, not having a nationality and being outside the country of his former habitual residence as a result of such events, is unable or, owing to such fear, is unwilling to return to it" (UNHCR). By reading the Convention in relation to North Korea, the constraints of the language and logic of human rights become visible in two crucial ways. First, the Convention conceives of persecution solely in terms of the state and as occurring for five possible reasons (that include race, religion, or political opinion); imagined in these terms, the refugee becomes legible as a minoritized subject that merits protection. In contrast, one kind of fear North Korean escapees often describe is the anxiety that they may be accused of having committed crimes against the state. This constant, low-grade fear is distinct from the kind of deliberate persecution imagined by the UN and cannot easily be translated into the restrictive language of the Convention. Second, human rights discourses position the rational citizen with access to political representation against the fearful figure of the refugee who, "caged within a depoliticized humanitarian space," is made invisible and passive (Nyers xiii). Located within these relations of power, the refugee becomes an irrational figure incapable of being heard by an international community.

And while North Korean escapees may not adhere to the UN's rigid definition of the refugee, as the example of Shin Dong-hyuk illustrates, they are nonetheless silenced by the discourses of human rights that seek to protect them even as these discourses forget the conditions under which they and North Korea emerged.

The difference between North Korea as a place lived by its citizens and one imagined by those outside of the DPRK is noted in another recent memoir, the aforementioned *Dear Leader: My Escape from North Korea* in which former high-ranking official and North Korean poet laureate Jang Jin-sung describes his harrowing experiences of fleeing his country of origin, travelling through China, and finally finding sanctuary in South Korea. Reflecting on his journey, Jang writes in the memoir's epilogue, "As I've written elsewhere: '[Back home] there are two North Koreas: one real and the other a fiction.' After my defection, I recognized the existence of a third North Korea: a theoretical one, one constructed by the outside world" (311). While the state propaganda of North Korea is familiar to most and forms the basis of what Jang calls a "fiction" of North Korea, what is less criticized is this "third North Korea," a fictional entity constructed by the rest of the world. For many, this third North Korea is produced through cultural representations that include commercial or documentary films about North Korea (e.g., Sony's *The Interview* or *Team America: World Police*), memoirs by former citizens such as Jang, and media reports that highlight nuclear threats, egregious human rights violations, and bizarre and even unfathomable actions (such as the execution of current leader Kim Jong-un's uncle by a pack of wolves or the institution of state-sanctioned hairstyles).

Collectively, these cultural representations function as a cultural fantasy of the inhuman for the rest of the world, one wherein the spectacular and macabre are pitched as the North Korean everyday. These cultural fantasies, which operate in stark contrast to Western notions of quotidian, "democratic" existence, serve as the primary backdrop for North Korean life writing and transform a survivor like Shin into a human rights star. In its wholesale accounts of unimaginable inhumanity and unending brutality, *Escape from Camp 14* renders urgent the need for human rights intervention; however, such calls for intervention are necessarily decontextualized, as evidenced by the narrative's nonmention of longer colonial histories, complex revolutionary moments, and convoluted sets of global relations. While life writing as a genre is certainly not obligated to tell national histories, historical framing becomes imperative vis-à-vis North Korean stories precisely given the systematic forgetting of its national histories by international audiences. Without such framing, Shin ran the risk of becoming an ahistorical figure or being reduced to a trope rather than an individual telling his particular story. This is consistent with how North Korea has, since its post-WWII creation, been as much an imaginary as it has been an actual space.

Cultural fantasies about North Korea not only reinforce how it is a country beyond the reach of human rights law and logic; such imaginings racialize North Korea as an inhuman entity. This becomes visible if we turn to the UNESCO statements on race, a set of documents produced conterminously with the UDHR. Here, it bears noting that UNESCO was also formed in the postwar context and "created in order to respond to the firm belief of nations, forged by two world wars in less than a generation, that political and economic agreements are not enough to build a lasting peace. Peace must be established on the basis of humanity's moral and intellectual solidarity" (UNESCO, "Introducing UNESCO"). At the core of UNESCO's mission are education, heritage, scientific cooperation, and freedom of expression. With these guiding principles in mind, UNESCO issued a series of statements (1950, 1951, 1964, and 1967) designed to address racial prejudice by debunking the biological determinism attached to race-based difference and emphasize difference as the product of culture and environment. Reinforcing the unity of humanity through shared potential, the authors of the 1950 statement state firmly that "the one trait which above all others has been at a premium in the evolution of men's mental characters has been educability, plasticity. This is a trait which all human beings possess. It is indeed, a species characters of *homo sapiens*" (UNESCO, *Four Statements* 32). In emphasizing the plasticity of humans over rigid limitations based on biology,[3] these statements mark a major shift in racial discourses and reflect the global changes underway during the post-WWII period.[4]

Within this modern terrain, North Korea functions as a peculiar anachronism due to its seeming resistance to transformation. North Korea remains a space whose state-controlled economy, authoritarian rule, and obedient citizens curiously seem to exemplify an outdated logic of biological racialism for a global cultural imagination. If the malleability of individuals is what makes them part of a collective humanity, then the perceived intransigence of North Korea marks it as inhuman. The international perception of North Korea as an historical relic, unwilling to develop economically and unable to change how it treats its citizens, illustrates how this metaphor of the inhuman operates in this context. Both the individual North Korean subject and the nation-state of the DPRK are constructed as inhuman through their inability to follow a progressivist trajectory, but such constructions do not take into account the complexities of North Korean history and revolutionary ideals as they have been shaped by Cold War politics, colonialism, and imperialism. In other words, while North Korea may not follow a progressivist trajectory to the Western gaze, it has not been a place of complete stasis and failure. Such a reading overlooks, for example, the relative prosperity of North Korea until about the 1970s and its rapid industrialization and the forms of assistance and relations it had developed with countries in Africa (Armstrong 192–193). These moments complicate a simpler narrative of the nation-state that fashions North Korea as the outside to the universality of human progress through adaptation.

As Cheah and Slaughter maintain, the construction of the human and humanity is always a limited and unequal project, one in which systematic exclusion must occur. And, while Cheah notes that even as the human is a construction, the "humanity effects are concretely real and efficacious and can be progressive and enabling" ("Humanity" 1556), I suggest that the effects of the inhuman are also concrete and real. It is paradoxically by being denounced as inhuman and irrational that, in terms of its international relations, North Korea has been able to exercise a form of power that, following Charles Armstrong, we might conceive of as a tyranny of the weak, an "ability of certain small or weak states to resist and even manipulate the more powerful" (3). In focusing on how the DPRK has navigated the pressures of the United States, China, and the former USSR for the past sixty years, Armstrong recognizes the survival of North Korea as "a remarkable achievement" (5). Nevertheless, it is the atypical position that North Korea occupies in a global landscape that locates it beyond the reach of the moralizing dimensions of human rights discourse.

What then can a discourse of human rights do for North Korea, a national entity conceptualized as inhuman and understood as signaling the limits of this discourse? In tracing how North Korea has come to mark the limits of the human, I argue that this metaphor is more powerful than it initially appears. As scholars researching forms of life such as plants, animals, and fungi have noted, the human is not the only actor within a network. Anna Tsing's anthropological research on fungi, for example, sketches out the interdependence between organisms and the valuable work that fungi do in terms of ecosystem renewal. She also points to the difficulties of recognizing species' interdependence, given collective beliefs in human control of nature ("Unruly" 144). Elsewhere, Tsing has interrogated the concept of the human by analyzing its relation to notions of progress: "Even when disguised through other terms, such as 'agency,' 'consciousness,' and 'intention,' we learn over and over that humans are different from the rest of the living world because we look forward—while other species, which live day to day, are thus dependent on us. As long as we imagine that humans are *made* through progress, nonhumans are stuck within this imaginative framework too" (*The Mushroom* 21). These ideas of agency and progress as central to human narratives are provocative for how they open up the distinction between the nonhuman world of plants, fungi, and animals and the inhuman figure of the Asian.

By unseating the logic of progress and shifting the focus away from the human and toward actants, this chapter rethinks the guiding logics of human rights. In using the conceptual framework of anthropocentrism to examine how North Korea is positioned within a global imaginary, my intention is to take stock of the audiences we speak to and for. While the primary distinction that cultural theorists such as Anna Tsing and Jane Bennett draw is between the human and the nonhuman, I understand North Korea as occupying within this framework a third space of the inhuman. The inhuman is denied the kind of subjectivity and recognition that the human is assigned not because it is a different species from the nonhuman is but because it represents the limitations of what can be recognized as human. If, as W.J.T. Mitchell suggests, "objects are the way things appear to a subject—that is, with a name, an identity, a gestalt or stereotypical template . . . [while] [t]hings, on the other hand, . . . [signal] the moment when the object becomes the Other, when the sardine can looks back" (qtd. in Bennett 2), then the inhuman might be understood as the other being turned into the object and not necessarily being invested in returning the subject's gaze. By being positioned outside of this economy of recognition, the inhuman is liberated from the regulatory powers of the subject, even as it serves as the basis of the economy of recognition. But within this framework, the question of what force the inhuman can exert must be reckoned with.

Bennett's project focuses on "vitality," which she defines as "the capacity of things—edibles, commodities, storms, metals—not only to impede or block the will and designs of humans but also to act as quasi agents or forces with trajectories, propensities, or tendencies of their own" (viii). Her investigation into "the material agency or effectivity of nonhuman or not-quite human things" (ix) calls to mind Armstrong's description of North Korea as a minor power that is nonetheless able to exert force on major powers and suggests that North Korea is a peculiar kind of actant within the sphere of global politics. Bearing in mind the capacity for inhuman actants to function as forces and exert influence, I return now to North Korean testimonials to examine what practices of writing and reading these inhuman voices reveal about our anxieties about the human.

## Inhuman Life Writing

In response to an interview question about whether he viewed North Korea to be a communist regime, Slavoj Žižek states that "we all know that North Korea is a total *fiasco*" (48). Žižek's blunt blanket statement seems to sum up a general global opinion on North Korea. And while it may be commonly understood that North Korea is an oppressive regime, details about it are few and far between. It is not, however, impossible to find information, as Armstrong notes when describing his approach for writing *Tyranny of the Weak*. While North Korea is closed to archival research for most people, archives of its allies, such as the former Soviet Union and nations in Eastern Europe, are open and declassified; People's Republic of China documents are also now available to foreign researchers. Armstrong argues that, by combing through these materials, it is possible to develop a strong sense of North

Korean history and politics. Another important source of information about North Korea is the memoirs written by former citizens, many of which read like dystopian nonfiction but are difficult to discredit given the levels of secrecy surrounding North Korea. To the best of my knowledge, fewer than five North Korean testimonials were published from the 1960s to the 1980s, while more than seventy have been published from the 1990s until now. These texts were often first published in either Korean or English (but some were also released first in Chinese or French) and were often translated into multiple languages. While the sharp spike in North Korean testimonials can be attributed to a host of factors that drove more people out of North Korea in the last few decades (including the worsening economic conditions, which peaked with the Arduous March, the title given to the famine of the 1990s by the North Korean government), it also indicates an increasing level of public interest in these stories.

While these firsthand accounts are valuable for their content and the desire to tell and hear North Korean stories they reveal, their accuracy is often suspect, and journalists have noted that it is difficult to verify stories before they go to print. This is part of the reason there is often much conjecture in news reports about North Korea. Harden, the reporter who published Shin's story as *Escape from Camp 14*, describes the real challenges this posed. Certainly, the controversy over the falsification of details of Shin's account speaks to these difficulties. While there may be a real desire to hear North Korean stories, there are few mechanisms in place to ensure the truthfulness of the stories that do circulate. As Harden's introduction to Shin's story notes,

> Fact-checking is not possible in North Korea. Outsiders have not visited its political prison camps. Accounts of what goes on inside them cannot be independently verified. Although satellite images have greatly added to outside understanding of the camps, defectors remain the primary sources of information, and their motives and credibility are not spotless. In South Korea and elsewhere, they are often desperate to make a living, willing to confirm the preconceptions of human rights activists, anticommunist missionaries, and right-wing ideologues. Some camp survivors refuse to talk unless they are paid cash upfront. Others repeated juicy anecdotes they had heard but not personally witnessed. (10)

It is important to note that Harden discusses the process he underwent in verifying Shin's story before the book went to press. He claims that the story seemed authentic to "survivors of other labor camps, to scholars, to human rights advocates, and to the South Korean government" (46).

How then do we understand the significance of the rising numbers of North Korean testimonials that have been written and consumed over the last three decades? Given that they clearly do not provide a reliable and unproblematic means of accessing life in North Korea, what might the popularity of these texts reveal about the desires and curiosities of a wider reading public? How does it speak to how North Korea is fashioned for global audiences? While Shin's text cannot be called a memoir because he is not the author of this story (and in this way, it and many other North Korean testimonials resemble more closely told-to narratives or even collaborative memoirs, as the subjects of the texts often rely on coauthors), I suggest that insights into the genre of memoir can be used productively to analyze the kinds of pleasures and anxieties generated by North Korean life writing.

One way of reading *Escape from Camp 14* is as the story of an inhuman North Korean subject as he fled the state and attempted to become human. By extending Slaughter's practice of reading human rights law and the bildungsroman as intertwined ways of writing the Western subject, we can see Shin's story as an extreme version of the bildungsroman: more than the story of an individual maturing into an adult, Shin was on a journey to becoming human, one that he did not complete by the end of the text. The incomplete journey of Shin toward humanity is crucial since, as Slaughter's work on human rights narrative demonstrates, there are multiple correspondences between the norms and forms of international human rights law and the literary form of the bildungsroman (1407). In the instance of North Korea, the failure to become the ideal subject of either the bildungsroman or international human rights means that North Korea is able to function as the limits of these forms. And here, we can see how the logics of race and the limitations of the nation-state work to position North Korea in discourses of human rights in highly circumscribed ways.

The bulk of the narrative tracks Shin's life in Camp 14, his flight from the prison camp and then North Korea, and finally his travels through China. It is replete with lurid details, such as the electrocution of the prison mate who tried to escape with Shin, Shin's use of his friend's dead body "as a kind of insulating pad" to protect him from the electric currents as he crawled over the live fence, and the burning smell of his friend's corpse (115). These sensationalistic descriptions make the text memorable, and it is perhaps unsurprising that relatively little of the story is devoted to Shin's life postarrival in South Korea, or after he then migrated to the United States. The story does not subject either of these two countries to the same degree of scrutiny that it has used to examine life in North Korea. *Escape from Camp 14* narrates the shocking tale of the inhuman subject's flight away from the repressive mechanisms and conditions of a dystopic state and toward the freedoms of capitalism and democracy symbolized by the United States, and it is this act that has captured the attention of countless readers and human rights advocates.

The appeal of this body of life writing is that it resonates with readers and audiences in ways similar to the genre of the memoir. In her overview of memoir as it has been produced for and consumed by a Western audience, Julie Rak highlights the changing market orientation of these texts. Although memoirs were being written earlier in Europe, a major shift occurred during the eighteenth century when prostitutes, libertines, and former courtesans anonymously published their stories. The popularity of these "scandalous memoirs" lay in the salacious details they provided (Rak 5). The anonymity of these authors suggests that, even as their stories found readers willing to buy copies, the market was for tales of vices and shocking appetites rather than for the stories of individual experiences. Much like narratives of North Korean refugees, these early memoirs could reach a wide audience by erasing the individual subjectivity of their authors and creating an almost interchangeable subject.

## Conclusion

The typicality of North Korean subjects is thus what makes North Korean life writing coherent as a genre and why it can reach millions of readers without necessarily changing perceptions of North Korea in any of its readers. Like Lukács's typicality of the nineteenth-century novel, the subject in North Korean testimonials stands in for a collective in order to telescope experience into one body or consciousness. The failure of the inhuman subject to realize the dream of being human is reenacted in each of these texts as the individual flees North Korea, and, in many ways, this limitation serves as the condition of possibility for this genre. It is the hope that the promise of humanity for the inhuman subject will eventually be realized that drives the reader to read multiple texts in this genre. However, since the bildungsroman is defined by the protagonist's ultimate integration into bourgeois society, Shin's struggle to adapt in his new home in the United States reminds us that these North Korean stories are failed bildungsromans. As Rak astutely observes of genre more generally, "Genre provides the conditions for understanding in everyday life because its operations do not work by a recognition of elements that are similar to ones that have appeared before. The temporality of these elements generates similar, but not the same, relations" (28). She cites the expectation that the same characters will appear when one reads one of the novels in the *Twilight* series or even the expectation that fruit purchased weekly at the same market will be of the same quality to illustrate how the principle of similarity operates in genre. And while the genre of North Korean life writing carries with it the risk of instrumentalizing stories and making them interchangeable in their sameness in order to emphasize the gravity of the human rights situation in North Korea, it also offers much potential for those advocating for North Korean human rights given the size of the audience it can reach. At the same time, the seeming sameness of North Korean life writing for non–North Korean reading publics reminds us that we need to develop sharper critical eyes to see the individual subjectivity of these writers.

In recognizing this double bind, I ask whether we can hold onto this frame of human rights discourse while enacting ruptures within it, ones that insert more complex understandings of what constitutes the human and which subjects consequently are entitled to these rights. Seen from this vantage point, the story of North Korean escape is not just a simple flight outward to freedom but also one that depicts a complex knot of family, obligations, national loyalty, and poverty that is never left behind. To return one final time to Shin's struggle to feel a range of emotion after betraying his mother and brother, this moment draws attention to the deep traumas inflicted by the North Korean state that dehumanized Shin. And yet an alternative way of reading that scene is that it reveals that Shin was never human, at least in the way that the category of the human has operated in human rights discourse. What *Escape from Camp 14* does not interrogate is the specificity of the emotions that define the human and why sympathy and sadness—rather than other emotions, such as self-loathing, or qualities such as resilience—are viewed as the hallmarks of the human. We can begin to productively engage with the limitations of how the human is conceptualized in human rights discourse by interrogating the historical frame that is implicitly employed as well as the cultural specificity of how the universal subject is imagined. In unpacking the human/inhuman binary logic that shapes human rights discourse and operates along national and racialized lines, we can begin to interrogate not just the cultural fantasies of North Korean inhumanity but also those that imagine the Western subject as universal and the fears and anxieties that underpin both.

## NOTES

1. Lankov's article continues with a description of the plight of North Koreans vis-à-vis other victims of poverty and violence that bears repeating for how it sketches out the struggles around being heard by international audiences:

> The story of the average North Korean refugee does not appear to be that remarkably different from the life stories of the countless millions of people from Africa and South Asia. Sadly, malnourishment, daily violence and for many women, thinly disguised institutionalized rape are ubiquitous in many parts of the poor world. . . . So, North Korean refugees—and their assistants—have to compete with the poorer elements of the rest of the world. This creates an incentive for them to deliver more dramatic and, if necessary, embellished stories in order to win some attention in a rather crowded media market.

2. As Pheng Cheah reminds us, the post-WWII institutionalization of human rights discourse was motivated by a desire to recognize the crimes committed by the Nazi regime as violations not just of individuals but of humanity as a whole (*Inhuman* 145). Within this concept of crimes against humanity, the human becomes a metaphor

that stands in for the Western subject and the citizen. I want to suggest that the timing of the adoption of the Universal Declaration of Human Rights in 1948 makes it clear that outside of those parameters lie the overlapping circles of North Korea and the figure of the Asian. This is perhaps unsurprising since, as Walter Mignolo points out, "In the eighteenth century, the 'rights of man and of the citizen' was formulated instead within the planetary consciousness of a cosmo-polis analogous to the law of nature, with Europe—the Europe of nations, specifically—as the frame of reference. There was a change but within the system, or, better yet, within the imaginary of the modern/colonial world system" (731).

3. My thanks to David Palumbo-Liu for drawing my attention to the emphasis on plasticity in these statements.

4. Michael Banton's reflections on the changes that had taken place since the UNESCO statements in the early 1950s speak to the changing international social and political conditions: "Educational campaigns were mounted. More important, probably, most colonial nations won their independence and were admitted to the United Nations" (19). And while this was a major shift, it did not necessarily lead to a lessening of racial conflict:

> New population movements occurred which brought previously separated peoples into closer contact and increased the points at which the sparks of hostility could be struck. African, West Indian, Indian and Pakistani workers migrated to their former metropolitan countries, the United Kingdom and France in search of work. Indonesians who had never previously left the land of their birth, but were Dutch citizens, took ship to the Netherlands. Negro farm workers in the Southern region of the United States were driven from the land as tractors and mechanical harvesters were adopted; they, and their families, travelled north and to the cities. In South Africa the government intensified its efforts to enforce a pattern of separation. Over much of the globe it seemed as if racial friction was growing more frequent and more intense. (Banton 19)

## WORKS CITED

Armstrong, Charles K. *Tyranny of the Weak*. Ithaca, NY: Cornell University Press, 2013.

Banton, Michael. "Social Aspects of the Race Question." UNESCO, *Four Statements*, 17–29.

Bennett, Jane. *Vibrant Matter: A Political Ecology of Things*. Durham, NC: Duke University Press, 2010.

Cheah, Pheng. "Humanity in the Field of Instrumentality." *PMLA* 121.5 (2006): 1552–1557.

———. *Inhuman Conditions: On Cosmopolitanism and Human Rights*. Cambridge, MA: Harvard University Press, 2006.

Harden, Blaine. *Escape from Camp 14: One Man's Remarkable Odyssey from North Korea to Freedom in the West*. New York: Viking, 2012.

Human Rights Council. *Report of the Detailed Findings of the Commission of Inquiry on Human Rights in the Democratic People's Republic of Korea*. Twenty-fifth session, agenda item 4. 2014.

Jang, Jin-sung. *Dear Leader: My Escape from North Korea*. New York: 37 Ink/Atria, 2014.

Jang, Lucia, and Susan McClelland. *Stars between the Sun and Moon: One Woman's Life in North Korea and Escape to Freedom*. Vancouver: Douglas and McIntyre, 2014.

Kim, Jodi. *Ends of Empire: Asian American Critique and the Cold War.* Minneapolis: University of Minnesota Press, 2010.

Lankov, Andrei. "After the Shin Dong-hyuk Affair: Separating Fact, Fiction." *NK News.org.* 13 June 2016.

Lee, Hyeonseo. *The Girl with Seven Names: A North Korean Defector's Story.* With David John. London: William Collins, 2015.

Lukács, Georg. "Art and Objective Truth." *"Writer and Critic," and Other Essays.* Ed. and trans. Arthur D. Kahn. London: Merlin, 1970. 25–60.

Mignolo, Walter. "The Many Faces of Cosmo-polis: Border Thinking and Critical Cosmopolitanism." *Public Culture* 12.3 (2000): 721–748.

Mitchell, W.J.T. *What Do Pictures Want? The Lives and Loves of Images.* Chicago: University of Chicago Press, 2005.

Nyers, Peter. *Rethinking Refugees: Beyond States of Emergency.* New York: Routledge, 2006.

Rak, Julie. *Boom! Manufacturing Memoir for the American Public.* Waterloo, ON: Wilfrid Laurier University Press, 2013.

Shoichet, Catherine E., and Madison Park. "North Korean prison Camp Survivor Admits Inaccuracies, Author Says." *CNN World+.* 20 January 2015. 13 June 2016.

Slaughter, Joseph. "Enabling Fictions and Novel Subjects: The 'Bildungsroman' and International Human Rights Law." *PMLA* 121.5 (2006): 1405–1423.

Tsing, Anna Lowenhaupt. *The Mushroom at the End of the World: On the Possibility of Life in Capitalist Ruins.* Princeton: Princeton University Press, 2015.

———. "Unruly Edges: Mushrooms as Companion Species." *Environmental Humanities* 1 (2012): 141–154.

"UN Dismisses North Korea's Claim That Damning Human Rights Report Is Invalid." *The Guardian.* 21 January 2015. 12 April 2016.

UNESCO. *Four Statements on the Race Question.* Paris: United Nations Educational, Scientific and Cultural Organization, 1969.

———. "Introducing UNESCO." www.unesco.org. 26 August 2015.

UNHCR. *Handbook and Guidelines on Procedures and Criteria for Determining Refugee Status.* 1979. Reissued 2011.

UNHDR. *The Universal Declaration of Human Rights.* United Nations, 1948.

United Nations. "History of the Document." *The Universal Declaration of Human Rights.* 26 August 2015.

Žižek, Slavoj. *Demanding the Impossible.* Ed Yong-June Park. Cambridge: Polity, 2014.

# Afterword

## *The Act of Listening*

Madeleine Thien

For a long time I did not listen to music. Music, as much as I loved it, felt like a pleasure that must wait. How difficult it seemed to turn away from the visual world, to quiet the din of my thoughts, to listen.

Yet music is everywhere around us. Music, John Cage writes, is the endless field of sound: "We can compose and perform a quartet for explosive motor, wind, heartbeat, and landslide" (3). Or, as Marcel Proust describes it, the sound "took on an order, a rhythm, became liquid, loud, drumming, musical, innumerable, universal. It was the rain" (102). Is there any animal on this earth that cannot hear (or feel) frequency? As far as I know, there isn't. Thus it follows that all creatures perceive silence. One could even say that silence, like sound, is a frequency; silence, as the composer Benjamin Britten has said, "is etched on the air" (qtd. in Scheinin). We hear it even when we are not listening, and we respond to it even without realizing.

To follow the path that music takes through time and space is a little like trying to map the fall of a drop of rain. So allow me to choose a gate through which we might enter: 433 B.C., the year the Marquis Yǐ of Zēng passed away. His tomb, stocked with everything a royal personage might require in the afterlife—wine cups, glass beads, weaponry, books, cauldrons, and chariot wheels—contained, as well, a magnificent collection of musical instruments. Most remarkable of all was a set of sixty-five bronze bells.

The bells, called *biānzhōng* in Mandarin Chinese, were laid out in three suspended rows. The smallest bell weighed 2.4 kilograms; the largest 203 kilograms. Astonishingly, each bell could produce two distinct and accurate tones, a quality achieved by precision modeling the bell's shape, density, thickness, and elasticity to produce two sets of vibrations. To put this art in perspective, nearly two thousand years would pass before the revered instrument makers of seventeenth-century Europe devised a way to tune a bell. Further, in the twenty-five hundred years that have since elapsed, the bells, tuned to twelve-note octaves, much like the modern Western chromatic scale, never lost their tuning.[1]

After twenty-five hundred years of silence underground, the bells of the Marquis Yǐ of Zēng were discovered when I was a child. That is another story, to which we'll return in a moment.

At the core of issues pertaining to personhood, and consequently to human rights, is unofficial history—the unofficial history of political collusion, vested financial interests, illegal bombing, and the occupation or disappearance of land, property, and people. Unofficial history, encoded in multiple and interlocking silences, is etched on the air; we could even say *it is the air itself.* For silence is not simply the absence of sound; silence is a form of expression when society requires that individuals speak in voices not their own and publicly declare selves that are fictitious.

In 1936, the Russian composer Dimitri Shostakovich, persecuted by authorities, chose to withdraw his Fourth Symphony. His brother-in-law, his sister, and his mother-in-law had all been sent into exile or labor camps, and close friends were disappearing. At the height of Stalin's Terror, a thousand people were executed every day. For years, in interviews, Shostakovich claimed to be working on a symphony celebrating Lenin, but no trace of any such composition has been found. Targeted again in February 1948, he was "subjected to vile public abuse" (Fay 182), and his works were removed from public performance. Shostakovich could only answer, "I will try again and again" (qtd. in Fay 160). That month, however, he began inserting a musical phrase, spelled out by the letters of his name, into his compositions—a hidden self that existed in the field of sound, audible but fleeting, present but surrounded. Shostakovich, surely one of the greatest composers of the age, told his students, "Work, play. You're living here, in this country, and you must see everything as it really is. Don't create illusions. There's no other life. There can't be any. Just be thankful that you're still allowed to breathe" (qtd. in Fay 269). Meanwhile, his fellow composer Sergei Prokofiev, increasingly ill, disappeared from public life. Asked by his young assistant why he allowed Party authorities to trample over and revise his creative work, Prokofiev had answered, "I no longer care" (qtd. in Meek).

In *The Semantics of Chinese Music*, musicologist and linguist Adrien Tien notes that the word *silence*—that is, the complete absence of sound—is an "Anglo-centric word which does not have readily available, lexical and translational equivalents in other languages, including Chinese" (38). Rather, Chinese uses concepts of sonic presence and absence and distinguishes between, for instance, *mò* 默 (nonspeech, someone having abstained from speech), *jìng* 静 (an adjective that denotes a space of tranquility), and *jí* 寂 (a state of isolation). What all concepts hold in common is the possibility that one does not hear with one's ears but that one may hear something in another way. Thus, value is placed on the gradations of "sonic contour" and what Frank Kouwenhoven describes as the "continuation of sounds beyond what the normal human ear can detect: silences [as well as] the dying away of audible sounds . . . that may continue for a while after any audible pitch has disappeared" (qtd. in Tien 42). Sonic absence, therefore, is commensurate with deep listening.

Among Shostakovich's most beloved works was Gustave Mahler's *Das Lied von der Erde*. In 1908, at what should have been the height of Mahler's storied career, he was forced out of his post as conductor of the Vienna Court Opera; he lost his five-year-old daughter, Maria, to scarlet fever; and he himself was diagnosed with a fatal heart condition. To a friend, Mahler wrote, "I simply say that at a single stroke I have lost any calm and peace of mind that I have ever achieved. I stand *vis-à-vis de rien* [face to face with nothingness], and now, at the end of my life, have to learn again to walk and stand."[2]

During this time, Mahler chanced upon a copy of *Die chinesische Flöte*, a volume of Tang Dynasty (eighth-century) Chinese poetry. Among the works was Wang Wei's famous poem "A Farewell":

*Off our horses, I offer you wine,*
*ask where you're going. You say*
*your work has come to nothing,*
*you'll settle at South Mountain.*
*Once you set out, questions end*
*and white cloud keeps on and on.*
(Wei 29)

Moved by the transience and lasting sorrow of the poems, Mahler began work on *Das Lied von der Erde* (The song of the earth), a six-piece song-symphony for orchestra and two voices. The words were written, or more aptly, remixed, by Mahler himself, who based the text on a German translation of an abridged French translation of the original Chinese. I like to think that as Mahler was walking toward the field of sound, he heard the "liquid, loud, drumming, musical, innumerable, universal." Ernest Bloch described the last words of "A Farewell," the sixth part of the song-symphony, as dissolving with "an unresolved suspension into an immeasurable forever" (qtd in "Wang Wei's Farewell"). *Das Lied von der Erde* premiered in Munich in 1911, six months after Mahler had passed away.

Just as Wang Wei arrived in Mahler's imagination, Mahler's symphonies, too, were carried back to the East, and *Das Lied von der Erde* was translated, its strangeness and sorrow intact, back into Chinese languages, a trajectory that playfully reproduces sonata form itself, exposition, development, and recapitulation—or to put it another way, arrival, departure, and return.

Meanwhile, in Shanghai in 1934, Russian and French composers initiated a competition for Chinese students, wherein they were invited to submit work with a "Chinese flavor." The inaugural prize was awarded to a student at the Shanghai Conservatory of Music. He Luting, born in a remote mountain village, was first introduced to Western classical music by a French textbook abandoned by his older brother. On receiving the prize in 1934, a year when China was at the height of a catastrophic civil war, He wrote, "My father passed away in June of this year and at home there is a great hunger. In order to live, I may have to temporarily stop my studies. My journey of life will always be circuitous" (qtd. in Melvin and Cai). More than thirty years later, He, now sixty-five years old, became the target of the first-ever publicly televised struggle session of the Chinese Cultural Revolution. By that time, He was one of China's foremost composers and the president of the Shanghai Conservatory of Music—a position abruptly terminated in 1966 at the start of the Cultural Revolution.

Organized by high-ranking leaders of the Shanghai Revolutionary Committee, the denunciation meeting began like countless others: arms tied tightly behind his back, the elderly man was pulled onto the stage by two Red Guards. His head was forced down. He's family, including his wife, daughters, and nieces, were paraded onstage. A massive, well-organized mob hurled slogans and accusations, accusing He Luting of betraying not only the Communist revolution and its ideals but Chairman Mao himself.

The Cultural Revolution (1966–1976) was, on its surface, a political campaign to renew and purify the Chinese revolutionary spirit. Beneath the surface, however, the Cultural Revolution was something else entirely. Its campaigns, whose function would be to cement Mao Zedong's power and legacy through a cult of personality, attempted to purge all political, artistic, intellectual, philosophical, and physical resistance. In ten years, the Cultural Revolution targeted more than 36 million people and took the lives of between 1.5 and 2 million.[3] The physical torture was unceasing, and repeated public shaming tormented their minds and placed them under enormous psychological duress. Thousands, including He Luting's daughter, were driven to suicide, from nameless teachers and workers to writers, artists, historians, scientists, literature scholars, physicists, musicians, law scholars, photographers, translators, and editors. The composer Li Delun said, "It was very hard to be a person then" (qtd. in Melvin and Cai). In a single institution, the Shanghai Conservatory of Music, seventeen professors, spouses, and students committed suicide, and still more died from physical abuse and privation.

In April 1968, workers from across Shanghai and the region were summoned to auditoriums and meeting halls to watch the live broadcast. When a thin and frail He Luting was dragged, for the second time, onstage, the violent conclusion seemed foregone. Immediately, a leading cadre accused him of opposing Chairman Mao. Shaking with rage, sweating under the glare of klieg lights, He Luting answered, "I am not guilty." The cadre denounced him as a counterrevolutionary. He Luting shouted back, "Your accusations are false! Shame on you for lying!" At that moment, a Red Guard stepped in to grab the microphone away.

Sheila Melvin and Jindong Cai, in their groundbreaking book about Western classical music in China, describe what happened next: "Before the surprised Red Guard could react, Hè Lùtīng grabbed the microphone back. 'Shame on you for lying! Shame on you for lying!' he repeated over and over before the stunned live audience . . . that was no doubt equally shocked—and awed—by his brazen courage. . . . The Red Guards twisted [his arms] so hard that Mr. Hè collapsed onto the stage in pain, but when they let go, he stood back up, and repeated his curse of shame. . . . Up in the control booth, the live broadcast was cut off" (239). In *The Rest Is Noise: Listening to the 21st Century*, Alex Ross writes, "No composer ever made a braver stand against totalitarianism" (565). To be clear, the Cultural Revolution did not simply target teachers or artists believed to be corrupted by Western influences; tradition, in and of itself, was the target. Tradition was the concrete stand-in for the past—the intangible realm of ideas, the vast field of sound, the world that could not be contained by Mao's closed narrative of the revolutionary present. A closed narrative sets limits on what is acceptable, what is viable, and, finally, what is human. This closed narrative—and the use of extreme violence to maintain its closure—would be adopted wholesale in Cambodia by Pol Pot and the Khmer Rouge revolution. There, too, musicians, alongside 1.7 million Cambodians of every age, from every stratum of life, holding every political belief, would be the targets of purification—they would be destroyed. For five years, as I worked on *Dogs at the Perimeter*, a novel about the long aftermath of the Cambodian genocide, I tried to learn the language of this closed narrative. The Khmer Rouge's fantasy of a revolutionary and glorious nation born from the destructive force of Year Zero, and of a country whose greatest enemies would be its own people and their "memory sickness," required new words and a new register in the Khmer language. The use of this new language—which sought to internalize in individuals the Khmer Rouge construction of reality—was surveilled; improper use would reveal spies, counterrevolutionaries, and internal enemies. But why was music, even pieces that had no words or lyrics, considered dangerous? Perhaps because music addresses and reaffirms our private worlds. We can arguably tell each other what a sentence means, but we can never guarantee the meaning of a phrase of music.

Music makes use of measures of time to recommence our perception of time—it is a heightened state of awareness that is made possible because, as the composer Aaron Copland has noted, we lend ourselves to it (*Music and Imag-*

*ination* 40). We lend ourselves to a sound that does not come from us; we lend ourselves to the arrival of something within us. As Pol Pot realized and the Khmer Rouge ideology put into practice, it is not enough to destroy an idea, a mode of expression, or a way of living. To erase an idea, it is not enough to erase its sound. You must destroy the listener. You must erase the human being.

In the winter of 1977, soldiers from the People's Liberation Army were sent out to level a hillside in Hubei province. Digging into the earth, they accidentally discovered the twenty-five-hundred-year old tomb of Marquis Yǐ. Their timing was fortuitous: Mao Zedong had died almost exactly a year before, and the Cultural Revolution had finally come to an end. Two months later, archaeologists lifted off the huge timber cover and discovered the sixty-five bronze bells, each inscribed with elaborate notes on musical theory that would change our understanding of music history. The following year, the composer He Luting, who had survived his extraordinary ordeal, was reinstated as president of the newly reopened Shanghai Conservatory of Music. One year later, violinist Isaac Stern came to China to tour and work with the country's young musicians. He told them, "Every time you take up the instrument, you are making a statement. Your statement. And it must be a statement of faith, that you believe. This is the way you want to speak."[4]

I have chosen music as the clearest way to express what I believe is the foundation of my own literature. The polyphonic language of music and its specific ability to speak to us across vast distances of time and geography, as well as profound differences in political and social conditions—from the three-thousand-year-old songs of the Shījīng and the vast repertory of J. S. Bach to John Cage's *I-Ching*–inspired avant-garde works—are at the heart of *Do Not Say We Have Nothing*, my novel about the unresolved histories of China's twentieth-century revolutions. Here is what I believe: what a writer attempts, over the course of his or her life, is to practice the art of listening. As literary theorist Mikhail Bakhtin writes, "A [person] never coincides with himself [or herself]. . . . [I]n each of [us] is a 'great and unresolved thought' . . . and in this resolution of a thought (an idea) lies [our] entire life and [our] own personal unfinalizability" (87). Bakhtin calls this the surplus of humanness, which is for me the subject of literature, the subject of how we, as people, believe or disbelieve in the personhood of others. To deny the personhood of others is to believe that the boundaries of their bodies do not exist and require neither reciprocity nor dignity. We, the fortunate, occupy the land they once inhabited, use the resources they once controlled, and take ownership of the labor we now demand from them. Thus diminished, it is only a matter of time before political and geopolitical forces seek to erase their bodies from the landscape and their voices from the field of sound.

Literature tells us that it is the act of listening, more than the act of speaking, that makes us human. The act of listening—the lending of the self, a bell capable of sounding two distinct notes simultaneously, a silence in which we may yet learn to hear in another way, the continuation of sounds beyond what the normal human ear can detect, the unresolved narrative attuned to the surplus of humanness—is necessary for any sound to exist. Silence continuously repeats, and its structures can still be heard.

## NOTES

1. At the time of writing, a musical performance created on reproductions of the Marquis Yi of Zeng's bells can be viewed and heard at https://www.youtube.com/watch?v=zhcCSeRj2PU (accessed 8 August 2017).

2. Letter from Gustav Mahler to Bruno Walter, as quoted in the Los Angeles Philharmonic program notes, written by Herbert Glass for a performance of *Das Lied von der Erde*.

3. These statistics are drawn from research conducted by MacFarquhar and Schoenhals; Dikotter.

4. At the time of writing, a clip of eleven-year old violinist Wang Jian performing Henry Eccles, *Sonata for Violin in G minor*, arranged for cello by E. Cahnbley in *From Mao to Mozart: Isaac Stern in China*, directed by Murray Lerner, can be viewed here: https://www.youtube.com/watch?v=-qK54RSndHg.

## WORKS CITED

Bakhtin, Mikhail M. *Problems of Dostoevsky's Poetics*. Ed. and trans. Caryl Emerson. Minneapolis: University of Minnesota Press, 1984.

Cage, John. *Silence*. Middleton, CT: Wesleyan University Press, 2013.

Copeland, Aaron. *Music and Imagination*. Cambridge, MA: Harvard University Press, 1952.

Dikotter, Frank. *The Cultural Revolution: A People's History, 1962–1976*. New York: Bloomsbury, 2016.

Fay, Laurel E. *Shostakovich: A Life*. New York: Oxford University Press, 2000.

Horton, Scott. "Wang Wei's Farwell." *Harper's Magazine* (blog). 29 November 2009. https://harpers.org/blog/2009/11/wang-weis-farewell/. 18 June 2019.

MacFarquhar, Roderick, and Michael Schoenhals. *Mao's Last Revolution*. Cambridge, MA: Belknap, 2006.

Meek, James. "Out of Stalin's Shadow." *The Guardian*. 17 January 2003. https://www.theguardian.com/music/2003/jan/17/classicalmusicandopera.artsfeatures1. 8 August 2017.

Melvin, Sheila, and Jindong Cai. *Rhapsody in Red: How Western Classical Music Became Chinese*. New York: Algora, 2004.

Proust, Marcel. *Remembrance of Things Past*. Trans. C. K. Scott-Moncrieff. New York: Random House, 1934.

Ross, Alex. *The Rest Is Noise: Listening to the 20th Century*. New York: Picador, 2007.

Scheinin, Richard. "S.F. Symphony and Baritone Hampson Shine in Mahler." *Mercury News* (San Jose, CA). 27 September 2007. http://www.mercurynews.com/2007/09/27/s-f-symphony-and-baritone-hampson-shine-in-mahler/. 8 August 2017.

Thien, Madeleine. *Do Not Say We Have Nothing*. 2016. New York: W.W. Norton, 2017.

———. *Dogs at the Perimeter*. 2011. New York: W.W. Norton, 2017.

Tien, Adrien. *The Semantics of Chinese Music: Analysing Selected Chinese Musical Concepts*. Amsterdam: John Benjamins, 2015.

Wei, Wang. *The Selected Poems of Wang Wei*. Trans. David Hinton. New York: New Directions, 2006.



# Contributors

**GUY BEAUREGARD** is Professor at National Taiwan University. His work has appeared or is forthcoming in *Amerasia Journal*, *Asian American Literary Review*, *Canadian Literature*, *Concentric*, *Inter-Asia Cultural Studies*, *International Journal of Canadian Studies*, *Studies in Canadian Literature*, *Tamkang Review*, and *West Coast Line*. He has coedited *Pacific Canada* (a special issue of *Amerasia Journal*, 2007) and *Asian Canadian Studies* (a special issue of *Canadian Literature*, 2008). He was the founding director of the Empire and Overseas Literature project at National Tsing Hua University and a collaborating member of the SIAAS collective, a multicampus initiative to further Asian American critical work in Taiwan and elsewhere in Asia.

**ANNIE ISABEL FUKUSHIMA** is Assistant Professor in the Ethnic Studies Division in the School for Cultural and Social Transformation at the University of Utah. Before joining the faculty at the University of Utah, she was Andrew W. Mellon Postdoctoral Fellow with the Institute for Research on Women and the Department of Women's and Gender Studies at Rutgers University. She earned her PhD in Ethnic Studies with a Designated Emphasis in Women, Gender and Sexuality Studies at University of California, Berkeley. She has published a variety of scholarly and nonscholarly works on immigration, violence, race, gender, and human trafficking and also served as an expert in the U.S. legal system. She is author of *Migrant Crossings: Witnessing Human Trafficking in the US* (Stanford University Press, 2019), where she examines Asian and Latinas/os who are trafficked in the United States.

**MAYUMO INOUE** is Associate Professor of Comparative Literature in the Graduate School of Language and Society at Hitotsubashi University in Tokyo, Japan. His work explores the intersection of literature and film, postcolonial studies, and aesthetic theories (of Jean-Luc Nancy, Adorno, Deleuze, et al.) in the context of imperialisms and their memories in East Asia and the United States. His essays on Theresa Hak Kyung Cha, Charles Olson, Kiyota Masanobu, and the politics of U.S.-Japan military alliance have appeared in *Criticism*, *Discourse*, and *American Quarterly*. His coedited collection of essays *Beyond Imperial Aesthetics: Theories of Art and Politics in East Asia* (coedited with Steve Choe) is forthcoming from Hong Kong University Press in 2019. He is also one of the founding editors of *Las Barcas*, an Okinawa-based journal devoted to innovative art forms and critical texts.

**MASUMI IZUMI** is Professor of North American Studies in the Department of Global and Regional Studies at Doshisha University in Kyoto, Japan. Her research focuses on wartime experiences of Japanese Americans and Japanese Canadians as well as their postinternment community activism. She has written numerous articles on these topics both in English and Japanese in journals including *Amerasia*, *Journal of Asian American Studies*, and *Peace and Change*. She is author of the forthcoming book *The Rise and Fall of America's Concentration Camp Law: Civil Liberties Debates from the Internment to McCarthyism and the Radical 1960s*, from Temple University Press.

**DINIDU KARUNANAYAKE** is a Visiting Instructor of English at Centre College in Danville, Kentucky. His research examines contours of the postcolonial South Asian security state and its relationship with Asian America in the terrains of memory, human rights, and transnational citizenships. His work has been published in *South Asian Review* and *The Oxford Encyclopedia of Asian American Literature and Culture*.

**CHRISTINE KIM** is Associate Professor in the Department of English and codirector of the Institute of Transpacific Cultural Research at Simon Fraser University. Her teaching and research focus on Asian North American literature and theory, diaspora studies, and cultural studies. She is author of *The Minor Intimacies of Race* (University of Illinois Press, 2016) and coeditor of *Cultural Grammars of Nation, Diaspora and Indigeneity* (Wilfrid Laurier University Press, 2012). She has contributed chapters to essay collections on Asian Canadian literature and theater and published articles in *Interventions*, *Mosaic*, *Studies in Canadian Literature*, and *Journal of Intercultural Studies*. Currently she is working on a SSHRC-funded book-length project on representations of North Korea, cultural fantasies, and Cold War legacies.

**MIN-JUNG KIM** is Professor in the Department of English Language and Literature at Ewha Womans University in Seoul, Korea. She received her BA in English from Ewha; her MA from the Department of English at the University of California, Berkeley on a Fulbright scholarship; and her PhD from the Department of Literature at the University of California, San Diego. Her research interests include African American and Asian American literature, narrative theory, postcolonial literature and theory, and critical issues in American studies scholarship and study of American culture and literature in Korea. She is coeditor of *Transnationality in US Immigrant Literature* (Ewha Womans University Press) and author of articles covering a wide range of canonical and minority writers. Her interest in U.S. imperialism in Asia, immigration, and memory is explored in essays such as "Moments of Danger in the (Dis)continuous Relation of Korean Nationalism and Korean American Nationalism" (*Positions*, 1997) and "Language, the University and American Studies in Korea" (*American Quarterly*, 2005). In 2003, Kim received the American Studies Association's Yasuo Sakakibara Award for her essay on Ronyoung Kim's *Clay Walls*. She was also the recipient of the Fulbright midcareer research grant in 2006–2007. Kim has served as associate editor (2014–2015) for *American Quarterly* and on its editorial board (2015–2018).

**CHRISTOPHER LEE** is Associate Professor of English and Director of the Asian Canadian and Asian Migration Studies Program at the University of British Columbia. He is author of *The Semblance of Identity: Aesthetic Mediation in Asian American Literature* (Stanford University Press, 2012), which received the literary criticism book award from the Association for Asian American Studies. He is currently associate editor of the journal *American Quarterly*.

**HSIU-CHUAN LEE** is Professor in the Department of English at National Taiwan Normal University. She authored *Re-siting Routes: Japanese American Travels in the Case of Cynthia Kadohata and David Mura* (2003), translated Toni Morrison's *Sula* into Chinese (2008), and participated in the Chinese translation project of *Global Identity, Local Voices: Amerasia Journal at 40 Years* volumes 1 and 2 (2012–2013). Her articles on Toni Morrison, Ruth Ozeki, Asian American studies, psychoanalysis, and film have appeared in journals including *ARIEL: A Review of International English Literature*, *Mosaic: An Interdisciplinary Critical Journal*, *Amerasia Journal*, *Concentric: Literary and Cultural Studies*, *Chung-wai Literary Quarterly*, and *Review of English and American Literature*. She was a collaborating member of the SIAAS collective, a multicampus initiative to further Asian American critical work in Taiwan and elsewhere in Asia.

**VINH NGUYEN** is Assistant Professor of English at Renison University College at the University of Waterloo. He holds a PhD from McMaster University, where he specialized in Asian North American literature and culture and critical refugee studies. He held a SSHRC Vanier Canada Graduate Scholarship, a Sir James Lougheed Award of Distinction, and a Harry Lyman Hooker Fellowship, among other honors. He is the 2017 recipient of the John C. Polanyi Prize in Literature. His writing can be found or is forthcoming in *Social Text*, *MELUS*, *ARIEL*, *Canadian Literature*, *Life Writing*, and *Canadian Review of American Studies*.

**CHRISTOPHER B. PATTERSON** is Assistant Professor in the Social Justice Institute at the University of British Columbia. His research focuses on transpacific discourses of literature, games, and new media through the lens of empire studies, queer theory, and creative writing. His academic book, *Transitive Cultures: Anglophone Literature of the Transpacific* (Rutgers University Press, 2018), traces identity-transition across Southeast Asian migrant narratives. His articles have appeared in *American Quarterly*, *Games and Culture*, *MELUS*, and the anthologies *Global Asian American Popular Cultures* (New York University Press, 2016) and *Queer Sex Work* (Routledge, 2015). He writes fiction under the pseudonym Kawika Guillermo and is author of *Stamped: An Anti-travel Novel* (Westphalia Press, 2018), as well as short stories in *Cimarron Review*, *Feminist Studies*, and *Hawaiʻi Pacific Review*.

**CATHY J. SCHLUND-VIALS** is a Board of Trustees Distinguished Professor of English and Asian/Asian American Studies at the University of Connecticut; she is also Associate Dean for Humanities and Diversity, Equity, and Inclusion in the College of Liberal Arts and Sciences at UConn. She is author of two monographs: *Modeling Citizenship: Jewish and Asian American Writing* (Temple University Press, 2011) and *War, Genocide, and Justice: Cambodian American Memory Work* (University of Minnesota Press, 2012). Her work on visual culture, popular culture, human rights, and Asian American studies has appeared in a number of collections and journals including *Modern Language Studies*, *Amerasia*, *Life Writing*, *American Literary History*, *LIT: Literature, Interpretation, Theory*, *Women's Studies Quarterly*, and *positions*. She has also coedited and edited a number of collections including *Disability, Human Rights, and the Limits of Humanitarianism* (Ashgate, 2014), *Keywords for Asian American Studies* (New York University Press, 2015), *Recollecting the Vietnam War* (a special issue of *Asian American Literary Review*, 2015), *Interrogating the Perpetrator* (a special issue of the *Journal of International Human Rights*, 2015), *Asian America: A Primary Source Reader* (Yale University Press, 2016), *Flashpoints in Asian American Studies* (Fordham University Press, 2017), and *Redrawing the Historical Past: Multiethnic Graphic Narrative* (University of Georgia Press, 2018). Most recently, she served as President of the Association for Asian American Studies (2016–2018).

**MADELEINE THIEN** is author of four books, including *Dogs at the Perimeter,* and a story collection, *Simple Recipes.* Her most recent novel, *Do Not Say We Have Nothing,* was shortlisted for the 2016 Man Booker Prize, the Women's Prize for Fiction, and the Folio Prize and won the 2016 Scotiabank Giller Prize and the Governor-General's Literary Award for Fiction. The novel was named a *New York Times* Critics' Top Book of 2016 and long-listed for a Carnegie Medal. Her books have been translated into twenty-five languages, and her essays and stories have appeared in the *New York Times, The Guardian, Brick, frieze, Granta,* and elsewhere. She lives in Montreal and New York, and is Professor of English at Brooklyn College.

**YIN WANG** is Associate Professor of English at National Cheng Kung University in Taiwan. She received her PhD from the University of California, San Diego. She specializes in African American literature since the Civil War, gender and sexuality, and black political thought. She is currently at work on a book on James Baldwin's engagement with discourses of U.S. nationalism from World War II to the 1980s.

**GRACE HUI-CHUAN WU** is Assistant Professor in the Department of English at National Central University in Taiwan. Her research focuses on the intersection between economy and culture across the transpacific in the twentieth century, tracing and unfolding connections between literary form, race, and economic development. Her current project examines the interrelationship between narratives of Chinese migrant workers and the discourse of human rights in a global context. Her work appears in *Journal of Modern Literature, Concentric: Literary and Cultural Studies,* and *Chung Wai Literary Quarterly.*

# Index

Also in the series *Asian American History and Culture*

Cherstin M. Lyon, *Prisons and Patriots: Japanese American Wartime Citizenship, Civil Disobedience, and Historical Memory*
Shelley Sang-Hee Lee, *Claiming the Oriental Gateway: Prewar Seattle and Japanese America*
Isabelle Thuy Pelaud, *This Is All I Choose to Tell: History and Hybridity in Vietnamese American Literature*
Christian Collet and Pei-te Lien, eds., *The Transnational Politics of Asian Americans*
Min Zhou, *Contemporary Chinese America: Immigration, Ethnicity, and Community Transformation*
Kathleen S. Yep, *Outside the Paint: When Basketball Ruled at the Chinese Playground*
Benito M. Vergara Jr., *Pinoy Capital: The Filipino Nation in Daly City*
Jonathan Y. Okamura, *Ethnicity and Inequality in Hawai'i*
Sucheng Chan and Madeline Y. Hsu, eds., *Chinese Americans and the Politics of Race and Culture*
K. Scott Wong, *Americans First: Chinese Americans and the Second World War*
Lisa Yun, *The Coolie Speaks: Chinese Indentured Laborers and African Slaves in Cuba*
Estella Habal, *San Francisco's International Hotel: Mobilizing the Filipino American Community in the Anti-eviction Movement*
Thomas P. Kim, *The Racial Logic of Politics: Asian Americans and Party Competition*
Sucheng Chan, ed., *The Vietnamese American 1.5 Generation: Stories of War, Revolution, Flight, and New Beginnings*
Antonio T. Tiongson Jr., Edgardo V. Gutierrez, and Ricardo V. Gutierrez, eds., *Positively No Filipinos Allowed: Building Communities and Discourse*
Sucheng Chan, ed., *Chinese American Transnationalism: The Flow of People, Resources, and Ideas between China and America during the Exclusion Era*
Rajini Srikanth, *The World Next Door: South Asian American Literature and the Idea of America*
Keith Lawrence and Floyd Cheung, eds., *Recovered Legacies: Authority and Identity in Early Asian American Literature*
Linda Trinh Võ, *Mobilizing an Asian American Community*
Franklin S. Odo, *No Sword to Bury: Japanese Americans in Hawai'i during World War II*
Josephine Lee, Imogene L. Lim, and Yuko Matsukawa, eds., *Re/collecting Early Asian America: Essays in Cultural History*
Linda Trinh Võ and Rick Bonus, eds., *Contemporary Asian American Communities: Intersections and Divergences*
Sunaina Marr Maira, *Desis in the House: Indian American Youth Culture in New York City*
Teresa Williams-León and Cynthia Nakashima, eds., *The Sum of Our Parts: Mixed-Heritage Asian Americans*
Tung Pok Chin with Winifred C. Chin, *Paper Son: One Man's Story*
Amy Ling, ed., *Yellow Light: The Flowering of Asian American Arts*
Rick Bonus, *Locating Filipino Americans: Ethnicity and the Cultural Politics of Space*
Darrell Y. Hamamoto and Sandra Liu, eds., *Countervisions: Asian American Film Criticism*
Martin F. Manalansan IV, ed., *Cultural Compass: Ethnographic Explorations of Asian America*
Ko-lin Chin, *Smuggled Chinese: Clandestine Immigration to the United States*
Evelyn Hu-DeHart, ed., *Across the Pacific: Asian Americans and Globalization*

Soo-Young Chin, *Doing What Had to Be Done: The Life Narrative of Dora Yum Kim*
Robert G. Lee, *Orientals: Asian Americans in Popular Culture*
David L. Eng and Alice Y. Hom, eds., *Q & A: Queer in Asian America*
K. Scott Wong and Sucheng Chan, eds., *Claiming America: Constructing Chinese American Identities during the Exclusion Era*
Lavina Dhingra Shankar and Rajini Srikanth, eds., *A Part, Yet Apart: South Asians in Asian America*
Jere Takahashi, *Nisei/Sansei: Shifting Japanese American Identities and Politics*
Velina Hasu Houston, ed., *But Still, Like Air, I'll Rise: New Asian American Plays*
Josephine Lee, *Performing Asian America: Race and Ethnicity on the Contemporary Stage*
Deepika Bahri and Mary Vasudeva, eds., *Between the Lines: South Asians and Postcoloniality*
E. San Juan Jr., *The Philippine Temptation: Dialectics of Philippines–U.S. Literary Relations*
Carlos Bulosan and E. San Juan Jr., eds., *The Cry and the Dedication*
Carlos Bulosan and E. San Juan Jr., eds., *On Becoming Filipino: Selected Writings of Carlos Bulosan*
Vicente L. Rafael, ed., *Discrepant Histories: Translocal Essays on Filipino Cultures*
Yen Le Espiritu, *Filipino American Lives*
Paul Ong, Edna Bonacich, and Lucie Cheng, eds., *The New Asian Immigration in Los Angeles and Global Restructuring*
Chris Friday, *Organizing Asian American Labor: The Pacific Coast Canned-Salmon Industry, 1870–1942*
Sucheng Chan, ed., *Hmong Means Free: Life in Laos and America*
Timothy P. Fong, *The First Suburban Chinatown: The Remaking of Monterey Park, California*
William Wei, *The Asian American Movement*
Yen Le Espiritu, *Asian American Panethnicity*
Velina Hasu Houston, ed., *The Politics of Life*
Renqiu Yu, *To Save China, to Save Ourselves: The Chinese Hand Laundry Alliance of New York*
Shirley Geok-lin Lim and Amy Ling, eds., *Reading the Literatures of Asian America*
Karen Isaksen Leonard, *Making Ethnic Choices: California's Punjabi Mexican Americans*
Gary Y. Okihiro, *Cane Fires: The Anti-Japanese Movement in Hawaii, 1865–1945*
Sucheng Chan, *Entry Denied: Exclusion and the Chinese Community in America, 1882–1943*

Also in the series *Asian American History and Culture*

Cherstin M. Lyon, *Prisons and Patriots: Japanese American Wartime Citizenship, Civil Disobedience, and Historical Memory*
Shelley Sang-Hee Lee, *Claiming the Oriental Gateway: Prewar Seattle and Japanese America*
Isabelle Thuy Pelaud, *This Is All I Choose to Tell: History and Hybridity in Vietnamese American Literature*
Christian Collet and Pei-te Lien, eds., *The Transnational Politics of Asian Americans*
Min Zhou, *Contemporary Chinese America: Immigration, Ethnicity, and Community Transformation*
Kathleen S. Yep, *Outside the Paint: When Basketball Ruled at the Chinese Playground*
Benito M. Vergara Jr., *Pinoy Capital: The Filipino Nation in Daly City*
Jonathan Y. Okamura, *Ethnicity and Inequality in Hawai'i*
Sucheng Chan and Madeline Y. Hsu, eds., *Chinese Americans and the Politics of Race and Culture*
K. Scott Wong, *Americans First: Chinese Americans and the Second World War*
Lisa Yun, *The Coolie Speaks: Chinese Indentured Laborers and African Slaves in Cuba*
Estella Habal, *San Francisco's International Hotel: Mobilizing the Filipino American Community in the Anti-eviction Movement*
Thomas P. Kim, *The Racial Logic of Politics: Asian Americans and Party Competition*
Sucheng Chan, ed., *The Vietnamese American 1.5 Generation: Stories of War, Revolution, Flight, and New Beginnings*
Antonio T. Tiongson Jr., Edgardo V. Gutierrez, and Ricardo V. Gutierrez, eds., *Positively No Filipinos Allowed: Building Communities and Discourse*
Sucheng Chan, ed., *Chinese American Transnationalism: The Flow of People, Resources, and Ideas between China and America during the Exclusion Era*
Rajini Srikanth, *The World Next Door: South Asian American Literature and the Idea of America*
Keith Lawrence and Floyd Cheung, eds., *Recovered Legacies: Authority and Identity in Early Asian American Literature*
Linda Trinh Võ, *Mobilizing an Asian American Community*
Franklin S. Odo, *No Sword to Bury: Japanese Americans in Hawai'i during World War II*
Josephine Lee, Imogene L. Lim, and Yuko Matsukawa, eds., *Re/collecting Early Asian America: Essays in Cultural History*
Linda Trinh Võ and Rick Bonus, eds., *Contemporary Asian American Communities: Intersections and Divergences*
Sunaina Marr Maira, *Desis in the House: Indian American Youth Culture in New York City*
Teresa Williams-León and Cynthia Nakashima, eds., *The Sum of Our Parts: Mixed-Heritage Asian Americans*
Tung Pok Chin with Winifred C. Chin, *Paper Son: One Man's Story*
Amy Ling, ed., *Yellow Light: The Flowering of Asian American Arts*
Rick Bonus, *Locating Filipino Americans: Ethnicity and the Cultural Politics of Space*
Darrell Y. Hamamoto and Sandra Liu, eds., *Countervisions: Asian American Film Criticism*
Martin F. Manalansan IV, ed., *Cultural Compass: Ethnographic Explorations of Asian America*
Ko-lin Chin, *Smuggled Chinese: Clandestine Immigration to the United States*
Evelyn Hu-DeHart, ed., *Across the Pacific: Asian Americans and Globalization*

Soo-Young Chin, *Doing What Had to Be Done: The Life Narrative of Dora Yum Kim*
Robert G. Lee, *Orientals: Asian Americans in Popular Culture*
David L. Eng and Alice Y. Hom, eds., *Q & A: Queer in Asian America*
K. Scott Wong and Sucheng Chan, eds., *Claiming America: Constructing Chinese American Identities during the Exclusion Era*
Lavina Dhingra Shankar and Rajini Srikanth, eds., *A Part, Yet Apart: South Asians in Asian America*
Jere Takahashi, *Nisei/Sansei: Shifting Japanese American Identities and Politics*
Velina Hasu Houston, ed., *But Still, Like Air, I'll Rise: New Asian American Plays*
Josephine Lee, *Performing Asian America: Race and Ethnicity on the Contemporary Stage*
Deepika Bahri and Mary Vasudeva, eds., *Between the Lines: South Asians and Postcoloniality*
E. San Juan Jr., *The Philippine Temptation: Dialectics of Philippines–U.S. Literary Relations*
Carlos Bulosan and E. San Juan Jr., eds., *The Cry and the Dedication*
Carlos Bulosan and E. San Juan Jr., eds., *On Becoming Filipino: Selected Writings of Carlos Bulosan*
Vicente L. Rafael, ed., *Discrepant Histories: Translocal Essays on Filipino Cultures*
Yen Le Espiritu, *Filipino American Lives*
Paul Ong, Edna Bonacich, and Lucie Cheng, eds., *The New Asian Immigration in Los Angeles and Global Restructuring*
Chris Friday, *Organizing Asian American Labor: The Pacific Coast Canned-Salmon Industry, 1870–1942*
Sucheng Chan, ed., *Hmong Means Free: Life in Laos and America*
Timothy P. Fong, *The First Suburban Chinatown: The Remaking of Monterey Park, California*
William Wei, *The Asian American Movement*
Yen Le Espiritu, *Asian American Panethnicity*
Velina Hasu Houston, ed., *The Politics of Life*
Renqiu Yu, *To Save China, to Save Ourselves: The Chinese Hand Laundry Alliance of New York*
Shirley Geok-lin Lim and Amy Ling, eds., *Reading the Literatures of Asian America*
Karen Isaksen Leonard, *Making Ethnic Choices: California's Punjabi Mexican Americans*
Gary Y. Okihiro, *Cane Fires: The Anti-Japanese Movement in Hawaii, 1865–1945*
Sucheng Chan, *Entry Denied: Exclusion and the Chinese Community in America, 1882–1943*

www.ingramcontent.com/pod-product-compliance
Lightning Source LLC
Chambersburg PA
CBHW030646270326
41929CB00007B/226

* 9 7 8 1 4 3 9 9 1 5 7 3 8 *